THE JUVENILIZATION OF AMERICAN CHRISTIANITY

The Juvenilization of American Christianity

Thomas E. Bergler

WILLIAM B. EERDMANS PUBLISHING COMPANY
GRAND RAPIDS, MICHIGAN / CAMBRIDGE, U.K.

Published 2012 by
Wm. B. Eerdmans Publishing Co.
2140 Oak Industrial Drive N.E., Grand Rapids, Michigan 49505 /
P.O. Box 163, Cambridge CB3 9PU U.K.

Printed in the United States of America

18 17 16 15 14 13   7 6 5 4 3 2

Library of Congress Cataloging-in-Publication Data

Bergler, Thomas E., 1964-
The juvenilization of American Christianity / Thomas E. Bergler.
        p.   cm.
Includes bibliographical references (p.   ) and index.
ISBN 978-0-8028-6684-4 (pbk.: alk. paper)
1. Christianity — United States — 20th century. 2. Christianity — United States —
21st century. 3. Christianity and culture — United States.   I. Title.

BR526.B455   2012

277.3'0825 — dc23

2011049264

www.eerdmans.com

To my students at Huntington University
who remind me every day of the value of youth ministry

Contents

Acknowledgments

It has been a long journey from initial idea to final publication of this book. I want to thank those who helped me begin the journey, especially my doctoral advisor, George Marsden, and the members of my dissertation committee, Gail Bederman, John McGreevy, and James Turner, for their valuable advice. George is a gracious man and I owe him a great debt of gratitude. Notre Dame friends Brian Bademan, Jay Case, Victor Hinojosa, Tommy Kidd, James McCartin, Steve Nolt, Kurt Peterson, John Turner, Bill Svelmoe, and John Wigger all provided encouragement and helpful comments on my work.

I also want to express my gratitude to those who funded this project. The University of Notre Dame Graduate School provided both a Presidential Fellowship and a Zahm Travel Grant. The Pew Program in Religion and American History provided a dissertation fellowship and an opportunity to share my work with other dissertation fellows and senior faculty members. The University of Notre Dame History Department provided funds for research trips. Most recently, President G. Blair Dowden, Academic Dean Norris Friesen, and the trustees of Huntington University generously granted me a sabbatical leave to complete this book. Huntington University also provided travel funds to present parts of this book at academic conferences.

I also want to thank the staffs of the University of Notre Dame Library, its Archives, and Special Collections for providing friendly support services and an enjoyable research environment. I offer special thanks to the staffs of the Archives of Catholic University of America, the Billy Graham Center Archives, the Methodist Center for Archives and History, the

Southern Baptist Historical Library and Archives, the Vanderbilt University Archives, and the Western Reserve Historical Society. Their cheerful service helped me go through reams of material in record time. Thanks are also due to Barbara Freese of the American Baptist Theological Seminary Library who went above and beyond the call of duty to help me find materials on the National Baptist Convention.

During the research phase of this project I was privileged to meet and worship with the members of First Baptist Church, Capitol Hill in Nashville. Dr. Evelyn Fancher connected me with church members to interview and helped me find materials in the church's archives. I am especially grateful to those who took the time to tell me their memories of the Rev. Kelly Miller Smith and of the church: Cecelia Adkins, Alice Archer, Virginia Bright, Calvin Calhoun, Inez Crutchfield, Zelma Ewing, Dorothy Fort, Evelyn Gaines, Ben Harris, Alice Smith Key, Dorothy and Sherman Webster, Mary Wickware, and Delois Wilkinson.

My students and colleagues at Huntington University have provided a congenial environment for discussion, thinking, and writing about youth ministry and the church. In particular, I want to thank my colleagues in the Ministry and Missions Department, Luke Fetters, Karen Jones, Bob Myers, RuthAnn Price, and Melanie Ross, for their support and friendship. Thanks to my colleagues in the International Association for the Study of Youth Ministry and the Association of Youth Ministry Educators who provided valuable feedback when I presented papers related to this book.

It was my pleasure to speak with many other people who took interest in the project and shared their own youth group memories. Thanks to all of you for encouraging me on the journey. I especially want to thank Jan Munk and her prayer group for praying that this book would find a publisher. My editor at Eerdmans, David Bratt, was always gracious and helpful. Thanks for believing in this project and expending such effort to see it in print.

I would also like to thank the members and leaders of the Methodist Youth Fellowship, Youth for Christ, the Catholic Youth Organization, and the Baptist Young People's Union of the National Baptist Convention, most of whom I have never met. I hope that they will correct me with gentleness and grace if I have misrepresented them or their organizations at any point. I respect each of these organizations for seeking to help young people come into a full experience of the life of Jesus Christ. Finally, I offer thanks to Sarah Bergler, who provided love and encouragement throughout the many years it took to finish this project.

We're All Adolescents Now

It's Sunday morning. Let's visit a typical middle-class American church. As we walk into the main worship area, notice that people are dressed less formally than they will be when they go to work on Monday morning. You can't tell just by looking at them, but quite a few did not grow up in this particular church or even in this denomination. Some ended up here only after shopping around for a church. They chose this one not because of its denominational affiliation, but because its worship services and other activities helped them feel connected to God and to other people. Church members will happily tell you all about their faith and its important role in their lives. But ask them to explain their church's beliefs and how they differ from those of other churches, and you might get an awkward silence.

During worship, the congregation sings top-forty-style songs addressed to God and heavily peppered with the words "I," "you," and "love." In the sermon, the pastor may talk about "falling in love with Jesus." With or without the romantic analogy, the preacher will spend a lot of time on the topic of God's love. Even in theologically conservative churches, you won't hear much about guilt, suffering, or judgment. Some pastors will describe the life of faith as a "search" or a "journey" and imply that constant restlessness is the mark of authentic spirituality. A member of the congregation may tell the story of his or her faith journey during the public worship service. Even in Protestant denominations long noted for their suspicion of idolatry, you can count on seeing some visual, dramatic, or even entertaining element in the worship service. It might be a musical performance, a dramatic presentation or film clip, or maybe an elaborate liturgy designed to appeal to the senses. It could even be just a vivid story or use of humor in the sermon. Ask the regulars, and they'll gladly tell you their favorite parts of the church service, just like they can tell you about their favorite movies, music, or television shows. Even if the church officially frowns on combining entertainment and worship, its members still tend to behave like spectators.

Although it might not happen on the week you visit, if you return often enough, you will hear someone praise young people as models of what every Christian should be. Their idealism will be contrasted with adult cynicism. Their zeal for evangelism or social justice will be contrasted with adult apathy. Their constant searching will be contrasted with adult stagnation. On rare occasions, young people will be criticized — but almost in the next breath, the speaker will be sure to say something like, "not all young people are like that" or "adults are really to blame." Again and again you will hear the "passion" and "authenticity" of youth lauded as the gold standard of Christian spirituality.

On your way out of the worship service, don't forget to check out the church's other offerings. Most likely, some Christian products such as CDs, books, or t-shirts are for sale. Even if the church itself is not much into merchandising, it's a safe bet that its most committed members purchase and use Christian products at home. They may spend precious vacation days attending Christian camps or conferences. They also contribute to at least one specialized Christian organization outside their congregation. Whether they are passionate about politics, international relief, or marriage enrichment, they can find an organization that captures their imagination and responds to their needs.

In part because of this intense competition from other Christian organizations, this local church probably offers quite a variety of programs. Especially in larger churches, specialized ministries cater to specific types of people, such as children, single parents, young couples, senior citizens, or recovering alcoholics. While some of these activities will emphasize traditional religious activities like prayer, Christian education, and service, others will focus on fun and socializing. The church probably offers some kind of "small group" ministry. Although no two small groups are exactly alike, all involve face-to-face encounters with fellow believers in an informal, intimate setting. Such groups provide a sense of belonging and a place to form supportive friendships. Whether in small groups or other venues, the church will be concerned to educate its members in the faith. But teachers and students alike look with suspicion on anything that smacks of indoctrination. Rather, leaders are supposed to encourage people to "discover" the truth or "decide for themselves" what to believe. Lecturing and rote memorization are out. Informal discussions are in. At their best these sessions make the truth come alive in people's personal experience. At other times, participants wonder if they are only pooling their ignorance.

The church is concerned about mission, but in a way that its members might describe as "relational" or "incarnational." Church people pride themselves on emphasizing "people not programs" and want their activities to benefit others holistically, including their bodies and relationships, not just their souls. For example, when it comes to evangelism, members will be quick to tell you that they no longer use aggressive tactics and canned gospel presentations. They prefer to build friendships, serve others, or just live a good life that will speak louder than words. In some churches, leaders try to build an intergenerational, inter-racial family. In others, they target a specific type of person, such as middle-class suburban baby boomers, often making use of the principle of "like attracts like." Both types of leaders intentionally shape church life to attract and serve the people they want to reach. The church also sponsors an annual "mission trip" in which congregation members travel (often overseas) and spend a week or more in Christian service. Most likely someone in the church has protested, marched, written letters, or otherwise engaged in religiously motivated political activism. The church may or may not officially encourage its members toward particular political causes and activities, but it almost certainly provides a place where its more politically inclined members can recruit others. In all of this activity, congregation members believe themselves to be just as important as the paid church staff. Most likely their pastor agrees, and urges his congregants to take more ownership of the church's programs.

Sometime during the week, there will be special activities for the youth of the congregation. Even in congregations of otherwise meager resources, a full-time youth minister often plans and leads these activities. The youth minister dreams of evangelizing the youth of the community or mobilizing the youth of the church for social action. But the majority of the youth group members are children of church members, and most of the church's youth activities revolve around making or keeping these young people Christian. Some parents even see the youth group as a convenient place to turn over the responsibility for Christianizing their offspring to a competent, paid professional. Attend a youth group meeting, and you will find more pop music, more spiritual searching, more refer-

3

ences to romantic spirituality, more fun, more informality — more of everything that you saw on Sunday morning.

Of course, no real congregation looks exactly like this composite portrait, and some may only show a few of these traits. But dig a bit deeper into the life of churches that don't fit the pattern and you will find that their members are agonizing or arguing over what they need to do to appeal to "the young people" and to remain viable as a faith community. This perceived need to adapt to constant cultural change is itself yet another element of the new shape of American Christianity.

The Juvenilization of American Christianity

Fifty or sixty years ago, these now-commonplace elements of American church life were rare. What happened? Beginning in the 1930s and 1940s, Christian teenagers and youth leaders staged a quiet revolution in American church life which can properly be called the *juvenilization* of American Christianity. Juvenilization is the process by which the religious beliefs, practices, and developmental characteristics of adolescents become accepted as appropriate for Christians of all ages. It begins with the praiseworthy goal of adapting the faith to appeal to the young. But it sometimes ends badly, with both youth and adults embracing immature versions of the faith.

Like other revolutions, juvenilization swept away both good and bad elements in church life. Youth ministries brought necessary and beneficial reforms to the churches, but they also made Christians more suspicious of authorities and traditions. They revitalized individual Christian lives, Christian organizations, and even whole denominations. In 1950, many American churches promoted a more serious, mature faith than they do today. But ironically, those same churches also often had less of a grip on people's lives. By personalizing Christianity and creatively blending it with elements of popular culture ranging from rock music to political protests, youth ministries helped ensure the ongoing vitality of Christianity in America. But these same ministries also sometimes pandered to the consumerism, self-centeredness, and even outright immaturity of American believers. For good or ill, American Christianity would never be the same.

Ask about any dramatic change in American society over the last fifty years and most people will point to the 1960s, but we need to back up to the 1930s to really understand the origins of juvenilization. At that time, Christians concerned about young people thought they were taking drastic

4

measures to save the world. Between 1930 and 1950, Americans got blasted by the Great Depression, World War II, and the Cold War. Many wondered if America and its "way of life" would survive. Many also worried that it might be impossible to grow up as a good Christian and good American in such a world of crisis. Concerned Christians launched dozens of new youth organizations in this period in the hopes of protecting young people from the evil effects of these crises and mobilizing them to make a difference in a dangerous world.

At the same time, the 1940s and 1950s saw the birth of the "teenager." Unlike the more diverse "youth" of previous eras, teenagers all went to high school and all participated in a national youth culture increasingly dominated by the same music, TV shows, movies, products and cultural beliefs. Of course not every young person fit this pattern, but enough did to reshape both the teenage experience of growing up and adult perceptions of that process.

It was in the 1950s that youth and youth culture hit the American mainstream in a big way. Although it may seem that the teenagers of the twenty-first century bear little resemblance to those of the 1950s, crucial similarities remain in the structure of adolescent life and its relationship to the church. The upheavals of the 1960s certainly intensified the process of juvenilization and expanded its reach so that it touched more and more believers and their churches, but the mechanisms by which teenagers influenced church life were already well established. It was probably in the 1960s that adolescent versions of Christianity began to make serious inroads among adult Christians. Yet this happened because both adults and teenagers reacted to the traumas and opportunities of the 1960s using patterns of thinking and behaving they had come to accept during the previous decade. Even today, American churches still respond to youth culture using a range of options they developed during the 1950s.

The story of juvenilization is a story not of a sinister plot or a noble crusade, but of unintended consequences and unquestioned assumptions. Even the "leaders" of juvenilization did not always realize what they were doing. In some ways, juvenilization was a byproduct of noble goals. In the years immediately following World War II, youth leaders set out to save America and the world by saving young people. Some dreamed of a youth-led crusade for Christian social reform; others saw a youth revival as the key to saving America from moral collapse. For their part, young people tried to figure out ways to be good Christians and make a difference in the world while still fitting in with their peers and having fun.

Youth groups proved to be key laboratories of religious innovation, because church leaders needed to compete for teenage loyalty against an increasingly powerful and pervasive youth culture. At the same time, these groups also functioned as social spaces in which to quarantine and contain change. Although cultural phenomena like pop music or racial integration might not yet be welcome in the church, adults sometimes permitted them in youth groups. Some adults intentionally used youth groups as a "back door" into the church; others hoped that threatening practices would stay in quarantine. In practice, adult fears usually faded, and what worked in youth group was eventually accepted in the church as a whole.

Youth culture and the desire to pass on the faith to younger generations are not the only engines driving juvenilization. Since the 1960s, the life experiences and cultural expectations of adulthood have also changed. Older cultural conceptions of adulthood encouraged responsibility, self-denial, and service of others. In the first half of the twentieth century, most people clearly entered adulthood in their teens or early twenties by virtue of getting married, getting a job, and having children. More recently, the passage to adulthood has been delayed and rendered more subjective for most middle-class Americans. In this new "psychological adulthood," the individual's "needs and wants" expand and his or her "obligations and attachments" contract. The seven deadly sins have been redefined: "pride has become self esteem . . . lust has become sexuality . . . envy is now channeled into initiative and incentive . . . sloth has become leisure." Of course, most adults still value virtue and deplore vice. But they also increasingly view life as an unending journey of self-development. And the contemporary landscape through which they journey has many paths that can end in self-centeredness or even narcissism. In short, at least some traits that should be included in Christian maturity have been decoupled from adulthood in post-1960s America, and this change has encouraged juvenilization in churches. Indeed, it is likely that the juvenilization of American Christianity and the emergence of the new immature adulthood have mutually reinforced one another.[1]

To give one example, consumerism and juvenilization reinforce one another. People who know who they are, who think carefully about purchases, and who exercise self-control are harder to persuade to buy products they don't really need. In contrast, impulsive people who are searching for a sense of identity, who are looking to salve their emotional pain, who desperately crave the approval of others, and who have lots of discretionary income (or are willing to spend as if they do) make ideal consumers. In other words, encouraging people to settle into some of the worst traits of adolescence is good for business. Not all businesses and advertisers operate on this basis, but enough do to encourage the cult of youth and discourage people from growing up. Considerable evidence suggests that consumers can see through these techniques and resist them to some extent. But immersed as we all are in the culture of adolescence, it becomes increasingly hard to embrace the self-denial and character formation necessary to achieve what used to be called mature adulthood.[2]

This book is about how and why this process of juvenilization got started, what keeps it going, and how it has benefited and hurt each of the major streams of Christianity in America. It is not about beating up on young people or youth ministers. Youth ministries are a necessary and valuable tool for the Christianization of young people in modern societies, and to be effective in that task, these organizations need godly, trained leaders. I hope that youth ministry leaders will be stronger and more faithful to their callings as a result of what they read in these pages.

This book is a work of history in the service of faithful Christian ministry. It tells the story of a key period in recent church history that continues to significantly shape American Christians, their churches, and to a lesser extent even American society itself. For example, when post-Christian Americans describe themselves as "spiritual but not religious" and pursue a "faith journey" characterized by mix-and-match spirituality, they are displaying the effects of juvenilization. My hope is that by understanding where we have come from and how we got here, we might be able to choose the best paths forward.

This book is *not* a manual for how to eliminate juvenilization. Indeed, it might prove impossible to shut down this process, even if we thought it worth the risks to do so. After all, without youth ministries and their adaptive appeals to youth, the churches would not have many of the loyal and productive members that they have today. Yet it may be impossible to appeal to American youth without also letting adolescent spirituality into the church. Indeed, after fifty or more years of juvenilization, adolescent spirituality powerfully shapes the religious identities of many adults. So churches that ignore adolescent spirituality will have as much trouble communicating effectively to adults as they do to teenagers.

Instead of holding out false hope for completely reversing the process, I hope to equip the reader to recognize the dynamics and effects of juvenilization. Understanding how and why youth organizations digest youth culture and send its nutrients (and sometimes its poisons) into the body of Christ will help all of us make wise decisions about how to work for the health of the church. At the very least, I hope that all of us will think carefully about which aspects of adolescent spirituality deserve to be championed and which need to be restrained.

From what I have said so far, it might sound like juvenilization is a uniform process that produces the same effects everywhere. That is not true. Some churches seem less dominated by adolescent spirituality than others — but they often pay a price for bucking the trend. During the key decade of the 1950s, each church tradition, and even each youth organization within a tradition, created a different version of adolescent Christianity. Each organization brought its own beliefs and practices to bear on the shared problem of getting young people to pay attention to their faith and do something about it. Some spiritual goals fit better than others with the desires of different 1950s teenagers. The combination of adolescent preferences, adult priorities, and environmental constraints created different paths of juvenilization.

By tracing these paths we will be able to identify the consequences of particular choices about how to shape youth ministry. Although youth leaders have tended to believe they can take on a wide range of tasks and priorities, the reality is that youth ministry is limited by many factors external and internal to the church. Those who attempt to do everything usually fail to do much of anything. On the other hand, those who "succeed" in one realm by narrow specialization often leave significant gaps in the spiritual and moral formation of their young people. The repeated cries for "holistic" or "integrated" youth ministry over the last fifty years testify to just how hard it is to comprehensively form young Christians in the faith. They also hint at one of the underlying causes of spotty Christian formation: disunity among adults.

What Is "Adolescent Christianity"?

Adolescent Christianity is any way of understanding, experiencing, or practicing the Christian faith that conforms to the patterns of adolescence in American culture. I am well aware that the tangled web of beliefs, practices, and experiences that we call "adolescence" is itself a product of human cultures and changes over time. Attempts to define a universal set of traits that apply to every adolescent are always gross generalizations that betray cultural biases. One reason juvenilization is so powerful and deceptively difficult to manage is that adults are constantly investigating, debating, and misreading the supposed "nature" of adolescents. Juvenilization is also driven by actual changes in the lives of young people, not just adult perceptions. So no matter how the experience of adolescence changes, churches will eventually conform to that new set of adolescent traits.

A reliable body of social science research has identified some common aspects of adolescent development in American society. And though some of the traits we ascribe to adolescents have changed over time, beneath these particulars lie some foundational realities that have remained relatively stable. Adolescents are people in a particular developmental life stage, who occupy particular positions in the social and economic structures of society, and whose lives provide important raw materials for creating meaning in American culture. Each of these aspects of adolescence shapes the process of juvenilization in the church, so each deserves some explanation.

Adolescence as a Developmental Life Stage[3]

Adolescents are people who are going through a particular developmental stage which begins about the time of puberty. I say "about the time of puberty" because the biological changes associated with puberty are not the only markers of entry to this life stage. Someone who turns thirteen, enters high school, starts dating, or even just dresses a particular way will be perceived as an adolescent whatever the status of his or her biological development. Nevertheless, physical development powerfully influences this life stage. Physical changes make adolescents self-conscious and concerned about their bodies. They begin to rival or even surpass adults in their physical strength, energy, and coordination. At some point during adolescence, the individual becomes capable of reproduction and begins to view herself, and be viewed by others, as a potential romantic or sexual partner. Adolescents spend much time and energy thinking about, discussing, and pursuing such relationships. Especially in early adolescence, romantic relationships serve primarily to help the individual achieve status among his peers and feel good about himself.

Adolescent spirituality favors physical activity, touch, and other bodily ways of expressing faith. Adolescent Christians are concerned about how their faith relates to their sexuality and their romantic relationships. They want to experience a "personal relationship with God" and like the idea of "falling in love" with Jesus.

Cognitively, adolescents are growing in their ability to think abstractly. They can now begin to grapple with concepts like love, truth, or justice. Since these ideals seem fresh and new to them, adolescents sometimes display an excitement about them which is rarer among older people. They also have a new ability to perceive the contradictions and hypocrisies of adult society, but may be unable to process this new knowledge charitably and responsibly. Some may respond with cynicism or apathy, while others will be tempted to believe that simply identifying and protesting against problems will easily solve them. Adolescent Christians sometimes throw themselves into projects that reflect their high ideals. Unlike many adults, they assume that positive change is both possible and desirable. They ask tough questions and shake up adults in ways that can be creative and energizing. They value discovering the truth for themselves more than receiving the wisdom of others. On the other hand, they sometimes fall prey to misdirected zeal in their excitement over a new cause, and they may not have the staying power of an adult. They can get frustrated when their simple solutions seem to fail, often blaming adults or the church.

Adults influenced by adolescent Christianity romanticize the supposed idealism and zeal of youth and try to force each other to conform to those patterns. Adolescent Christians blame someone else for the world's problems and seldom recognize their own role in evil social systems. In an ironic twist, some adults influenced by juvenilization blame teenagers for society's problems. Adolescent Christians spend their energy denouncing evils and staging symbolic protests rather than engaging in the less glamorous work that can lead to long-term change.

Socially, the influence of friends grows relative to the influence of parents during adolescence. Adolescents lean heavily on a few close friends who provide companionship and a sense of emotional security, advice, and acceptance. These groups of friends tend to be similar in age, race, economic status, school achievement, and pop-culture tastes. Through these relationships young people learn what is "normal" and what is "weird," and how to behave in relationships so that people will like them and treat them well.

Adolescent Christians seek out intimate, nurturing groups of friends who will support their faith journey. They care more about the quality of their religious friendships than about truth. Adolescent Christians are most comfortable around believers who are just like them, and they may have a hard time widening their circle of friendship. Some can become obsessively conformist in their religious beliefs or behaviors, while others pride themselves on their self-conscious rebellion against the crowd — although they often need a group of friends with whom to share their rebellion!

Another reason for the power of friends in the lives of adolescents is that friends play a key role in the process of identity formation. Adolescents want to know who they are and how they compare with others. Questions like "what sort of person am I?" or "who will be my closest friends or my romantic partner?" or "what will I do with my life?" or "what do I believe?" take on a new importance. Adolescents might not consciously ask themselves these questions, but they form the subtext of personal relationships. Because they are experimenting with new beliefs, behaviors, and self-images, adolescents tend to have a less stable sense of self than the typical adult. Adolescents tend to think everyone is watching them and can become obsessed with what others might think of them. They fantasize about being the hero in their personal life story of romance and adventure. Older adolescents sometimes go through a period of intense questioning in which they may wholly or partially reject the beliefs and sense of self they have built up so far in their lives. Because they are absorbed in the crucial developmental task of identity formation, adolescents can sometimes seem narcissistic.

Adolescent Christians are preoccupied with self-exploration and personal transformation. They want to personalize their faith and use it as a resource in identity development. They want to know how their faith can help them with important life decisions like marriage and career. Adults affected by juvenilization will glorify spiritual searching and look suspiciously on believers who have "settled" beliefs and habits. Because juvenilized Christians are still figuring out who they will be, they are free to experiment with new ways to live out their faith. They may see themselves as potential heroes in the drama of redemption. On the other hand, without a settled sense of identity, they find it hard to make strong commitments to particular beliefs, people, or religious institutions. Indeed, they may see institutions and commitments as impediments to personal spiritual growth. Even if they like church, such Christians are tempted to see it as a tool for personal fulfillment.

Emotionally, adolescents tend to experience higher highs and lower lows than adults. They feel strong emotions toward things that seem trivial in the eyes of adults, but which loom very large in their world. Some also experience more frequent emotional changes than adults and less ability to control their behavior in the midst of those changes. Yet contrary to much that has been written about adolescence, it is not always a time of "storm and stress." Conflict with parents does often increase, and emotional swings or even depression can occur, but most adolescents' lives are not characterized by dramatic external rebellion or damaging internal turmoil. Most develop in a relatively peaceful manner.

Adolescent Christians see the faith as incomplete unless it is affecting them emotionally. They are less likely than adults to settle for a faith that offers only a dutiful adherence to particular doctrines, rules, or institutions. On the other hand, they have a hard time keeping religious commitments when their emotions are not cooperating. They are drawn to religious practices that produce emotional highs and sometimes assume that experiencing strong feelings is the same thing as spiritual authenticity. They may be tempted to believe that God's main role in their lives is to help them feel better or to heal their emotional pain. Juvenilized adults agree that a main purpose of Christianity is to help them feel better about their problems.

Adolescence and Social Structure

Adolescents occupy a dependent and highly regulated place in the social and economic structures of society. Almost everywhere they go, adolescents are subordinate to adults. Adults group them together in schools and other age-segregated environments in an attempt to regulate them and train them to be good adults. But by bringing them together, adults create the opportunity for young people to form their own peer cultures with distinctive dress codes, slang, behaviors, and moral norms. These "youth cultures" often put a premium on character qualities and behaviors which oppose adult expectations for youth. Age-segregated environments also tend to constrict the life vision of adolescents. They spend much time focusing on the narrow and sometimes even selfish range of concerns that go along with adolescent development, to the neglect of the "outside" world. For example, the social hierarchy of the high school and one's place in it holds some power to shape the happiness or unhappiness of every adolescent. A student who gets identified with the football players or cheerleaders really does have a different life experience than one pigeonholed with the "geeks." Although most young people chafe against this stereotyping, they care about such markers of social status. Adults want the schools to form good citizens, but these environments are even more effective at creating good shoppers, gossips, romantic partners, and sports fans.

Adolescent Christians insist that their faith adapt to their social world. They want to know how their faith can make a difference in their daily social interactions at home, school, and work. They are impatient with a faith that offers only abstractions and no personal life applications. On the other hand, this intense need to apply the faith has a downside, because the adolescent world is sometimes so isolated from "real life." Even fervent adolescent Christians always keep one eye on how their religious activities and relationships help or hurt their status in the claustrophobic world of the high school. And many are only superficially interested, if at all, in how their faith impacts others outside their narrow world.

The powerful place of the high school in the structure of adolescent lives puts pressure on churches. Except for students at Christian schools (and sometimes even for them), faith is pushed into the realm of extracurricular activities. Youth groups must compete against an appealing array of sports teams, clubs, dances, and other adult-sponsored activities. Although experts regularly scold parents for not caring better for their children, the structures of adolescent life teach parents to leave the educating to the teachers, sports training to the coaches, and spiritual development to the youth ministers. Christian youth leaders find themselves under incredible pressure to make a significant impact on young lives using only a few hours a week.

Economically, adolescents are restricted to low-level, part-time employment. Those who favor this arrangement claim society is protecting young people and making sure they get an education that will prepare them for better jobs later. More suspicious observers wonder who really benefits from keeping young people out of the full-time labor force. Perhaps young, part-time workers are easier to control than older workers and can be paid less. Or perhaps we keep adolescents out of the labor force to artificially open up more jobs for older workers. Although it is not at all clear that the current work and school arrangements are in the best interests of teenagers, especially those who will not be going to college, there is little will to change the system.[4]

Meanwhile, the economic growth of the last fifty years has meant that more families have not needed to rely on their children's income to survive, and many even have surplus income to spend on their children. In addition, adolescents are not typically supporting a family of their own. As a result, adolescents have enough spending money that whole industries have arisen to sell them products and experiences. During the 1950s, enterprising adults began to create and market products and entertainment just for teenagers. Today, to be a teenager is to be bombarded by up to 3,000 advertising messages a day designed to play on desires for popularity, fun, domination of others, and sexual fulfillment.[5] Christianity must compete effectively in the smorgasbord of sensuality that is the youth market.

Adolescent Christians expect their faith to be fun and entertaining. They want the church to make use of the latest music, technology, and cultural trends. Some revel in a completely parallel Christian youth subculture, complete with its own music, celebrities, and clothing, all modeled on the offerings of the wider popular culture. Adolescent Christians construct their religious identities through consumption of products and experiences. Because these can be expensive, youth groups and the juvenilization they bring are primarily phenomena of the white middle class, although as more people get a share of the "American dream," juvenilization spreads to their churches as well. Juvenilization is also a middle-class phenomenon because middle-class parents worry that their children will "fall" into lower economic classes through poor life choices.[6] So middle-class adults are more than willing to pay for youth groups that provide appealing Christian alternatives to more risky, lower-class ways of having fun.

Adolescents occupy an ambiguous legal and social status — and this "in-between" life stage lasts a long time. Today adolescence begins earlier and ends later than it did 100 years ago. In 1900, young women did not get their first menstrual period until they were 15 or 16; today the average age is 12.5. In 1900, most teenagers were in the work force, not in school. For most of the twentieth century, some combination of full employment, marriage, and the birth of a first child marked the transition to adulthood. As more and more people have delayed these life transitions, full adulthood has receded into the distant future for most teenagers.

In addition, there seems to be little consensus regarding when a person becomes an adult. Students graduate from high school by age eighteen, but in some ways that does not make them full adults. They can vote and die for their country at eighteen, but in many states they still may not drink alcohol. The legal system sometimes treats juvenile offenders according to different rules than adults; at other times, juveniles are tried as adults. Earlier puberty and later "settling down" has made it harder and harder for adolescents to maintain sexual purity. In addition, the lengthening of adolescence has made this life stage seem semi-permanent, a place to settle in, not a place to quickly pass through on the way to adulthood.

Adolescent Christians don't expect to be adults for a long time, so they don't particularly care if their Christianity prepares them for adulthood. They tend to be much more aware of their religious "rights" than their religious responsibilities. Meanwhile, the churches have a hard time spanning the chasm between childhood and adulthood. Many churches have high school youth groups, but few have viable ministries to college students or working young adults. Even though high school graduation is not an effective rite of passage to adulthood, church structures assume that it is.

A certain number of young people "drop out" or rebel significantly against the constraints imposed upon them by society. Young members of street gangs, radical political groups, or religious cults see themselves as rejecting the surrounding society and ignoring its demands that they join the economic and political "establishment." In reality, these groups and their members depend in one way or another on the larger society for their daily bread either by crime, family support, or subsistence employment. These youth subcultures gather around shared music, slang, modes of dress, and sense of community. They want to shock "normal" people and repudiate mainstream institutions and values — so much so that some Marxist and postmodern scholars in the 1980s wistfully looked to these groups as a sort of new proletariat and debated the political meanings of their hairstyles and piercings.[7] In fact, these alternative lifestyles are almost always temporary and generate little political clout. For some, their participation in radical youth subcultures ends tragically, with imprisonment or even premature death. In other cases, participants eventually rejoin "normal life," hold down jobs, and raise families, although they may do these things with a countercultural style. As they are temporary and economically derivative, extreme youth subcultures should be viewed as part of the larger social structure, not something separate from it. They may well function as "safety valves" that allow a certain amount of youthful unrest to be dissipated. These groups also take up the slack when young people find themselves in conflict with or abandoned by families, schools, employers, and other institutions that should be helping them.

Few adolescent Christians come from the ranks of gangs or other extreme subcultures. The structures of youth ministry, born among the middle class, have little appeal in these alternative worlds. In addition, middle-class parents have little desire to see their children hanging out with these scary characters. Those who do minister to these groups must do so using different strategies and often separate structures not closely connected to middle-class congregations. On the other hand, the dress, slang, and music of extreme youth subcultures are often attractive to middle-class kids. So the most aggressively juvenilizing youth ministers try to use some of these subcultural styles, while trying to purge them of their more offensive content. Even in the most conformist, middle-class, white youth group, you will find at least metaphoric talk of rebellion against the status quo. Often adolescent Christians dream of rebelling against the system, and dread turning out just like their parents. They create churches that often settle for symbolic rebellion rather than substantive social change.

Adolescence and Culture

The developmental and structural elements of adolescence provide raw materials for meaning making. For example, adults assign threatening meanings to the physical changes that come with puberty. Girls are now potential sexual deviants. Boys are now potential criminals. Why not reverse these stereotypes? After all, more boys than girls are sexually active, and have been for at least a century. But the facts rarely get in the way of a powerful cultural belief. Adults spend a lot of time talking about whether young people are basically good or bad, idealistic or apathetic, spiritual or secular, and so on.

Adolescence is a life stage perfectly suited to be a screen upon which adults can project their worst fears and highest hopes. In the lives of teenagers, adults think they are getting a first glimpse at the future of their society and its institutions. Do adolescents seem to be embracing the values and behaviors we want them to embrace? All is well. Are they dropping out and forming their own deviant subcultures? Our society must be fundamentally flawed. And often, the next step is, "We have the solution to the crisis, and you must support our organization before it is too late." Because adults readily accept extreme, unsubstantiated pronouncements about young people, almost any program of juvenilization can be sold to a church so long as leaders push the right buttons.

Adolescent churches are more likely to conform to the supposed needs or desires of young people than they are to shoulder the more difficult task of spiritually forming the young. Indeed, in adolescent churches, leaders use talk about the preferences of "young people today" as a ploy to avoid the conflict that would result if adults talked openly about their opposing visions for the Christian life. At other times, adults use cultural beliefs about youth as an excuse to delegate their problems and disagreements to the next generation.

The structures of adolescence also provide grist for the mill of meaning making. For example, in the 1930s, thousands of young people were unemployed due to the Great Depression, so adults discovered a problem group they called "out of school youth." Suddenly adults decided that all teenagers needed to get a high school diploma in order to become good citizens and productive workers. In earlier, more prosperous decades, when industries needed more unskilled workers, fewer adults cared whether young people were in school or in the factory.

The meanings adults read into the lives of young people take on the power to shape the experience of adolescence itself. For example, once adults decided that every teenager needed a high school diploma, students who did not earn one were stigmatized as "dropouts." Those who stayed in school found themselves subjected to a curriculum that was often far removed from the realities of their lives and did little to provide the skills they would need upon graduation. Instead of aspiring to become adults, many settled into the new and exciting youth culture developing among their peers at school. Although adults often complain about the misbehavior of the young, these behaviors are logical outcomes of the contradictory messages adult society has been sending them. Adolescent behavior often reflects the actual, lived values of society, not just its ideals.

In addition, adolescence as a grab bag of meanings has come to shape even the experience of being an adult in American culture. Americans are ambivalent about whether they want to grow up or not. On the one hand, most high school students want to be treated like adults, and many demand full adult privileges regarding alcohol use, sex, and other behaviors. On the other hand, many college students do not consider themselves adults. Developmental psychologists have even identified a new life stage they call "emerging adulthood" as a way to acknowledge that even many college graduates do not see themselves as adults. They have many years left of their youthful searching and self-development.[8] One reason for this confusion about adult status is that the very idea of becoming an adult has taken on negative connotations. As a result, many young adults find the forced transitions to adult status that may come with full-time employment, marriage, or childbirth to be emotionally traumatic. Many Americans don't like to think of themselves as adults, because it implies that the good part of their lives may be over. Advertisers recognize this fact and market products with the promise that they will perpetuate the buyer's youthfulness.

Individual adolescent development, the social structures that house adolescents, and the cultural beliefs that we assign to them constantly influence each other. Because this three-way relationship is so complex and powerful, juvenilization is hard to recognize and even harder to influence. With everything moving at once, it can be hard to find a secure place to stand, take a breath, and make wise choices. Misunderstanding this dynamic interaction or neglecting one of its elements leads to bad decisions about how to adapt the Christian faith to the needs of rising generations.

A Vision for Spiritual Maturity

Why should anyone care about juvenilization? Early in my college teaching career, I asked a group of my students, "What does a mature Christian look like?" They disliked the question and resisted answering it. "I don't think we ever arrive in our spiritual growth." "We're not supposed to judge one another." "No one is perfect in this life." Sadly, these evangelical college students did not believe that Christian maturity was either attainable or desirable. The churches that had nurtured these young people well enough to get them to pursue a Christian college education had not managed to inspire them with a biblical vision of spiritual maturity.

Neither the life stage of adolescence nor individual young people are ultimately to blame for creating an immature faith. Adolescents have good developmental reasons for at least sometimes thinking and acting in an immature fashion. But it is harder to explain why adults feel free to neglect the character traits of Christian maturity. Of course, we must also celebrate the fact that some very good things have come from injecting more "youth" into American Christianity. And it is important to recognize that not everything that a culture labels as "adult" is necessarily a good reflection of Christian maturity.

Still, unchecked juvenilization does tend to undermine Christian maturity over time. Only by learning from the victories and defeats of the past can we hope to achieve spiritual maturity in our individual lives and in the corporate lives of our churches. And only intergenerational communities of people devoted to mature Christianity can build seawalls high enough to hold back the tide of juvenilization that has now risen high enough to threaten all of us.

CHAPTER 1

Youth, Christianity, and the Crisis of Civilization

All politics today is youth politics.

The Doom of Youth, 1932

No part of the population is affected more vitally or occupies a more essential position in time of war or world crisis than youth.

A Program of Action for American Youth, 1939

Youth ministry as we know it today, with its power to shape the future of American Christianity, was born in an hour of world crisis. As the traumas of the Great Depression, World War II, and the Cold War followed each other in quick succession, people started to speak of a "crisis of civilization." They had reason to fear that their children might see the end of economic prosperity, democracy, and religious freedom.

Young people seemed to be both key actors in the international political drama and especially vulnerable victims of the times. So an amazingly broad spectrum of leaders both inside and outside the churches proclaimed that youth held the key to saving civilization. Most Americans not only nodded their heads in agreement, they opened their wallets to fund new youth organizations.

By capitalizing on fears about youth and the crisis of civilization, Christian youth leaders and young people were able to launch some much-needed reforms in their churches. Young people pioneered racial integration, created new and exciting methods of evangelism, and gained a newfound sense of their own political power. These changes were at first restricted to youth environments, but they would eventually reshape the lives of adults as well. Although they may not have single-handedly saved civilization, the Christian youth leaders of this era did help thousands of young people become stronger, more active Christians who made a difference in their society.

Youth leaders believed they were catching the wave of the future and channeling the innate power of young people. They were also building one of the engines that would drive juvenilization in subsequent decades. In a world of impending doom, who could argue against doing whatever it took to Christianize and mobilize the young saviors of the world?

The Crisis of Civilization and the "Youth Problem"

The Great Depression and World War II created significant suffering and new temptations for young people, but adults too easily assumed a close connection between these problems and the possible shipwreck of their civilization. For one thing, unemployment hit young people hard. As of 1936, an estimated 4.7 million Americans between the ages of 16 and 24 were unemployed. This number represented about one-third of all the unemployed in the country. In 1932 a railroad policeman in El Paso estimated that he saw 200 transients come through each day, at least half of whom were under twenty-five years old. The problem of indigent youth took on a threatening racial and sexual significance with the arrest of the Scottsboro boys in 1931. This widely publicized incident happened among the swarms of young people who were wandering from city to city by catching illegal rides on freight trains. Two young white girls accused nine African Americans of raping them. Although the boys were convicted, years later it would become clear that the accusations were false. African American and white parents had radically different interpretations of the case, but all found it deeply troubling.[1]

Adults responded to the threat of unemployed, unsupervised young people by pushing them all to go to high school. Ironically, this new expectation that most teenagers should go to high school made the dropout problem seem worse than it had before.[2] In their dreams about the possible benefits of a high school education, most adults chose to ignore the way that they were using schools as a place to warehouse young people and keep them off the streets.

But keeping kids in school was not enough. Adults also worried that unemployed young people would get in trouble during their leisure time. One 1942 curriculum designed to lead high school students through a study of the youth problem contained the following exercise: "Study the life of the French nobility during the 75 years preceding the French revolution. Was there a fruitful and creative use of leisure?"[3] In hindsight it seems ridiculous to think that the young men hanging out on street corners or the young women trying to pick up soldiers would somehow lead America down the path of bloody political revolution. But at the time no one batted an eye at such outrageous ideas.

To be fair, anything seemed possible in a world in which a tyrant like Hitler could rise to power with the help of a fanatical youth movement. Many feared that communists or fascists could manipulate unemployed, idealistic young Americans just as easily. The Student Strikes for Peace in 1934 and 1935 and youth marches on Washington organized by the American Youth Congress seemed to confirm these fears. Some believed the AYC was a "communist front" and viewed its activities with alarm. President Roosevelt addressed the young people who marched on Washington and scolded them for listening to political extremists. The American Communist Party was at its zenith of strength during the Great Depression, so fears about it were not entirely unfounded.[4]

Whether or not young Americans were about to sign on with the communists or fascists, many adults insisted that something drastic had to be done to properly direct the political power of youth. Literature on the "youth problem" proliferated with titles like *How Fare American Youth?; Youth a World Problem; The Lost Generation: A Portrait of American Youth Today; Christian Youth and the Economic Problem* and even *Doom of Youth.*[5] Adult fears about the fate of America came to rest squarely on the shoulders of young people.

Preaching the Youth Problem

Christian youth leaders seized the day and proclaimed that they held the key to saving youth and civilization. In the process, they also convinced themselves of the political power and apocalyptic significance of young people. Mainline Protestants proclaimed that the world was doomed unless Christian young people would devote themselves to social action. Participants in the 1935 national youth conference of the Methodist Episcopal

Church, South, heard talks with titles like "The Church and the World Crisis" and "Youth and World Trends." In the latter address, Dr. Ivan Lee Holt described conditions in Europe and Asia where he had seen "armies of fighting youth who are willing to give their lives in mad devotion to the cruel policies of dictators." Like many adults of the era, Holt used these young people as a double warning to Americans. On the one hand, American youth needed to be careful not to be duped by demagogues. At the same time, they should imitate the intense devotion of Communist and Hitler youth. Many in attendance assumed that young people would lead the way in transforming the world, and that the rest of the church might need to scramble to keep up. As Sterling F. Wheeler, a senior at Southern Methodist University, put it in his speech at the same conference, "youth today realizes that the Church offers the greatest promise, youth stands ready and eager to live faithfully, fight courageously, yes, to die for the Church if need be. But youth is not willing to sit idly by and do nothing in the face of world crises!"[6]

Evangelical Protestants insisted that only mass evangelization of young people could save the world from destruction. At the founding convention of Youth for Christ International in 1945, Rev. Torrey Johnson warned that if they failed in their task of world evangelization, "we who are here will be held responsible for the greatest tragedy in human history — we are headed either for a definite turning toward God or the greatest calamity ever to strike the human race." He called for an all-out evangelistic effort directed at postwar Germany to prevent that country from going Communist. He reassured the delegates that "if Hitler could make the youth in a nation move with his program, God, by the Holy Spirit, ought to be able to get the same youth into a program of His kind and it has to be done." The secret to saving the world, Johnson insisted, was to "challenge young people with the job that needs to be done around the world."[7]

African American Baptists used the specter of angry young men to argue that adults needed to get rid of segregation and discrimination before it was too late. In 1934 George E. Haynes, Executive Secretary of the Federal Council of Churches Department of Race Relations, addressed the National Baptist Convention on the topic "The Crisis Confronting the American Negro and the Negro Churches." Integral to his diagnosis of the crisis was his concern that "our young people will no longer accept the soft pabulum" they had traditionally been fed in church. Instead, they were becoming increasingly open to communist propaganda. Unless the church led society in offering real-world solutions to the economic crisis, chaos and tyranny might overtake America. Sounding a similar note in 1945, William H. Jernagin, President of the Sunday School and Baptist Training Union Congress, warned that "Johnnie G.I." would not put up with the old injustices. He proposed a comprehensive program of reform that included anti-lynching legislation, voting rights, and federal employment regulations.[8]

Roman Catholic Bishop James Kearney gave an especially revealing speech in 1937. While participating in a radio panel on the potentially boring topic of "The Organization of a Youth Program," he felt the need to give an electrifying warning. "We are blind to what is happening around us if we do not see that we live in a truly critical and crucial age in which changes are being brought about that will control course and direction to ensuing generations — or perhaps even centuries," he said. Kearney articulated what many Americans felt when he described a future offering two contrasting paths. One led to "liberty, economic security, and human dignity," the other to "state control and regimented slavery in the economic, social and spiritual order." What would decide the outcome? His answer was clear: "the character of the ensuing age will be determined by the philosophy of life which we give to the young people of this present generation." Kearney drew a parallel between adolescence and the crisis of the age. The young person faced the "hottest stage" in the warfare of life "when he is assailed by a tumultuous confederacy of lawless passions and desires; and it is in that awful crisis, that period on which, like a pivot, may hang his triumph or defeat, he needs all the aids of religion."[9]

The battle for the future of civilization became quite literally the battle for the souls and bodies of youth. One reason young people acquired such symbolic power during the crisis years was that the potential, peril, and confusion of adolescence seemed to parallel the distress of American civilization. Whatever the truth behind such sentiments, many Americans heard these messages and started to agree.

Christian Youth Work Gains Public Influence

Through their relentless campaigning, Christian youth leaders influenced the public conversation about the youth problem. The American Council on Education established the American Youth Commission in 1935 to study the problems of youth in light of the "long-continued world crisis."[10] In 1939, the AYC issued a report that included praise for the role of religion in solving the youth problem: "for moral action, there is only one rational basis, namely, the conviction of our accountability to the Power that gave us being. The brotherhood of man is an idle dream unless there is a recognition of the fatherhood of God." The report went on to observe: "it is significant that every attack by contemporary tyrannical governments on human rights has begun with an assault on religion." Although the economic needs of youth had to be tackled, the report concluded that "a program for strengthening the nation that looks to youth and to the future will in itself be a source of vitality and of spiritual strength even though physical accomplishments are still to come." In other words, youth programs could at least protect youth and teach them good values, even if they couldn't solve the problem of unemployment. The report called for an all-out effort to help youth, because "national survival" hung in the balance.[11] Even this non-sectarian panel of youth experts believed that religion would play a crucial role in saving the nation by saving its youth.

The reports of the American Youth Commission were widely quoted by those concerned about the youth problem and prompted the establishment of the National Youth Administration. The NYA tried to provide job skills and political indoctrination for young people who were out of work, while keeping them off the streets and out of trouble. Compared to other New Deal departments, the NYA never accomplished much and its programs remained tiny. The better-known Civilian Conservation Corps impacted more young people. But whatever their scope, the very existence of such programs confirmed that at the highest levels, Americans saw the "youth problem" as important.[12]

Because theirs had been some of the most persuasive voices proclaiming the youth problem and offering solutions, Christian youth leaders gained new power to influence public policy and new respect in society at large. Catholic educator George Johnson played a prominent role in the American Youth Commission.[13] African American Christian educator Mary McLeod Bethune served as the Director of the Division of Negro Affairs for the National Youth Administration. NYA staff member Charles Taussig courted Protestant youth organizations and hoped to start a "democratic education" program in churches to indoctrinate youth in the politics of the New Deal.[14] Even fundamentalist leaders like Jack Wyrtzen could wield political influence at times. When a local military officer refused to release his men to attend Wyrtzen's Saturday night youth rally in New York City, a quick appeal up the chain of command straightened things out. The Hearst newspapers and several national news magazines portrayed the fledgling Youth for Christ movement as a potential answer to the problem of wartime juvenile delinquency. On one occasion, President Truman praised Youth for Christ as just what America needed.[15]

Christian leaders did more than just revel in their newfound respect. Across the spectrum of American churches, concerned leaders founded new youth organizations between 1930 and 1945. The National Council of Churches put new efforts into their United Christian Youth Movement. Mainline Protestant denominations founded new youth ministries or re-organized their national youth programs with an eye toward youthful social action. Evangelical Protestants founded new interdenominational youth organizations like Youth for Christ and Young Life, which used innovative methods to evangelize the young. Roman Catholics founded the Catholic Youth Organization, Young Christian Workers, and Young Christian Students. They also created a Youth Department in the National Catholic Welfare Conference. African American Christians did not found new organizations, but their efforts to help young people garnered new support from both church members and outsiders as a result of national concerns about the youth problem. Not since the late nineteenth century had there been so many new Christian youth programs. Considering the scarcity of resources during the Great Depression and the national mobilization for World War II, it is amazing that so much time, effort, and money went into Christian youth work.

Christian leaders agreed that they needed to solve the "youth problem" if the nation was to survive its "crisis of civilization." But they did not agree on how best to protect young people from evil influences or mobilize them to save the world. The powerful drive to save the world created space for a rich variety of religious innovations. Young people and their leaders found themselves able to ignore their critics and do things they had never done before. Some actively tried to rebuild America using Christian economic and political principles. Others tirelessly preached the gospel so that young people would be converted to Christ. Still others tried to provide recreational and educational programs for young people in order to turn them into productive citizens. These innovations strengthened the churches and convinced both adults and young people that youth really were politically powerful.

Youth Building a Christian Social Order

Mainline Protestant youth leaders like those who ran the Methodist Youth Department dreamed of mobilizing young people to build a "Christian social order." In the early 1930s, Blaine Kirkpatrick and Owen Geer took over the Youth Department of the main northern branch of Methodism. According to their plan, each local youth fellowship would elect officers and establish committees on devotional life, world evangelism, social service, and recreation. Adults would serve as advisors whose role was to help young people discover the truth for themselves and become solid democratic citizens and leaders. A popular manual promised that through their discussions, committee meetings, group projects, and wholesome recreation Methodist youth would not only "win folks to Christ" but also "help build a Christian social order."[16]

Aware that local church youth clubs might struggle to create a "Christian social order" on their own, Kirkpatrick and Geer also organized the National Conference of Methodist Youth in 1934. Since they believed young Methodists could play a key role in the crisis of civilization, it seemed natural to them to create an organization modeled on a legislative assembly. They intended this group to be a "democratic" organization that would serve as the voice of Methodist youth, and they hoped that this voice would be politically progressive. The 1,000 college students and teenagers elected each year to the conference more than fulfilled their leaders' expectations. They endorsed the Student Strike for Peace, raised money to help carry the Hamilton-Reynolds case against compulsory ROTC training to the Supreme Court, and adopted resolutions containing statements like "we denounce our present capitalistic system." They also protested racial segregation at major denominational conferences. Many young Methodists pledged themselves not to participate in any war declared by the United States. Their ideal was one of "Christian citizenship" that put loyalty to the ideals of Jesus above loyalty to the state. They deplored both the capitalist greed and the virulent nationalism that were pushing the world toward war.[17]

Such successes are all the more striking in light of the strong opposition these pioneers faced. Alarmed by what seemed to be a rising tide of communist-inspired activism, some church members pressured the Methodist Board of Education to fire Kirkpatrick and Geer in 1936. Young Methodists strongly protested this action, as did *The Christian Century*, the leading voice of liberal Protestantism. Although the young officers of the

National Conference of Methodist Youth did not sever their relationship with the denominational Youth Department, relations were strained for some years.[18]

But conservative opposition did not dampen youthful enthusiasm. The young Methodists who attended national conferences became even more active in the late 1930s and early 1940s. They lobbied against the draft, made national news by writing an open letter to President Roosevelt denouncing his support for the war in Europe, and disrupted the Methodist General Conference in 1940 by passing out handbills denouncing guest speaker Senator Martin Dies as a pro-war legislator. Some young Methodists even refused to register for the draft, while others accepted conscientious-objector status.[19]

Young Methodists were also very active in the cause of racial justice. When the northern and southern Methodist churches reunited in 1940, members of the National Conference of Methodist Youth lobbied denominational leaders asking them to create an integrated governing structure for the new denomination. Unfortunately, the church retained the segregated Central Jurisdiction for its African American congregations. Members of one Methodist Youth Fellowship in Dallas successfully pressured local officials to build a new black high school. Others raised money for the relief of interned Japanese Americans and spent part of their summer vacation providing services to victims of internment. In the summer of 1945, teenagers at one Methodist youth camp in Iowa reportedly treated their two Japanese American campers as "heroes." Regional youth leaders integrated their summer camps by inviting African Americans in at least token numbers during the war. Even in the Deep South, young whites protested the exclusion of black Methodists from their camp facilities.[20] These interracial and anti-war activities were extremely countercultural and demonstrated the power of national youth conferences and regional camps to foster a vision for social reform among young Methodists.

This rising tide of youthful activism caused politically progressive Methodists, both young and old, to see young people as a natural opposition party in church and society. In 1941 Herman Will exhorted his fellow delegates to the National Conference of the Methodist Youth Fellowship to become a "democratic" and "creative" force in church and society. By "creative," he meant that they "should break new ground where institutional boards and commissions often bound by red tape and conservatism dare not venture." Young Methodists learned to see themselves as potential leaders. A Catholic bishop who was an adult convert from Methodism complained in the 1950s that as a young Methodist he had been taught to expect to exert influence as a leader in society, whereas Catholic young people did not seem to get that message.[21]

At the end of the war, many socially concerned Methodists were confident that youth would take the lead in their church's bold plan for postwar reform. Bishop G. Bromley Oxnam helped launch a church-wide campaign for social reform labeled the "Crusade for a New World Order." At a Methodist youth conference in 1946, renowned liberal Dr. Kirby Page told the attendees that if they could just educate 1 million Methodists to support "world government" and oppose the arms race with Russia, they could sway the entire church, and the church could influence the United States government. Page delivered this stirring exhortation at a Methodist camp in Fayetteville, Arkansas, which had just that year agreed to feed and house a black conference speaker even though white young people had been demanding a change in the camp's policy since 1938.[22] Perhaps swaying the Methodist church might be hard enough, never mind creating a "new world order." Despite ongoing opposition from social and political conservatives, Methodist reformers interpreted their successful national youth conferences of the 1930s and 1940s as clear evidence that they stood on the cusp of a dramatic Christian transformation of society that would begin with the young.

Saving the World by Launching a Youth Revival

On Memorial Day 1945, some 70,000 people gathered at Soldier Field for a "Victory Rally" sponsored by Chicagoland Youth for Christ. Organizers provided an exciting spectacle that combined intense evangelistic fervor with staunch patriotism. The event began with a posting of the American and Christian flags by a color guard of local high school ROTC cadets. A choir of 2,500 young people provided music. Four hundred nurses marched in the form of a giant cross. Servicemen and their families received recognition in the form of a twelve-foot gold star. Sergeant Bert Frizen testified to the need for Christian faith among young soldiers. Champion runner Gil Dodds ran an exhibition lap before testifying to the crowd that "running is only a hobby. My mission is teaching the gospel of Jesus Christ." Finally, Percy Crawford, fundamentalist youth ministry pioneer, preached an evangelistic message and asked for a show of hands of those who wanted to accept Jesus Christ as savior. One pastor in attendance crowed that the event "out-colossaled the movies." Youth for Christ president Torrey Johnson later recalled that on that May afternoon in 1945 more war bonds were sold than at any other single gathering held during the war. Just days after this event, Johnson wired Rev. Martin Niemoller in Germany to offer Youth for Christ's services to bring Nazi youth back to Christ.[23]

Youth for Christ had its roots in the independent efforts of a new generation of fundamentalist preachers like Jack Wyrtzen in New York and Torrey Johnson in Chicago. These men raised money with the help of local businessmen and rented public auditoriums in downtown areas. The typical Saturday night youth rally featured a live radio broadcast, upbeat music that mimicked the crooner and big-band styles of the day, brief "testimonies" by recent converts, and short, fervent sermons tied to current events.[24]

This mix of entertainment, evangelism, and patriotism sounded just the right note during the fearful days of World War II. On weekend evenings during the war, the streets of many cities filled with a crowd of soldiers and local youths all searching for a good time. YFC rallies adapted to the mobility and emotional needs created by wartime conditions more effectively than traditional Sunday schools and youth meetings. Both participants and sympathetic outsiders stressed YFC as the answer to wartime restlessness and danger. One sailor converted at a rally told reporters,

> I have felt almost adrift, with no sense of security. I don't want to get caught in the current of vice. I need something to stabilize me and in my new faith in Christ, I have found it.[25]

But in the eyes of YFC enthusiasts, the conversions at these rallies did more than just keep young people out of trouble. They also contributed to the war effort. The souvenir program for the 1944 Chicago Victory Rally told the story of Kenneth Kirby, another young sailor who had made a point of witnessing to "every man on board" his ship. No doubt readers felt a pang of both grief and excitement when they read that "faithful to that task, sailor Kirby went down with 165 others when his destroyer sank recently. Some of them are in Glory tonight because of his testimony."[26] Young people continually exposed to such stories learned that their conversion and witnessing for Christ would not only provide a sense of inner peace but might also play a role in America's war effort. They also may have learned, by implication, that a death in service of country could be viewed as a sort of Christian martyrdom.

YFC leaders saw themselves as the solution to the wartime problem of "juvenile delinquency." Reporters once asked Johnson what Youth for Christ could have done for the university sophomore in Chicago who had recently been arrested for burglaries and murder. In reply, he told them the story of Perry Jackman, a thirteen-year-old from Salt Lake City. One Saturday night Perry, with a gun in his pocket, approached a young woman with the intention of robbing her. Instead, with "God-given courage" she invited Perry to the Youth for Christ rally. They rode the streetcar together to the rally, and while there, Perry was converted.[27]

By the end of the war, about 1 million teenagers gathered every Saturday night in 900 churches and auditoriums across the country for Youth for Christ rallies. Overseas, military servicemen started their own rallies and discovered a taste for Christian service that would lead some of them to found missionary, humanitarian, and evangelistic organizations in the postwar era. Chief among these was the Billy Graham Evangelistic Association, whose leader got his start as a preacher for Youth for Christ.[28]

The leaders of Youth for Christ did not think they were just providing a wholesome alternative for young people on Saturday night. They planned to solve the world's problems by evangelizing youth. Torrey Johnson, the newly elected president of Youth for Christ International, presented his vision for the group in two sermons delivered at its 1945 youth convention. Johnson believed that YFC rallies held the key to saving the world because "after all, who are the people that are saved in revivals? The answer is — YOUNG PEOPLE!" Yet his vision went beyond the youth of America. YFC needed to reach Germany with the gospel, because a communist postwar Germany would "directly affect us."[29] He exhorted evangelical teenagers to solve the crisis by devoting themselves to world evangelization. "America cannot survive another twenty-five years like the last . . . If we have another lost generation . . . America is sunk," he warned. He blamed the failure to reach the "lost generation" of the 1920s on the adults of the inter-war years: "all you older friends, get this: It's your fault that we have to speak simply to our young people, and I'll tell you why. It's because our young people have been betrayed by the generation that went before." Although they had failed to pass on the faith before, they must not fail now, because "fellows that were out in the hell of Guadalcanal and through the thick of the invasion of Normandy and on the Anzio beachhead — they are the boys that will rule this country. We have to reach them for Christ, or God help us."[30] According to Johnson and his fellow Youth for Christ leaders, an army of teenage evangelists could rebuild the world and root out evil political systems. No doubt the young people present felt a heightened sense of their own significance in God's plan for saving the world.

Although most of the public attention generated by the massive Youth for Christ rallies was positive, a few voices questioned the political leanings of the movement. Harold Fey of the *Christian Century* observed that at YFC rallies, "the war is presented as a holy crusade" and "the service of Christ and the military service of country are equated." He worried that many of the financial backers of the movement were "theologically and socially conservative business men" and even quoted one such supporter who liked the fact that YFC provided an alternative to "the social gospel kind of preaching." Less careful critics assumed that YFC was a front for right-wing politics. They noted ominously that conservative newspaper baron William Randolph Hearst gave the movement extensive coverage. Even worse, fascist sympathizer and fundamentalist preacher Gerald L. K. Smith, who had been recently charged with sedition, had publicly endorsed the movement. At one point, the *Christian Century* tried to rein in the escalating accusations by publishing an article, "Has Youth for Christ Gone Fascist?" The author recalled that from the beginning some had feared the movement might be "a cloak to cover the efforts of a group of fascist-minded business men to capture the mind of American young people for their own purposes." But such charges had never been proven. Recently, plans to establish a Youth for Christ rally on the south side of Chicago in a heavily black neighborhood had prompted cries of "Jim Crow Christianity" in some quarters, much to the dismay of the black church leaders involved in the planning. In response to the uproar, the author offered a cautious defense of the movement, admitting that since its leaders were "little concerned with the social or ethical bearing of the Christian life" they might blunder into alliances with groups who would try to exploit their mass appeal. He concluded that so far the group had not been drawn into such unholy political alliances, but implied that socially progressive Christians should keep an eye on the group.[31]

When asked to comment on these allegations, Torrey Johnson insisted that YFC had no ties with William Randolph Hearst or Gerald L. K. Smith and that they wanted nothing to do with "anyone with a political axe to grind" because their movement was "100% religious." Early promotional materials for the movement insisted that it was "inter-church, non-political, and non-sectarian." One brochure even claimed that the overwhelmingly white movement was "inter-racial." In fairness, even one of

YFC's critics had to admit that "at every YFC meeting I have attended, I have noticed a few Negro members."[32] It seems ridiculous in hindsight to see Youth for Christ as fascist, but then again, the Methodist Youth Fellowship was not communist, either. These feverish accusations on all sides vividly demonstrate the political significance many Americans read into youth groups during the crisis years. On the other hand, it was naïve and somewhat misleading of Johnson and other YFC leaders to claim political neutrality when their rallies dripped with patriotism and rang with calls to save the world from political disaster and the nation from moral corruption.

Youth for Christ leaders considered their movement a success against the crisis of civilization. They modernized revivalism, won respect in the secular press, and appealed to young people by combining entertainment, an appealing spirituality, and the powerful language linking youth and the crisis of civilization. It remained to be seen whether their appealing combination of youth-friendly revivalism and American patriotism would produce the army of young evangelists needed to save the world.

Saving America by Making It More Catholic

Roman Catholic youth leaders were sure that their church could solve the youth problem and save the world. But they could not agree on whether to save America by keeping youth Catholic, by making them better Americans, or by mobilizing them to create a society based on Catholic social teaching.

The traditional approach had been to create separate youth institutions to form young Catholics in distinctive ways of thinking and living. One of the main purposes of Catholic schools had always been to form strong Catholic identities so that young people would grow up resistant to the influences of Protestant (or secular) America. As Bishop Kearney put it, the most crucial task of youth work was to give young people the right "philosophy of life," by which he meant a Catholic philosophy of life. In the 1930s, many Catholics believed that Catholic schools should be their first choice for forming their children. Pope Pius XI's 1929 encyclical *The Christian Education of Youth* had insisted that only the Church and the family could provide the type of education that could produce a good society.[33] The 1917 code of canon law had commanded Catholic parents to send their children to Catholic schools.

Although many Catholic parents in the United States took this obligation seriously, Catholic elementary school attendance typically outpaced high school attendance. Even though the number of pupils in Catholic high schools rose 54 percent between 1934 and 1945, the majority of young Catholics still attended public high schools, or none at all. Yet throughout this period high school attendance was on the rise, meaning that more and more young Catholics breathed the spiritually harmful atmosphere of the public high school. Believing that the "youth problem" demanded a vigorous and innovative response, Catholic clergy, educators, and parents began exploring ways to spiritually influence young Catholics who did not take the preferred path of Catholic schooling.[34]

The leaders of the National Catholic Welfare Conference seized the moment and began planning a national youth program that would protect and care for young Catholics not covered by the Catholic school system. The NCWC had been created by the American bishops during World War I to coordinate Catholic social, political, and humanitarian efforts. The organization had pioneered lay leadership by forming National Councils of Catholic Men and Women. In 1934, at the urging of papal delegate Amleto Giovanni Cicognani, these lay councils convened meetings to discuss the improvement of Catholic youth programs.[35]

Over the next few years, these conferences combined extreme rhetoric about youth and crisis with recommendations for recreational programs and a dose of spirituality. In an address to the National Council of Catholic Women, Bishop Joseph Rummel warned of the urgent need for effective youth programs by noting that "at no time in the history of human experiences was there manifest such a vying and striving for the possession of the mind, the heart and the brawn of youth as is almost universally in evidence today." But it seemed that this historic crisis was to be met with the same old recreational programs. As part of "The Call to Youth" radio broadcasts sponsored by the National Council of Catholic Women in 1938, Anne Hooley outlined a four-fold program providing opportunities to "play, create, think, and pray." She insisted that "if we could supply these, there would be no talk of a lost generation, no mournful head shaking over the outcome of youth." By providing activities like "dramatics or music or painting or one of the crafts," leaders would be satisfying deep human needs and saving civilization.[36]

In 1940, the National Catholic Welfare Conference established a Youth Department, headed by Rev. Vincent Mooney, CSC. Both Mooney and his successor, Rev. Paul Tanner, tried to build a network of diocesan youth directors and support them with resources to improve Catholic youth work.

They also dreamed of establishing a system of youth councils that would begin at the parish level and culminate in a National Council of Catholic Youth. But unlike the National Conference of Methodist Youth, Tanner hoped these councils would have a pro-war, anti-communist influence. He wrote that the "possibilities of a Christian peace" depended upon American Catholics and that "upon articulate, informed youth groups depends the formation of popular American Catholic opinion." Tanner urged his fellow youth leaders to keep up the good fight against subversive youth groups with their "pacifistic disloyalty to God and country" and replaced them with the American majority values of "religion, filial piety, humility."[37] Nothing much came of these efforts during the war, but they laid the foundation for the postwar emergence of a model of Catholic youth work that emphasized purity, piety, and patriotism.

Many Catholic leaders of the 1930s and 1940s claimed to possess a definitive Christian blueprint for social reform — and a mandate from the pope to put it into action. Emboldened by the desperate needs of their nation, they dreamed of reforming society along the lines of what they called "Catholic social teaching." The Catholic answer to social ills received renewed attention with the promulgation of *Quadragesimo Anno* in 1931. Following Pius XI's direction in this encyclical, progressive Catholics condemned communism, fascism, and unrestrained capitalism alike. In place of these they preached economic cooperation between labor and management to be achieved via the "living wage" and other social welfare measures. Even as they criticized inequity in America and supported labor unions, many Catholic activists also insisted that papal social teachings and true American values were fully compatible, usually without explaining just how the two fit together. The pope also created a new term, "Catholic action," to describe his ideal of lay activism in which committed Catholics, working in close cooperation with the clergy, would re-Christianize society. American Catholics of all stripes seized on this label and applied it to their activities.[38]

But the mere existence of a Catholic social blueprint and a stirring ideal of "Catholic action" did not eliminate all questions of how to solve the "youth problem" and save America. Some, like Bishop Bernard Sheil of Chicago, tried to take Catholic youth work into the mainstream by creating agencies designed to benefit the entire community. In 1930 he founded the Catholic Youth Organization in direct response to his experience as a chaplain for young offenders in the Cook County Jail. The CYO worked to keep kids off the streets using boxing tournaments, community recreation centers, and vocational schools. Sheil also promoted Catholic social teaching by adding the Sheil School of Social Studies and a Social Services Department to the CYO. His strategy was to offer the resources of the church to the public as a solution to the crisis of youth unemployment and crime. He insisted that "youth is not a problem" but realized that working-class Catholic boys were especially well represented among unemployed and delinquent youth. He presented Catholic recreational activities as providing political help to the nation by protecting young Americans from the communists. He even claimed that boxing had brought many young men back to the sacraments. Teaching boys moral and democratic values through sports was a way to establish American middle-class credentials for a Catholic population still viewed with suspicion by the Protestants who ran the country at the time. His portrayal of the CYO boys as "America's team," drawn from every race and religious background, reflected his fond hope that Catholics could be full partners in American society without losing their distinctiveness.

Sheil's model gained national recognition and prompted imitators. When he called these leaders together for a national conference in 1938, sixty-five dioceses sent 102 delegates. By 1940 the CYO claimed to be touching the lives of 250,000 young people annually. Forty summer day camps served 14,600 participants with a staff of 1,133 volunteers. In a show of cooperation typical of Sheil's programs, employees of the Works Progress Administration, National Youth Administration, and Chicago Park District joined nuns, seminarians, and Catholic college students to staff these "vacation schools." Many were held in city parks. Of course such cooperation limited the explicit religious content of the vacation schools; no longer did the youngsters learn to sing the mass as they had in the early days. On the other hand, Sheil did not soften his staunchly progressive political agenda. He publicly criticized the right-wing radio priest Father Charles Coughlin. He also denounced racism and the exploitation of labor. One conservative critic even accused him of being a communist.[39]

Sheil's vision of an inclusive, politically progressive, yet distinctively Catholic youth-serving agency still seemed too compromising in the eyes of other Catholic activists. Since everyone in the 1930s claimed they were doing "Catholic action," some leaders, like Monsignor Reynold Hillenbrand of the Chicago Archdiocese, started describing their youth organizations as "specialized Catholic action." The leaders of this movement modeled their activities on those of Cardinal Joseph Cardijn in Belgium. Cardijn had created the "Young Christian Workers" as a Catholic alternative to the heavily communist labor movements of Europe. The idea was for Catholic factory workers to meet in small groups called "cells" that would "observe" conditions in their neighborhoods and workplaces, "judge" those conditions in light of Catholic social teaching (often under the guidance of a priest advisor), and "act" together to improve their workplaces and neighborhoods. This process of "observe, judge, act" was called the "inquiry method."

Leaders of the movement in the United States believed that the best hope lay not in creating a mass movement of Catholic youth, but rather in training and deploying an elite corps of what they liked to call "young apostles" who would transform society. The leaders of the Young Christian Workers also differed from other socially concerned Catholics like Sheil in that they took a more critical stance toward American society and its institutions. They were much more likely to see America as unchristian and in need of some serious reform.

The young Catholics who joined the Young Christian Workers in the 1930s and 1940s felt the excitement of participating in a world-changing movement. One early participant recalled:

> I was attracted to the YCW by the people involved in it and by the potential for revolutionizing the face of the earth and therefore being involved in an important historical event which I anticipated as being immediate. (Oh, maybe it would take ten whole years to straighten things out!)[40]

Whether it was through parochial schools, CYO boxing tournaments, Specialized Catholic Action, or parish youth councils, Catholics claimed to be able to fix America by saving its youth. World War II in particular provided a choice opportunity for Catholics, African Americans, and other "outsiders" to prove their loyalty and value to America. Young Catholics seemed to be mobilizing on every front to save America: on the battlefield, in the factories, and in their schools. Perhaps young people would lead Catholics from the margins to the center of American society.

Rebuking America for Its Failed Promises to Youth

Like other Christians, African American Baptists believed that young people might hold the key to saving civilization. At a regional youth gathering in 1935, the Rev. W. H. Jernagin, president of the Sunday School and Baptist Training Union Congress, proclaimed that "young people can do more toward bringing the world back to God than all the other organizations or set-ups you might mention."[41] Lethia Craig, president of the Women's Auxiliary Convention of the National Baptist Convention, called for more extensive and efficient youth programs in the church using the following argument:

> Today as never before the nations of the world are realizing the importance of the training of youth. All are seeing that tomorrow's world depends on today's youth. The leaders of our great national organizations are realizing that the security of their power depends on what they put into the young people.[42]

Stating explicitly what others left implicit, Craig argued that youth were a source of power.

Yet unlike their white counterparts, African American Baptists did not create new youth organizations during the crisis years. Instead of segregating young people into separate organizations, African American Baptists tended to integrate them into the life of the church. Rev. William H. Jernagin's Baptist Training Union Congress drew adult and youth delegates to an annual conference for training in how to teach Sunday School and run youth programs. The local Baptist Training Union meeting typically took place on Sunday night and drew adults, teenagers, and children to a program of shared social activities and Bible lessons. The Women's Auxiliary of the National Baptist Convention organized an age-graded program of clubs for children and youth, but at their national meetings, young women joined in common sessions with their elders.[43] Besides Sunday School, the most common Baptist youth activity was a monthly "Youth Sunday" at which young people led the prayers, took up the offering, and sang in the choir. Preachers often used their sermons on Youth Sunday to exhort adults.[44] During the 1930s and 1940s, young African American Baptists shared a similar pattern of spiritual life with their elders and benefited from close interaction with adults.

Several factors account for the fact that black Baptist leaders tended to integrate young people into the life of the church rather than creating separate organizations. Limited resources, especially in small rural congregations, forced churches to offer a narrower range of program options. Yet even larger urban congregations did not build separate youth organizations on the scale of their white counterparts. Separate youth organizations were less needed in the black community because families, churches, and schools cooperated more closely than they did in the white community. Many schools began the day with Bible reading and prayer. Preachers often addressed school assemblies. Educators intended the strict discipline and vigorous morality of the schools to impart confidence and ambition to young black people who faced a society intent on keeping them down. These dynamics proved especially powerful in middle-class urban congregations in which young people often interacted with their teachers both at school and in church.[45] The Rev. Kelly Miller Smith, pastor of First Baptist Church in Nashville and noted civil rights leader, hinted at a deeper reason for the generational integration of the black church. In an address to Christian educators he complained that "too often we want our young people to be confined to certain categories. Indeed we wish to segregate them."[46] As victims of racial segregation, African American adults may have instinctively avoided the white model for age segregation.

Perhaps because they had personally suffered injustice, African American church leaders were even less likely than whites to blame young people for the problems of the world. W. H. Jernagin told gatherings of young people that "the fault is clearly with Age" and that "the militancy of Christ's gospel appeals especially to young people." He criticized adults for creating a nation in which "The Bill of Rights are a mere scrap of paper, for millions have not the right to work." He insisted that "The primary duty of the Christian church is to deal with the problems of this world here and now." He denounced the "hypocrisy and duplicity" of white clergy who occasionally talked about "brotherhood" but did little about it. The new social order that so many Christians sought would be "impossible without first a new Christian attitude towards races."[47] Although young people needed to take an active role, African American youth leaders believed that adults were clearly to blame and held the greatest responsibility to fix the world.

More often than their white counterparts, African American clergy combined both the spiritual consolations of "old time religion" and an aggressive priority on social justice. The struggle to balance these sometimes competing priorities shaped the lives of well-educated clergy who began their pastorates in the 1930s and 1940s. For example, as a young man in a sharecropping family, Rev. Wade Hampton McKinney underwent a conversion experience, and especially remembered the spiritual sung at his baptism which emphasized separation from "the world." While in seminary he suffered from doubts as he learned more theology, but the memory of his conversion sustained him. Over time he became increasingly concerned with social justice. During his first pastorate in Flint, Michigan, he aroused controversy within his church because he got involved in labor disputes.

In his second pastorate in Cleveland, McKinney combined the roles of social prophet, community organizer, and gospel preacher. He unambiguously preached that only spiritual regeneration could save individuals and society. Yet he also told white community leaders that rates of crime and infant mortality were higher in the black community because "they are the most exploited group of any in our city." McKinney worked closely with Sylvester Williams of the Christian Community Center to help meet such needs. He also organized a junior church, Boy Scouts and Girl Scouts, a youth fellowship, and sports teams. He criticized the modern tendency to call youthful sins "adolescent impulses" but he also denounced Americans for promoting sexual vice and greed while fighting a war to save the world. Like many African American leaders, he predicted that victory in the war could not save America unless it led to racial justice. "No immoral or selfish civilization can endure in a moral universe," he warned. He also saw youth as key to the crisis. After the dropping of the atomic bomb, he often preached that "the only power that can save us from our science is moral power. If we cannot persuade the children of the next two or three generations to open their hearts to this moral power, then our world is doomed." His efforts inspired many young men and women to pursue higher education and the Christian ministry. One young church member praised McKinney for being a wise counselor, an inspiring preacher, and most of all because "he stands for the right and fights courageously for the welfare of the Negroes of Cleveland."[48] Compared to white Protestants, African Americans found it easier to combine concern for social justice with traditional gospel preaching. But like their white counterparts, African American youth leaders tended to idealize young people and overestimate their political clout.

Saving the World by Saving Youth

In the name of saving civilization by saving young people, Christian youth leaders juvenilized Christian political action and social concern. From now on, young people would be held up as the ideal political activists, social re-

39

formers, and patriots. Each branch of American Christianity had a different plan for saving young people and civilization. Yet they all believed that the young had a natural idealism, boundless energy, and an innate tendency to devote themselves to important but unpopular causes. Youth leaders sometimes blamed adults and called on them to fix the world for the sake of young people. But most often, youth leaders and those they influenced got in the habit of thinking of youth, not adults, as the most important reformers in church and society.

The people who most often heard this message were the young Christians who participated in the many large youth gatherings of the era. These future leaders learned that youth would always be the most important political and social force in the world, and by implication, not to expect much from themselves or others once they reached adulthood. According to this line of thinking, if adults were to accomplish anything of value in the political realm, they needed to become more like young people. In point of fact, young people are rarely in a position of political and social power, so this way of thinking led to a skewed view of reality that could easily lead to discouragement or frustration.

In the heat of battle and seemingly on the verge of dramatic victories, Christian youth leaders of the 1930s and 1940s found it easy to ignore some otherwise pressing questions that linger to this day. Are young people the problem, or the solution? Are American youth ready to be saviors of the world, or do they need to be saved first? Are young people natural political progressives? Do they really have the power to change society? Do adults really want them to be politically powerful, or would we prefer them politically quiet? How can young people fix adult problems? Do young people really fit the images we have of them, or want the "savior" roles we often demand of them?

Such questions could be ignored in the 1930s and 1940s, because the crisis of civilization allowed little room for armchair theologizing. The politically exciting Christian youth gatherings of that era also seemed to prove that young people were poised to save the world. Christian youth leaders and the young people who followed them unleashed a new and powerful engine of change in the churches. From then on, almost any innovation could be justified in the name of saving young people. Who could worry about the long-term impact of youth work on the church when the fate of civilization hung in the balance?

CHAPTER 2

Misreading the Signs of the Times:
From Political Youth to Trivial Teenagers

We just like to live and have a good time. We're not in a hurry to grow up and get all serious and morbid like older people.

"Teenage Girls," *The March of Time* newsreel, 1945

By the end of the 1940s, those committed to enlisting youth in the serious business of saving the world competed against the all-encompassing social world of the high school, the enticements of youthful consumerism, and even the temptations of drinking, sex, and crime that contemporaries lumped together under the label "juvenile delinquency." A few youth leaders occasionally worried that providing entertaining programs for teenagers might have little to do with solving the world's problems. But for the most part they banished such doubts and clung to their belief that young people were a powerful force that would reform the church and save the world.

In one sense, it's easy to see how youth leaders could have made this mistake. Although Americans felt intense jubilation at the end of World War II, their sense of relief gave way to renewed apprehension as they attempted to adjust to the idea of a potential nuclear war and a Cold War with no end in sight. Perhaps there *was* something new and different in their world, a perpetual "crisis of civilization" which could only be solved by shaping the next generation of Christian leaders. Many also feared a postwar economic depression. The outbursts of juvenile delinquency that many had blamed on wartime conditions seemed if anything to be waxing stronger after the war. With their imaginations held captive by such dramatic problems, Christian leaders assumed that the newly emerging middle-class youth culture was either a safe tool to use, or a trivial trend to ignore. For their part, young people pushed their leaders to provide both exciting, entertaining experiences *and* ways to participate, at least symbolically, in world-saving crusades. Youth leaders set the stage for the juvenilization of Christianity by overestimating the political power of youth and underestimating the long-term effects of accomodating youth culture.

The Tip of the Iceberg:
Juvenile Delinquents and "Bobby-Soxers"

Two stereotypes of troublesome young people grabbed headlines during the 1940s: juvenile delinquents and "bobby-soxers." As with other youthful stereotypes, these images had some basis in fact. There was in fact a surge of youth crime, or at least heightened awareness of it, during the war, and there was a new and more visible girls' culture. As often happens when adults observe teenage behavior they don't like or understand, these new young people provoked much hand-wringing and even outrage. But in terms of the real experiences of young people, the juvenile delinquent and the bobby-soxer were but the tip of the iceberg. Beneath these often discussed but seldom understood stereotypes lay more foundational changes in the lives of a majority of young Americans that few adults truly recognized at the time.

Two newsreels of the 1940s illustrate what adults thought about juvenile delinquents and bobby-soxers. These newsreels appeared before feature films in theaters across the nation. Like most media products, these reports both reflected public opinion and helped to shape it. A newsreel entitled "Youth in Crisis" began by noting that many young men were being rejected by the military due to psychological problems. The narrator hinted that something must be deeply wrong with America if so many young men were mentally unfit to serve their country. The film went on to suggest that the psychological tensions of the war created race riots because young people "absorb the new spirit of violence and recklessness." Mothers working in war industries supposedly produced a generation of "door key kids" living in "squalid trailer settlements." Teenage boys turned to pornography, marijuana, alcohol, and property destruction as "abnormal outlets for their wartime excitement." Other boys now earning a man's wages were rebelling against their parents and staying out all night. Some young women became "victory girls" who believed it to be their patriotic duty to "deny nothing" to servicemen.

The film echoed the beliefs of many adults at the time when it speculated that boys and girls were getting into trouble because they longed to make some contribution to the war effort, but were thwarted by their age, gender, or both. The film preferred not to explore the possibility that these misbehaving teenagers were just taking advantage of looser supervision during the war to have some fun. FBI director J. Edgar Hoover appeared in the film, insisting that the "solution is in the home." The newsreel also praised daycare centers, after-school programs, and "dry night clubs" or "teen canteens" set up using community funds and run by teenagers themselves.[1] The teenagers who organized their own "teen canteens" would supposedly learn democratic procedures even as they provided wholesome fun for their peers. When even teen recreational centers are touted as training grounds for democracy, the hopes for training young people to be political saviors have run way ahead of reality.

Christian youth leaders were quick to offer their services as a solution to these wartime problems. Young Life, a brand new evangelical Protestant youth organization founded by Jim Rayburn, presented its meetings as the solution to the "victory girl" phenomenon. The first issue of *Young Life*, published in 1944, promoted the movement using contrasting photographs. At the top of the page was a photograph reprinted from *This Week* magazine showing a teenage girl sitting at a bar with two soldiers. The caption read, "These girls come from good homes — they're lonesome, need attention." Below was a picture of teenagers at a Young Life club. The caption read "Young Life has the answer. These kids prove the falsity of 'only sissies read the Bible.'"[2]

Young Life was not the only organization that tried to present itself as a "manly" Christian response to the challenges of the age. Lurking behind such language was the corresponding fear that Christian youth work (and Christian youth workers) might not be so powerful after all. But in the excitement of saving the world by saving Christian youth, most youth leaders ignored such thoughts.

In 1945, theatergoers were treated to yet another newsreel about youth, this one entitled "Teenage Girls." As the film began, a girl sat at a conference table with a collection of white-coated scientists attempting to explain the mysterious values held by her species. "We just like to live and have a good time," she said. "We're not in a hurry to grow up and get all serious and morbid like older people." In sharp contrast to the somber tone of earlier newsreels like "Youth in Crisis," this portrayal of female youth culture adopted an amused tone as it described fashions, music, slang, slumber parties, excessive telephone use, and other traits of these young ladies who had recently been labeled "bobby-soxers." Yet the final scene showed girls singing in a church choir as the narrator reassured the audience that "Youth's boundless energy will in the end direct itself to worthy goals" if adults offered understanding and guidance.[3]

Although the film took note of recent efforts to design and market products to the bobby soxers, it called these girls "a product of wartime" and implied that it was all a passing fad. But these young women represented the wave of the future for middle-class youth cultures. Adults who agreed with this film portrayal saw teenagers as threatening only in the sense that they seemed preoccupied with trivial things and not serious enough about life. After almost fifteen years of hand wringing over the "youth problem," adults could perhaps be excused for wanting to find teenage girls less threatening than "juvenile delinquents" or young political subversives. Yet in hindsight, it seems worth considering that the potentially powerful world inhabited by political "youth" was contracting into the trivial consumer lifestyles of "teenagers."

The young people portrayed in "Youth in Crisis" and "Teenage Girls" captured adult imaginations, but deeper changes were also underway. In reality, the juvenile delinquency scare of the 1940s was a response to a temporary trend created by a combination of wartime social disruptions, media hype, and misleading crime statistics. But that wouldn't stop juvenile delinquency from being a major concern for adults throughout the 1950s.[4]

More significant for the long-term history of youth and youth ministry were two institutions whose power was just beginning to be felt in the 1940s: the high school and youth consumerism. By 1940, for the first time ever, the majority of fourteen- to eighteen-year-old Americans attended high school. They spent more time with each other and less time with adults. Crowded together in age-segregated environments to learn how to be productive adults, young people instead began to create their own language, values, and styles, which sociologist Talcott Parsons would soon label "youth culture." Youth cultures had come and gone before, but never before had young people from across the country shared so many of the same tastes and experiences. Their lives increasingly revolved around school activities, dating, music, and movies. Rural, poor, and minority youth participated less, but it was becoming harder to escape the power of youth cultures.

Since young people seemed to be increasingly different from their parents and finally had some spending money of their own, a few pioneers in entertainment and other industries began intentionally marketing their products to teenagers. For example, in 1942 Frank Sinatra became one of the first true "teen idols" who attracted throngs of screaming and swooning bobby-soxer fans. The first teen magazine of the new era was *Seventeen*, launched in 1944. Its first editor, Helen Valentine, had already proven to the business world that college girls were worth some marketing attention, but it took several years before she could convince them to take high school girls just as seriously. Meanwhile, in 1945 a nineteen-year-old sales clerk named Eugene Gilbert noticed that shoe sales in his store increased dramatically when he changed the advertising approach to attract younger customers. Within two years he had an army of 300 teenagers on the streets interviewing their peers about their consumer preferences.

But like the makers of the film "Teenage Girls," these youth marketing pioneers tried to reassure adults that the changes in teenagers' lives were wholesome. For example, the early issues of *Seventeen* took a serious approach, including articles and editorials that exhorted young readers to get ready to build a better world in the postwar era and to participate in the upcoming presidential campaigns. The typical article also exhorted young girls to earn more privileges from their parents by behaving responsibly, not staying out too late, and maintaining sexual purity.

These early examples of youth consumerism also took place on a small scale and showed signs of being temporary. During the postwar consumer buying boom, the staff of *Seventeen* had to scramble to convince advertisers that teenage girls were still worth courting as a unique market.[5]

Advertisers were not the only ones who needed to be convinced that youth cultures were more than a passing fad. Since these emerging youth cultures could be dismissed not just as fads, but as *female* fads, Christian youth leaders held firm to their stereotypes of powerful, world changing young people. Yet the lives of the high school students who attended Christian youth groups were beginning to diverge more and more from those of the young adults who had recently made headlines as political activists and soldiers.

A shift in terminology both reflected and promoted these changes in the lives of young people. In the 1930s people talked about "youth" as a collective noun, and they talked about it as if it were a powerful force of nature. "Youth" also included a wide range of ages from older childhood through young adulthood. But in the 1940s, the term "teenagers" emerged to describe a narrower, age-defined group of thirteen- to eighteen-year-olds who all attended school, listened to the same music, bought the same products, and behaved in similar ways. "Youth" was a powerful force; "teenagers" were a sometimes irritating, sometimes amusing, but less often threatening group. Most Christian youth leaders missed the significance of the shift from powerful youth to trivial teenagers. So despite their successes at the time, these leaders did not lay a good foundation for dealing with later youth culture developments.

Reluctant Social Crusaders

Throughout the 1940s, mainline Protestant youth leaders like those who ran the Methodist Youth Department remained confident that youth would save the world in its time of "crisis" by devoting themselves to a crusade for a more Christian, politically progressive America. But they tended to ignore contrary evidence. The firing of Blaine Kirkpatrick and Owen Geer from the Youth Department in the 1930s demonstrated that powerful adults in the denomination did not approve of the Youth Department's political agenda. Even worse, it seemed that not all young people would be easy recruits to the crusade for a new world order. If progressive Methodists were really right in their assumptions about "youth," young people should have flocked to opportunities to make a difference and contribute to the war effort by building a better America. But in fact Methodist work camps and other opportunities to build a "Christian social order" mobilized far too few young people during the war.

As a result, Methodist Youth Department leaders gathered groups of young people to help them figure out how to recruit more youth for social service. Staff member Walter Towner began one of these meetings by noting that young people in the typical "small church out in the country" had not yet enlisted in the social reform crusade. One participant in the consultation noted with dismay that many young Methodists did not see the Jim Crow system of racial segregation as unchristian. Participants in these meetings debated several competing strategies, but in the end did nothing to change their fundamental methods for recruiting youth. Some called for more "indoctrination," and argued that their strategy should be to recruit and train a smaller group of young Methodists to actively work on unpopular causes. Others insisted that since millions of young people were just waiting for an opportunity to serve, only practical obstacles stood in the way. Still others suggested that slogans and billboards might help, since these tools seemed to work well with war bonds and scrap drives. After vigorous debate, these youth leaders and teenagers shrank back from marketing their cause and reaffirmed their assumption that all young Methodists could be turned into progressive social activists using the traditional methods of conferences, camps, youth committees, and publications.[6]

But would success at regional and national events be sufficient? The challenges of launching a progressive youth movement through local church youth programs were aptly, if unintentionally, illustrated in the 1941 manual *Young Leaders in Action* by Isaac Kelley Beckes. In this fictionalized account the kindly pastor Dr. Morrison advised the new youth fellowship president Ed Smith on his duties. Significantly, Dr. Morrison had to help Ed overcome ridicule at school for being "elected president of a sissy society." Evidently progressive Christian youth activities were not popular in the high schools of the 1940s and did not seem quite so "manly" and influential in the eyes of teenagers as adults hoped.

In addition, the call to sacrificial service probably competed poorly with the emotional consolations of old time religion. Thus Dr. Morrison had to explain to Ed that the meaning of conversion had changed since the old days. Now it meant not an emotional experience of the Holy Spirit, but personal dedication to the "life of service." Dr. Morrison explained that when Ed had committed himself to serving his community through the Methodist Youth Fellowship, it was such a powerful religious change that "Your Grandmother probably said that you had been converted."[7] In this idealized portrait, running an educational and social-service youth club somehow became a manly way to save the world and overcome outdated religious sentiments.

Although the fictional Dr. Morrison projected optimism, his remarks hinted that Methodist youth experts themselves feared that local church youth fellowships would prove politically impotent after all. Even worse, local Methodist youth meetings might be boring and unattractive to young people immersed in the excitements of popular culture. Attendance at Sunday School and the Sunday evening meetings of the Methodist Youth Fellowship fell during the war. Methodist Sunday schools registered a decrease of 279,447 in 1941 and 45,793 in 1942. Enrollment in high schools also dropped during the war, as more and more young people either enlisted in the army or dropped out to take jobs in war industries. In some places the high school dropout rate was as high as 35 percent. Yet even taking into account the disruptions of war, Methodist youth programs competed poorly against the available alternatives during the 1940s.[8]

Because of their progressive views on religious education and the re-sistance they encountered from many white Christians in the South, na-tional Methodist youth leaders tended to view revivalism, conversion, and other elements of traditional Methodist piety as obstacles to their crusade. Trained in theories of religious education that insisted on gradual spiritual growth, Youth Department leaders viewed emotional conversion experi-ences with suspicion. Although they insisted that "true" commitment to Christ would "automatically" produce social concern and activism, they had a hard time defining and fostering such commitment. Staff member Walter Towner told one group of leaders that "we don't want old time reli-gion" but claimed they did need to foster "warmth and enthusiasm." Cur-riculum editor Rowena Ferguson insisted that "volunteer service and evangelism are identical." Although they claimed that old-fashioned reviv-alism would no longer appeal to modern youth, Methodist leaders felt threatened by the Youth for Christ rallies that sprang up during the war.[9] They disliked revivalism, but they didn't have a compelling social-justice spirituality to replace it. Instead they just kept exhorting young people to commit themselves to social action.

Of course, revival meetings weren't their only competition. Adult leaders promoted songs, picnics, and "rhythmic games" as an alternative to the kind of dancing emerging in youth culture. But such alternatives only worked for young people who shared their elders' fears about bobby-soxers dancing to the latest swing records at the "teen canteen." Methodist leaders reassured themselves that "youth does not want the cheap type of entertainment" found in teen canteens. Yet a 1944 issue of *The Planner*, a newsletter designed to help local Methodist Youth Fellowships with their programming, offered recreational ideas for Methodist youth meetings and warned teenagers to keep "holding the line" on the home front through a "high type of personal living." The author insisted that if young people became "jive hounds," "hepcats," or otherwise "loose in their moral life," "they have become moral and spiritual saboteurs who will be of no aid" to the war effort and to returning soldiers.[10] Of course, some young Methodists preferred movies, music, dances, and other youth culture amusements to sacrificial service. But if that was the case, Methodist youth leaders were naïve to believe that most young people were just waiting for a chance to serve.

Even in these circles in which the most politically progressive Method-ists tested their mettle, some worried about the long-term effectiveness of their activities. In 1944 Harold Bremer, secretary of the National Conference of Methodist Youth, told a national gathering of his fellow young Methodists that he had begun his work with high hopes that he represented "young people capable of developing a Christian America." But he now wondered if adult church members might be dismissing their hard-hitting political resolutions as "a necessary safety outlet for the enthusiasm of youth, knowing full well that it will end there and nothing very dangerous will happen." Bremer responded to this discouraging possibility with more of the crisis rhetoric he had learned through his involvement in the Methodist Youth Fellowship. At a 1945 youth conference he warned that "the issues you deal with, if not dealt with adequately, will result in forces that will destroy you and your children and your children's children." Even the recently unveiled atomic bomb was now counted among the "forces" that demanded an effective response from Methodist youth.[11] Were young Methodists saving the world from destruction, playing around at politics, or simply ignoring the whole question and getting on with their lives as teenagers? Progressive young Methodists like Bremer preferred to ignore the possibility that their fellow teenagers might not be as politically engaged or powerful as they had hoped.

Saving the World by Entertaining the Bobby-Soxers

One early insider account of the Youth for Christ movement described it as a "Twentieth-Century Wonder." The phrase aptly captured the early ethos of the movement. Its leaders combined the miraculous wonders and emotional consolations of old-time religion with modern marketing techniques aimed at the newly discovered "teenage" population. YFC leaders did not worry about the potential corruptions of catering to teenage tastes because they thought they saw a world-transforming youth revival on the horizon.

The mainstream press offered bemused praise for Youth for Christ and hinted that it might provide the answer to wartime juvenile delinquency, or that it might at least tame the bobby-soxer phenomenon. One reporter from *Colliers* visited a YFC rally in Chicago complete with a tribute to servicemen, a swinging trumpet solo by the "Harry James of the sawdust trail," and numerous converts evenly divided between service personnel and young civilians. He concluded that these teenagers who had "taken to the straight and narrow" seemed to be "having as much fun as other juveniles who haunt the night spots and keep their parents sleepless until dawn." A *Newsweek* reporter described Torrey Johnson as a religious Frank Sinatra: "He, too, has a Voice and curly hair, wears bow ties, and speaks the language of bobby soxers."[12]

Although the press joined YFC leaders in hoping that such rallies would prevent male juvenile delinquency, both news copy and photographs highlighted the large numbers of teenage girls in attendance. YFC rallies featured female singing groups, testimonies by young women, and armies of young female ushers. In contrast to many other wartime settings, teenage girls probably felt themselves to be valued participants at these rallies.

Young people, many of whom had never seen old-time religion anywhere but in church, found it exciting to attend rallies in theaters, civic auditoriums, and even stadiums. In the age before television, participating in a live radio broadcast was a thrilling media event. An army of traveling evangelists and musicians made Youth for Christ rallies their full time work. Many teenagers also got the chance to become Christian "stars." Local rally directors recruited and trained teenage musical acts that performed old gospel music favorites in contemporary musical styles; at a rally in Kansas City in 1947, a trio sang "I Have a Great Salvation" in the style of the popular Boswell Sisters.[13] Indeed, the music at YFC meetings was close enough to the crooner, girl trio, and big-band styles of the day to arouse the ire of some fundamentalists and the scorn of mainline Protestants. But teenagers loved it.

The leaders of Youth for Christ claimed to be solving the problem of juvenile delinquency, but this claim was as much public relations as reality. Appointed in the summer of 1945 as YFC "Vice President at Large," Billy Graham traveled 135,000 miles over the next twelve months and reported "eight thousand professions of a straight-forward invitation to accept the Lord Jesus Christ as Savior, besides thousands of others who have consecrated their lives to the Lord Jesus Christ." In every town, Graham spoke to Rotary clubs, Kiwanis clubs, and ministerial associations with the goal of, as he put it, "promoting and selling" Youth for Christ. His standard strategy when he arrived in a city was to interview the police chief, juvenile judge, and other local leaders for information on juvenile problems. He then presented this information to community groups and offered Youth for Christ as the solution. Many communities were amazingly supportive. In San Antonio, Graham and his traveling companion T. W. Wilson not only preached to all the civic clubs and ministerial associations; they also held assemblies in every high school and grammar school. Because of its all-American, clean-cut image, YFC appealed to adults who feared that their children might become the next young criminals.[14] Groups like YFC had a broad appeal because they offered to inoculate middle-class kids against such insidious moral diseases. And the warm civic welcome they received reassured YFC leaders that they were leading an important youth movement that just might save the world.

Since the fate of the world depended upon winning as many youthful converts as quickly as possible, preachers at YFC rallies didn't worry about ways they might be subtly altering the gospel message. To appeal to teenagers, YFC preachers painted Christianity as the most attractive way of life available, and tried to dispel fears that it was boring or restrictive. Billy Graham claimed that "the young people around the world today who are having the best time are the young people who know Jesus Christ." Jim Rayburn, founder of Young Life, agreed; as he put it, "It's a sin to bore a kid." Evangelical leaders like Graham and Rayburn insisted that accepting Christ as savior did not mean giving up pleasure and wearing a long face. Instead, it meant acquiring a new hero and falling in love with Him. At the same time, they stressed that following Christ included absolute obedience to his commandments and separation from "the world."[15] This seemingly contradictory combination of fun and moral strictness would prove crucial to evangelical youth work and to the juvenilization of the gospel message in the decades to come.

Sermons about how "fun" it was to follow Jesus were only one of the ways in which the early Youth for Christ leaders marketed old-time religion to teenagers. In their book describing how to set up a YFC rally, Torrey Johnson and Bob Cook crowed about beating "the world" at its own game. They advised local rally directors to "have something to sell" to their communities. Good music was crucial, because "radio has spoiled things for the careless gospel musician; for your young folk can hear, if they wish, worldly music, *perfectly produced,* any hour of the day or night." Although only God could save souls, new times demanded professional production and promotion. When organizers in Grand Rapids, Michigan, brought in Billy Graham for a series of meetings they called "Christ for this Crisis," supporters roved the streets in sound trucks, paraded through the city in sandwich boards handing out flyers, dropped literature from airplanes, posted a banner across a main intersection in town, and conducted high school assemblies. The local paper was full of coverage of the campaign for weeks. Local YFC leaders put together twenty radio broadcasts designed to be "promotional not devotional." At the meetings themselves, a brass quartet called "The Silvertones," a men's quartet called "The Couriers for Christ," and a women's quartet called "The King's Karollers" all performed. Strat Shufelt led the exuberant singing with dramatic arm movements, and Billy Graham emphasized his points with force. This "campaign" proved so successful that it became a model for rally promotion.[16]

In sharp contrast to Methodists who discarded ideas about advertising their social action crusade, Youth for Christ leaders instinctively embraced marketing techniques and business terminology in their evangelistic efforts. In these early days of commercial youth culture, the Youth for Christ rallies could compete with some of the best that the entertainment world had to offer. Quite a few non-Christian young people came along for the ride. But even in these early stages of the movement, the core audience was probably conservative evangelical and fundamentalist teenagers who were forbidden to attend movies, listen to "worldly" music, or otherwise indulge in questionable entertainment. For such teenagers, YFC was quite literally the best show in town.

Still, some fundamentalists criticized the movement for selling out to worldliness and cheapening the faith by using vaudeville-style gimmicks like the "gospel horse." (How many persons in the Trinity? The horse stamps its hoof three times.) Youth for Christ leaders answered that their rallies were not church services, so it was fine for them to be entertaining. They also insisted that in light of the world crisis and the imminent end of the world, youth needed to be reached by any means necessary. Since most evangelical adults already believed that winning young converts was crucial to saving the American way of life, YFC quickly won this argument.

More probing criticisms came from some mainline Protestant youth leaders who visited early rallies. In 1945, Methodist Youth Department staff member Hoover Rupert attended a YFC rally in Nashville that showed a more ragged side of the movement. Although rally organizers had promised a 150-voice youth choir and an attendance of 1500, the meeting began with cajoling people from the audience of 350 to 400 to come up and sing in the choir. The singing seemed to evoke little life or excitement from the crowd, one-third of which was adults. When called on to give their "testimonies" of faith, teenagers offered stereotyped and selfish sounding statements like "I am happy in the Lord," "Jesus satisfies," and "If you want happiness and if you want to sing and whistle all day, take Jesus." The speaker of the evening concluded his sermon with a long, drawn-out altar call — to which no one responded. Rupert concluded that the Nashville group was being supported by a handful of conservative churches and was "not touching the unchurched youth."[17]

In 1947, Rupert visited another rally in Kansas City. He had higher hopes for this one, since it was one of the "better" YFC centers and would feature YFC president Torrey Johnson as speaker. Rupert noticed the strong emphasis on entertainment in the first half of the program. A xylophone solo was followed by thundering applause, which was unheard of in churches of that era. A song leader charged through several up-tempo numbers like "Whosoever Hear Us, Shout, Shout," complete with hand motions. In between songs the leader kept things moving by asking questions like "How many are having a good time?" and calling on the audience to stand up or shake hands with their neighbors. Rupert found this frantic activity distracting and inappropriate when singing Christian hymns and songs, but grudgingly acknowledged that the teenagers in attendance seemed to be enjoying themselves. Torrey Johnson gave a report on YFC rallies underway in Europe, noting that U.S. Army chaplains overseas were calling on YFC to help the youth of Germany. Johnson went on to preach on the theme "It Pays to Be a Christian" and concluded with an extended altar call, but only two young people came forward. Rupert disliked the fact that at both of these rallies, it seemed to be adults who were firmly in charge and presenting a program to youth, with no opportunities for youth to lead either the rallies or the organization.[18] Probably more significant were the motivations Torrey Johnson drew upon to attract converts. For the leaders of Youth for Christ, Christianity was increasingly becoming a product to be sold to customers via entertaining promises of personal fulfillment — with an added benefit of saving the world.

Mainline Protestant youth leaders took note of Youth for Christ because they rightly saw it as competing with their programs. They reluctantly admitted that many young people seemed to like the simple message of salvation being served up at YFC rallies. But they objected to this as a deficient gospel. As one put it, "in vain did we listen for a challenge to build a new world or better community life in the name of Christ." These mainline observers noted that the YFC rally ignored the local council of churches and did not cooperate with the local Christian Youth Councils sponsored by the National Council of Churches. Yet YFC did approach these organizations in some cases, and did not find them cooperative. Rally visitors sometimes caught local YFC leaders publicly criticizing the mainline denominations, but even critics had to admit that usually YFC leaders scrupulously avoided criticizing other Christians. It seems that mainline youth leaders saw YFC as a dangerous competitor, while YFC leaders simply did not pay much attention to the mainline youth programs. As a result of this one-sided competition, a few liberal youth leaders began to wonder if they should create their own youth rallies. One Unitarian and Universalist minister, Rev. G. Richard Kuch, actually suggested that "liberal youth" should copy YFC by publicizing their activities more aggressively and by having more singing, more chances for participation, and more "vim and vigor" in their youth meetings.[19] Although liberal youth rallies did not develop at the time, Kuch's observations would prove prophetic. Like it or not, all youth organizations would eventually follow in the steps of Youth for Christ by trying to create Christian versions of youth culture entertainment.

Youth for Christ leaders sometimes worried about whether they had adequately tamed teenage culture. Torrey Johnson warned at the 1946 YFC convention that "some of us who are leaders in Youth for Christ are entirely too cocky. We think we are glamour boys." Johnson feared that some of his fellow YFC preachers took too much pleasure in their flashy clothes and the line of autograph seekers after each meeting. He also insisted that "if all we have to offer is entertainment and a wholesome atmosphere in which young people may spend their evenings" without "the winning of lost souls," then "we are not measuring up" to our "God-demanded responsibility."[20] YFC leaders sometimes preached sacrifice and told stories of believers who suffered for their faith. But these same preachers, along with Christian musical performers, were becoming a new breed of Christian celebrities.[21] Celebrities certainly inspired devotion and imitation among teenagers. But as Johnson sensed, such devotion probably differed in important ways from Christian discipleship.

Despite both favorable public relations and a steady stream of youthful conversions, by the time Bob Cook became president of Youth for Christ in 1948, even some supporters were asking, "How long can it last?" Cook saw many positive signs in the movement, but he did worry that the rallies had lost their evangelistic edge. "Stop merely inviting Christian youth to come and listen to a charming program!" he told rally directors. He took a hard look at YFC rallies and concluded that the minority at any rally was unchurched and few if any came from "the so-called 'seamy' side of town."[22] Cook's observations raised a troubling possibility: instead of saving the world and stamping out juvenile delinquency, YFC rallies might be nothing more than entertainment for Christian teenagers.

All-American Catholics or Young Apostles?

Catholic youth workers of the 1940s were divided between a majority who thought youth culture could be easily tamed or ignored and a minority who recognized that it posed unprecedented challenges. The mainstream Catholic response to the rise of the American "teenager" was similar to that of Youth for Christ: create a parallel Catholic youth culture. This strategy was adopted by many of those who imitated Bernard Sheil's Catholic Youth Organization but didn't share his progressive political commitments. But the most prominent architect and promoter of this approach became Fr. Joseph Schieder, who directed the National Catholic Welfare Conference's Youth Department from 1948 to 1961. Ironically, Schieder never claimed to be creating a passive Catholic youth culture. Instead, like other leaders of his era, he set his sights on reforming America and saving the world.

Early in his career with the Youth Department, Schieder confidently announced that his plan for combining spiritual devotion, recreation, and a system of youth councils would produce young Catholic leaders who would reform society. He believed that if his fellow Catholics would join him in establishing councils of Catholic youth, they would together establish "a bulwark against materialistic secularism which could not otherwise be achieved." He placed a high degree of confidence in the effects of spiritual programs like communion breakfasts, retreats, discussion groups, and special prayers called "First Friday Devotions."[23] At the same time, he continued to insist that "formation must come in and through concrete action within and upon the immediate community." He envisioned two basic modes in which this goal might be accomplished. First, the CYO would influence young Catholics as individuals to "act upon and transform their immediate community" by "creating, as it were, contrary social pressures which are thoroughly Christian." In order to exert such influence, CYO adult leaders should especially "work with those who have a natural influence in the 'crowd.'" Schieder sensed that a new social hierarchy was arising in the world of the high school — and that youth leaders needed to exploit it for good.

The second and most important method for developing the "apostolic mentality" in CYO members was the community action discussion group. Schieder believed that gathering Catholic young people to discuss social and spiritual problems in society would teach them not just that "they must transform their own lives to fit the Christian pattern" but also that "it is both necessary and possible for them to act effectively upon those about them." Schieder hoped that his national organization would discourage youth and their leaders from drawing themselves "apart from others into ghettoized, completely isolated groups."[24] In practice, local Catholic youth programs majored in dances and athletic competitions, and a whole generation would later describe their upbringing as taking place in the Catholic "ghetto." Community action discussion groups were less common than recreation, and when they did happen, they rarely resulted in social action. Even the social activism that did result tended to be moral crusades against indecent literature and films, rather than care for the poor or other forms of social justice. As the generic youth programs promoted by the NCWC youth department spread throughout the country, many local leaders settled for a mission of providing students in public high schools with recreational activities that paralleled the extracurricular activities in Catholic schools.

The one outward-looking, reform-minded element in Schieder's ideal program was the youth council plan, but he found this a hard sell, even though the idea of "education for democracy" was in vogue at the time. Whether through "teen canteens," public school "citizenship" curricula, or Christian youth assemblies, adults of the era were obsessed with forming good democratic citizens. An organization called the National Social Welfare Assembly promoted community youth councils to advise local government and provide a voice for youth in civic affairs. As of 1948, 1,000 copies of their promotional film "Youth United for a Better Home Town" were in constant use, and the pamphlet version showed up in Catholic youth worker files and in the NCWC Youth Department publication *Newsnotes*.[25] At a meeting of diocesan youth directors held in May 1948, Schieder warned that Protestant, Jewish, and cooperative councils were quickly organizing, and that Catholic young people dared not be left behind. Even more ominously, he insisted that only Catholic young people organized and trained to work through youth councils could thwart communist subversion of international youth movements.[26] But even though Schieder was using all the right language about powerful, political youth and threats to democracy, he still struggled to get Catholic youth councils up and running. The first meeting of the National Council of Catholic Youth did not take place until 1951, and only a minority of Catholic dioceses ever established youth councils.

There were several reasons for this resistance. First, many adult youth leaders worried that their organizations would be swallowed up by the youth council structure. They feared that youth councils would get to decide which youth activities were allowed in a given parish or diocese. Second, youth councils did not really fit into the adult *or* teenage social worlds. Young Catholics found the idea of serving on councils and committees less attractive than the emerging world of high school social and athletic activities. Adults were reluctant to give youth council members much authority to make real decisions. As a result, young people may have rightly sensed that youth councils were largely "make work" or "make believe" intended to reassure adults that young people were learning how to be good democratic citizens.[27]

Schieder and his circle of Catholic youth leaders were not the only ones who struggled to adapt to the new realities of high school youth culture. Participants in the Young Christian Workers were hard-pressed to adapt their social action labor movement strategy to the lives of the new teenagers. Fewer and fewer Catholic teenagers were factory workers; they were in high school instead. One response was to create a new organization, the Young Christian Students. But many early YCS cells got started in Catholic high schools rather than in more secular settings. How exactly would young Catholic activists reform Catholic schools? Was reform even needed there? A student in a Chicago Catholic high school explained that he refused to join his school's Young Christian Students cell because of what he perceived as its elitism and secretive tactics, adding, "isn't a Catholic high school really a big cell in itself?"[28]

Even worse, many of the early participants in YCW and YCS did not seem to grasp the mission and methods of the organization. One of the first cells of young female workers began meeting in 1939. They read Frank Sheed's *Map of Life* in order to learn more about their faith. Their action steps included looking up answers to common criticisms of Catholic doctrine and writing a letter to *Look* magazine protesting an article on birth control by Margaret Sanger. Such activities were pretty mild compared to the progressive social-reform agenda of the movement's leaders. During the war, Monsignor Hillenbrand sharply criticized the Young Christian Workers in San Francisco for not being true to "specialized Catholic action," since their main "social action" seemed to be wholesome social events for soldiers and other young people. Even worse, some parish clubs seemed to have dispensed with the inquiry method.[29] Of course, in an era in which many people spoke as if "teen canteens" were an important tool for training democratic citizens, these young people in San Francisco can be excused for not seeing the subtle distinctions Hillenbrand had in mind.

More fundamentally, they were reflecting the deeper confusion caused by the political paradigm of youth work. If all youth work is political, then anything being done to help young people is saving the world, even if it's just arranging wholesome dances for soldiers.

Still, these Catholic Action organizations did make some significant progress in educating young Catholics in a countercultural version of their faith. Chicago Inter-Student Catholic Action, led by Fr. Martin Carrabine, S.J., from 1934 to 1950, worked hard to educate young Catholics about their social responsibilities. The core of the CISCA program under Carrabine's leadership was a Saturday morning forum that attracted at least 400 college and high school students each week. On Saturday afternoons, student leaders met with Carrabine for a "bull session" to prepare the next week's program. Each year the sessions tied into a theme in Catholic doctrine like the beatitudes, the mystical body of Christ, the Christian family, or the liturgy. Carrabine hoped to form doctrinally sound and socially aware young Catholics. He called on them to rise above the youth culture; "You kids are being gypped," he said. He insisted that "compared to the drama-packed existence of a Christian fighting for the cause of Christ, living fully the life of Christ as a member of the Mystical Body, the current crazes lose their fascination, look pale, lifeless, trivial." One problem, of course, is that it was difficult to keep the vision of being involved in a spiritual battle in the midst of a full high school social life. Despite Carrabine's disdain for the "fads" of youth culture, CISCA gradually took on leisure and entertainment functions, just like other youth groups. Even under Carrabine's leadership, members started presenting plays and an annual variety show.[30]

Some young people resisted the progressive political messages they heard through CISCA and similar organizations. One Saturday morning in 1947, about 1,200 Catholic teenagers and college students gathered for the weekly CISCA forum. The featured speakers, Carol Jackson and Edward Willock, editors of *Integrity* magazine, lectured on "Sanctity in This Highly Mechanized World." Jackson and Willock were rising stars in the reform wing of Catholicism that preached an "integrated Catholicism" in which lay Catholics did not allow their faith to be privatized. Instead, they believed, ordinary people steeped in Catholic doctrine, liturgy, and social teaching could work strategically to save America from secularism, immorality, and injustice. On this particular occasion, they especially criticized the American economic system for being "oriented to Mammon; the profit motive is supreme." Willock warned students that in the world of work they would "develop a split personality. You will either compromise on

58

serving Mammon or you will work to reorient the system." Many young people in the audience balked, and several complained that his advice seemed "impractical and unreal." One young man complained, "It doesn't seem as if there are many things left for me to do except scrub floors or establish another *Integrity*." This same teenager resented Willock's statement that most jobs made it "almost impossible to achieve sanctity," because it insulted Catholic fathers who had worked so hard to provide for their families.[31] Such reactions are not surprising; they reflect normal American middle-class values, as well as the pull of the newly emerging youth consumerism. But such opposition should have served as a warning to Catholic Action leaders that economic prosperity might kill youthful interest in social reform.

Despite such opposition, young leaders in the Catholic Action movements were among the few people of their day to develop a prophetic critique of the emerging youth culture. For example, the early readers of *Today*, a Catholic Action youth paper published in Chicago, could not miss its critical stance toward popular culture and consumerism. The last page of each issue carried an editorial by teenage editor John Cogley, satirizing elements of the teen world like predictable movie plots, the cult of movie stars, *Reader's Digest*, perfume advertisements, and comics. Cogley even went so far as to criticize the insipid Catholicism portrayed in the popular film "The Bells of St. Mary's." Readers reacted with confusion. Some thought the paper's coverage of "The Bells" was too harsh, while others took the back page satires too literally.[32]

In dismay, Cogley wrote an editorial insisting that he and his staff did not mean that watching movies or buying perfume was sinful. He insisted instead that "we have tried desperately to develop that critical spirit in our student-readers which would enable them to recognize phoney-baloney solemnity for what it is; to recognize the shallow basis for much of what high-powered advertising passes off as serious stuff; and to counteract the drugging effects of slick elegance, meretricious glamour, and ersatz popularity." He further argued that Catholic school graduates, while on guard against the "big dragons of Divorce, Birth Control, Communism, and Euthanasia," easily fell victim to "the deadening-to-the-spirit, petty distractions which nip the development of the spiritual life and of the Christian Apostolate right in the bud." The youthful staff of *Today* recognized remarkably early on in the process of postwar youth culture development that "the students' real world in America today is not obviously patterned after the terrible place of the religion class and the penny catechism."

Cogley and like-minded Catholic youth saw that pop culture distractions could be more spiritually deadening than direct attacks. Thus he argued that one story in the "slick magazines" or the Hollywood gossip columns did more to reshape opinions on birth control than "fifty platform lectures by Margaret Sanger."[33]

Despite periodic campaigns by young Catholics against indecent literature and movies, Cogley and some of his fellow Catholic Action teenagers suspected that most young Catholics did not take a truly critical stance toward popular culture. In 1947 he reprinted an article criticizing Frank Sinatra written by a young Catholic named Marguerite Ratty. She deplored Sinatra's pandering to publicity and felt embarrassed at his public profession of Catholicism since he seemed to be a poor role model. In response, Charles Smith, executive director of the Chicago Catholic Youth Organization and personal friend of Sinatra, defended the young crooner: "He has tried his best to maintain a certain dignity and I know that he is deeply disturbed and worried by the responsibilities he bears toward the thousands of young people who flock to see and hear him." This interchange provoked more letters from young readers on both sides of the debate. But several teen writers recognized neither extreme as accurate and advised their peers to avoid Catholic celebrities as role models altogether. As one put it, Sinatra was not the "only Catholic in Hollywood not living up to his faith."

Nevertheless, the very need to debate Sinatra's merits revealed the lure of success and celebrity, even for young Catholics in the reform camp. Perhaps Cogley meant to create a damning exposé, but when he published an interview with Betsy Weer, founder of the Sinatra Fan Club, many of his readers might have agreed with her when she gushed that even Sinatra's "imperfections are perfect."[34] What Cogley did not foresee is that teenagers might be increasingly unable to understand and imitate his thoughtful critiques of pop culture. His readers could only see two alternatives: withdraw from pop culture, which they didn't want to do, or accept it and ignore Cogley's critique. Cogley's approach to pop culture, while more nuanced and deeper than that of Youth for Christ, may have been beyond the grasp of his audience, who didn't seem prepared for it.

Roman Catholic youth leaders were divided on the question of whether to create an alternative Catholic youth culture, embrace Catholics like Frank Sinatra in the mainstream media, or maintain a critical distance from all of it. For their part, most young Catholics seemed to want some combination of these three options. They liked Catholic parish dances,

Frank Sinatra records, and Catholic social concern, so long as that social concern didn't get too radical and threaten their economic future. Even those young Catholic leaders who took the dangers of the emerging youth culture most seriously typically saw it as a sideline, a skirmish in the larger battle to create a new America based on Catholic social teachings. Catholic youth councils might save America by helping young people practice their democratic political skills; political discussion groups might mobilize armies of young activists. But more likely, everyone would get down to the business of helping Catholic young people continue to identify as Catholic as they fit into the emerging world of middle-class youth culture.

"Worldly" Christians Saving the World

For the most part, the emerging teenage culture remained a sidelight in the African American experience. To some extent, segregation and racism pushed adults and young people together and united them against shared enemies, though some church leaders did worry that "worldly" activities would detract from serious pursuits among young people. African American Christians did not make many adaptations to youth culture in their churches during the 1940s, but neither did they fully come to grips with the emerging differences between "youth" and "teenagers."

Throughout the 1940s, African American churches continued to have "Baptist Training Union" meetings, Youth Sundays, and other activities that brought together children, youth, and adults; groups dedicated only to teenagers were rarer there than in white churches. While this intergenerational approach had many benefits, there were drawbacks as well. The Rev. J. Pius Barbour, editor of the *National Baptist Voice*, wondered if attendance at Baptist Training Union meetings had declined during the war because "Old folks sit around and attack with vigor any discussion that seems to them to vary from their conception of religion." Rev. L. M. Terrell of Atlanta insisted that "you will drive a boy away from the church if you put a six foot youth in a class with boys four feet tall."[35] Evidently the extended family culture of African American congregations was running up against teenage desires to carve out a collective identity separate from both adults and children.

A more threatening problem, at least in the eyes of adults, was that some African American young people seemed to be indulging in "worldly" forms of entertainment once considered taboo among churchgoers. One response was simply to accept the looser behavior of the younger generation in the hope that it would not interfere with their world-saving mission. Rev. R. C. Barbour complained in the 1930s that the "average Negro youth is at home in a jazz dive." By 1940, while attending his twenty-year reunion at Morehouse College, Barbour observed that times had changed since his day: "We slipped away from campus to dance and smoke in the old days. Today the young generation smoke and dance on the campus in the presence of their teachers." Despite such scandalous behavior, Barbour remained upbeat about the political power of youth: "This new generation is going to give us a new world — a world free from war and all the other scourges that [afflict] our generation."[36]

Some theologically and politically progressive churchmen like Barbour even tried to use youthful misbehavior as a tool to push for reform in the church. He blamed old-time religion for youthful rebellion: "Our Pharisaic religion has driven our young people to the debauching dancing hall and the degenerating moving picture show," he argued. He insisted that only a pastor "able to discuss the pressing social questions of the day can preach with effectiveness to youth." Only if adults got on board with social activism could they hope to keep a hold on their young people. Barbour claimed he did not know "one conservative intelligent young person in America."[37] Of course, Barbour was just one of thousands of adults throughout the years who have tried to turn unsupported generalizations about young people into calls for adults to get with the program. The fact that he felt it necessary to make this appeal also illustrates that many African Americans of all ages were probably not as concerned as he was about progressive political causes.

But the majority of socially concerned African American Baptists recognized that old time religion was not the problem. Instead, with greater insight than some of their white counterparts, they realized that youthful amusements, even some of the more innocent ones, would likely distract young people from more important tasks. Rev. M. D. Dickson of Peoria, Illinois, called on the youth of his church to "quit so much foolishness and frivolity" and to "get prepared because doors of opportunity are opening."[38] Similarly, William H. Jernagin called on youth to invest in political and social reform the same "enthusiasm you put into your sports, your social affairs, your plans of life, and America may yet realize its full glory as the land of opportunity to all."[39] He called on youth and adults alike to "live our lives in such a way as to be of greatest service in the fight against Hitler abroad and against Hitler-like practices at home." He claimed that "the new social order — the new world — will be largely determined by the youth of today" and complained of some young people who had secured important government jobs and yet "abused the privileges afforded them" by arriving late to work and smoking.[40] Of course the need to regularly rebuke young Baptists for their "frivolity" suggested that youth culture amusements were indeed proving more attractive than saving the world. Or perhaps, unlike their elders, young people thought they could have some fun while they saved the world.

Church leaders also recognized that "frivolous" or "worldly" youth behaviors were symptoms of deeper social injustices. Rev. Wade Hampton McKinney of Cleveland repeatedly told city officials that young African Americans in the city's "central district" were victims of white lust and prejudice. Turning the tables on those who saw the district as a den of sin and vice, he called it "the most widely sinned against and exploited area in our city" and took note when white sex offenders received mild penalties for their dalliances with young black women. He expressed outrage that in the midst of a "war that threatens our democratic way of life" city officials allowed white criminals to escape while the "flower of our youth" gave their all on the battlefield.[41] The young people who listened week after week to preachers like McKinney must have realized that white society and its injustices, not young people and their amusements, were the greater source of society's problems.

The debate in the black church over the relationship between worldliness and political influence reached a crescendo over the troubling emergence of new forms of gospel music. Religious education expert Jesse Jai McNeil called it the "invasion of jazz into many of our churches." McNeil insisted that "any church which must yield to methods and devices of the world to perpetuate itself is doing a futile thing because it is already dead."[42] Reverend Henry T. McCrary of Philadelphia was typical of many older preachers who objected to this "jazz band evangelism" because it produced "emotional pandemonium" and led to "snake hipping and buckdancing." McCrary admitted that, to his dismay, even as a minister he felt like dancing when he heard this music.[43] Rev. D. V. Jemison of Mobile, Alabama, blamed youth and commercial entertainment for debasing the church. He rejected the argument that "the young must have amusement" and insisted that he would rather have the church "be blotted from the face of the earth than to surrender its principles at the demand of worldly-minded professors of religion."[44]

But these views did not win over the majority of adults, and certainly made little headway with young people. Even though the new gospel music sounded "worldly" because of its affinity with jazz and the blues, some Baptist leaders recognized its appeal to young people and tried to tame it rather than reject it outright. Lucie Campbell, who served as music director for the National Sunday School and Baptist Training Union Congress, was definitely an "old school" Baptist when it came to purity and propriety. Yet she helped song writers like Thomas Dorsey and performers like Mahalia Jackson gain exposure at Baptist youth conventions. She learned from these younger artists, and even wrote some songs, such as "Jesus Gave Me Water," that showed the influence of their new styles. Although Campbell, like Dorsey himself, disliked the driving beat of some gospel music, her influence helped keep a bridge open to the tastes of the younger generation.[45] The new gospel music fostered youthful devotion to the church through powerful religious experiences. Singing in a gospel choir was one of the primary ways that young people participated in many African American churches.

Meanwhile, some observers in the African American community questioned whether the churches were reaching and helping young people at all. In a study of "Negro youth" sponsored by the American Youth Commission, sociologist E. Franklin Frazier argued that regardless of social class, young people criticized the churches for pushing an "otherworldly outlook" that ignored "the problem of the status of the Negro in this world." He also quoted many young people who complained that preachers asked for money too often and preached too much against drinking and dancing. He concluded that the black church had "nothing in its ideology to cause Negro youth to have greater respect for themselves as Negroes."[46] But Frazier's evidence was hard to interpret. Were young people alienated from the church? Or was the church providing them spiritual strength to help them deal with the struggles of their daily lives? At the very least, the study hinted that the church might not be as central to the lives of young people as their elders hoped.

Most African Americans rightly believed that their churches could provide crucial support to young people in their struggle for racial justice. What was less clear was whether young African Americans would choose to lead the battle for racial justice or would turn aside to pursue youth culture amusements. One key difference between African American and white young people, however, was that African Americans could not fully participate in the emerging middle-class youth culture and the broader patterns of consumption and upward mobility in American society without first fighting the battle against racial segregation. Perhaps African American churches put less effort into creating separate youth groups to protect their young people because they sensed that black teenagers could not wander off into the white world of teenage indulgences until the walls of segregation came down. Other than adopting more youth-friendly music, African American Christians did not cater to teenage tastes in the 1940s. But they also did little to understand the emerging youth culture and to plan for the day when racial solidarity would not be enough to keep teenagers in church.

The Birth of Juvenilization

The 1940s saw the emergence of an enduring dilemma in Christian youth work: to adapt to youth culture and tamper with the faith, or to ignore that culture and suffer the loss of youthful loyalty. The newly labeled "teenagers" would from now on be increasingly seduced by the siren song of high school social life dominated by fun, sports, dating, movies, music, and fashion. While adult values and youthful tastes have often clashed over the centuries, what was changing was the relative balance of power between the two and the length of time between puberty and full adult status.

Largely unaware of the real changes going on all around them, the adults of the 1940s tended to push their politicized religious goals whether those agendas fit the changing lives of young people or not. Methodists insisted that young people were natural political progressives in an era of world change, so they wrongly assumed that church-based social action crusades would compete effectively against the high school social scene. African Americans managed to adapt very little to youth culture while sustaining political vision among young people, but the extreme injustice they experienced was a key force that helped hold the generations together. Leaders of the Catholic Youth Organization and Youth for Christ claimed to be saving the world and building democracy by entertaining teenagers with wholesome social activities. This approach not only widened the gap between rhetoric and reality, it subtly changed the content of the faith that was being communicated. Meanwhile, a small minority of young Catholics in the Catholic Action movement recognized that the biggest problem with youth culture was not the immorality of its content but rather the sort of persons it tended to create: passive consumers with poor critical-thinking skills. Such leaders realized that despite all the apocalyptic rhetoric surrounding young people, they were more likely to be lulled to sleep by the trivial world of teenage social life than to be directly defeated by the devil (let alone the communists).

Of the many words swirling around about young people in the 1940s, only this message of the insidious deadening effect of popular culture still rings true. Unfortunately, few at the time heeded this warning. Instead, most remained optimistic that youth culture could be easily tamed or ignored. But in such an atmosphere, it was unlikely that anyone would pay much attention to how youth and their preferences could — and would — dramatically reshape the face of American Christianity.

CHAPTER 3

Social Prophets or Silent Generation?
The Failed Juvenilization of Liberal Protestantism

Christians must be at once the happiest and yet the most dissatisfied citizens in a community — dissatisfied, that is, with all that is wrong.

                    Handbook of the Methodist Youth Fellowship, 1953

Where is the prophetic voice of the church?

                    Methodist teenager John Waggy, 1959

At the 1952 National Conference of Methodist Youth, George Harper warned his fellow young leaders that they stood "in an historical place of opportunity and danger." Since youth had always served as "the opposition party" in church and society, Harper worried about the current atmosphere of Cold War–induced apathy among young people. Young Methodists needed to keep taking risky political stands even when others might accuse them of being communists. He tried to turn the rhetoric of the Cold War to his own ends by warning his fellow Methodist youth that "the followers of the easy life will never extend freedom in today's world; they won't even keep it for themselves." He continued, "Communists have answers to economic questions. Do we?" He predicted that unless "we instead of the Communists become the great revolutionaries of our age" the developing nations would turn to Russia for leadership. Harper ominously reported the words of one Indian communist youth: "We will win. I live, eat, drink, and if necessary die for our cause. I have no luxuries in my life. You Christians only give leftovers."[1] Would young Protestants devote themselves to the grown-up work of political activism, or would they settle into the teenage "easy life"?

In some ways, mainline Protestant youth organizations like the Methodist Youth Department scored amazing victories during the 1950s. In an era when criticizing America's Cold War foreign policies could cost people their jobs and fighting for racial integration could lead to beatings, jail, or even death, it is significant that *any* young people participated in such dangerous activities. Conservative Christians of the day smeared progressive Methodists as "communists" for holding political ideas that have now become common. Today, the vast majority of Christians agree that racism and racial discrimination are evil and have no place in the church or society. Most consider social activism and political demonstrations to be legitimate religious activities, and expect that Christians should feel free to criticize their government's policies. It's even possible to find conservative Christians who use the word "revolution" to describe their ideal for Christian influence in society. Among white Christians of the 1950s, only liberal Protestants held such views and put them into action. And their Christian youth movements proved crucial in popularizing these ideas and practices.

On the other hand, George Harper's fear that "the followers of the easy life will never extend freedom in today's world" also seemed to be realized as the decade of the 1950s progressed. By 1959, Youth Department staff members and liberal Methodist young people were wringing their hands over the "conformity" and "apathy" of the "silent generation." And by 1970, the Methodist church, like other mainline Protestant denominations, would enter a period of declining membership that was especially pronounced among the young. What went wrong?

Many factors contributed to numerical decline in the mainline Protestant churches, but youth leaders like those who ran the Methodist Youth Department bear some responsibility. Although they were among the few white Americans of their time to recognize and fight against the evils of racism and segregation, their powers of prophetic discernment did not extend to a deep understanding of the new world of American teenagers. They succeeded dramatically in mobilizing a small number of young people for social justice, but they could not spark a mass movement of socially concerned young people because they did not find a way to overcome the deadening effects of middle-class white youth culture. But it was not just the inhospitable times that caused this failed juvenilization of social gospel Christianity. Bad decisions by denominational youth leaders, opposition from teenagers, and a mismatch between the methods of juvenilization and the requirements of social justice Christianity guaranteed that only a minority of young people would embrace the social action crusade. Those few made a big long-term impact on church and society. But denominational youth programs left most young Methodists either bored or alienated, with long-term consequences for the vitality of the Methodist church.

Early Successes

In the early 1950s, numerous signs seemed to confirm that young Methodists stood poised to save the world. The Methodist church affirmed the importance of youth by declaring a church-wide "Quadrennial Emphasis on Youth" from 1953 to 1956. To promote the emphasis on youth, Youth Department staff member Harold Ewing spoke on the National Council of Churches radio show "Church of the Air" on September 6, 1953. He called the twentieth century the "century of the pursuit of power" and cited the atomic bomb as a prominent example. But, he insisted, "the greatest stockpile of power in the world today is the power-potential in the lives of young people." He told the young members of his audience, "in you lies the power to change the world and make it the world of your dreams — or the power to bring the world toppling down about your ears."[2] Youth leaders of the 1950s commonly compared the power of youth to the power of the atomic bomb and used the Cold War to motivate youth and to rally support from adults. Adults were probably drawn to this analogy because, just as they wavered between seeing the "atomic age" either as a dawning technological utopia or as a terrifying harbinger of the end of the world, in the same way many attached high hopes and desperate fears to young people.

During the Quadrennial Emphasis on Youth, the Youth Department sponsored hundreds of "Christian Witness Missions" in which Methodist teenagers and college students went door to door inviting young people to church and to the local Methodist Youth Fellowship. These efforts paid off by reversing the attendance losses of the 1940s. Still, although national leaders had set the ambitious goal of adding 500,000 new youth members during the Quadrennial Emphasis, the actual gains were smaller. After recruiting over 70,000 in 1954, Christian Witness Missions added only 39,308 more by the end of October 1955.[3] The declining returns suggest that much of this evangelism had been recruitment of lapsed Methodists and other types of easy growth. Nevertheless, adding 100,000 new members in just a few years was a significant achievement. No wonder Methodist youth leaders thought their programs would prove popular and effective among American teenagers.

Meanwhile, delegates to the National Conference of Methodist Youth continued to pass progressive resolutions on important political and social issues. They opposed the nuclear arms race. They denounced communism but also criticized the House Un-American Activities Committee, which was harassing American citizens suspected of communist ties. They supported labor unions and complained about the inequities of the capitalist system. They attacked racial segregation in their church and in society. Unlike most Americans at the time, they questioned America's foreign policies that included propping up right-wing dictatorships in the name of containing communism.[4]

Delegates to the National Conference of Methodist Youth did more than pass resolutions. They appointed a full-time secretary from among their number to carry out a program of religious and political advocacy. Over the years, these secretaries testified before Congress on matters of concern to the National Conference such as universal military training. They raised money for the defense of James Lawson, a young African American Methodist and vice president of the Conference who had been jailed in 1951 for his refusal to register for the draft. And they kept their fellow Methodist teenagers informed of national and international political issues.[5]

Beginning in the late 1930s, young Methodists had staged yearly protests to pressure adults to integrate Methodist camps like Lake Junaluska in South Carolina and Mt. Sequoyah in Arkansas. The first victories came in the 1940s, as camp officials reluctantly agreed to house African American speakers on the camp grounds. These may seem like small victories today, but they were radical enough to provoke threats of violence at the time. In 1949, Charles B. Copher had to leave Mt. Sequoyah early due to anonymous threats from some townspeople who disliked what he later called his "unrestricted freedom of association, especially with the lady folk." The campers were outraged and criticized camp officials for caving in to these threats.

Such experiences made a profound impression on white Methodist teenagers and often provoked them to question the racist practices of their society. Rebecca Owen, who grew up in Lynchburg, Virginia, remembers that she participated in a boycott of the Lake Junaluska camp pool in 1956 in order to protest segregated facilities at the camp. At the time she barely knew what a boycott was, but this experience contributed to her questioning of segregation and her pilgrimage toward participating in a lunch counter sit-in as a college student in 1960.[6]

A few young Methodists even risked their lives to work for racial justice. In the summer of 1956, an interracial work camp sponsored by the Youth Department almost blew up in their faces. The interracial group of young people stayed at a black Methodist school in Camden, South Carolina, to paint the boys' dormitory and to participate in what they called "a Christian fellowship." Members of the Ku Klux Klan burned a cross on the front lawn and sent a message through the local sheriff that they planned to burn down the school if the group stayed. Joseph Bell of the Youth Department rushed down from Nashville to try to defuse the situation. He and the campers met with local white leaders, including the Methodist pastor and a prominent Methodist layman who acted as intermediary with the Klan.

Local leaders resented these young people they assumed to be northern outsiders and accused them of "coming down here to show us how to live inter-racially." Mayor Savidge baldly stated, "the colored people are inferior. They can not live with the white." Others complained that such provocative interracial living would "set race relations back even further." Although the local white Methodist minister, Rev. Kilgo, commended the group for working together interracially, he also complained that "you came down here to tell us that you are right and we are wrong." One of the campers quipped, "Sir, I didn't come down from anywhere. I'm from Louisiana." The brief moment of laughter that followed did little to defuse the tension. Mayor Savidge told the group, "I'm behind any move you decide to make." One of the campers courageously called him on his hypocrisy: "Yes, you are behind us. You are behind us with a kick."[7]

Such stories show that Methodist youth leaders had reasons to be hopeful. A few young people seemed to be courageously working to make America a more Christian society. Thousands of young people were joining local Methodist Youth Fellowships. On the other hand, there were signs that society would exact a high price from those who insisted on fighting racism, opposing the Cold War military buildup, and criticizing capitalism — and even the less daunting effort of recruiting young people for youth groups tapered off quickly. The limits of their idealism were all too easily exposed.

Shaky Foundations

It soon became apparent that successes at the national and regional levels rested on shaky local foundations, and a conservative backlash drove national Methodist youth leaders toward some dubious strategies. Conservative Christians embraced the anti-communist witch hunts of the era. In 1950, Stanley High published an article in *Reader's Digest* entitled "Methodism's Pink Fringe." He claimed that "a powerful and growing minority" of communist sympathizers were making a bid for control of the church. He described the Rev. Jack McMichael, director of the Methodist Federation for Social Action, as a "young, personable and dynamic" speaker who was much in demand "among young people and students." Even worse, McMichael was former chairman of the American Youth Congress, which High called "one of the Communists' most notorious fronts." As further evidence of communist influence in the church, High noted that the executive secretary of the National Conference of Methodist Youth was also a member of the MFSA.[8]

When liberal Methodist Bishop G. Bromley Oxnam spoke at the 1955 National Convocation of Methodist Youth, one Methodist newsletter asked, "Do you want COMMUNIST dupes counseling METHODIST YOUTH?" In Houston, Methodists formed watchdog organizations called the "Circuit Riders" and the "Minute Women" to put pressure on ministers with ties to the MFSA. Many prominent segregationists, including Bull Connor and not a few Klan members, were Methodists. Methodist ministers who favored labor unions and racial integration got kicked out of their churches, especially in the South.[9] Threats of violence, ostracism, and loss of income kept many people from embracing the righteous cause of racial integration. And shamefully, much of that intimidation came from people who claimed to be good Christians.

Racist adults especially feared corruption of their children through interracial "mixing," so right-wing Christians kept a close eye on liberal Protestant youth organizations. Robert Thompson, editor of *The High Point Enterprise* in North Carolina, was disturbed by reports from those who had attended the 1951 National Convocation of Methodist Youth. He particularly objected to the re-election of James Lawson as vice-president of the National Conference of Methodist Youth because Lawson was a "Negro youth who is serving a three year term in federal prison for violation of the draft law." He also saw the "Communist line" in conference resolutions that condemned ROTC units in church colleges, called for "independence and freedom of the people of Asia and all other lands from foreign domination," and insisted that all nations, including China, be admitted to the United Nations. Thompson saw these resolutions as support for a "surrender" of Korea and China to the Communist Party. He also found it sinister that these resolutions did not come to a vote, but were simply presented to the convocation. In a letter to Thompson, national youth secretary George Harper explained that only elected members of the National Conference of Methodist Youth could vote, and insisted with regard to communism that "you cannot possibly stand more against it than we do."[10] It is unlikely that Thompson and like-minded anti-communists were convinced.

Methodist youth leaders expected opposition from conservative adults in the church since they had experienced this all their lives. But because they believed that young people were naturally members of a liberal "opposition party" in church and society, they did not take youthful resistance to their agenda as seriously as they should have. Some young people were only reluctantly going along with the progressive agenda at camps and conferences. For example, in 1956 one white girl attending the Methodist camp at Lake Junaluska caused trouble when she agreed to room with an African American girl at camp, then complained about it when she got home to Georgia. In addition, members of the National Conference of Methodist Youth sometimes complained that their quadrennial convocations did not draw enough young people and did not provoke social action at home. As a representative body, even the National Conference itself felt the pinch of conservative pressure, as the political opinions of some delegates weakened resolutions against McCarthyism, war, and ROTC programs.[11]

Speaking in favor of racial integration and criticizing the ways unregulated capitalism harms the poor was enough to get someone labeled a communist in the 1950s, and this general atmosphere of suspicion definitely put a damper on youth recruitment to the Methodist social crusade. In addition, it is important to recognize that the staff of the Youth Department could only indirectly shape local programs. But more was at work than just a hostile environment and structural distance between national and local programs. Youth Department staff made several decisions that compromised their ability to forge a compelling, socially concerned and spiritually grounded youth movement at the local level. As a result, they found it harder and harder to recruit teenagers to their program of Christian social concern.

First, Youth Department officials rejected the idea that a conversion experience should be the foundation of the Christian life. But they did not replace conversion with an equally powerful experience of spiritual transformation that could sustain social concern. It was one thing to argue, as many did, that it was preferable to grow up in the church as a lifelong Christian, with no need for a dramatic conversion experience. But in the process of fighting for this view, many lost any sense that being a Christian included a personal encounter with God leading to a transformed life. For example, a youth evangelism manual published in 1949 drew no clear distinction between Christians and non-Christians and said little about how a person might make the transition to Christian belief and identity. Instead, the author focused on techniques for getting people to visit the Youth Fellowship meeting.[12]

Many of the 100,000 or so young people who joined or rejoined the Methodist church in the early 1950s probably did not do so as the result of any powerful religious experience. Materials for the Christian Witness Missions of the early 1950s asked teenagers to visit their peers with a "commitment card" in hand. Some young Methodists resisted this hard-sell approach and stated a preference for "fellowship evangelism." Instead of pressing for conversion, they invited prospects to the local MYF meeting.[13] These young Methodists pioneered a form of evangelism more in keeping with the adolescent need for peer acceptance, and their example has spread throughout American Christianity. But such approaches can also wrongly equate joining an organization with spiritual transformation.

There was a lot of confusion in Methodist and other mainline Protestant circles during the 1950s regarding evangelism, conversion, and the process of eliciting spiritual commitment among young people. As late as 1957, the author of another evangelism manual admitted that "at the present time in the Methodist church the term 'evangelism' does not have a clear cut meaning that conveys the same idea to all people." Throughout the 1950s, the Youth Department staff spent lots of time debating how best to induce "Christian commitment" in young people and worrying about how to combine it with social activism. A few youth leaders and local churches tried to launch church membership or confirmation classes as alternative models for evoking Christian commitment, but these approaches never really gained popularity. Even when implemented, such classes seldom if ever had the emotional power to elicit commitment and life change.[14] Without a viable spirituality to launch and sustain it, the high ideal of Christian social activism could easily degenerate into what its critics labeled a spiritually dry "do-goodism."

Methodist leaders sometimes came close to admitting that the more conservative evangelical groups had something that they lacked when it came to fostering powerful religious experiences among young people. In 1953, staff member Wallace Chappell criticized Young Life for its tendency to treat young Methodists as "pagans," but he admitted that such groups reached kids that Methodists were not reaching, and wondered whether their success came from "a greater feeling of certainty and zeal than one usually finds in liberal religion." Nevertheless, he asked, "can we accept a doctrine of personal salvation that ignores the world about it?" Chappell consulted the Anti-Defamation League and the NAACP for information on Young Life, and they assured him that the group and its leader, Jim Rayburn, were "anti-Negro, anti-Jew." Yet outside headquarters, many Methodists warmly embraced the new evangelical groups. Throughout the 1950s, pastors and church members wrote to headquarters for help with refuting their fellow Methodists who wanted the local MYF to be more like one of the evangelical groups. As of 1960, Methodist youth leaders were still publishing articles in their youth magazines with titles like "Young Life: In Competition with the Church." These articles always offered the same solution: a revitalized Methodist Youth Fellowship program. The authors and the good Methodist teenagers they interviewed always reassured readers that young people didn't really want the brand of Christianity being served up by the evangelical groups. But the ongoing need to warn Methodists about these groups suggested otherwise.[15] Too many Methodist youth leaders underestimated the hunger among 1950s teenagers for powerful experiences of God and a comforting spirituality.

Second, Methodist Youth Department leaders did little to provide compelling alternatives to youth culture enticements. Methodists condemned dancing and drinking, as did the leaders of Youth for Christ and Young Life. Yet unlike the evangelical groups, Methodists did not provide engaging alternatives. The Methodist Youth Department sponsored Youth Caravans throughout the 1950s, in which teams of young Methodists spent the summer traveling to local churches. They performed Christian dramas, taught wholesome recreation, and otherwise strengthened local Methodist Youth Fellowships and Sunday schools. Between 1939 and 1958, a total of 1,163 caravans employing 4,435 students traveled the country. Caravaners led sing-alongs and taught "rhythmic folk games" hoping to replace pop music and dancing. Despite such efforts, a national survey in 1955 found that 75 percent of Methodists aged 18 to 24 opposed drinking, but only 10 percent opposed dancing.[16] Apparently the typical Methodist alternatives to dancing and popular music didn't do what they were intended to do.

Methodist curriculum writers also underestimated the pull of teenage culture. Sunday school materials of the 1950s discouraged petting, reckless driving, and obsessive pursuit of popularity, but these topics did not receive much attention. Lessons all but ignored popular music. Where previous generations would have condemned an activity as "worldly" or "sinful," Methodist leaders of the 1950s tried to teach young Methodists neither to repress their "drives" nor to express them indiscriminately. Rather, they advised young people to guide their desires into "co-ordinated movement toward a worthy goal." They gently chided young people who as a result of "our modern civilization" were "less concerned with preparation for life" than "with the enjoyment of the present moment." One lesson advised teenagers to "sublimate" their sexual desires by giving themselves to worthwhile causes — such as those available through their local Methodist Youth Fellowship.[17] But church youth committees turned out to be an unattractive alternative to foreplay.

Methodist curriculum writers seemed to be clinging to a Victorian ideal of self-discipline and hard work that did not mesh with the growing value teenagers placed on fun and emotional fulfillment. At the same time, they also lacked an incisive critique of youth culture and its deadening effects on Christian discipleship like the one present in "Catholic action" circles. Thus young Methodists heard a weak message of abstinence from youth culture vices that was not supported either with a satisfying range of Christian alternatives or with a sense that one's self-denial would ultimately contribute to some important mission in the world. National conferences with stirring calls to world transformation provided some powerful religious experiences for a minority of young Methodists. But for the majority who never made it to a national conference, the Methodist Youth Fellowship provided neither an exciting introduction to Christian social activism nor even a fun Christian youth club.

Third, those who wrote the curriculum materials for Sunday schools and Methodist Youth Fellowship meetings actually toned down their social justice messages during the 1950s. During the 1940s, Methodist teenagers had received regular reminders in Sunday school about racism, world peace, and other aspects of social Christianity. Lessons had often drawn direct application to momentous contemporary events and had challenged young people to rise to the historic opportunities that faced them in a world in revolution. In 1944, teenagers in Methodist Sunday schools studied lessons with titles like "Building a New World Together" and "Working Toward a Christian Nation." Lessons cited racial and economic injustice as obstacles to this Christian world order and tried to convince young people of their important role in remaking the world. Students read in one lesson that "civilizations flourish when the individuals of ability within them are harnessed to some great task." Later that same year they studied a seven-lesson series on postwar reconstruction called "The Church and World Order."[18]

In the 1950s, instead of reading stirring calls to build a Christian world order, young Methodists learned about being good citizens. They did study the occasional lesson like "Home Should Never Be Like This," which listed social evils like substandard housing, alcohol, and racial prejudice. These lessons typically asked young Methodists to investigate conditions in their community, such as housing problems, and then make a report to authorities. But such activities often seemed both ineffective and too much like schoolwork. Lessons about social issues tended to settle for advising young Methodists to "not be discouraged if they find opposition to their methods of inquiry or their proposals for the eradication of community evils."[19] Conceding defeat in advance, while realistic for the times, was probably not a great motivator. Despite growing opposition in church and society, the authors of these lessons still optimistically assumed curriculum materials with watered-down calls for societal transformation would be enough to create socially concerned young Methodists at the local level.

In the Methodist curriculum for twelve- to fourteen-year-olds, strong condemnations of segregation actually decreased in the late 1950s due to the heightened controversy over *Brown v. Board of Education* and the emerging civil rights movement. Those who prepared the Methodist youth curricula never reversed their stand against racism and segregation, and their teachings became more vocal again in the early 1960s.[20] In addition, the suggested programs for Methodist Youth Fellowship Sunday evening meetings more frequently addressed social issues.[21] Still, social and political issues became easier to ignore in the curriculum materials of the 1950s. In 1954, the editorial division estimated that 50 percent of Methodist churches used Methodist materials exclusively, 25 percent combined them with other materials, and 25 percent did not use Methodist materials at all.[22] Since Methodist Youth Fellowships were led by youth officers, it seems likely that a significant minority of young Methodists did not like the emphasis on social action in the standard curriculum materials. Even Sunday school classes, which were always led by adults, had to cater to some degree to teenage tastes. And of course in the age of McCarthyism, Methodist curriculum writers knew they needed to tone down their political messages or conservative adults would stop buying their materials. As a result of all these factors, many teenagers probably heard diluted political messages in their Sunday school and MYF meetings.

Fourth, despite growing evidence that their social action agenda was losing appeal, Youth Department leaders continued to insist that young people were natural idealists and social activists. They assumed that youth programs that provided opportunities to exercise leadership and practice politics would have broad appeal. Methodists made much of "democratic" procedure in their design for the local Methodist Youth Fellowship. They believed that only if young people learned how to vote, serve as officers, sit on committees, and engage in lively group discussions could democracy be saved. In an example of risky commitment to this principle, some Methodist summer camps even called on teenagers to come up with the camp rules.[23] National leaders always insisted that if adults would only allow young people to lead the local Sunday night youth meeting, all would be well. Privately they admitted that meetings planned and led by teenagers often seemed to fall flat, and that this hurt attendance. Even more disturbing to Methodist youth experts was evidence that the curriculum materials they had designed to train young leaders sometimes went over their heads.[24] Youth Department staff members assumed that the "nature" of youth would do much of their work for them, so they did not develop the programs of intensive intellectual, spiritual, and political formation that were needed at the local level to train young people for social action on behalf of unpopular causes.

As a result of all these factors, Methodist youth work at the local level could be rather uninspiring, even in its ideal form. In 1955, the Youth Department released a film entitled *The Tell-Tale Arm* that portrayed the ideal Methodist Youth Fellowship in action. As the film opens, Bill and his friend Jim are working on Jim's car together. Bill invites Jim to church, telling him, "I've never had such kicks in my life" and "we discuss every problem a young person can have." Jim seems intrigued, but hesitant.

In the next scene, Bill and the other MYF officers hold a business meeting at which they discuss how to "bring in" more kids like Jim. They agree that they need to be more welcoming and have "well planned, significant meetings." When Jim gets in an auto accident, his father yells at him and refuses to hear his side of the story. After their fight, Jim is suddenly seized by intense pain in his arm, and his parents call in Dr. Billings, who also happens to be the adult advisor for the Methodist Youth Fellowship. It turns out that at the age of six, Jim broke his arm, but his busy parents did not take him to the hospital immediately. Ever since then, conflict with his parents induced pain in his arm. Although his father is a successful lawyer and both parents are involved in "civic affairs," Dr. Billings tries to explain to them that Jim needs "some tenderness, some understanding," from them.

Later, after yet another fight with his dad, Jim goes to Dr. Billings and says of his father, "I hate him." Dr. Billings replies, "That's alright. I guess you needed to say that for a long time." At that moment, Jim's arm stops hurting. By now Jim is active in the Methodist Youth Fellowship and participates in a discussion with other teenagers about how their parents subject them to suspicious "cross-examinations" and treat them like "delinquents" or "children." Eventually, Jim's parents come around. They realize that they must spend time with Jim and treat him with understanding and respect.

The clear message of the film was that a little friendly guidance, some pop psychology, and participation in "democratic" discussions at Methodist Youth Fellowship meetings would solve all the normal problems of middle-class adolescence.[25] In the film, the mission of the MYF seemed to be helping parents and teenagers get along better, not mobilizing young people to change their communities. Like many of the curriculum materials and youth fellowship manuals of the day, this film downplayed the real mission of the MYF in an attempt to appeal to a broad audience. But ironically, these efforts at broad appeal just made the MYF look boring. The only drama in the film came not from young Methodists doing something important, but from Jim's injury and his fight with his parents. The drama was what the MYF was trying to eliminate.

Methodist youth programs in local churches often stagnated because conservative and liberal influences neutralized each other. Given the intense opposition to racial integration and other elements of the Christian social agenda, it is amazing that liberal youth leaders and teenagers accomplished as much as they did. But national Methodist youth leaders made a strategic blunder when they continued to insist that most Methodist young people could be easily converted to the liberal political agenda and so invested too little in creating spiritually transformative local programs. They wanted young people to overcome the pull of youth culture and the pressure of their communities, but they did not provide them with the necessary tools and support.

"Hip" Methodism Fails to Reach the "Silent Generation"

Perplexed by youthful apathy, denominational youth leaders looked to the experts of the day to understand what was going on among American youth. David Riesman's *The Lonely Crowd: A Study of the Changing American Character* (1950) was one of the first major shots fired in the assault on postwar conformity. He appeared on the cover of *Time* in September 1954, and his "inner-directed" and "other-directed" personality types became part of the vocabulary of educated people of the day. With the title of his 1956 book *The Organization Man*, journalist William H. Whyte added another memorable phrase to the language Americans used to understand their society's problems. That same year Paul Goodman published an expose of the crippling apathy among American teenagers entitled *Growing Up Absurd: Problems of Youth in the Organized System*. Hollywood even got in on the act with films like *The Man in the Gray Flannel Suit* (1956) and *Rebel without a Cause* (1955).

All these sources agreed that conformity and apathy were the main problems in modern American society. The apathy came because government, schools, and corporations had all become large, impersonal organizations that valued "getting along" and fitting into the bureaucracy more than independent thought or innovation. Individuals knew that they couldn't make a difference, so they were giving up. Even worse, the whole system of American life seemed to be shifting gears to help people "adjust" to the new realities of the "organized system." Permissive parents, teachers who emphasized group work over individual achievement, churches more interested in socializing than in serious religious faith, tyrannical teenage peer groups, and degrading mass entertainment all pushed Americans, especially younger Americans, toward conformity. In Riesman's words, the young person was "the product of his peers . . . the other kids at school or on the block." What bothered Riesman was his belief that the other-directed person conformed to his peers not just externally but "in the very quality of his inner experience." With the recent horror of Nazism and the contemporary menace of communism firmly in their minds, these critics wondered if the "organization man" might be so willing to go along with the crowd that he could become easy prey to a political tyrant. So-called "normal" adolescent rebellion and exploration seemed to be disappearing into a vast sea of peer conformity. As Riesman put it,

> In a profound sense he never experiences adolescence, moving as he does uninterruptedly with the peer-group, from the nursery years on.

He learns to conform to the group almost as soon as he learns anything. He does not face, in adolescence, the need to choose between his family's world and that of his own generation or between his dreams and a world he never made.

Or as Goodman put it, faced with a world that offered them no meaningful work or roles, young men became resigned Beats, fatalistic juvenile delinquents, or "humanly wasted" conformists. What made all this especially tragic was that it supposedly deadened individual initiative and pursuit of noble dreams. "How rarely one hears," Goodman lamented, "the mention of some lofty purpose."[26]

It's easy to see how such ideas appealed to staff members of the Methodist Youth Department and other mainline Protestant youth workers. If youth seemed apathetic, it was because "the organized system" was deadening their natural idealism, not because they really didn't care about racial justice or labor unions. And in fact, viewed superficially, these social critics seemed to be endorsing the Methodist youth program and its view of young people. Yet every one of these authors criticized the churches for being just one more agency in the "organized system." Would it be possible to rescue youth from the organized system and oppressive peer conformity from within a denominational bureaucracy that relied heavily on "group work" in its educational methods? Even worse, the experts offered few proposals for reversing the effects of the organized system. Indeed, they sometimes admitted that the best that could be done was to help some people resist bowing to the crowd on the inside.

As is often the case, it fell to church leaders to come up with their own solutions to the problems exposed by the experts. Of course, complicating the picture even further was the fact that the "experts" may have been wrong. They certainly projected their own fears about young people and society onto their analyses. At any rate, the supposed conformity and apathy of young people would reverse with a vengeance just a decade later.

But for now, Methodist youth leaders accepted the analysis of the critics of conformity and, like them, cast about in 1950s American culture to find some inspiring rebels. Their first idea was to seize on the emerging "Beat" culture and existentialism as resources for political dissent. In hindsight, Beat authors like Allen Ginsberg and Jack Kerouac, with their drug use, sexual immorality, cursing, and dabbling in eastern religions, seem like unlikely choices for Methodist heroes. Even if it was possible to ignore some of their objectionable personal habits, Methodist youth leaders did not really want young people to imitate the Beats' cynicism, rage against American society, and dropping out of the system to become wandering gypsies in search of "authentic" (or at least drug-induced) experiences. In addition, Methodist teenagers living at home and attending high school lived lives that had little in common with the independent Beat authors, who were free to travel and explore. Yet the need to overcome the apathy of Methodist teenagers caused youth leaders to overlook these major differences between the "Beat generation" and the "silent generation."

Harold Ehrensperger of the Youth Department organized the 1955 National Convocation of Methodist Youth, and he filled the program with existentialism. He and his team developed a series of evening sessions that used drama and worship to provoke young Methodists to "love the questions" and "live the questions" rather than seek pat answers.[27] The first evening of the convocation began with vignettes showing humanity's search for God through different world religions. Then a narrator and a "speaking choir" raised a literal cacophony of questions about God, life, and the world. On another night, in an updated dramatic version of *Pilgrim's Progress,* Christian found that the City of God was quite near the City of Man. Echoing existential dogma, Christian's friend Faithful taught him that "to find the answers is asking an awful lot. But one must stake a stand." Later a judge and mob transparently modeled on the anti-communist, politically conservative critics of the Youth Department unjustly condemned and executed Faithful in the name of "democracy" and "patriotism." Finally, Christian met a character named Ignorance, who looked suspiciously like a fundamentalist. Christian asked Ignorance what he thought about war, the atomic bomb, universal military training, and refugees. After hearing his unsatisfactory replies, he somewhat self-righteously told Ignorance, "We shall pray God that you cease knowing the answers and ask a few good questions."[28] As this allegory heavy-handedly illustrated, the real point of "loving the questions" was not in fact to achieve a state of perpetual existential angst, but to jar complacent middle-class young people out of their political apathy and provoke them to embrace the liberal political agenda.

For Ehrensperger and other Youth Department staff members, this use of existentialism arose out of frustration with past attempts to mobilize young people. Instead of leading to local action, inspiring programs that offered an "answer" had often led to a "let down." He believed that because they faced "unanswerable," overwhelming questions, "enormous numbers of young people" simply gave up and said, "Well, what difference does it make?" Behind this assessment lay the liberal assumption that young people were by nature progressive political activists. If the "silent generation" seemed apathetic, it must be because they were overwhelmed with angst. Ehrensperger believed that if young people learned to "live the questions" they could tap into the power of the human soul, which would eclipse the power of the atomic bomb. Existentialism also dovetailed nicely with the reigning orthodoxies of Christian education that defined religious growth as a lifelong process to be promoted through carefully supervised experiences.[29] The seminarians who led the Youth Department in the 1950s had read Christian existentialists like Paul Tillich and Søren Kierkegaard. Although a philosophical chasm loomed between optimistic progressive Christian educators like George Albert Coe and pessimistic French existentialists like Albert Camus, Methodist youth leaders could easily combine their insights because of their common emphasis on experience. Indeed, the ongoing search for a suitable substitute for the old-time conversion experience encouraged just this sort of eclectic borrowing.

Protestant youth leaders also turned to psychology as a tool for fixing apathetic members of the "silent generation." In the 1930s and 1940s, social gospel leaders had simply taught young Methodists that religious devotion would give them "power" to implement the social teachings of Jesus. By the mid-1950s, young Methodists were more likely to hear that they needed some intensive internal reconstruction before they could remake the world. At the 1955 convocation, Henry Hitt Crane, speaking on the topic "An All-In Victory," claimed that "the world of struggle begins within ourselves." He called on young Methodists to "confront" themselves and "choose" among their conflicting identities. At the conclusion of his talk, two dancers portrayed the "reach of the soul for the highest" and its struggle against "the lesser self."[30] Although this use of dancers was all the rage in modern artistic circles, it was probably a bit shocking to the rank-and-file Methodists in attendance.

Yet at the same time, Methodist leaders seemed uncertain whether the introspective, psychologically therapeutic trend they detected in society could be turned to useful advantage or not. Another speaker at the same convocation, Dr. James Thomas, noted that "there is in our time a deep desire to understand our inner lives," yet worried that this could easily lead to superficiality and pride. Still, he hoped that the turn inward would eventually lead to "the active witness in the world of affairs." Thomas told the young people assembled that if they lived "as if life is good," they would tap into an "inner power" more substantive than the contemporary fad for "peace of mind" and more dynamic than the atom. Gerald Kennedy called on the young Methodists to be "Pioneers of Life" who would not give in to the "lust for security" or Cold War hysteria. Instead of giving in to those who demanded "adjustment and conformity," young Christians could tap into the "immeasurable" power "bound up in a man's life" by cultivating a "divine discontent."[31] Perhaps some young people did take up the challenge to introspection as a preparation for social engagement. But the need to talk about psychological barriers to social activism was yet another sign that mainline Protestant liberals did not fully understand the new realities of teenage life.

Rebecca Owen's experiences at the 1955 conference illustrate the strengths and the weaknesses of such events. Rebecca grew up in rural Virginia and was excited to travel out of state for the first time: "I expected a great revival, with five thousand students dedicating their lives to Jesus. This did not happen, but all was not lost. I held hands for the first time with a boy from Oregon, and other events paled in comparison." While it is not surprising that teenage romance loomed so large in her experience, the conference organizers seemed to largely ignore such mundane concerns of teenage life. But Methodist leaders would have been truly dismayed to hear from Rebecca that "the conference was a little over my head theologically." Instead, racially integrated dorms and African American speakers made a more positive impact on her. She had never before been to an integrated event, and the experience changed her political views:

> I was not able to escape the feeling that there should be some relationship between what I heard in my larger church and the segregation I knew in my community. I returned home deeply puzzled and talked with my MYF leader and other persons whom I respected. I was rebuffed, but it was suggested that I might give some of my outgrown clothes to a colored family. For the first time I felt resentment toward my church, but I quickly became quiet.[32]

Rebecca's story was no doubt repeated across America as young people newly awakened to the immorality of segregation got shut down in their home churches and "quickly became quiet" without support from local youth leaders.

Youth Department staff members also sensed that what they saw as the "conformity" or "apathy" of the "silent generation" was somehow linked to popular culture and entertainment. In planning for the 1959 National Convocation of Methodist Youth, they struggled to untie that knot. Several of the youth representatives on the planning committee had strong things to say. In response to a discussion of how to reach the "silent generation," John Waggy said, "Where is the prophetic voice of the church? Maybe life is a *Peyton Place,* and we just aren't realistic enough to recognize it." Don Cramer complained that "'commitment' has lost its meaning." Others perceptively wondered if the very format of the convocation as a "show" put on for teenagers would somehow undermine their true goals. Staff member Rene Pino observed that "a convocation is another affirmation or product of our culture; we put on another extravaganza — but we are not 'saying anything.'" Although they provided for optional afternoon sessions to address youth "needs" in the areas of family relationships, dating, and sex, the planning committee devoted the main substance of the convocation to counteracting the "conformity" and "apathy" produced by "the organized culture."[33] There seemed to be little recognition that the teen world of relationships might be one of the obstacles to the political activism they sought.[34]

As they groped toward an understanding of the relationship between entertainment and "apathy," the organizers of the 1959 convocation turned to popular music to communicate their message. They hoped to help conference attendees through an "exploration of the religious situation that produces such music as Boone's 'Sugar Moon' and 'The Man Upstairs.'" Some members of the convocation committee wanted to invite popular singer Pat Boone, but others objected to his "apparent fundamentalism." In the end, they settled on jazz as the genre that would appeal to youth as "*their* music" yet allow for political interpretations.[35] In fact, for millions of young white Methodists, jazz was probably not "their music." Like other white American teenagers in 1959, they probably spent more time listening to Pat Boone.

The convocation organizers commissioned daily performances of a jazz setting of John Wesley's Service of Morning Prayer. This piece later appeared on Ecclesia Records and NBC television. The crowds at these optional worship services reached 3,500 on the last day. Organizers also put together several evening programs that combined jazz, dance, and drama. Young actors performed dramatic readings from *Our Town, Epitaph for George Dillon, Auntie Mame, Death of a Salesman, Diary of Anne Frank, The Catcher in the Rye,* and *Saint Joan.* As this selection of materials shows, middle-class hypocrisy and apathy were the targets.

On Wednesday evening, the Dave Brubeck Quartet performed the jazz accompaniment for a program of readings, dance, and song by Odetta, a popular African American vocalist. The performance included black and white dancers acting out conflict and reconciliation between the races. Brubeck and Odetta were major acts of the day, albeit a bit "edgy" for the largely white, middle-class Methodist crowd. And the racially integrated dance performances would have been deeply offensive to white southerners. In optional afternoon sessions, participants could view episodes from the National Council of Churches TV show for youth called *Look Up and Live*. The episodes screened included "The Delinquent," "The Hipster," "The Square," and "Toward a Theology of Jazz."[36] Here again, the mainline Protestant celebration of the Beat generation and its culture came through. Young people who performed in or watched these spectacles probably were impressed by the cutting-edge messages, styles, and technologies, even if the content made them a bit uncomfortable.

Meanwhile, plenary speakers at the convocation sent out confusing messages about just how an existentially aware teenager should engage the world. Theodore Gill, a controversial Presbyterian liberal, insisted that "the church is here to join the world." Joining Youth Department leaders who were attempting to put the best face on the "silent generation," he argued that "listening is our generation's job." He applauded the use of the arts in the conference as a way to listen to the world. He especially liked the use of jazz because it was "born of the human situation that mingles so variously our hopes, despairs, fears, expectations, promises, denials, aspirations, degradations, freedoms, slaveries." Indeed he rejoiced that "for once, we in the church caught up with the savages in the jungles in our worship." He deplored revivalist spirituality with its "whiny, weepy, sentimental, girly pictures of Jesus and that sort of slush." His comments revealed not only a level of racism and sexism shocking to us, but also a thinly disguised anxiety about the power of Christianity in the modern world. Was the church "weak," as women supposedly were, or strong and manly?[37]

Rising just after these comments by Gill, and trembling with emotion according to one young observer, Chester A. Pennington said, "I feel like David facing Goliath without a slingshot." He tried to qualify Gill's statements, which seemed to call for the church to be absorbed into the world. Pennington rejected the old view of an "angry" God, but he also criticized the newer conception of a "benevolent deity who merely wants his children to be good little boys and girls." He took liberal Christianity to task for becoming "just another religion like all the rest — tiresomely telling us

86

what we ought to do," and insisted that "the Christian promise is that we must allow God to make us new creatures." Young people in the audience sensed the conflict with Gill's world-affirming and church-dissolving message. Some misinterpreted Pennington's comments as a vindication of their conservative theological beliefs. The issues at stake were so divisive and confusing that Pennington later wrote to convocation organizer Charles Boyles, expressing regret that some had been "supporting what I said for the wrong reasons."[38]

Charles Boyles claimed later that he was "swamped" with reactions to the event. Apparently the controversial use of drama and jazz made for good copy in the Methodist press. Such controversy may have even contributed to Boyles's decision to resign from the Youth Department soon after the convocation.[39] Some participants who already shared the liberal agenda did express glowing praise; they especially liked the way the program "shook up" both young people and adult leaders. In New Jersey, young Methodists immediately began using music and drama in their own programs. But even those who praised the convocation typically observed that much of the material went "over the heads" of the youth. They also complained that although the theme of the convocation was "Man's Need and God's Action," the programs dealt almost exclusively with "man's need." Don Barnes, a minister of Christian education from Fort Worth, Texas, perceptively noted that this tendency came straight from the wellsprings of existentialism that fed the convocation program. Others doubted that the use of jazz, drama, and dance actually furthered the liberal political agenda. They called for more direct treatment of social problems like gangs and segregation.[40]

Not surprisingly, many conservatives raged against the conference. An anti-communist newsletter sent to Methodists in Mississippi and Louisiana criticized the use of jazz, especially in worship, because it brought "inspirational religion DOWN to the level of today's teenager." What clearly bothered the author was the underlying message of racial integration. "With the need for the winning of young people to Christ through evangelism, and with national problems of divorce in marriage and lesser but acute social ills such as vice and dope with us . . . WHY should such a major place be given to the race question?" the editor asked.[41]

Yet more was at work than simply racism. By transgressing boundaries between the sacred and secular in the hope of "shaking up" complacent young people, Methodist leaders unwittingly tainted their entire political program with an aura of sacrilege. For example, Mrs. Bernard Miller complained that in her adult class one of the leaders had said that "John Wesley had his greatest inspiration while sitting on the john." At this, another participant had quipped, "Does this mean the world is going to pot?" Mrs. Miller, who was from Indiana, insisted that she was "not a prude" and that her district sponsored dancing and "popular jazz programs." But like many others, she objected to what she perceived as the sacrilegious mixing of jazz and worship. The Rev. John N. Grenfell of Wisconsin wondered why the church could "discard" its programs of evangelism because of their "emotional appeal" and yet replace them with interpretive dancing and jazz: "Since when did jazz fail to have any appeal or stimulation for the emotions?" Similarly, Mrs. Edwin Close of Pennsylvania saw the same corrupting influence at work in producing the jazz program and in the declining emphasis on evangelism in Methodist Sunday school materials.[42]

Some teenagers also objected to what they saw as the irreverence of the program. Judy Carr, a teenager from Indiana, gave a scathing report to her church in which she called the convocation "disgusting." She too was scandalized by Methodist ministers who seemed to reject traditional Christian doctrines, and by dramatic presentations containing cursing and irreverent humor. She did not object to the jazz program promoting racial integration or to the liberal internationalism preached by Eleanor Roosevelt and other speakers. Theodore Gill aroused her deepest ire because she sensed his revolutionary message would destroy the very basis of her faith by dissolving any distinction between the church and the world.[43] By entangling their social agenda with attacks on the church and celebrations of Beat culture, Methodist leaders mainly succeeded in alienating many of the young people they were trying persuade.

The Prophetic Voice of the Church
and the Failed Juvenilization of Liberal Protestantism

In 1959 Methodist teenager John Waggy asked in dismay, "Where is the prophetic voice of the church?" Actually, the outlook was not as gloomy as he thought. Because of progressive youth programs, the prophetic voice of the church could be found among a significant minority of young Protestants. Liberal Protestant young people were among the few voices of their generation to speak out against nuclear proliferation and racial segregation. Officers of the National Conference of Methodist Youth like George Harper, Harold Bremer, and James Lawson embodied the ideal of "Christian Citizenship" that put loyalty to their Christian principles above loyalty to the state or to public opinion. They made sacrifices and worked tirelessly to improve society according to the progressive Christian blueprint. Where else in the 1950s could you find an African American elected to leadership of a largely white youth organization?[44]

Young women also exercised unprecedented leadership in mainline Protestant youth organizations. May Titus grew up in Methodist youth programs, became a staff member for the Methodist Youth Department and proudly listed her memberships in the NAACP and the Fellowship of Reconciliation in her employee biography. Peggy Billings participated in the Methodist Youth Fellowship in McComb, Mississippi, and went on to a lifetime of civil rights activism. In 1968 she became secretary of the race relations department of the Women's Division of Christian Service. Young women like Rebecca Owen who first heard the message of social justice Christianity at national conferences of the Methodist Youth Fellowship went on to become leaders in the Methodist Student Movement and active in the civil rights movement as college students in the early 1960s. And many of these same women also later became leaders in the feminist movement.[45] The ongoing strength of social justice Christianity owes much to the tireless efforts of the denominational youth leaders of the 1950s who helped young people — both male and female — discover and use their own prophetic voices.

Young Methodists and the youth programs that encouraged them also helped change attitudes and beliefs in the church at large. In 1955 a national survey found that only 56.4 percent of Methodists favored a policy of removing racial barriers to church membership. But younger Methodists were more likely to favor integrated churches, and those with more contact with the church and its teachings tended to favor integration more than those who attended sporadically.[46] The young Methodist prophets were right about race, and over time they helped other white Christians see the light. Even more fundamentally, the social prophets of the 1950s would eventually be vindicated in their view that the church should be an agent of the Kingdom of God in society. In the long run, even many theological conservatives would come around to the idea that the Christian mission was not just "saving souls" but working to bring God's ways into every corner of human society.

The political successes of the era came when adults provided opportunities for young people to escape the increasingly narrow teenage world. At national conferences, young people learned about the important political issues of their day and flexed their political muscles. For those young people most active at the national level, it proved truly empowering and inspiring to form interracial friendships and see their own ideas for activism put into practice. This youth-friendly social concern captured the imaginations of a generation of young leaders and, through them, transformed mainline Protestant churches and society at large.

But locating the fulcrum of social change among young people and putting them more or less in charge of it also had its dangers. If young people were the best activists because of their "natural idealism," their lack of prejudice, or other innate qualities, where did that leave adults? Perhaps they would need to become more "adolescent" in their political views and practices. Indeed, the political naiveté of some liberal Christian activists may come from this unquestioned and even unrecognized assumption that Christian political activity should imitate the idealism, innocence, and symbolic protests of youth. Also, if adolescents were the model Christian activists, then rebelling against adult institutions like the church might seem to be the best type of political activity. Fortunately the rhetoric tended to be stronger than the reality here. Through youth organizations, young Methodists learned quite well how to run the committees and departments of the church. But during the 1960s, more and more liberal young people would take these messages to heart and reject the church that had nurtured them.

The most effective political activism also took place in youth environments that bore little relationship to the centers of power in society. Youth conferences, camps, and service projects could be good places to practice racial integration and other unpopular activities. Indeed such "artificial" environments were crucial in an era that was so suspicious of progressive politics. But like the artificial environments created in schools, Methodist political activities could sometimes seem like busywork with little real impact. Even worse, Methodist youth leaders did not always recognize the significant differences between the lives of college students and the lives of high school students. The college students of the Methodist Student Movement led the way in liberal activism during the 1950s in part because they could better understand liberal political arguments and existential theology than high school students. Most importantly, high school students still lived at home and attended churches where their fledgling political views were often squelched. But because they still tended to think of all "youth" as the same, the national leaders of the Methodist Youth Department probably expected too much of high school students and underestimated how much support it would take to keep even the willing ones engaged when they returned home from conferences.

Methodist youth leaders pioneered the use of edgy entertainment in youth work. Although controversial at the time, this juvenilized form of religious instruction has since become widespread not just in other Christian youth movements, but in the churches at large. Even some conservative evangelicals who are impatient with the stodgy scruples of their upbringing now like to talk about "engaging" the culture and "seeing God" in what their parents would have called "worldly" entertainment. The "hip" religious entertainment pioneered by Methodists and other mainline Protestants in the 1950s takes advantage of the adolescent pleasure in shocking parents and other members of the older generation. But it does better at pointing out the flaws in adult society than in offering solutions. As young Methodists found in 1959, getting inspired or offended by edgy entertainment is not the same thing as experiencing the transforming power of God. Hip religious entertainment can easily become just one more set of products to consume. It does not necessarily lead to social action.

Hip Methodism proves that it is not enough to "engage" the culture and use popular forms of entertainment to "reach" youth. It is not enough even to be on the right side of history. Methodist youth leaders correctly identified racism and segregation as among the worst evils in American society. They experimented with culturally cutting-edge ways to get this message to teens. But they failed to identify and foster compelling practices and religious experiences at the local level that could attract and sustain young social activists. Indeed, the failed effort to create a popular hip Methodism channeled resources and creativity away from the crucial task of fostering the sort of social justice spirituality needed for long-term effectiveness.

Methodist leaders also underestimated the power of popular culture to undermine the beliefs and practices they hoped to inculcate in youth. The young Methodists most immersed in the world of conventional entertainment and high school life viewed hip Methodism with disinterest or anger. Meanwhile, those teenagers who managed to beat the odds and get on board with the progressive agenda often held an increasingly negative view of the church. On the eve of the sixties, neither the conventional majority nor the radical minority got much help in loving the church. This failure to compete effectively for youthful loyalty of any kind would prove decisive in the decades ahead.

CHAPTER 4

The Black Church and the Juvenilization
of Christian Political Activism

*Because of these demonstrations the soul of America is in the process
of redemption.*

Rev. Kelly Miller Smith, "Creative Disruption"

In the spring of 1960, young African Americans shocked the country and
transformed the civil rights movement by staging sit-ins at department
store lunch counters and restaurants across the South. By the time the sit-
ins were over, an estimated 50,000 African American young people had
participated in more than thirty cities. They endured beatings and imprisonment in order to dramatize the evils of segregation and the hatred that
sustained it. Both whites and African Americans noticed the contrast between the well-dressed and well-mannered protesters and the leather-
jacketed white "hoodlums" who verbally and physically abused them. The
African American protesters behaved like adults, while white teenagers
demonstrated the worst elements of youth culture.

The African American churches played a key role in training, inspiring, and supporting the young people who led these protests. Their success
is even more striking because it happened during the very same decade
that other youth leaders were struggling to get through to the "silent generation" of young white Protestants. To the extent that young African
American Christians embraced the dignified behavior, sense of responsibility, and commitment to Christian political activism preached by their
elders, we can say that juvenilization had made little headway in the black
church as of 1960.

On the other hand, not all young African American Christians devoted their lives to civil rights activism. The first group of protesters

tended to be the elite young people of the black middle class, or at least those on their way into the middle class by means of higher education. Most young people in this elite group preferred to focus on getting a good education and preparing for successful careers. Of course, many also preferred popular music, parties, or fraternity and sorority life to the dangers of Christian political engagement. Yet overall, African American youth culture proved less deadening to more serious moral purposes than white youth culture. Unlike white Protestants, African Americans did not need to create a "hip" version of Christianity to provoke young people to embrace social justice. Nor did they need to create a Christianized version of teenage entertainment to convince young people to get saved. African Americans could avoid these detours because dramatic injustices forced every young person to realize that some things were more important than fun and entertainment. And many black adults proved to young people that the church cared about both civil rights and personal salvation.

Yet it would be a mistake to conclude that juvenilization was absent from the African American church during the 1950s. The process was certainly slower to gain momentum than in the white churches, but African American young people did push their elders to adopt new styles of music and to create youth-friendly church activities. But since youth were less often segregated into separate youth groups, this type of juvenilization only went so far. Meanwhile, the successes of the civil rights movement laid the foundation for the juvenilization of Christian political activism. Adults came to see youthful demonstrations as the model for Christian politics. For their part, some young activists came to see the protests, imprisonments, and community they experienced with peers in the movement as the most authentic forms of Christian life they had ever experienced.

By 1960, African American church leaders stood at the pinnacle of youth work success as it had been defined by adults during the 1930s and 1940s. African American young people seemed to have become the spiritual and political saviors of the nation. The student movement was at its most powerful when for a brief historical moment its leaders combined the piety and politics of African American church life into a mature challenge to segregation. But even in these early stages of the movement, young leaders and their adult supporters also planted the seeds of juvenilization that would eventually destroy this fragile synthesis.

Growing up in Racist America

Growing up black in the 1950s was so difficult and dangerous that even some young African Americans today find it hard to believe the stories they hear from their elders.[1] In order to see just how astonishing it was that young people launched a nonviolent movement of civil disobedience in 1960, we need to remind ourselves of the harsh conditions of their upbringing. Even the simplest life experiences, like going shopping, were often tainted by racial humiliations. Myrna Carter grew up in Birmingham and remembered a painful visit to a department store:

> This sales person was showing some white people hats. Another white lady began to open the drawers and look at hats. A black lady standing there thought that while she was waiting she could do the same thing. So she opened the drawers. The saleslady acted like she had committed a crime. She told her "You don't go in those drawers. You wait until I get to you!" That stayed with me a long time. I was about ten or eleven when that happened and I could not understand it.

Most African American children of the era experienced similar insults. They learned the hard way that they could not use the drinking fountains, bathrooms, restaurants, swimming pools, and parks that white people enjoyed. They knew that their schools were not as well equipped as those that white children attended. And they knew that many white people would prefer that they not get a good education and improve their lives.

Even worse, young people soon learned that when they broke the rules of racial etiquette, their parents could do little to help them. James Roberson was in for a shock when he and his family moved back to Alabama from Cincinnati. When his train stopped in Decatur, Alabama, he made the mistake of going through the front door of the station and looking for a place to get something to eat.

> A lady said, "Get out of here, nigger! You get out of here!" I was shocked. I ran out and got back on the train. I told my mom what had happened. She said, "Baby, you back down south."[2]

These were not isolated experiences. Every young African American experienced insults, humiliations, and even physical threats. They quickly learned that their parents could protect them only so much. All too often, white people seemed to be an alien, hostile group that held all the power.

Every African American who was alive at the time remembers hearing news of the 1954 Supreme Court ruling in *Brown v. Board of Education* that declared segregated public schools to be unconstitutional. This decision and other positive steps like the Montgomery Bus Boycott inspired hope in young people. They came to believe that, at long last, racist America might be changing. Yet even hopeful events like these could also put young people in danger. The day that news came of the *Brown* decision, seventh grader Melba Patillo did not know what it might mean. But she did notice that the teachers at her black school in Little Rock seemed nervous rather than happy. They sent the whole school home early with instructions to "Pay attention to where you're walking. Walk in groups, don't walk alone." Melba ignored this advice and found herself alone in a vacant lot, where a white man attacked her and tried to rape her. As he tore at her clothing he said, "I'll show you niggers the Supreme Court can't run my life." Just then another black girl came to her rescue and helped her escape. Soon after this incident, Melba wrote in her diary:

> It's important for me to read the newspaper, every single day God sends, even if I have to spend my own nickel to buy it. I have to keep up with what the men on the Supreme Court are doing. That way I can stay home on the day the justices vote decisions that make white men want to rape me.

No black person in America in 1954 would have been shocked by this story. But many would have been surprised to learn that this same girl who barely knew what the *Brown* decision meant in 1954 would become one of the Little Rock Nine who integrated Central High School in 1957.[3]

The murder of Emmett Till in 1955 also made a big impact on a generation of young African Americans. The fourteen-year-old Till was visiting relatives in Mississippi when, on a dare from his cousins, he joked with a white woman in a store. Although it is difficult to know for sure exactly what he said or did, it was at most mildly flirtatious. Till's mutilated body was found three days later in the Tallahatchie River. The men who murdered Till were acquitted by an all-white jury, and later brazenly admitted to the crime. At his mother's insistence, photographs of Emmett's body in an open casket were printed in the African American press. Cleveland

Sellers, who was a high school student at the time of the murder, remembers that it made a big impact on him and his friends:

> I was one of those students that grew up knowing we had to avenge the murder of Emmett Till. We had long discussions at school about it. We would be the generation that would step into the pages of history and create change not just because society had allowed this to happen but because a judicial system appeared to actually condone the murder of Emmett Till.

Sellers would go on to become a key leader in the Student Non-Violent Coordinating Committee in the 1960s. Many others remember that hearing the news of Till's murder was a turning point in their lives that profoundly altered their perspectives on American society. And Till's murder was only the best-known case. Claudette Colvin and her friends in Montgomery raised money for the defense of a boy named Jeremiah Reeves, who was falsely accused of raping a white woman. The authorities held him in jail until he was old enough to be executed. Years later Claudette said, "That anger is still in me from seeing him being held as a minor until he came of age."[4] African American young people knew that their lives were constantly in danger, and that the legal system might not protect them. Seeing their peers die unjustly convinced some that they needed to fight for change. It convinced others to keep their heads down and avoid trouble.

Although conditions were somewhat better in Northern and Western states than in the South, there was still plenty of racism to be overcome everywhere. To give just one example, in 1956 tensions between white and African American teenagers flared into violence at an amusement park in Buffalo, New York.[5] Whites unfairly blamed African Americans for such "race riots." They also blamed African Americans for the poverty and crime in their neighborhoods, even though police and city officials did little or nothing to provide protection and services in those districts. Whites looked at African American boys as criminals and African American girls as sexually loose and more likely than white teenagers to get pregnant.[6]

The majority of white Christians, both Protestant and Catholic, either tacitly or overtly approved these arrangements, and a few even participated in the violence. The Ku Klux Klan, operating in both Northern and Southern states, claimed to be protecting "Protestant Christianity" against Catholics, Jews, and African Americans. Wherever they were in power,

Klan members attacked, beat, and killed any African Americans they be-lieved to have become too "uppity." They also harassed any whites foolish enough to befriend African Americans or speak in favor of racial integra-tion. In many communities, the Klan operated with full or at least tacit ap-proval of elected officials and other powerful whites. White Roman Catho-lics and Protestants in many Northern cities worked hard to keep African Americans from moving into their neighborhoods, even turning to violent harassment when necessary. Many white Protestants in the South helped form "White Citizens Councils" to fight school integration. White Chris-tian teenagers and college students formed violent mobs and made daily life a living hell for young African Americans who dared to integrate for-merly all-white schools.[7]

Even many white Christians who thought segregation was probably wrong did little about it. White liberals used talk of "gradual" change as an excuse to do nothing. Martin Luther King's famous "Letter from a Bir-mingham Jail" was written to several such clergymen, attempting to con-vince them that gradual change was the same as no change. White Evangel-icals in the North and the South claimed that the "race issue" would just detract from the more important work of spreading the gospel and saving souls. Whites who claimed that they had no problem with integrated churches also admitted they would prefer not to have an African American attending their *own* church.[8] There was little in the white Christianity of the 1950s to inspire love in the hearts of young African Americans.

Given the dangers, discrimination, and humiliations of everyday life, it is amazing that so many African American young people of the era con-tinued to dream of a better day. No one could have blamed them for giving in to despair or violence, but instead they changed the world. With so many reasons to hate, what could have possibly motivated them to love their enemies and launch a Christian, nonviolent movement for civil rights? At the national, regional, and local levels, the black church made the difference.

Learning to Combine Racial Uplift, Nonviolent Protests, and Fun

In the 1950s, African American church leaders urged young people to be serious, well educated, and well mannered. Adults worried that youthful frivolity could jeopardize the progress of the race. Many church leaders also believed that the time had come for more aggressive political protests in order to win the struggle for civil rights, but most did not envision children and adolescents participating. Adults didn't foresee that young people would combine propriety and aggressive political action with a dash of teenage fun. But by preaching both aggressive action and personal propriety, national and regional youth conventions of the 1950s laid the groundwork for the student sit-ins of the early 1960s.

The National Sunday School and Baptist Training Union Congress, led by Rev. William H. Jernagin of Washington, D.C., promoted an aggressive stance toward racial injustice. In 1953, civil rights activist Rev. L. K. Jackson from Gary, Indiana, told the group that "we come to you at the most critical period in the annals of history," in which "the so-called Democracies and Totalitarian states . . . are vying with each other for dominance." He spoke with scorn of the "traditions, customs, and mores" which made men "slaves of the status quo." He argued that "people who embrace the religion of the Lord Jesus" would "never be content to be slaves for any individual, race, or nation."[9] Young people who heard messages like this knew that they had to do more than just get a good education, dress neatly, and have good manners. They heard the call to rise up and throw off their oppressors.

Each year Jernagin staged a parade and youth rally as part of the convention. An observer at the 1953 meeting in Brooklyn entitled his report on the event "Jernagin's Youngsters Take Over Brooklyn." The author commented that:

> Dr. Jernagin was in Germany under Hitler and he saw Hitler rise to power by the mechanism of showmanship. He has been to Europe recently and he has seen how the reds have been taking YOUTH with Parades. Mossbacks fail to understand that nothing sweeps Youth as parades.[10]

Adults who had lived through the crisis years continued to use the political movements of Europe as a benchmark for the mobilization of youth. For his part, Jernagin did more than talk. In 1953 he modeled civil rights activism by personally integrating movie theaters and restaurants in Washington.[11] For their part, teenagers who grew up in Baptist circles in the 1950s knew the power of a public march to build solidarity and dignity well before civil rights leaders used that technique more directly in the struggle. Such militancy was all the more striking given that the main work of the

Congress was to train Sunday school teachers, youth leaders, and officers of young people's societies.

Nannie Helen Burroughs, President of the Women's Auxiliary of the National Baptist Convention, was one of the foremost proponents of racial uplift. Although primarily an organization for adults, the Women's Auxiliary established a Youth Department that sponsored organizations for children, adolescents, and young single women. At the 1950 convention, Burroughs praised the accomplishments of the Youth Department and told its delegates, "Make no little plans, they have no magic to stir your souls. Attempt great things for God." In keeping with the theme of sacrificial service, a young soloist performed "Is Your All on the Altar?"[12] A play entitled "Youth on the Auction Block" dramatized the call to resist the "temptations of life" in favor of "Social Service for the Lord." As the title of this allegory implied, young Baptist women learned to view their lives as a valuable resource not to be wasted.

Corenne Watts, director of the Southern region of the Youth Department, exhorted young delegates to have "the mind of Christ," which was "that of a complete self-surrender and self-dedication" to a life of service. She warned, "Around us today are wars and crisis," and reminded the young women that "youth has always fought the battle of the world" so that "with every new generation a turn is in civilization that is determined by the spirit of youth." As with other leaders who operated out of the political paradigm of youth work, Watts believed that young Baptist women would save the world in its hour of crisis. "Would one control the future? Then let him lead youth in the right way," she advised.[13] Leaders of the Women's Auxiliary taught young Baptist women to see themselves as important leaders in the arduous task of Christianizing and uplifting their race.

Proponents of racial uplift like Burroughs did not blame African Americans for their problems, but they did warn young people that equality could not be achieved by lazy, immoral people. Burroughs was quick to point out the damaging effects of oppression: "the moral breakdown in the Negro masses stems from the fact that laws, practices, and attitudes that are basically unchristian and undemocratic are practiced in race relations with impunity and defiance."[14] On the other hand, she rebuked African Americans for not exerting themselves to make the best of their limited opportunities. "The time has come for the educated, well advantaged Negro to become concerned about the mass in his own race and unite in a crusade of redemption and uplift," she told the 1956 convention delegates. She rebuked middle-class people for their selfishness: "Keeping up with white people, showing off in what they give us or allow us to use is no achievement."[15] Although the prophets of racial uplift could sound harsh and paternalistic, they also fought for a new and different self-image among the black middle class that would emphasize sacrificial service rather than self-centered success.

Although young people could get inspired by the ideal of sacrificing themselves to lift up their race, they probably chafed a bit more under exhortations against the fun and fashions of youth culture. Burroughs complained about teenage fashions: "it is a dark, unpromising, evil, foreboding time in the life of any people when its teen-age girls parade the streets in pants, overalls, slacks, trunks, dungarees and halters." She worried that the "very souls of the next generation are in pawn," and predicted that unless these fashion trends could be reversed, "Decent womanhood and pure motherhood are doomed." She counseled that the best way to overcome white opposition to school integration would be a campaign of "intensive teaching in the home and in every church" that would train every African American child to "come clean, dress properly, have good manners, show deep interest in learning . . . stand erect, walk with a clear stride and determine to excel and go on about his business as becometh free Americans."[16] Middle-class teenage girls heard such messages at home, in church, and in school, not just at national conventions. It's hard to say how many African American girls really believed that wearing pants would jeopardize school integration and the future of their race, but they certainly felt the pressure. Whatever their personal preferences in clothing, the college women who participated in the 1960 sit-ins had learned as teenage girls that dressing up and carrying themselves with dignity could be politically powerful — and as it turned out, it was.[17] But the fact that Burroughs had to make this exhortation about clothes also suggests that African American girls were beginning to write their own rules about how to combine teenage fashions with service to their communities.

Even in this bastion of racial uplift, elements of 1950s youth culture made inroads. A yearly queen competition held at the Women's Auxiliary Convention honored young women who had established an outstanding record of service. Rather than placing a premium on popularity and beauty, this contest taught young women to value strong character and sacrificial service as a way to build their self-esteem. Yet in 1955, a "Queen of Beauty" and "Queen of Talent" were crowned along with the "Queen of Service."[18] In an era in which white society constantly undermined the dignity of young African American women and promoted only white ideals of beauty, such contests could inspire them with self-confidence that could spill over into other areas of their lives. But beauty and talent contests were also hugely popular among teenagers of the era more broadly, and young people had their own reasons for participating in them and their own interpretations of what winning meant. Beauty and talent contests reveal that young women were successful in pushing their elders to provide new ways to combine teenage fun with racial uplift.

Burroughs denounced the new gospel music, claiming that young people were starting to "prostitute sacred hymns and heavenly music to earthly imagination and sensual emotionalism."[19] Burroughs feared that the hedonism of youth culture would dissipate the energies that teenagers should use for service to the race. But other youth leaders did not agree. Musicians and choir directors like Lucie Campbell thought it was more important to build bridges to young people than to condemn their tastes in music. Campbell wrote music that offered the consolation of heavenly reward to those who would endure the labors and crosses of life. One of her most famous songs was "He Understands; He'll Say, 'Well Done'":

> If when you give the best of your service
> Telling the world that the Savior is come
> Be not dismayed if men don't believe you
> He understands; He'll say, "Well done."

> Oh, when I come to the end of my journey
> Wearied of life and the battle is won
> Carrying the staff and the cross of redemption
> He understands; He'll say, "Well done."

Her songs "Heavenly Sunshine," "When I Get Home," and "Footprints of Jesus" all shared this theme of earthly service as a participation in Christ's sufferings that would lead to eternal reward. Like the spirituals of the previous century, her hymns and gospel songs offered both consolation and motivation to continue the struggle. One of her most popular songs, "Something Within," prefigured the determination of the student activists:

> Preachers and teachers would make their appeal,
> Fighting as soldiers on great battlefields;
> When to their pleadings my poor heart did yield,
> All I could say, there is something within.

Have you that something, that burning desire?
Have you that something, that never doth tire?
Oh, if you have it, that Heavenly Fire
Let the world know there is something within

Chorus
Something within me, that holdeth the reins;
Something within me that banishes pain;
Something within me, I cannot explain
All that I know, there is something within.

Such music could both comfort the oppressed and inspire civil rights demonstrators. James Bevel, one of the Freedom Riders, faced down a Mississippi jailer by singing Campbell's song "The Lord Is My Shepherd."[20] African American leaders at the time and ever since have debated whether the comforting element in black Christianity was at odds with its prophetic call to social justice, but that contrast probably did not occur to most teenagers growing up in the 1950s. Gospel music played a crucial role in African American youth work because these songs provided encouragement in the face of suffering and sacrifice. Teenagers also liked them because they were fun to sing and entertaining to hear.

The leaders of national youth organizations taught the African American teenagers of the 1950s to be proper Christian ladies and gentlemen who would devote themselves to community service. They also claimed that by direct political action, young people could save America from the evils of racism and segregation. Young people pushed for more youth-friendly music, contests, and fashions, and refused to believe that teenage fun was incompatible with serious life goals. Yet the majority of African American teenagers never attended a national conference. They learned their faith and political attitudes in local churches and schools. It was at the local level that young people synthesized Christian piety, racial uplift, nonviolent direct action, and teenage fun into a powerful but ultimately unstable engine of social change.

Raising a Generation of Christian Activists: Local Church Youth Programs of the 1950s

The First Baptist Church of Nashville, Tennessee, was fairly typical of local congregations that worked hard to foster both spiritual growth and political activism among young people during the 1950s. Rev. Kelly Miller Smith, who took over as pastor in 1951, combined a passion for social justice, deep theological insight, and personal warmth. He connected well with young people. Evelyn Gaines remembered, "He was young too, with young ideas. That was stimulating to young people." She also remembered that "he just seemed to involve those youngsters in more things at the church." Gaines concluded, "The church was rather stiff before that, and he brought more warmth and loving care to the church and friendliness too."[21]

First Baptist Church was a warm community in which young people felt loved and protected. Zelma Ewing remembered that adults would regularly greet her with a hug at church and give her candy. "We were a family," she recalled. Part of the feeling of safety came from the realization that misbehavior would be caught and quickly punished. Not only was the black community close-knit as a whole; the membership of First Baptist included many of the teachers from the local black schools. Dorothy Fort recalled, "I lived in a well organized, sheltered or protected community" in which adults always made sure "we had activities to keep us busy so we weren't wandering off." Living in the closely supervised, self-contained middle-class black community, she and her friends did not dream of getting into any serious trouble. At the same time, Dorothy insisted that she and her friends were "very happy" and that "I didn't feel deprived."[22]

Smith established new programs and strengthened existing activities for children and youth. He revived the Red Circle Girls, which was the teenage branch of the Women's Auxiliary. He also established graded choirs for youth, hired a youth minister, and strengthened the "junior church," which provided worship for children and youth each Sunday morning before the main worship service. Although some older children had been in the habit of leaving after junior church to wander the streets with friends from other downtown churches, Smith insisted that all young people stay for the adult worship service.[23] Smith organized a Youth Committee in which youth and adults shared the responsibility for programming. He also placed young people on many other committees, because he believed that they should be integrated into the church.

One of the duties of the Youth Committee was to plan the monthly Youth Sunday. Teenagers provided the music, offered prayers, made announcements, and collected the offering. Ben Harris, who served as an adult advisor to the Youth Committee in the late 1950s, remembered that his strategy in recruiting participants was to "try to pull those kids in that are a little shy to give them an opportunity." A typical service included a

call to heroic devotion to Christ and his cause as well as comforting reminders of God's help. Musical selections ranged from comforting reminders of God's love such as "Come into My Heart, Lord Jesus" to more
militant hymns like "The Son of God Goes Forth to War." As in white
mainline Protestant settings, a perennial favorite for youth gatherings was
the hymn "Are Ye Able?" which includes the lines:

"Are ye able," said the master,
"to be crucified with me?"
"Yea" the sturdy dreamers answered,
"to the death we follow thee."

Sermons typically drove home this theme of sacrifice and devotion with titles like "Panoply for Fighting Youth" and "The Discipline of Difficulty."
One Youth Sunday included a special afternoon meeting with civil rights
leader Rev. Fred Shuttlesworth.[24] Youth Sunday programs often combined
the call to conversion with the call to social action.

Another annual youth activity sponsored by First Baptist Church was
Youth Week. Special worship services, panel discussions, and social activities marked this event. In the program for Youth Week in 1954, youth minister John L. Edwards wrote that the purpose of Youth Week was "to enlist
young people for the cause of Christ" and a "continuous program of evangelism and Christian Action." Educators and other community leaders,
many of whom were also members of First Baptist, led nightly discussions
on topics that included "What Does God Require of the Student?"
"Keeping Physically Fit," "Choosing a Life's Career," and "Love, Courtship,
and Marriage." This list of topics suggests that the church tried to help
teenagers with their everyday concerns, rather than focusing exclusively on
politics. The week concluded with a special evangelistic service featuring
seventeen-year-old preacher Rev. Howard Chubb.[25] Both the monthly
Youth Sunday and the yearly Youth Week provided young people with visi-
bility, leadership opportunities, and recurring exhortations to attempt
great things for God.

In his sermons on Youth Sundays, Smith tried to provide spiritual resources that would sustain young people against the opposition of a cruel
world. In a 1951 sermon, "God in the Morning," he claimed that "youth is
the morning of life at which time the sunrise of God should take place
within the soul." The young person with such a vital connection to God
"pulls away from the crowd, denying himself of popularity, and says 'I'll

take the way with the Lord's despised few.'" This sense of consecration would lead to commitment to Christian service and perseverance in the inevitable times "when the way will be confusing and dark."[26] Unlike many white youth leaders, Smith emphasized to his young audiences that the way of obedience to Christ would involve suffering. Without becoming pessimistic, he communicated a sense of realism to young people and called on them to embrace the suffering that would come from working for the Lord in racist America.

Like many adults of his generation, Smith also tended to idealize young people, sometimes implying that their potential for devotion to God and to civil rights was higher than that of adults. In a youth sermon entitled "Consecrated through Faith," Smith recognized the problems of youth, but noted that "youth and childhood already possess an abundance of faith," so the chief task became "channeling their faith in wholesome directions."[27] He recognized that young people faced sexual and other temptations, but quickly set these aside to focus on their potential. He reminded his audience that "armies are composed of young men, thus, the well-being of our nation is based upon our faith in the young." Smith exhorted the young people in the audience, "Have faith enough to be laid on the altar of God. Whatever life has to offer you, you will be laid on some altar. Why not let it be the altar of God? He can be trusted."[28] Smith's picture of adults putting their faith in young people who would make heroic and redemptive sacrifices would find fulfillment in the later student protests. But it also planted the idea that young people were naturally better Christians and activists than their elders.

Smith praised young people for their courage, their enthusiasm, and their healthy dissatisfaction with the status quo. For this reason he thought that despite the "age war" young and old could fruitfully work together as "the counsel of the older members must be adhered to while the young man wages the battle." Smith primed his fellow Baptists to see youth as the natural foot soldiers in the struggle for justice. He also called on adults to make their youth programs and worship services more relevant to real-world concerns in order to compete with the distractions of youth culture. He worried that "the places of amusement have us beat miserably." He also worried that the emphasis on heaven and consolation in old-time religion might alienate young people: "young people can find very little enjoyment in singing 'Before this time another year I may be dead and gone' or 'steal away, I ain't got long to stay here.'" Similarly, he believed that young people "can find very little interest in sermons that are more concerned with the business of making noise than that of conveying ideas," adding, "It is important that the social issues of our times strike young people aright."[29]

Smith taught young people not to settle for what he called the "snail's pace" of change. When white people told him things like "don't push too hard" or "wait for the next generation," he responded, "When we say freedom we do not mean for the next generation, nor for tomorrow, but we want our freedom now!" Smith practiced what he preached. Early in his pastorate he established a Social Action Committee that organized programs to educate the congregation and community on local social and political issues.[30] He also played a prominent role in the local effort to integrate the public schools. As the head of the local chapter of the NAACP he led groups of black children to schools in an attempt to register them for classes. When school officials refused them, he and his fellow activists took legal action to pressure the school board.

In 1957, when white officials finally agreed to begin integrating one grade per year, beginning with the first grade, Smith's daughter Joy was one of thirteen black students to attend white elementary schools. He walked his daughter to school that first morning, amid crowds of angry whites yelling racial slurs. Early the next morning, a bomb destroyed part of another elementary school that had been integrated the previous day. Smith played a key role in calming the rage in the black community and redirecting it into nonviolent action. In 1959 he organized and led the "Youth March for Integrated Schools." Children, parents, and teenagers joined together to march across Nashville to protest the slow pace of integration.[31]

Young people growing up in First Baptist Church saw their pastor standing up to the segregationists and working nonviolently to improve the lives of African Americans in their community. They were inspired and challenged by his example and even got to participate with him in the struggle. If they were listening closely, they also learned that young people like them would naturally become more devoted Christians and more effective soldiers for justice than their parents.

The Sit-Ins and the Juvenilization of African American Christianity

During the student sit-ins in Nashville, Fisk University student Earl Mays told a reporter, "There is no organization behind us. There is none! I can assure you of that!"[32] Perhaps Mays simply didn't know about all of the planning and preparation that had gone into the demonstrations. Perhaps he was trying to protect the adults in the African American community who might face reprisals from angry whites. But he was almost certainly caught up in the excitement of what seemed to be a spontaneous uprising of young people. Young African Americans were the first of a new breed of political activists that would become commonplace in the decade to come: young people aggressively protesting against the system. Although Mays and other young participants in the movement claimed to be acting on their own, they were actually indebted to local civil rights leaders, supportive churches, and the beliefs and practices they had learned in their own religious upbringings.[33] But the belief that young people had somehow single-handedly accomplished something that adults had failed to do for a hundred years would eventually became a powerful driving force in the juvenilization not just of African American politics, but of the political left in America more broadly.

Politically active ministers like Kelly Miller Smith and their congregations helped lay the groundwork for the student movement. In 1957, Smith attended a conference sponsored by the Southern Christian Leadership Conference, where he discussed civil rights tactics and philosophy with Fred Shuttlesworth, C. K. Steele, Ralph Abernathy, and Martin Luther King.[34] In January of 1958, Smith called together local ministers to discuss the possibility of a voter registration drive. At the meeting, the ministers decided to set up a local branch of the SCLC.[35]

In March 1958, the group sponsored its first workshop on nonviolence. They invited Glen Smiley and James Lawson of the Fellowship of Reconciliation to teach them about the philosophy and techniques of Christian nonviolence. Many prominent black leaders from the community attended this workshop. Soon after, when Oral Roberts visited Nashville, several members sat in the main-floor section reserved for whites, and refused to move despite threats and intimidation. Armed with this personal experience, in January 1959 Smith and other leaders of the local SCLC chapter targeted the downtown department store lunch counters as a strategic place to confront and hopefully defeat segregation. They asked James Lawson to provide training sessions for student protesters.[36]

Lawson worked through relationship networks in the black community provided by the churches, the American Baptist Theological Seminary, and the black universities. From his personal experiences in the youth and student movements of the Methodist church, in the Fellowship of Reconciliation, and as a draft resister in the Korean War, Lawson had learned how to recruit students for social action. Lawson also knew from experience what it was like to be thrown in jail by a white judge who was irritated by his stubbornness. This experience would prove crucial in convincing students to follow him down such a frightening path.[37] Smith offered First Baptist Church as a rallying point for student protests. Many students already attended First Baptist, and its downtown location made it a perfect staging point for the demonstrations to come.

Many of the students Lawson attracted to his workshops came from strong church backgrounds, which helped motivate their activism. Curtis Murphy grew up in a devout Baptist family in rural Tennessee. James Bevel, Bernard Lafayette, and John Lewis were all students at the American Baptist Theological Seminary. Lewis was deeply religious from an early age, going so far as to play church with the family chickens; he preached to his "flock," baptized, and even buried them. Bernard Lafayette was a leader in Baptist young people's activities in his church in Tampa. He was chosen to represent the youth group by offering a speech on Mother's Day. Since Mother's Day drew the most worshipers of any Sunday of the year, such a speaking opportunity was a great honor. Lafayette was typical of the Nashville student protesters in being one of the best students in his high school, and treated as "special" by his family and church. He also heard the typical contradictory messages about southern racial etiquette from his proud but wary father: "Now, always stand up for your rights, and don't let anyone walk over you and don't ever be afraid. And don't get in any trouble with white folks."[38] Although the parents of the early protesters would worry about their children's activism, many of these same parents had modeled a potentially explosive mix of propriety and assertiveness.

Such young people emerged from their strict upbringings with both a deep emotional tie to Christianity and a religiously inspired sense of moral obligation to their families and race. Gloria Johnson remembered her mother using God to keep her children in line and spur them on to high achievements. When Mrs. Johnson came home from work on a Saturday and found that her children had not done their chores, she would get down on her knees in front of her children and pray, "Lord I don't know where I got these lazy children." Her prayer went beyond manipulation to become an exhortation to heroic action for the good of the race:

> Lord, my people were proud people. If there was a slave revolt they were part of it, and if there was an Underground Railroad, they worked on it. They were good people and fearless, and they were *never* lazy, Lord. So why are my children so lazy, Lord?[39]

When the children obeyed and achieved good grades in school, their mother praised them highly. She also supported them in their moral and political convictions; when a high school principal threatened to sabotage Gloria's college plans because she refused to salute the American flag, Mrs. Johnson backed him down. Sometimes parents didn't realize that their children were simply putting into practice the messages they had learned at home and in church. When John Lewis's mother pleaded for him to "get out of the movement," he wrote back, "I have acted according to my conviction and Christian conscience. I can do no less."[40]

Many students at the black colleges in Nashville had similar backgrounds, yet most of them were not directly involved in the sit-ins. Some even criticized and resisted the movement, especially at first. Fisk University students often saw themselves as above the movement; they preferred fraternity and sorority life and preparing for a comfortable future. Marion Barry recalled that the more popular a young man was in campus social life, the less likely he was to be involved in the movement. At Tennessee State, many students from humbler backgrounds feared jeopardizing their chance to fulfill not only their own ambitions, but their families' dreams for a better life.[41] No one can blame these young people for being cautious — they had grown up in a world in which African Americans who got out of line were beaten or killed. They knew that a college education was a privilege not to be lightly cast aside. In hindsight, the surprising thing is that *any* young people risked their lives and futures on a gamble to change a system that had crushed all dissent for more than a century.

James Lawson and his seminars on nonviolence made the difference, but his task was not easy. Unlike later students who could join the sit-ins after they had become a proven technique, these pioneers had to be convinced on philosophical and theological grounds that such a counterintuitive, dangerous strategy could work. Only a deep faith that God would work through nonviolence could convince these young people to try it. Lawson insisted that nonviolence was not a technique, but a Christian way of life: "You have to do more than just not hit back. You have to have no *desire* to hit back. You have to *love* that person who's hitting you. You're *going* to love him." The underlying belief was that love for enemies and enduring public suffering at their hands would unleash spiritual and moral power to change society.

Eventually, Lawson's confidence began to rub off on the students. Lewis recalled, "There was something of a mystic about him, something holy, so gathered, about his manner, the way he had of leaning back in his chair and listening — really listening." Lawson convinced the students that the righteousness of their cause and the nature of God and His universe would inevitably combine to grant them success. Significantly, growing up black and Christian in the Jim Crow South had given many of these students an instinctive understanding of the power of suffering. "We talked a lot about the idea of 'redemptive suffering,' which from the first time Jim Lawson mentioned the phrase made me think of my mother," Lewis remembered.[42] Although the participants in Lawson's seminars learned about the theories of Reinhold Niebuhr, Thoreau, Lao-tzu, and Gandhi, it was their experiences growing up in African American Christian families that probably made much of it ring true.

As John Lewis began to believe the message of Christian non-violence, he came to see it as a fulfillment of all he had learned in church:

> I'd finally found the setting and the subject that spoke to everything that had been stirring in my soul for so long. This was stronger than school, stronger than church. This was the word made *real*, made whole. It was something I'd been searching for my whole life.[43]

Like Lewis, many who participated in the movement came to see it as the most authentic version of Christianity they had ever experienced. In the process they came to redefine the faith of their childhood.

By January 1960, the Nashville Christian Leadership Conference and its student recruits were planning a massive test of department store lunch counters to begin in March. Several times in January, the group tested lunch counters, but these efforts led to no arrests or violence, and very little press coverage. The sit-ins launched in Greensboro, North Carolina, on February 1 prompted Lawson and the Nashville students to speed up their plans. But as late as Saturday, February 27, the very day that the students planned to fill the jails with protesters, the older leaders hesitated. As students filled the sanctuary of First Baptist Church, adult and student leaders held a tense meeting in the Sunday school area in the basement.

Smith and the other adults saw some serious obstacles to success. Chief of Police Douglas Hosse had made it clear that unlike previous sit-ins, the next attempts would be met by massive arrests. The black community was largely unaware of the impending showdown, and their support could not be taken for granted. Smith reminded the students that the NCLC had only $87.50 in its account, and no legal representation to deal with arrests and bail. Adult leaders worried about how they could justify such recklessness to school officials and parents. Since it was a Saturday, they expected crowds of white youths, who could easily become violent. Adults worried that since many of the protesters were teenagers themselves, they might be goaded into violent retaliation. The adults understood that a race riot would ruin their chances to integrate the lunch counters.[44]

Smith began the meeting with reassurances that the adults were ready to go to jail when the time was right — "In fact, perhaps we will all be locked up before this thing is over," he said. But when he and other adult leaders advised that the demonstration be postponed, the student leaders vehemently disagreed. One student leader said, "If we wait until next week we may be asked to wait until next month, and then the next month and on and on. Personally, I'm tired of this business of waiting." Bernard Lafayette and other theological students said that their upcoming protest, like the cross of Christ, would involve redemptive suffering. Finally, Smith and the other adults realized that sit-ins would be happening that day with or without their support. After some hesitation, Smith said, "We are all in this together — when you go down to the stores, you will go with our full support." As the student leaders left the meeting, obviously irritated at the delay, one of the ministers joked, "Some of those kids seem to have a crucifixion complex." But Smith remembered a thrilling feeling that he had just witnessed more than "simply an encounter with rebellious youth." He believed these were young people "armed with a dream."[45] For adults like Smith, watching young Christian protesters became a powerful religious experience that confirmed their beliefs that young people were somehow more natural Christian social activists than their elders.

Smith watched as several hundred well-dressed, well-mannered young people filed out of the church, headed toward the department stores. The dignified manner of the protesters contrasted sharply with the shouts and threats from white onlookers. Some eighty-one students were jailed that day, and at least three were badly beaten first. None of the students retaliated against their young white attackers. Under police custody, they sustained themselves by singing freedom songs. One of the first they sang was an adaptation of the spiritual "Amen" that substituted the word "Freedom."

The dramatic actions of the young protesters that day galvanized the adults of the black community. Z. Alexander Looby and a dozen other black lawyers offered their services, and other adults put up bail money. Looby was visibly moved by the courage and spirit of the protesters. The imprisoned students refused bail, and even managed to endure prison with flair. Upon release, one student complimented the chief of police on running "the best jail I've ever been in."[46]

In the weeks and months that followed, Smith and the members of the First Baptist Church continued to provide crucial support for the movement across generational lines. Church member Ben Harris, who worked as a freshman counselor at Tennessee A&I, regularly went downtown to get students out of jail, and spent hours on the phone trying to calm the fears of angry parents. Other local adults gave money sacrificially. Some even reportedly mortgaged their homes in order to provide bail, transportation, and legal services for the students. During the height of the sit-ins, Dorothy Webster and many of the other female members of First Baptist Church went downtown to the church every day. They prayed with the students, fed them, and bound up their wounds when they returned from the front lines. African American adults also organized a boycott of the department stores that helped to break the back of segregation.[47] Thus although both adults and students would later reinterpret the movement as entirely student led, it was actually cooperation between the generations that made it so effective.

Early Nashville protesters saw their cause and even their imprisonment in dramatic religious terms. John Lewis later compared his first civil rights arrest to Christian conversion:

Now I had crossed over, I had stepped through the door into total, unquestioning commitment. This wasn't just about that moment or that day. This was about forever. It was like deliverance. I had, as they say in Christian circles when a person accepts Jesus Christ into his heart, come home. But this was not Jesus I had come home to. It was the purity and utter certainty of the nonviolent path.[48]

Growing up in the black Baptist church taught young men and women to see a life as a battle between good and evil, to value total life commitment, and to expect emotional release to accompany that commitment. The emotions and moral convictions they found in the civil rights movement would therefore reassure them that their cause had divine approval and ultimate significance. The religious experiences of childhood certainly prepared activists like Lewis to act courageously and to understand their political experiences as redemptive. But those same political experiences then became a lens by which to reinterpret their Christianity. The intense emotions provoked by the dangers and exhilarations of student protests became a new kind of conversion that seemed superior in some ways to the old. Neither black politics nor black Christianity would ever be the same.

When store owners finally backed down and integrated the lunch counters in May 1960, the student movement did not disband. Instead, the student leaders pursued their advantage and insisted that God demanded full equality and integration of the races in Nashville. A recruitment flyer issued in the fall of 1960 told fellow students that "SEGREGATION and discrimination make men slaves in their minds, and God did not make men to be slaves. God made men to be free and to walk the earth with dignity." The flyer went on to call segregation "a great sin against man and against God." A 1961 statement issued by the "Nashville Non-Violent Movement" dripped with theological language as well as moral outrage:

> Police officers stand guard over the customs of segregation while valuable citizens of our nation are heckled, molested and then arrested. Such acts obviously deny all intellectual, moral, Christian and democratic principle. But do not such acts indicate that the immorality of racial pride, the sin of separation from God and from one another remains in our so-called "good city"?

The statement went on to declare that protests would continue not only until all people found "better jobs and housing; more educational and vocational opportunities, and expanded social and recreational facilities" but until Nashville became "a city of genuine brotherly love," concluding, "Nothing less will satisfy the purpose of God."[49]

There is much to admire in the idealism and Christian vision of these young people. Their theology motivated them to make great sacrifices and to work for immediate rather than gradual change. But their unrealistic expectations for how quickly a segregated city could become a bastion of "brotherly love" set them up for considerable disillusionment later. That disillusionment would eventually push some of them to deeply question the Christian basis of the movement and their own loyalty to the church.

Theology was not the only Christian resource that sustained the student movement. Just as gospel music had been crucial to the black church youth activities of the 1950s, freedom songs provided spiritual encouragement to the young protesters. One of the most popular songs of the movement was "We Shall Overcome," which updated the old church song "I'll Overcome Some Day" to celebrate current, not just future, spiritual victories. Similarly, the spiritual "I'm Gonna Sit at the Welcome Table" was also a favorite in Nashville. This song tied the lunch counter struggle into the biblical image of the marriage supper of the Lamb to be celebrated by the church in heaven. Its message in the context of the sit-ins was that heaven was coming down to earth and a new beloved community was replacing the old segregated world of hate. Yet another popular song with the Nashville students was the spiritual "We Are Soldiers," which managed to combine their martial spirit, their intense identification with the cross, and the warmth of family feeling:

> We are soldiers in the army
> We've got to fight although we have to cry
> We've got to hold up the freedom banner
> We've got to hold it up until we die.
>
> My mother was a soldier, she had her hand on the gospel plow
> One day she got old, couldn't fight any more
> But she stood there and fought on anyhow.

The student protesters of 1960 drew heavily on the resources of their churches to create a new youth-friendly synthesis of spirituality and political activism.[50]

Participants also drew on more secular elements of black youth culture to express their cry for freedom. James Bevel had tried his hand at rock and roll, performing in a group with his brothers. Bevel and Bernard Lafayette rewrote popular songs to reflect movement sentiments. Their song "You'd Better Leave Segregation Alone" borrowed the tune from Little Willie John's rock and roll song "You Better Leave My Little Kitten Alone." Bevel and Lafayette's lyrics ridiculed segregationists by claiming that "they love segregation like a hound dog loves a bone." They also used humor in their rewrite of Ray Charles's "Moving On," which claimed, "Old Jim Crow's moving on down the track, he's got his bags and he won't be back." One of their original songs, "Your Dog Loves My Dog," built on Bevel's childhood experiences in Mississippi in which his dog played with the white neighbor's dog, even though the children could not play together. The Nashville student group also produced an album that included dramatic reenactments of the sit-ins and performances of popular movement songs. Cordell Reagon, a high school student from Nashville, later helped found a SNCC performing group called the Freedom Singers.[51]

These young black activists used their musical talent to raise money for the cause. As with other elements of their African American heritage, these students pushed their musical performances in more aggressive directions than had been common in the past. They were less afraid than their elders to combine fun, entertainment, and secular music with their Christian political activism.

The new political activism among college students soon began to influence even younger African Americans. After Z. Alexander Looby's home was bombed, most of the student body of Pearl High School joined college students in a march to city hall. Zelma Ewing's father, who taught math at Pearl High, hesitated to let her march, but in the end he reluctantly agreed. Several other teenage members of First Baptist participated in the march. Cordell Reagon recruited his fellow high school students in the cafeteria. When the students marched by, these teenagers jumped into line before anyone could object. Reagon remembered that many of his fellow high school students seemed to be looking for excitement rather than pursuing a particular political agenda.[52] Student activism was indeed serious, but it was also an exciting way for young people to escape the grind of everyday life and find adventure.

The student sit-in movement of 1960 revolutionized adult perceptions of youth, Christianity, and race relations in America. Indeed, Kelly Miller Smith's speeches can be dated by their use of the student movement as a paradigm for God's action in America on behalf of justice. One reason for the dramatic impact of these events on adults like Smith was simply the emotional intensity of watching young people face physical danger in obedience to God. In a 1963 speech to an NAACP mass meeting, Smith recalled fighting back tears as students prepared themselves to face hostility and violence by singing the "Battle Hymn of the Republic." He was especially moved by the lines, "As He died to make men holy/Let us die to make men free/While God is marching on." The spectacle of young Christians possibly walking to their deaths was especially moving because it combined powerful dreams, intense fears, and a sense of redemptive significance. Just as generations of adults had wept to see their children answer the call to conversion, civil rights leaders wept to see them answer the call to nonviolent protests.[53]

The students provided more than an emotionally powerful moral example. Smith placed the student movement at the center of his theological and political reflections on the problem of race in America. In one speech he began by recalling an experience from the movie theater "stand-ins." As he watched student protesters lining up to buy tickets under a movie marquee for the film "The Misfits," it had struck him that the title applied equally well to these students and to all true Christians. Smith believed that these students showed the way out of "Casper Milquetoast religion" and into "a disturbing and disruptive faith." Smith claimed that "prophetic misfits are likely to engage in disruptive acts."[54] In the mind of church leaders like Smith, the oppositional politics of youth became the new ideal for all Christians, and other approaches to faith and politics seemed weak by comparison.

Smith came to see the students and their "creative disruption" of an evil society as part of God's action to redeem America. He quoted a letter he had received that asked, "why do you people create so much disorder and ill-will; don't you know that God is a God of order, not disorder?" In reply, Smith recounted the long-deferred promises of justice and equality in America and claimed that the current demonstrations were part of "a struggle between light and darkness, between good and evil, between right and wrong." He continued, "although the methods have not always been perfect in their application and the motives of the participants have not always been pure, I submit that the sit-ins, the stand-ins, the wade-ins and the freedom rides are the best form of treatment this ailing America has had for a long time." Why? "Because of these demonstrations the soul of America is in the process of redemption." Smith believed that the successes of these demonstrations proved that "the posture of non-violence is far more powerful and meaningful than that of retaliation." Indeed, he thought that "our experience has taught us that through the means of non-violence men can be changed from within." Nonviolence worked because of the power of redemptive suffering:

> By his willingness to take abuse, the nonviolent demonstrator reveals both his recognition of his involvement in the evil which is being attacked and his willingness to make whatever sacrifice necessary to have it corrected. As James Lawson of our Nashville movement puts it, he is willing to absorb the hostility of the opponent with his own body.[55]

The dramatic success of the early student movement convinced church leaders like Smith that youth-led protests really would save America.

The religious intensity of the Nashville student movement left its mark on the ethos of the Student Nonviolent Coordinating Committee (SNCC) that formed in 1960 as a result of the nationwide sit-in movement. The

Nashville group was especially prominent in the early leadership of SNCC. Marion Barry was the first president; John Lewis took over the job in 1963. James Lawson spoke at the early SNCC conferences and imparted his theological vision for nonviolent action. Under his influence, the students adopted an official statement that affirmed the redemptive power of nonviolence and the high hopes they had for the outcome of their movement:

> Through nonviolence, courage displaces fear; love transforms hate. Acceptance dissipates prejudice; hopes ends despair. Peace dominates war; faith reconciles doubt. Mutual regard cancels enmity. Justice for all overthrows injustice. The redemptive community supersedes systems of gross social immorality.[56]

Although Smith and other Christian civil rights leaders celebrated the young "misfits" who "disrupted" society, the possibility remained that youthful political activists would abandon their loyalty to the church, with its middle-class ideals of racial uplift and propriety. Hints of this future development could already be seen at the founding conference of SNCC in April 1960. In his speech to the students, James Lawson called the sit-ins "a judgment upon middle-class, conventional, half-way efforts to deal with radical social evil."[57] Indeed, one early study of SNCC labeled it a "moralist" or "redemptive" organization, unable to compromise and increasingly suspicious of conventional politics.[58] The religious backgrounds and training of the Nashville student leaders helped create this ethos. Who needed conventional politics when the miraculous lifestyle of nonviolence was producing such dramatic successes? Who needed to listen to the older generation when even they were saying that young people were the new saviors of America?

A Powerful yet Fragile Synthesis

By 1960, young African Americans had created an impressive new form of Christian life that combined the powerful spiritual resources of the black church with a commitment to nonviolence and a dash of fun and excitement. In the process they really did bring redemption to America. They accomplished great things and defeated great evils. God worked through the black church to create one of the most powerful Christian youth social movements in history.

The very successes of the student movement convinced many that youth-led marches and protests would be the wave of the future. Meanwhile, there were already signs that some young people had begun to see the movement as their new church, and nonviolent protests as the center of their spirituality. Many came to believe that they really were better political activists than their elders, and consequently they undervalued the co-operation and support of the older generation.

In hindsight, we can ask some probing questions about this fragile early 1960s synthesis of nonviolent protest, Christian piety, and youth culture excitement. Would the student movement maintain its ties to older adults, or would young protesters create their own youth subculture and isolate themselves? Would young leaders continue to value Christian maturity, love their enemies, and actively try to build the "beloved community," or would they come to see American society as almost irredeemably evil and to be torn down? Would they treasure the Christian foundations of the movement, or would they leave the church behind in their quest for the perfect society and spiritual authenticity? And, meanwhile, what would the church do to help the majority of young people who were not participating in civil rights demonstrations? What would happen to young people and the church if civil rights victories, white backlash, and youth rebellion combined to weaken the very African American institutions that had so successfully formed generations of young people?

Few, if any, asked such questions at the time, because young people seemed to be fulfilling adult dreams. But what would happen if the student movement did take one or more of these detours into juvenilization? The resulting youth-culture religion of political protest might hold as many pitfalls as promises for the future of young people, the church, and society.

CHAPTER 5

Why Everyone Wanted to
Get out of the Catholic Ghetto

It was a ghetto, undeniably. But not a bad ghetto to grow up in.

Garry Wills, *Bare Ruined Choirs,* 1972

Christians have often dreamed of a world in which their children could grow up hearing the same positive messages and learning the same godly behaviors at school, at home, in church, and even in society at large. If they could just create a unified set of Christian institutions, many adults believe their children would turn out just the way they want them to. This dream continues to be powerful, especially among morally and theologically conservative Christians.

In the period between 1945 and 1965, Roman Catholics came as close to achieving this ideal as any group in twentieth-century America. The young Catholics of this era were much better educated about their faith and practiced it more faithfully than Catholic teenagers today. Yet the story of 1950s Catholic youth work proves to be a cautionary tale to those tempted to imitate its methods. Many of these same young people later repudiated what they called the "Catholic ghetto." And in some ways, the American Catholic church has yet to recover from the chaos and confusion that resulted from the collapse of its 1950s system of spiritual formation.

What went wrong? Roman Catholics adapted too much to youth culture in some ways, and not enough in other ways. The parts of teen culture they tried to suppress by force came back to haunt them later. The youth groups of the 1950s did little to equip Catholics to provide successful spiritual formation once the supportive institutions of the Catholic ghetto collapsed.

The Catholic experience shows that it is possible to create a juvenilized faith that seems strong for a while. But when that version of the faith depends too much on particular institutional arrangements and coercion, it can collapse suddenly. It becomes vulnerable when conditions inside or outside the church change.

"Catholic Action" Youth Groups Fall on Hard Times

The opposition to "Catholic Action" that began to emerge in the 1940s reached full flower in the 1950s. Because most Catholics were desperate for acceptance in the American political system and hated anything that smacked of communism, economic and political critiques of the sort proposed by Catholic reformers fell on deaf ears.[1] In addition, the economic prosperity of the postwar period reduced the pool of discontented young people who might swell the ranks of groups like the Young Christian Workers. Even though the Young Christian Workers' ideal member was a male factory worker, by 1957 most local groups were 75 percent white collar. And YCW always struggled to attract male members. In the sixties, the membership voted to change the organization's name to Young Christian Movement.[2] A working class social action movement held little appeal for the upwardly mobile young Catholics of the 1950s.

Catholic Action leaders also noticed that economic prosperity seemed to be making some young Catholics more conservative. One such leader reported on an evening socializing with young Catholic school graduates. He found these couples in their late twenties to be obsessed with financial success and disgusted with pro-labor and "pro-Negro" priests. He believed that Catholic education had failed to cure these young people of the "secularism" that proved more dangerous than a "frontal attack from communism or fascism" because it promoted tolerance of "the social evils on which the totalitarianisms thrive."[3] For their part, many teenagers resented the pressure they felt from Catholic Action youth leaders. One young man complained that if he and his fellow teenagers joined reformers in rejecting "so many things that are part of our society," then Catholics "would never make any progress in this country." He blamed reformers for stirring up anti-Catholic prejudice with their constant attacks on the American way of life.[4]

Postwar teenagers' lives were dominated not by oppressive factory conditions or labor unrest, but by high school social life, with its sports, clubs, and dances. Even teenagers who joined the Young Christian Students or Young Christian Workers tended to remake them into recreational and educational clubs much like all the other youth organizations of the day. At their best, these organizations recruited and trained leaders who knew how to identify social injustices and work to change them. Young leaders in these movements worried that social concern might become just another activity to keep kids busy. One asked, "Are listening to the popes' pleas, re-making society, bringing Catholic principles and the Christian spirit to a cynical and tired world . . . just something for whiling away time in school, on a level with basketball games and chemistry clubs; fit objects for the sophomore's native idealism and nothing more?"[5] Now that Catholic Action seemed like just another extracurricular activity, there was a danger that teenagers might leave it behind when they grew up and entered the real world.

Finally, Catholic Action youth organizations received little support, and occasionally even faced opposition, from the church hierarchy. One reason for this lukewarm reception was undoubtedly Reynold Hillenbrand's autocratic and independent leadership style. Catholic Action leaders never really wanted to build a mass movement, preferring to strongly influence a small number of leaders toward a more countercultural form of Catholicism. But they also realized that their version of Catholicism was a hard sell to the teenagers of the 1950s.[6] Although these organizations operated on a model more likely to succeed once the Catholic ghetto collapsed, they failed to capture the imaginations of most young Catholics and their parents.

All-American Catholicism

The main institutional competitor to the Young Christian Students was the Youth Department of the National Catholic Welfare Conference. This body appropriated the name "Catholic Youth Organization" and promoted a network of diocesan youth programs more compatible with middle-class American sensibilities. The CYO and the NCWC Youth Department tapped Catholic hunger for national recognition, effective organization, and visible proof that the next generation of Catholics remained faithful to the church. Many bishops were looking to unify and expand their diocesan youth programs in the late 1940s and early 1950s.[7] The NCWC offered support and a ready-made program combining anti-communism, fun activities, and devotionalism into an all-American Catholicism that met all these needs. This juvenilized version of Catholicism kept kids busy praying and demonstrating their patriotism in a way that promoted cultural assimilation more than deep commitment to a countercultural way of life.

Fr. Joseph Schieder, who directed the Youth Department of the National Catholic Welfare Conference from 1948 to 1961, inherited several aspirations that had shaped Catholic youth work during the depression and war years. First, he embraced the view that youth held the key to the crisis of civilization. Second, he pursued the dream of establishing Catholic youth councils that would both unify Catholic youth work and train young Catholics in democracy. Third, he promoted the "four-fold program" of spiritual, cultural, social, and physical activities. Finally, Schieder inherited the general mission of the National Catholic Welfare Conference to organize Catholics and give them a voice in national affairs.

In 1951 Schieder finally succeeded in establishing a national network of youth councils and its capstone, the National Council of Catholic Youth. At the founding national conference, Schieder and other adult participants rejoiced that "not a voice was heard from the observers' section, for it was the young people's show." The spectacle of young Catholics practicing a devout democracy seemed especially important to adult observers throughout the fifties. Such spectacles were also moving for their young participants. William Kernan, a delegate from the Archdiocese of Baltimore, called the conference "the most outstanding experience of my life." In a sentiment typical of the youth council movement, he lauded the convention as "a group of young people from all areas, all environments, and all walks of life, working not for their own personal proposals or advancement, but rather working for the good of everyone." Another delegate broke down and wept as he exhorted the group to pursue genuine spirituality in their new organization. The delegates responded as they had to the election of their national officers: with a standing ovation.[8]

Filled with a sense of making history and setting the stage for world impact, youth council members found themselves largely occupied with perpetuating the council system and its four-fold program of spiritual, cultural, social, and physical activities. The four-fold program, not political involvement, became the core of 1950s Catholic youth culture. Although young leaders periodically condemned the "dance of the month club," much of their energy went into organizing teen social activities rather than mobilizing young people for social action. Like other politically oriented youth conferences of the era, the National Conference of

Catholic Youth had very little real influence in society. It was a pretend political organization, and it touched only a minority of Catholic teenagers. Adults like Schieder ignored the differences between a gathering of hand-picked teenagers practicing democratic procedures and a truly powerful political movement. And it is likely that the vast majority of young Catholics were indifferent to the political aspirations of their elders.

Schieder and the NCWC Youth Department also organized numerous large youth conferences and national publicity campaigns during the 1950s that had two main goals: to encourage young people to be good Catholics and to prove to the public that Catholics were good Americans. National CYO conventions held every two years became large-scale spectacles of Catholic piety, patriotism, and national influence. The 1955 convention held in St. Louis featured nationally known speakers ranging from Catholic publisher Frank Sheed to former president Harry S Truman. The convention climaxed with a pontifical mass attended by 17,500 and declared to be a "breathtaking, awe-inspiring sight."[9] Such spectacles proved that Catholics were a powerful force in American society.

Schieder also created National Catholic Youth Week as a public relations campaign to promote a positive public image of Catholic young people and of the church. For the first observance of Youth Week in October 1951, Schieder lined up celebrity endorsements from Bing Crosby, Ed Sullivan, Jimmy Powers, and Walter Winchell. Locally, diocesan youth directors solicited proclamations from city governments and orchestrated elaborate celebrations with full radio and press coverage. In New York, acting mayor Joseph Sharkey praised the CYO before a crowd in City Hall Plaza that included 5,000 Catholic schoolchildren. "In our troubled world of today, with confusion and overtones of war raging, there is among us an organization which faces the future with courage, confidence, and vision," he said.[10] By 1953 television spots joined radio and billboard announcements reminding the public of the importance of Catholic young people.

Such eager use of public relations and celebrities contrasted sharply with the 1940s debate in the pages of the Catholic Action youth magazine *Today* over whether Frank Sinatra was a good spokesman for Catholicism. Schieder and like-minded Catholic leaders did not fully realize the implications of creating an image of clean-cut, all-American teenagers, lining up celebrity endorsements, and selling that image to the American public. They were turning Catholicism and even young Catholics themselves into products for the American public to consume. Their image of the ideal Catholic did little to help ordinary teenagers with their everyday needs and concerns. If anything, such tactics put more pressure on teenagers, since their failures would now harm not just themselves, but their church's reputation.

Some teenagers eagerly participated in the public relations campaign. To identify a yearly theme for Youth Week, Schieder turned to his council of national youth officers. These outstanding Catholic teenagers, who had been elected by their peers, chose to emphasize the positive contributions of Catholic youth to American society. In 1953, their chosen theme was "America's Hope: Youth with Faith." Hoping to counteract the negative publicity surrounding juvenile delinquency, they chose "Youth . . . America's Richest Heritage" as the theme for 1954. By 1956, Youth Week themes, poster designs, plays, poems, and prayers came from young people across the country who competed for top honors in Youth Department contests.[11]

Promotional materials for Youth Week often proclaimed that Catholic teenagers held the key to defeating communism. To depict the 1955 theme, "Youth — Our Hope," the official Youth Week poster featured an old-fashioned balance-style scale. On one side, a teenager helped his companion onto the scale. On the other lay a cracked globe. The message was clear: Catholic youth thrown "into the balance" would save the world. The 1959 poster, bearing the motto "Spiritualize Youth . . . Vitalize Nations," showed a young man gazing at a globe oriented to display the United States and the Soviet Union. In 1958, the prayer intentions for Youth Week included "that more Catholic youth will be called to fill the need for Catholics in the field of (physical) science."[12] This obvious response to the Sputnik crisis signaled that Schieder and the Youth Department intentionally linked Catholic youth, piety, and American national interest. Young Catholics got the message that by promoting a positive image of Catholic youth they would help not only themselves, but the nation as a whole. At St. Joseph High School in Camden, New Jersey, it was the Civics Club that made Youth Week promotion its special project.[13] But what could teenagers really do to win the Cold War?

The Youth Department of the National Catholic Welfare Conference promoted an all-American Catholicism that simultaneously tried to sell young people on being devout Catholics and sell America on the idea that Catholics were good Americans. Some young Catholics did pick up on the political messages and public relations techniques promoted by Schieder and the Youth Department. But the most powerful influences on young Catholics were still their local parishes, schools, and youth groups. These influential institutions sent similar messages that combined piety and pa-

triotism, but they also added a sometimes contradictory intellectual formation, an emphasis on fun, and a heavy emphasis on sexual purity.

The Juvenilization of Catholic Piety

Young Catholics grew up immersed in a world of prayers, candles, holy
water, crucifixes, pictures of Jesus and Mary, and countless other devotional objects, with weekly or even daily mass at the center of it all. Some of
the most powerful religious experiences for young Catholics happened
during mass and other devotional activities. The Latin masses of the era
were suffused with mystery and grandeur. Garry Wills remembered moments when "communion was not cannibalism but its reverse, body taken
up in Spirit." Attending a weekday mass gave him a sense of participating
in something that set him apart from others while somehow helping the
whole world. He wrote, "eight o'clock Mass on a Monday 'in the old days'
did have a feel of the catacombs about it, of underground good rendered
to a world still bound in sleep." After recounting at some length the sights,
sounds, and smells that made the Catholic devotions of his boyhood so
memorable, Wills concluded:

> All these things were shared, part of community life, not a rare isolated
> joy, like reading poems. These moments belonged to a *people,* not to
> oneself. It was a ghetto, undeniably. But not a bad ghetto to grow up
> in.[14]

On the other hand, to some, mass could be boring or scary. Other than
standing and kneeling at the right times and being careful while receiving
communion, the liturgies of the era did not require much participation.
Altar boys were the only ones expected to recite the Latin responses to the
priest's prayers. Both the words of the priest and those of the altar boys
were often unintelligible to members of the congregation, even if they
happened to understand Latin. Everyone else was free to pass the time in
any non-disruptive way available. The devout prayed the rosary or followed the service in their missals; many children and teenagers spent the
time daydreaming or examining the statues, paintings, and architecture in
their churches. Meanwhile, the altar boys who assisted the priest lived in
dread of offending God and the priest by making a mistake, and every
child was drilled in how to receive communion and warned not to chew it.

Homilies were extremely brief or non-existent. Catholics didn't expect to learn anything in church; they expected to watch the miracle of the mass and receive God by partaking of communion. The old Latin mass also sent strong messages about the distance between the worshipper and God. Wills saw in the mass a "hierarchic dance arranged around the Host, bowings, blessings, kneelings, liftings, displayings and hidings of It." Even though Catholics could receive Jesus by partaking in communion, they were supposed to bear in mind the vast distance between him and them. Children and teenagers told each other scary stories about what happened to those who misused a consecrated communion wafer.[15]

Perhaps because many teenagers did feel distant from what happened at mass, Catholic youth leaders came up with creative ways to make it more accessible. They offered special youth masses followed by breakfast and a guest speaker with teen appeal. These speakers included athletes, entertainers, and local celebrities. Catholic youth programs also abounded in other eucharistic practices like holy hours, benediction of the Blessed Sacrament, and first Friday devotions. Deanery and diocesan youth rallies often imitated national ones, combining several of these elements into a memorable religious experience. Adults believed that if teenagers attended these events in sufficient numbers, all was well. In his youth prayer book, *Spiritual Lifts for Youth*, Schieder reminded young Catholics that "we can positively say that the answer to every problem of youth rests in the frequent reception of Holy Communion."[16] Since teenagers sometimes didn't see mass and communion as really for them, adults needed to create juvenilized versions of these sacramental observances.

Confession also loomed large in Catholic childhoods. Confession could be a profound experience not just of personal cleansing, but of a world made new. Mary Gordon remembered, "After you had made a good, and sometimes, a difficult confession, walking out of that church and feeling a lightness and singleness was beautiful and very valuable, and I don't think the secular world has any replacements for it." Garry Wills agreed that sometimes "Confession did not mean cleaning up oneself . . . but cleansing a whole world, the first glimpse of sky or grass as one came out of church. . . . Moments of purity remembered, when the world seemed fresh out of its Maker's hands, trees washed by some rain sweeter than the world's own."[17]

On the other hand, confession provoked all sorts of fears. First confession was often an especially scary experience for young children. As teenagers, young Catholics feared the embarrassment of having to reveal sexual sins to a priest they would see on a regular basis in their school or parish. To avoid this problem, some went to distant parishes. Young Catholics feared the excessive prayers some priests imposed as penance, so they shopped around for confessors who were known to offer easier penances. Teenagers also tried not to take too long making their confession, so that others waiting in line would not wonder what horrible sins they had committed. Young Catholics worried that if they committed a mortal sin and died before they could get to confession, they would go straight to hell. One catechism of the era showed a drawing of a man held at gunpoint to illustrate the condition of a person who had forfeited the "state of grace" by committing a mortal sin.[18]

Catholic practices surrounding sin and the sacrament of penance, at least as understood by many young people of the era, helped create a heavy burden of guilt and fear that today is not remembered fondly. Like other elements of the Catholic ghetto, weekly confession would not survive the 1960s. Catholics first experienced this system of sin management in childhood and adolescence — stages of life in which fear and guilt could easily trump their limited cognitive abilities to grasp a more balanced theology. In other words, the problem of "Catholic guilt" may have been partly caused by the adolescent misunderstandings of confession. Perhaps post-Vatican II adults wanted to leave behind the practice of confession as eagerly as they wanted to escape the other fears and restrictions of adolescence.

Devotion to Mary was also popular, and served both as spiritual consolation and as a way to see God in control of history. American Catholics devoutly believed that in the early twentieth century, Mary had appeared at Fatima in Portugal and warned of an impending apocalyptic showdown between good and evil. In the 1950s, they interpreted the Cold War as a fulfillment of these prophecies. Many Catholic youth groups prayed the rosary for peace and for the defeat of communism. For one such prayer session, a group of young Catholics took as their motto, "appease God, not Stalin." During the Korean War, one CYO newsletter told teenagers, "You are a soldier in the greatest army of all times, in the Army of Our Lady. Yours too is the power to end all conflict." By using prayers viewed as exotic and threatening by Protestants to pray for American victories in the Cold War, young Catholics could combine a sense of religious distinctiveness with staunch patriotism. They could also receive comfort that Mary was watching over them and keeping their country safe from nuclear war and communism. Mary seemed very close to young people of the era, who remembered experiences like "fishing pennies and dimes out of pockets pebbled with the fifty-nine beads and assorted medallions of a rosary."[19]

During the month of May, Marian festivals dominated Catholic youth activities. One typical celebration took place in Springfield, Illinois, in 1951. The festivities began with a procession that included clergy, Catholic Boy and Girl Scouts, and the Catholic Youth Organization May Court. The May Court was composed of a queen and her eight attendants. Other teenage girls formed themselves into what was called a "living rosary" on the front yard of the Sacred Heart Academy, with each girl in matching skirt and blouse representing one of the rosary beads. Together, the young people recited an Act of Consecration to the Sacred Heart, listened to a sermon, and participated in the ceremony of Benediction of the Most Holy Sacrament. Following these devotions, all adjourned to the Knights of Columbus hall for the Queen's Dance. Pope Pius XII sparked an outpouring of such public devotion to Mary by declaring 1954 a "Marian Year." In Detroit, the Councils of Catholic Men, Women, and Youth combined forces to sponsor a Marian Day at University of Detroit Stadium attended by over 80,000 people.[20] Even the relatively private practice of saying the rosary and expressing devotion to Mary became the occasion of public spectacle in the 1950s. The Catholic press eagerly reported such events because they publicly demonstrated the vitality of Catholic piety among young people.

The drive to keep kids Catholic and to sell Catholicism to America as a patriotic religion combined to make even Catholic devotions into products to be marketed to young people. From the beginning, National Catholic Youth Week included National Youth Communion Sunday, which claimed 3 million young communicants in 1953. But in 1954, Schieder instituted the National Youth Communion Crusade as well. In each diocese, a parish CYO or Catholic school promoted daily communion for one week. Then the crusade moved on to the next parish or set of parishes. The crusade climaxed with another National Youth Communion Sunday on Pentecost. Each year special prayer intentions, often for increased numbers of religious vocations, marked this eight-month observance. In 1957, this National Youth Communion Day on Pentecost became National Youth Adoration Day. This celebration encouraged local groups to mobilize as many young people as possible to keep a continuous prayer vigil in front of the Blessed Sacrament.[21]

Some young Catholics embraced the use of public relations and advertising techniques to promote religious devotion. Teenagers at St. Monica Parish in Rochester recruited more of their friends to attend the monthly holy hour at St. Joseph church by chartering a bus. In Toledo, members of the spiritual committee of the Catholic Youth Council promoted daily communion using posters with slogans like: "Get up and Go to Mass and Holy Communion *daily* during Lent. There will be plenty of time to sleep after you're dead."[22] Although a majority of American Catholics still attended mass weekly during the 1950s, young Catholics were beginning to see religious devotions as products that could be "sold" to their friends.[23] It is not a stretch to see such advertising as one contributing factor to a later tendency for middle-class Americans to view religious practices not as duties to fulfill but as commodities promoting personal fulfillment for those who wished to partake.

Getting Serious:
The Physical and Mental Disciplines of Catholic Schools

Although there was fun to be found in dances, clubs, and sports, many teenagers who grew up in the era especially remembered the mental and physical discipline taught in Catholic schools. In their schools, Catholic adults fought hard against what they perceived as the enemies of their faith and got serious about forming young Catholics. Catholic schools made few concessions to youth culture, and served as a bulwark against juvenilization. Yet these same schools could seem stifling and backward to young people and loomed large in their memories of wanting to escape from the Catholic ghetto.

Catholic school children learned how to control their bodies. They learned to line up and file silently into their classrooms. The sisters taught them to stand and greet any adult who entered the room. When seated, they learned to keep their hands folded on top of their desks. Confession, first communion, and confirmation all required preparatory drills. Edward Stivender grew up in Philadelphia and remembered that in preparation for confirmation, the sister drilled his classmates until all could genuflect in unison. On the big day, each child received a light slap on the cheek from the bishop, symbolizing his or her induction as a soldier for Christ. The bishop exhorted this class of third graders to do their part to defeat the communists.[24]

Sometimes the physical rigor of Catholic school life far exceeded its intellectual rigor, but much depended upon the school and which order of nuns ran it. Mary Gordon went to school in New York and remembered,

We had Josephite nuns, who were very strict but also very dumb. They managed to combine being very ill educated with being very strict about all the wrong things. Everything seemed to center on neatness and appearance, and content was really pretty irrelevant.

In sharp contrast, Sister Joan Chittister, O.S.B., remembered of her Catholic schooling, "I loved it. I was crazy about the sisters. They were kind. They were omniscient, they were present, they were beautiful people, and I loved it."[25]

Most commonly, Catholic schools both pushed young people to become rigorous logical thinkers and forced them to accept church teaching on faith. Garry Wills reminds us that growing up Catholic in that era could equip a person with an elaborate theological and moral vocabulary that included distinctions like "*ex opere operato* and *ex opere operantis,* homoousian and homoiousian, mortal sin and venial sin, matter of sin and intention of sin." Wills claimed he could identify Senator Eugene McCarthy as a Catholic just by the phrases he used in conversation.[26]

Single-sex schools provided special opportunities for young Catholic women to practice intellectual assertiveness in a way that bypassed the gender stereotyping and intensive search for male approval that dominated public high schools. Mary Gordon attended a school that she later criticized as proof that "learning, to the Church, was not something to be treasured but something to be feared." Yet she and her classmates enjoyed a camaraderie based on their furtive forays into the writings of Camus and D. H. Lawrence. More importantly, she later appreciated the "separate but equal world for women" of the Catholic girls' school. In hindsight, she valued an atmosphere in which she did not need to "refrain from saying something in class for fear of seeming smart and therefore losing the love of boys."[27]

Some young Catholics learned their lessons so well that they put their teachers on the spot. Ed Stivender remembered of his high school religion classes,

> Discussions of doctrine often ended with the priest against the wall claiming, "It's a mystery of Faith," when the doctrine wore thin on the abrasive washboard of logic and common sense. Discussions about sex and Hell, when the touchstone of fairness was used, backed the priest into the confessional, where such issues were decided on a one-to-one basis.[28]

Peggy Scherer, who attended a Catholic high school in Cincinnati, recalled an incident in which she argued with her teacher, claiming, "I cannot believe that everyone who is not a practicing Catholic is going to hell." The teacher told her she was wrong, but provided no convincing explanation.[29] Many who grew up in this era would later forget that their Catholic education provided some of the intellectual tools that made such critiques possible.

Millions of young people benefited from Catholic schooling. They learned valuable mental, moral, and physical disciplines. On the other hand, many would remember seeing apparent contradictions in the system of Catholic faith and morals. They also remembered being taught by priests and nuns who could not give satisfying answers to their questions. Children and teenagers sometimes even grew up with a strong sense that their faith was on the defensive and had little to offer intellectually.[30] As we shall see, both the intellectual and sexual restrictiveness of the stereotypical Catholic school would loom large in the minds of those who later came to repudiate the Catholic ghetto.

Sports and Competitions:
Having Fun While Proving Catholics Are Good Americans

Although doubts about Catholic beliefs and practices did trouble some Catholic teenagers, most did not spend lots of time worrying about such issues. Instead, they devoted their energies to Catholic sporting events and other competitions. Competitions of all kinds were hugely popular among teenagers and in society at large during the 1950s. Television game shows drew huge audiences, and successful contestants could become national celebrities. Advertisers sold products by creating contests for their customers. Public and parochial schools joined secular and religious youth groups in providing an endless array of contests, with something for every type of child. Teenagers who were top athletes or who won a place on the school homecoming court became celebrities in their schools and stood at the pinnacle of the emerging teenage social hierarchy. The pressure to elect "kings" and "queens" for special high school social events was so strong that all Christian groups had to provide a version of this activity, even if they disliked popularity and beauty contests. The youth culture of the 1950s was dominated by sports and contests of every kind, and Roman Catholics catered heavily to this teenage preference.

Sports not only kept young people interested in the CYO and pro-tected them from less wholesome activities; they also contributed to Cath-olic pride and a positive public image for Catholicism. In Chicago, two highlights of the high school sports year were the championship games in basketball and football between Catholic and public high school leagues. Catholic youth leaders struggled to tie sports explicitly to Catholic piety. Some argued for the spiritual benefits of sports as a character-building ac-tivity. Others tried to combine devotionalism and recreation. In addition to the prayers or meditations led by priests before games, many dioceses sponsored communion breakfasts and holy hours for CYO athletes. On Fridays during football season, Catholic sisters commonly led their paro-chial school students in prayers for the University of Notre Dame football team. Just as the Notre Dame football team functioned on the national stage as a symbol of Catholicism winning a place in American society, local CYO and Catholic high school sports functioned as an all-American way to assert Catholic superiority.[31] But it is likely that most young Catholics just liked competing or enjoying the social occasion as spectators. Ameri-can teenagers loved the fun of sports; adults tried with limited success to make sports into spiritual activities.

Obviously sports leagues thrived on competition, but so did cultural activities. Drama contests, oratorical contests, and essay contests abounded in the CYO. Essay and oratorical contests divided evenly between devo-tional topics like "Prayer and Penance for Universal Return to Christ" and patriotic themes like "Can a Catholic Be a Good American?" These contests too were thinly disguised attempts to get young Catholics to promote the values of all-American Catholicism. Thus in 1956, contestants in the na-tional oratorical competition spoke on "The Place of Private and Church-Related Schools in American Education." There were some themes in these contests that related to Catholic social reform; for example, contestants in the 1956 contest also had to deliver an extemporaneous speech on a selec-tion from the papal social encyclical *Quadragesimo Anno.* Some local CYO chapters sponsored religious quiz competitions, modeled on the popular quiz shows of the day. Virtually every Youth Department project, from Na-tional Catholic Youth Week to crusades for modest clothing, involved teen-age competition. A typical issue of the NCWC youth magazine *Youth Newsnotes* contained reports on Christmas Crib, writing, music, photogra-phy, and talent contests.[32]

Adults had a harder time purifying the popularity contests so prevalent among teenagers. Most diocesan CYO programs sponsored annual formal dances, which usually included the crowning of a king and queen. Sometimes these teenage sovereigns won by means of a simple popular vote. At other times, a teenage girl could win the crown by selling more tickets or raising more money for the building fund than any of her competitors. Most often, however, priests and adult advisors tried to tie positions like "CYO Queen" to more exalted criteria. In Wheeling, West Virginia, students selected "Mr. and Miss CYO" based on their virtues of "hard work, initiative, and motivation." Using similar criteria, CYO leaders in Los Angeles presented their "Girl of the Year Award" at the Annual Chrysanthemum Ball. In St. Louis, Fr. Louis Meyer set up a system of recommendations and applications extending from the parish to the diocesan level. In his system, the boy members of the Archdiocesan Council of Catholic Youth chose the queen based on "her interest in the Church, her personality and her accomplishments." For the all-important interviews, the young ladies had to dress alike in plain skirt and blouse. In Springfield, Illinois, May Queen Margie Murphy participated in the 1953 May Day celebration by crowning a statue of Mary.[33] Adults wanted CYO "kings" and "queens" to be model Catholics, but it proved difficult to get middle-class teenagers to value whatever that included as highly as popularity and beauty.

Perhaps in part to correct this embarrassing ambiguity, in 1955 the Youth Department established an award for Outstanding Catholic Youth of the Year. For the first few years, the award went to a young Catholic coed who had proven herself to be a leader in the CYO and at college. The fact that young women won this contest so often suggests that teenage girls tended to conform more to adults' expectations for young people than boys did. It also suggests that girls may have been more involved than boys in the activities of the Catholic Youth Organization. In fact, the available evidence strongly suggests that boys participated in sports and dances, but were much less involved in the spiritual and service activities of the CYO.

But whatever its gender implications, the Outstanding Catholic Youth of the Year award provided a chance for Catholic youth leaders to once again remind everyone that Catholics were good Americans and that young Catholics would save the world. In 1957, the episcopal moderator of the Youth Department, Archbishop Leo Binz of Dubuque, Iowa, presented the award to Peggy Nichols in her parish church in Milton, Massachusetts. In his presentation speech he noted that "in this age of desperate competition among men and nations, the prizes to be won too often are tarnished by materialism." He went on to remind his audience that the award "transcends the individual upon whom it annually is bestowed" because through it "all our Catholic young people are recognized and newly valued." Binz also insisted that the award directed to all Catholic young people an "exhortation to excellence." Monsignor Schieder, who created the award, could not have agreed more. In commendation of the first male recipient of the award in 1958, Schieder said, "this is an inspiring example of a young man's gaining notice and publicity for worthwhile and extraordinary achievements — in contrast to the many juvenile delinquents and youthful offenders all too frequently glorified by the public."[34] Here again, young people were presented as the ideal Catholics — and potential saviors of the world.

As hinted in Binz's comment about "competition between men and nations," young Catholics competed for high cultural stakes that mingled the international threat of communism with hopes for Catholic influence in America. These high stakes, and their link to the earlier rhetoric of youth in crisis, emerged most clearly in the furor surrounding the successful launch of the Sputnik satellite in the fall of 1957. This Russian success sparked a national uproar over the state of science education in the public schools. Catholics had helped to create this cultural connection between international threats and youth problems, so they participated fully in the Sputnik sensation. Editorials in *Youth* during 1958 carried titles like "In the Present World Crisis . . ." and warned that "as never before, the future is uncertain and threatening." In typical fashion, Schieder used the crisis to push traditional Catholic concerns. Parochial schools and Catholic social teaching came in for praise as keys to a better America. But a major theme of the Sputnik crisis, and of the Cold War as a whole, was competition. Catholics had long noted the competing Catholic and communist holidays in the month of May. But in 1958, when "competition between Christianity and Communism is especially intense," the editor of *Youth* urged young Catholics to observe the Marian festivals as never before and to recognize that they shared in a titanic struggle between good and evil, between "the two forces struggling for supremacy in modern society."[35]

These examples suggest that Catholic youth groups abounded in contests not just because they were fun or helped prepare young people for a competitive marketplace, but because adults saw a connection between youthful excellence and victory in the Cold War. At the same time, the youth culture could be an uncertain ally in the titanic struggle of the era. Although they dutifully competed for high honors in the endless round of CYO contests, young Catholics also responded in more playful ways to the Sputnik crisis. In Cleveland, CYO members organized a dance called the

"Satellite Swish," while in Springfield young Catholics danced the night away at the "Sputnik Spin."[36] The adult need for reassurance of cultural victory did not always mesh with teenage desires for fun. Although the all-American Catholicism of the CYO remained popular throughout the 1950s, the apocalyptic views that adults sometimes attached to it increasingly contrasted with the youth culture "fun" of Catholic youth groups. And while these ostensible extremes could be combined surprisingly well, teenage sexuality proved to be an especially difficult case that threatened the survival of the Catholic youth ghetto.

The Explosive Combination of Sexual Purity and Patriotism

During the 1950s Catholic adults thought they were equally emphasizing piety, patriotism, and sexual purity. But some teenagers would later associate their Catholic upbringing especially with sexual repressiveness. Certainly the much-touted 1960s "sexual revolution" introduced an anachronistic reading of some of these memories. At the time, many young Catholics did participate in purity crusades of various types and asked for more instruction regarding dating and marriage. Indeed, the teenage appetite for sexual advice at times crowded out the social concerns that interested some of their elders. Even those who remember this sexual regime with little fondness sometimes recall its benefits as well. Still, freighted with the fate of individual souls, the future of civilization, and the purity of the faith, the intense policing of adolescent sexual purity could sometimes make the Catholic ghetto seem like a prison.

The Cold War context definitely intensified the fears surrounding teen sexuality among 1950s Catholics. A 1953 editorial in the NCWC Youth Department magazine *Youth Newsnotes* drew an unfavorable comparison between communist and Catholic young people. Arguing that Catholic youth organizations often failed to "inspire their members with the burning zeal and self-sacrifice" common among communist youth, the editor wondered "what the Communists would be able to do to the United States did they possess the schools, colleges, and youth facilities we Catholics control." What was the secret to influencing America and defeating communism?

Youth's immense capacity for loving is the only answer to the problem. It was love, romantic love, not rules and organized projects, that made young Francis of Assisi capture the admiration and breathless wonder of all . . . and it is romantic love touched with the Divine spark that will make our youth militant, hot with Faith and love of God. . . ."[37]

By making "great demands" on young Catholics, leaders could channel romantic love into spiritual renewal and political influence. But by making "romantic love" the ideal of Christian spirituality, talk like this also contributed to the juvenilization of Catholic piety and politics. Romantic love is a powerful force, but it doesn't produce mature spirituality; it keeps people in the adolescent state of "falling in love," which focuses on the individual's internal happiness.

War also became a prominent image in Catholic exhortations to purity, especially those addressed to boys. Fr. Joseph Conroy established a club called the "The Fighting 69th." Members pledged to uphold the sixth and ninth commandments, which forbade adultery and coveting their neighbor's wife. They carried a membership card to remind them of their pledge. In an exhortation typical of the era, Conroy told a gathering of 500 Catholic teenagers that "the system of dating that obtains among our teenagers can be construed as an occasion of sin." He blamed this problem on "commercial and social interests." He drew a parallel between these purveyors of American youth culture and the communists: "The pattern for Communistic endeavor among the youth in the countries behind the Iron Curtain has always been to drive a wedge between these youth and their rightfully approved spiritual and civil authorities."[38] In their obsession with fighting the communists, Catholic youth leaders misconstrued the way that youth culture worked. Yes, popular culture promotes different sexual values among teenagers than the ones held by conservative parents, but these values are absorbed unconsciously, not through a frontal attack.

Adults claimed that sexual purity was crucial for keeping all sorts of evils at bay, so teenagers experienced intense pressure to conform and fear of the horrific consequences of sexual sins. Mary Gordon believed that the Josephite nuns who taught in her school in New York saw themselves as "beleaguered" by enemies ranging from "Communists, Jews, Protestants, or atheists" to "pornographers, intellectuals, and sociologists, almost without distinction." In hindsight she also recognized a parallel in the attitude toward men that these nuns hoped to instill in young Catholic women: "Not only were you beleaguered as a Catholic, but you were beleaguered by males, who were out of control. And the message was always, 'We know that you're not interested in these things, but you know how boys are.'"[39]

Growing up in such environments, it is small wonder that many young Catholics came to see sexual purity as the linchpin of Catholic identity. Nor is it too much of a stretch to imagine that those who grew up under this regime might cry "Enough!" when the papal encyclical *Humanae Vitae* renewed the church's prohibition on the use of contraception by married couples.

But the emphasis on sexual purity was not simply imposed by adults. In 1951, diocesan youth leaders in Hartford surveyed CYO members in order to identify their top concerns. Most of the teenagers they surveyed wanted more information on the Sacrament of Marriage and how to hold out against temptations to impurity that came from their friends, movies, radio, magazines, and television. In response to teen interest, CYO forums and conferences increasingly addressed issues surrounding the dating culture and condemned the practice of "going steady." A youth panel at the Queens County Youth Day Rally in 1954 on the topic "The Challenge to Catholic Youth Morality Today" was well attended and sparked many questions from the floor. The young participants concluded that "there is surely a Catholic way to dress, to date, to drink, to behave at home, at school and among associates but because of the constant pressure and publicity of low, worldly standards it takes plenty of prayer to 'go against the stream.'"[40] The Catholic system of moral instruction seemed to be working with these teenagers, but later generations would be much less likely to believe there was a distinctively Catholic way to behave in everyday situations.

Another popular tactic was for parents and teenagers to agree together on a teenage code of conduct that would be shared by all in the parish or community. The typical code established a common curfew and allowance and asked teenagers to give up drinking, going steady, and reckless driving.[41] As the decade of the 1950s wore on, a typical CYO member would be far more likely to encounter a group discussion on modesty, indecent literature and films, or the spiritual dangers of going steady than to participate in a brainstorming session on social action. But like the patriotic themes of National Catholic Youth Week, these concerns about youthful purity arose from youthful demands as well as adult fears.

Teenagers also flocked to marriage preparation programs. Particularly for young women, marriage just after high school was a common experience, so marriage preparation programs for high school students made sense. In the Archdiocese of New York, 20,000 young people attended marriage forums between 1948 and 1951. Young men and women attended separate sessions and heard talks by a priest, a married person, and a Catholic doctor. The priest taught Catholic moral perspectives on courtship, marriage, birth control, and child-rearing. The married person covered practical issues like money and relations with in-laws. The doctor discussed birth control and pregnancy. Catholic leaders hoped to strengthen marriages against divorce, to prevent "mixed marriages" to non-Catholics, to discourage "going steady" among teenagers, and to strengthen resolve against the use of birth control. Young Catholics flocked to these events, which promised to impart spiritual blessing and temporal success to their marriages. Diocesan youth directors in Detroit, Baltimore, Buffalo, and Philadelphia all reported that such seminars drew some of the largest crowds of any of their programs.[42]

Fears about "mixed marriages" also sometimes drove the development of Catholic youth clubs. For example, twenty-five-year-old Florence Hangach of St. Mary's Parish in Chardon, Ohio, noticed early in 1953 that Catholic teenagers in her rural community frequented Protestant church social functions. Alarmed at the possibility for spiritual drift and mixed marriages, she helped parish teenagers organize the "Mariateen Club." After eight months of square dances, song fests, swimming parties, and weekly religious discussions with Fr. James Maher, the club had fifty members. *Youth Newsnotes* editorialized, "thus Catholic youngsters, who may otherwise have lost their faith, are now providing themselves with Catholic fun and frolic — and Catholic truth."[43] "Catholic fun and frolic" may have appealed to teenagers, but they amounted to a more adolescent version of Catholicism. Such social segregation also institutionalized a defensive, negative posture toward the non-Catholic world which would later prompt some young people to tie together youthful rebellion and escape from the Catholic ghetto.

But for the time being, plenty of young Catholics worried about mixed marriages and exhorted each other to steer clear of romantic involvements with non-Catholics. Mary Jo Wahle, a junior at Notre Dame Academy in Covington, Kentucky, won the Catholic Youth Week writing contest with her essay, "Ro Could Be You Without CYO." Mary Jo told the fictional story of a young woman named Rose Baxter who took Holy Communion three times a week and said her rosary daily. Despite taking her faith so seriously, one Monday morning found "Ro" pouring out her spiritual fears to "Sister" at school. "Sister, I'm going steady with a non-Catholic boy," she said. "For how long?" asked Sister. "Since Saturday night," she replied. But after hearing a sermon on Sunday against going steady, Ro had realized that going steady with a non-Catholic was even worse. Still, she worried about breaking up with the boy so soon. Mary Jo went on to editorialize that Ro's problem started with her frequenting of a "public canteen." If more young people like Ro got involved in Catholic youth activities, Mary Jo believed, "we can double the influence of the CYO throughout the country and prevent many mixed marriages and unhappy homes." Evidently Mary Jo was not alone. A 1961 survey of Marquette University students found that only 17 percent said it was morally acceptable to be in a serious dating relationship with a non-Catholic.[44]

Catholics saw sexual purity as not just a personal issue, but also a public cause. Catholic teenagers willingly campaigned against indecent films, books, comics, magazines, and music. They visited local merchants, asked them to get rid of indecent literature, and presented awards to those that complied. In Syracuse, New York, young Catholics saw their 1954 "war against indecent literature" as a "major offensive against juvenile delinquency."[45] Even groups explicitly founded with a strategic emphasis on social action tended to drift toward purity crusades in this era. For example, Fr. Joseph Baglio of Minneapolis founded the Contact movement in 1950, which he modeled on the Young Christian Students. But by the late 1950s, this group's activities focused on youthful purity more than on social transformation. Some Contact members made dresses for the "Create Your Own" modest formalwear contest. Others came up with humorous slogans to promote good morals. Winning entries in these slogan contests got printed and distributed on cards bearing titles like "Ten Reasons Why I Tell Off-Color Stories."[46]

Events in Chicago, the national center of "specialized Catholic action," especially illustrated the power of sexual purity to eclipse other social issues. Chicago Inter-Student Catholic Action sponsored a Marian Art Contest, a teen variety show, a "Modesty Crusade" fashion show, and a yearly dance. Members organized a "Decent Disc Crusade" to alert the music industry to "Catholic teenagers' disapproval of objectionable lyrics." Chicago teenagers also launched Supply the Demand for the Supply, a national campaign to promote modest clothing that won approval from thirty-seven bishops in which young Catholic women fought to influence dress makers and retailers to carry modest formal wear. The Chicago example sparked CYO fashion shows in other cities in which young women designed, sewed, and modeled their own modest dresses. One catechism showed pictures of "Marian dresses" and emphasized the spiritual benefits of wearing such modest and blessed attire.[47]

Still, while sexual purity and modesty are laudable Christian ideals, when adults and teenagers chose to focus on campaigns against going steady, immodest clothing, and indecent entertainment, they narrowed the range of Christian social concerns to the activities of the adolescent world. Some teenagers felt highly engaged in these social issues that affected them directly, but this approach did little to overcome the adolescent tendency toward narcissism and self-absorption. Even as adults these young Catholics might see only those social issues that affected them directly as worthy of their interest.

And of course not all Catholic teenagers supported the purity crusades. One teenage observer wondered how boycotts and marches against indecent literature and movies could succeed when after one such protest some Catholic students lined up to see a "notoriously indecent movie" starring a woman who had made her reputation deriding chastity. With keen prophetic insight, he predicted that without a "large, articulate Catholic laity" that practiced an "integrated Catholicism," periodic crusades for decency would one day no longer succeed.[48] In other words, young Catholics may have willingly participated in purity crusades in part because these were socially acceptable ways to engage the public sphere during the sexually conservative 1950s. But once society came to regard such purity crusades as intolerant or even quaint, few Catholics would have the convictions necessary to sustain the cause. Juvenilized social concern gets left behind when teenagers become adults, or when opposition becomes too strong.

Attempts by adults to offer high-minded counterpoints to worldly temptations met with mixed results. It could hardly have been otherwise. For example, their attempts to spiritualize dances sometimes had limited success. Fr. Edward Juraschek, diocesan youth director in San Antonio, sponsored weekly dances for high school students and monthly "Senior Socials" for college and working singles. These dances, which regularly attracted 300 or 400 participants, ended promptly at 11:15 p.m. with night prayers and an examination of conscience. At the founding convention of the National Council of Catholic Youth, delegates "danced the night away" at the Saturday night cotillion — until it came time to sing a hymn, at which time "every eye fell upon the statue of Our Blessed Lady, appropriately placed in a niche of honor."[49] At formal dances, nuns sometimes scrutinized gowns and added bolts of cloth to cover plunging necklines. Some chaperones tapped couples on the shoulder and asked them to stop dancing so close in order to allow room "for your guardian angel" or "for the Holy

Spirit." But the attempt to spiritualize dancing could have unintended consequences. In his Philadelphia parish, Ed Stivender attended dances held in
the same hall in which the priest celebrated mass. Stivender's favorite spot
to slow dance was in a corner near the confessional and the plaques depict-
ing the Stations of the Cross.[50] Even holy places could become associated
with romance and sexual arousal.

Adults worked hard to control dating rituals through intensive surveillance. Catholic high schools were often segregated by sex, although not
as universally as is sometimes assumed.[51] Even in sex-segregated schools,
surveillance extended outside the building, often because boys' and girls'
schools were built near one another. Teenagers from neighboring Catholic
boys' and girls' high schools in Philadelphia were forbidden to speak to
one another at the trolley stop or to walk one another home from school,
not only because it might produce dangerous intimacies, but because it
would undermine the public image of their schools. In response, many
high school students like Ed Stivender frequented dances and tried out for
the plays at both schools in order to meet members of the opposite sex.[52]

Teenagers in the 1950s traveled in packs, and dated as groups. Often
the pairings within these groups were arranged by the girls and merely reported to the boys. Good girls, Catholic or not, did not allow kisses on the
first date. Good *Catholic* girls added prohibitions against petting and
French kissing on any date. Ed Stivender remembered marathon sessions
of "dry" kissing in which he would not have dreamed of pushing for more
because his date was the niece of the Catholic school board superinten-
dent.[53] Catholics may have been stricter than the general population when
it came to sex, but it helped that society was largely supportive. The entire
system depended heavily on keeping young people ignorant of sex and
afraid of negative consequences. Growing up in Norwood, Ohio, Richard
Schwartz learned from priests who were "too edgy when it came to sex"
that arousal was a sin. But he also learned from his teenage friends that
"women never became aroused. At least hardly ever."[54] Some Catholic
teenagers spread legends about couples who had gone too far and had died
suddenly in car accidents, presumably resulting in a one-way ticket to hell.
Although such a regime could be frightening, many teenagers found ways
to work within the system. Ed Stivender remembered that he and his
friends planned their dates for Friday nights so that they could go to confession on Saturday.[55]

Although it may have been paranoid and overly dependent on dubious claims about victory in the Cold War, this culture of sexual purity had

some advantages over later alternatives. The Catholic ideal of modesty spared young women from the increasingly intense scrutiny of their bodies that teenage girls endure today. Similarly, teenagers who wanted to avoid premarital sex could more easily do so under such a system.

All teenage girls of the 1950s, Catholic or not, bore the burden of policing not only their own sexuality, but that of their boyfriends and of the other girls in their schools. Girls were taught that it was their job to keep the boys from going too far. And a girl who was too free with her sexual favors became "cheap" and lost favor with "good" girls. She also supposedly lost favor with the "right sort" of boys — though this claim did not always hold true.[56] This burden bore heavily on 1950s teenage girls, but at least Catholic girls had help. A strong system of church teachings, relationships and practices protected both the young people who wanted to remain chaste and those who thought they were "ready" for sex but in fact were not.[57]

In addition, Catholic teaching and sexual surveillance actually worked against the "double standard" in teenage sexuality, because it was strict for both boys and girls. Mary Gordon later strongly disagreed with the Catholic teaching on sex she had heard while growing up, but admitted,

> In some ways, because the Church hated sex across the board, at least it was fairer. To get a message that sex is all right for men but it's not all right for women is more difficult than to get the message that it's not all right for anybody. At least that's more democratic.[58]

Just how effective was this system in shaping teenage sexual behavior? Compared to later systems, the 1950s Catholic sexual regime did a better job at getting teenagers to profess strict moral beliefs about sex. Only 6 percent of Marquette University students said in 1961 that "heavy necking with a steady date" was morally acceptable; by 1971 the number had jumped to 75 percent.[59]

On the other hand, many young people spent considerable time and effort figuring out ways to get around the sexual restrictions of their environment. Richard Schwartz remembered trying to find a way to see the racy movie *La Dolce Vita*, which had been banned by the Legion of Decency and his local archbishop. Schwartz found out that across the Ohio River in Covington, Kentucky, the archbishop had ruled the film acceptable for mature audiences. So he called his friend and former teacher Fr. Stottlemaier and asked him "why the opinion of one archbishop should carry more weight than the opinion of another, and what about the notion of morals changing in the middle of the Broadway Bridge?" "We both knew that we were now talking turf and bureaucracy, not faith and morals, and no one wants to believe in a God who will send you to hell for eternity . . . over a jurisdictional distinction," he remembered.[60]

Young Catholics remained chaste in much larger numbers than today, but they didn't do as well as adults hoped. Mary Gordon remembered that at eighth grade graduation parties, "you would go into these basements and you would neck with ten different boys with the lights out." More seriously, of the two hundred teen weddings approved in the Diocese of Fort Wayne-South Bend in 1962, 47 percent were motivated by the bride's pregnancy.[61]

What Turned "Integrated Catholicism" into the "Catholic Ghetto"?

The Catholics of the 1940s had dreamed of an "integrated Catholicism" in which young Catholics would grow up learning how to apply their faith to every aspect of life. By the time leaders met in 1958 to discuss "The Aims, Purposes, and Philosophy of Catholic Youth Work," they concluded that the typical CYO was not working. Monsignor John Kiley, Youth Director for the Archdiocese of Newark, claimed that for too long Catholic youth leaders had been toying with "adding the supernatural." Now it was time to move on to a "method of integration" whereby youth would be trained in a "way of living" in which all aspects of life contributed to sanctification.[62] But something about the lives of modern Catholic teenagers made it hard for them to live an "integrated" Catholicism.

Catholic young people also wondered at times about the effectiveness of the typical round of CYO activities. At the 1959 CYO convention, student leader Richard Baker asked, "how can we fight a militant enemy like Communism with the training gained at roller skating parties?" He concluded, "the challenge of the times is Communism and the need is for good Catholic citizens and leaders." Baker hoped such Catholic leaders would "bring the world back to Christ," "fight the materialistic attitude of our times," and foster democracy at home and abroad.[63]

In hindsight, it seems incredible that anyone could seriously think that dances, sports, and CYO queen contests could produce integrated Catholicism or victory in the Cold War. Grand visions seemed to founder on the rocks of keeping young people entertained. Clearly the political paradigm of youth and the crisis of civilization also had enduring power to distort thinking about youth ministry.

By combining civic Catholicism, Cold War hysteria, and a focus on adolescent purity, youth leaders forged a version of Catholicism that succeeded in helping millions of young people feel distinctively Catholic even as they fit in to the American middle class. For these architects of all-American Catholicism, crusades for modest clothing and boycotts of comic books and movies seemed to keep Catholic teenagers pure and enlist them in the battle to clean up America. Meanwhile, for those more on the margins of such efforts, parish and urban recreation programs promised to prevent delinquency.

As of the Marquette University poll of 1961, this system seemed to be working. Overwhelming majorities of young Catholics condemned "heavy necking," cheating, reading obscene magazines, and getting drunk. According to a 1957 Gallup poll, 100 percent of Catholic college graduates attended Mass weekly, and 87 percent of them believed in life after death.[64] Of course people tend to answer such opinion polls as they believe they should — perhaps even more fifty years ago than now — but at least these results show that the overwhelming majority of young Catholics knew, and wanted to give, the "right" answers to the questions. Although they surely did not all live up to these ideals, many probably sincerely believed in them.

Yet these same Catholic youth environments also created a juvenilized version of Catholicism that was much more fragile than it appeared at the time. How did this happen? First, Catholic teenagers pushed adults to provide them with more fun and entertainment than they would have otherwise offered. Adults were forever trying to "spiritualize" activities like dances and sports teams; teenagers were just happy to have safe Catholic places to socialize and have fun. Catholic teenagers willingly attended discussion groups on social problems, boycotted indecent literature or films, and raised money for the poor, but they avoided organizations or activities that required a negative stance toward normal middle-class life. Although they were happy to be countercultural in their prayers, they wanted to be "normal" in most other aspects of their lives. Even though many adults still hoped that young Catholics could reform American society, in practice both the pleasures of the Catholic youth culture and the push to prove Catholic patriotism all but destroyed the Catholic reform movements of the 1940s.

Second, religious instruction in the 1950s drilled young people in the doctrines of their faith, but didn't do as well at answering their tough questions. Young Catholics could recite the answers to the questions found in the Baltimore Catechism. But when they asked why certain things were true or how seemingly contradictory ideas could be reconciled, they seldom got satisfying answers. On the other hand, Catholic education helped young people develop critical thinking skills and gave them a rich moral and theological terminology that was stronger than most anything being offered to young Christians of any stripe today. Unfortunately, this intellectual environment encouraged some to think that perhaps growing up meant leaving behind the doctrinal formulations they had memorized. Some of the most intelligent and sensitive young Catholics of the Baby Boom generation came to see "indoctrination" as a bad word and instead embraced religious "searching." Predictably, teachers who celebrated searching over finding and questions more than answers would create a catechesis that was long on experiences and individual choice and short on content. The result would be the catechetical disasters of the 1970s.

Third, the schools and youth groups that created all-American Catholicism did little to prepare the Catholic Church to weather the storms of the 1960s. Catholic successes depended heavily on a dense network of mutually reinforcing institutions which kept teenagers in line. So Catholics had too little practice in creating attractive youth environments that would draw young people even if social pressures weren't forcing them to come. Even more significantly, leaders did not successfully link calls for sexual abstinence with a sense of participating in a powerful, important mission in the world. African American young people also lived in a ghetto, but theirs was imposed by racism and segregation, and their faith provided hope and strength to break free. Evangelical Protestants lived in their own restrictive Christian subculture, but adults taught them to believe that by avoiding sex, dancing, drinking and movies they became powerful witnesses who could evangelize the world. In contrast, Catholics had a more defensive stance, in which the Catholic youth subculture and even the individual teenager's own body became an embattled fortress. Adults talked more about keeping young people Catholic than about mobilizing them to change the world. As a result, the Catholic youth ghetto often became a claustrophobic subculture in which young people heard that they must win the Cold War by keeping sexually pure, saying the rosary, and participating in Catholic social clubs. Despite their best efforts, many parish and diocesan youth programs did not teach young Catholics how to be responsible, active adults, but rather taught them how to be adolescent consumers of Catholic identity markers. But it was hard to believe that this form of Catholicism was really changing the world. Without this sense of making a difference, young Catholics often just felt trapped. Some would later feel that they had to break free of the Catholic ghetto in order to grow up.

CHAPTER 6

How to Have Fun, Be Popular, and Save the World at the Same Time

Stand up, stand up for Jesus
Ye soldiers of the cross

Singing Youth for Christ, 1948

I've found something else that has given me more of a thrill than a
hundred Presley's ever could! It's a new friendship with the most
wonderful Person I've ever met, a Man who has given me happiness
and thrills and something worth living for.

Youth for Christ Magazine, 1960

In 1951, with the help of Ken Anderson of Gospel Films, Youth for Christ produced a thirty-minute color film called *Counterattack*. The film opened with familiar high school scenes. Then a "sweep of realism" portrayed dramatic teenage problems that culminated in "a narcotic rendezvous of high school students." At this point YFC representative Jack Hamilton appeared on screen before an eager group of students and explained how they could "put Christ and the Bible back into their school" by starting a Bible club. The film concluded with dramatizations of three true incidents. In the first, a girl stood up for the doctrine of creation in her science class. Next, a high school football player faced "ridicule to maintain his witness" but came out "on top." Finally, the film portrayed how a "Bible clubber leads his buddy to Christ." The advertisements for the film presented Bible clubs as the answer to juvenile delinquency.[1] The film portrayed the white evangelical Protestant ideal for young people during the 1950s. In the words of a popular gospel hymn often sung at Youth for

Christ rallies, young people would "Stand Up for Jesus" in their schools, and in so doing save the world.[2] YFC leaders saw their teenage converts as a Trojan horse in which to sneak the Bible and Christianity back into public high schools.

Youth for Christ leaders promised teenagers that they could have fun, be popular, and save the world at the same time. But in order to do so, they had to give their lives to Jesus and maintain a pure "witness." Many teenagers internalized the call to separation from "worldly" corruptions, but in return, they demanded that Youth for Christ leaders provide them a Christian youth culture complete with fun, popularity, movies, music, and celebrities. This combination of spiritually intense experiences, bodily purity, and youth-culture fun transformed thousands of young lives and guaranteed the long-term vitality of white evangelicalism.

But adapting Christianity so well to white, middle-class youth culture brought its share of compromises to the Christian message. The faith could become just another product to consume; a relationship with Jesus might become just another source of emotional fulfillment. And the obsession with teenage bodily purity made it difficult for white evangelicals to respond in love to those perceived to be impure outsiders, such as juvenile delinquents and African Americans.

In other words, white evangelical youth leaders and the teenagers who influenced them set the stage for the widespread juvenilization of American Christianity. These youth leaders wanted teenagers to make sacrifices for Jesus, not just have fun. But in the long run, the pleasurable side of this spirituality would prove to be overpoweringly enticing — and its rigors all too easy to avoid.

Crisis, Consecration, and Fun: A Teenage Evangelical Spirituality

Evangelical Protestants faced a dilemma in appealing to teenagers during the 1950s. On the one hand, they were fiercely committed to conservative moral and theological positions. On the other hand, they recognized the need to foster a spirituality that was less severe and more appealing to teenagers. Jim Rayburn, the founder of Young Life, remembered that a major turning point in his ministry came when he read in the book *He That Is Spiritual* by Lewis Sperry Chafer, a professor at Dallas Theological Seminary,

How misleading is the theory that to be spiritual one must abandon play, diversion, and helpful amusement! Such a conception of spirituality is born of a morbid human conscience. It is foreign to the Word of God. It is a device of Satan to make the blessings of God seem abhorrent to young people who are overflowing with physical life and energy.[3]

Rayburn instinctively sensed that combining fun and spirituality could have a powerful appeal to young people, and the leaders of Youth for Christ agreed.

In order to authenticate this new fun spirituality, YFC leaders urged teenagers to "consecrate" their lives to Jesus. "Consecration" denoted a further commitment, which could coincide with conversion or could happen later, in which a young person would "yield" or "surrender" her life to God. Consecration implied not only moral purity, but also the willingness, should God require it, to become a missionary or full-time evangelist. One young woman told of her consecration while attending a national YFC convention:

When I came here, I was cold and careless. I had no burden for souls. But as the week wore on, conviction came more and more heavily upon my heart, and yesterday in the early hours of the morning I knelt by my bed and poured out my heart to God. I yielded my life without reservation to him.[4]

Such testimonies reassured adults that even though teenagers were having lots of fun, they were also becoming spiritually radicalized and motivated to reach out to "lost souls."

YFC combined dispensational theology and fears about nuclear war to exhort teenagers to make sacrifices for the sake of world evangelization. Writing in *Youth for Christ Magazine* on the topic "Time is Now Fleeting," Norman King reminded his young readers of the "folly of investing life only in that which matures in earthly rewards." In a world in which young people may "never have the opportunity to realize any appreciable amount of life experience," they should be all the more eager to devote their lives to evangelism for whatever brief time remained to them.[5] Either nuclear war or the rapture of the church was going to happen any day, so teenagers should drop everything and evangelize. Evangelical youth spirituality came to include a powerful, if contradictory, mix of fun and fear.

YFC teenagers had weekly reminders to "get saved" or "rededicate their life to Christ." Some undoubtedly renewed these commitments regularly as they experienced the ups and downs of adolescent life combined with the preacher's appeal to elicit an emotional response. Young people who gave their lives to Christ at a YFC rally could imagine that by doing so they were helping to save the world in its hour of crisis. But the emotional power of these experiences could have negative effects as well. YFC President Bob Cook worried about "emotionalism without subsequent action" at the rallies, because this could easily become "a kind of addiction."[6]

All the talk of world "crises" may have pushed evangelical teens to seek out the comforting side of their spiritual heritage. In 1953, 93 percent of YFC teenagers answered "no" when polled on the question, "Are you disturbed about your future in an atomic age?" Although the pollster called this statistic a "thrilling witness of what Christ means in a Christian young person's life," it also hinted that YFC teenagers did not really live in fear of the imminent end of the world and so might not be dropping everything to devote their lives to evangelism.[7] Still, the spirituality of conversion and consecration created a direct link in teenagers' lives between powerful religious experiences, moral purity, and a sense of daily mission. This combination proved extremely effective in attracting and keeping teenagers in the evangelical fold.

These sober calls to consecration before the world came to an end existed side by side with lots of fun activities. In the early 1950s, leaders developed the "funspiration." As the awkward name indicates, this event mixed pie-in-the-face stunts and skits with a brief gospel message at the end. It was not uncommon to see conversions at "funspirations," hay rides, "singspirations," and roller-skating parties. In many cities, these events drew hundreds.[8] Teenagers came to associate Christianity with fun and bodily pleasure. In some ways, this fun spirituality was an improvement on the often dour fundamentalism of previous generations. And because teenagers' experiences of conversion and consecration seemed to be the same, adults didn't worry about how the content of the gospel may have been subtly altered in the creation of this new fun spirituality.

Evangelical Youth Culture and the Conquest of Public Space

The leaders of Youth for Christ did not take a very critical look at the new youth spirituality of "fun consecration" because they had set their sights on evangelizing the world and winning public influence in America. Bible clubs emerged in the early 1950s as an exciting way to meet these goals. Not only would they win converts and funnel teens into the local YFC rally, these clubs would provide a strategic point of entry and a public presence for Christianity in the "pagan" stronghold of the public schools. In the process, they would also accelerate the development of a white evangelical youth culture.

Bible clubs began in Kansas City in the 1940s, where local YFC director Al Metsker hired Jack Hamilton to promote clubs in local high schools. In the fall of 1947, just after Hamilton had succeeded in establishing twelve clubs, the Supreme Court handed down a decision restricting "release-time" religious education in public schools. Although the Court did not specifically prohibit Bible clubs, the decision caused school officials across the country to re-examine their policies toward religious activities. In Kansas City, the fledgling YFC Bible clubs found themselves ousted from school facilities. Undaunted, Hamilton and local students raised money to purchase a bus and fit it out as a mobile chapel.[9] When the bus pulled up outside each school, students boarded it to conduct their Bible club meetings. Although the Kansas City clubs continued to thrive, and their exclusion from school facilities was only temporary, Hamilton keenly felt the sting of exile. He began to see the clubs not just as a convenient way to get more students out to the Saturday night rallies, but as a way to put the Bible back into the schools.

Metsker and Hamilton promoted the Bible club idea at the 1949 YFC convention. Given that they could point to one hundred conversions and sixty seniors headed for Bible schools as the fruit of their clubs that year, it was not a hard sell. The idea fit well with YFC president Bob Cook's growing conviction that the "rally is just the show window. Let's get something on the counters the rest of the week." Cook appointed Jack Hamilton as national director of the new Bible Club Department in 1950. By the end of the 1951-52 school year, 700 clubs had been established nationwide. The number of clubs more than doubled in the next four years, reaching a total of 1,956. Hamilton insisted that clubs were "a movement of the students, by the students, and for the students,"[10] but throughout their history clubs relied heavily on adult directors like Hamilton.

Teenagers flocked to Bible clubs because they offered fun, a place to belong, and a role in restoring the public presence of their faith. Hamilton intended the clubs to be miniature YFC rallies, complete with "peppy singing," "punchy prayer," student testimonies, guest speakers, and even Christian musical performers. The main goal was always supposed to be evangelism. But by 1954 Hamilton worried about clubs becoming inwardly focused, so he warned club leaders that "Christian fellowship, wonderful as it is, is the least important aim of your club."[11]

Club directors and students adapted many elements of high school youth culture in order to enhance the appeal of their clubs. Several YFC groups published citywide club yearbooks, complete with senior photos, reports of each club's activities, and blank pages for autographs. The "Senior Ballot" identified the young men and women "most likely to succeed" or "most popular." In many cities, club members replaced the senior prom with a YFC banquet complete with an elected king and queen. Clubs often reported that showing a gospel film produced the best attendance of the year. A Christian ventriloquist and a program modeled on the popular television show "Dragnet" also drew large crowds. Bible Club members carried their Bibles to school and wore distinctive pins, sweaters, and jackets — group identifiers that closely resembled those of other high school clubs, cliques, and gangs.[12] Although they did not drink, dance, or go to movies, YFC Bible clubbers of the 1950s appropriated many elements of white, middle-class youth culture with full approval of their adult mentors. The combination of adherence to old standards of right and wrong and the drive for evangelistic success allowed this Christian youth culture to develop relatively unhindered.

Another way that Bible clubs successfully imitated popular culture was through the Bible quiz competition. Local Bible clubs competed in tournaments that culminated in annual championships at the YFC convention in July. Such competitions attracted even non-Christian spectators in the early 1950s, and remained popular well into the 1960s. By 1965, 60,000 teenagers participated in the nationwide quiz program. Because these quiz competitions appealed to teens and taught them the Bible, several denominations established their own versions of the competition. WMBI, the radio station of Moody Bible Institute, broadcasted the national championships live each year. Teams in elaborate uniforms and costumes waited tensely for the questions from Jack Hamilton, while supporters shouted out cheers in between questions. Members of championship teams typically memorized entire books of the Bible and interrupted the quiz master with the answer well before he had finished reading the question. Preaching, singing, song leading, and instrumental music contests also drew heavy teen participation and enhanced the appeal of clubs and rallies.[13] Bible clubs and Youth for Christ rallies offered teenagers a chance to participate in Christian versions of the hugely popular television quiz shows and variety shows of the era. Just as sponsorship of *The $64,000 Question* made Revlon the industry leader in cosmetics, YFC's sponsorship of Bible quizzes and other competitions expanded the evangelical market share among American youth.[14]

In addition to sparking interest through fun and competition, many clubs did win converts and produce teen evangelists. Jack Merjimakian, a football player at Evanston High in Illinois, thought that when he went to the local Bible club he was "in for a dull time." But after hearing the club leader talk about salvation he became intrigued, and later reported, "I gave my heart to Christ." Instead of weightlifting and football dominating his life, he said, "I want others to know Christ can change their lives too." By her aggressive witnessing, Joan Gorton of Kearny High in San Diego helped her club meet its ambitious goal of winning at least one convert per week.[15]

YFC Bible clubs made a significant impact on the world of the 1950s high school. The most successful clubs tended to be led by teenagers at the top of the high school social hierarchy, and YFC leaders intentionally cultivated relationships with such young people. Three young men from Winfield, West Virginia, attended the YFC convention at Winona Lake in July 1956. That fall, they started a Bible club in their high school of 400 students. By November they had 147 in attendance at one of the meetings. Tom Howell, student body president and football captain, was president of the club. The football coach was the club sponsor, and the school principal was a born-again Christian. By February 1957, the club attendance averaged 200 per week. Although such dramatic growth was not uncommon, many clubs were smaller. A survey of 59 cities conducted by Jack Hamilton in 1956 identified 461 clubs with an average attendance around 25. Still, that meant that across the nation as many as 48,000 teenagers were attending 1,956 Bible clubs each week. With such explosive growth in the first half of the decade, it was easy for Hamilton to claim that YFC clubs were indeed "bringing the Bible back to the American high school through the lives of consecrated teen-agers."[16]

In his monthly club column in *Youth for Christ Magazine*, Hamilton especially liked to highlight stories of student-body presidents, athletes, and homecoming queens who participated in their local Bible club. In so doing, he hoped to show that Christianity was fully compatible with success as defined in the teenage world. Some teenagers shared his aspirations for combining youth culture popularity and Christian witness. Molly Eichert of Santa Barbara wrote that her election as one of three "pep leaders" for her school revealed "the Lord's hand" at work. "Since being elected, I have come in contact with so many kids that I am able to witness to about my Lord," she explained. Both evangelical adults and teenagers helped to sanctify teenage popularity by linking it to effective witnessing. In fact, when such popular students were involved, there was a fine line, or no line at all, between witnessing and peer pressure.[17] But if the felt need of Hamilton and other YFC leaders to convince Christian teenagers that they could be popular and religious at the same time is any indication, such cases were probably the exception rather than the rule.

Even though he delighted in teenagers who combined popularity and a Christian "testimony," Hamilton also hoped to nurture a sense of opposition to high school culture. As he saw it, when the Supreme Court and Kansas City school officials kicked his clubs out of the schools, they proved that America was becoming "pagan." Citing the fall of Rome and the horrors of Nazi Germany as examples of what happened to civilizations that rejected God, he called on Christian students to infiltrate their high schools: "You know, gang, they can take the Bible as a book out of school, but you can put it back in by the life you live!" He urged students to carry their Bibles at school, and "not a tiny Testament, but a big one that everyone can see." With their usual combination of marketing savvy and evangelistic zeal, Youth for Christ leaders sold a special edition of the Bible with a bright red cover. Hamilton and his fellow YFC staff members liked to tell stories of students who gave bold answers to taunting peers. When friends mocked one Bible-carrying convert with the words, "Bill, you turnin' sissy on us?" he replied, "Here, you carry it for a week, and we'll see who the sissy is!" Like the liberal Protestants who called young people to social action, evangelicals tried to present carrying the Bible to school as a courageous way to exert Christian influence in the public realm.[18] But this story also reveals that conservative Christianity was not perceived as manly and courageous by many teenage boys during the 1950s.

Teenage resistance pushed YFC leaders toward ever more extreme exhortations to "stand up for Jesus" at school. In one of his editorials entitled "Branded," Hamilton began by noting that some teenage gang members tattooed marks on their bodies "so that everyone would know who they belonged to." Similarly, he reminded his young readers that "the world today is brand conscious" and that teenagers could even buy miniature dog collars for their steady girlfriends to wear on their ankles. Since Paul had boasted, "I bear in my body the marks, or brands, of the Lord Jesus," Hamilton urged Christian teens to do no less. He then recounted a story he had heard from a young woman named Norma that left "tears standing in my eyes." After her conversion, Norma refused to have anything to do with her old gang. They repeatedly threatened her and finally slashed her face with a knife. Despite being "branded" with such a wound, Norma's faith in God did not waver. Hamilton asked his young readers, "Are you made of that caliber stuff? What kind of a brand are you carrying?" He further exhorted them: "talking about the Lord is not enough; we should be branded for Him. Carry your Bible, not as a holier than thou, but as a brand to get the world watching your actions, which should prove the life in Christ is the best."[19] In a way that was just beginning in the 1950s, teenagers would increasingly shape their identities by consuming products and experiences. Hamilton was encouraging teenagers to carry the "brand" of Jesus — without asking whether this made Jesus just another brand.

Hamilton and other YFC leaders saw Bible club members as embodiments of the Bible, as free samples of the Christian "brand" of life that would attract other youthful customers. In this light certain YFC promotional devices take on a new significance. YFC members commonly used their bodies as walking billboards for their clubs. In one club, members wore a drawing of a banana on their shirt or sweater. When asked why, they replied, "I'm one of the bunch that goes to the YFC Bible club!" YFC members loved to route their hayrides through central business districts and enter floats in parades. On their way to a 1954 YFC convention in Vancouver, 172 Portland YFC members turned their stopover at the Seattle train station into a religious service.[20] Every victory of this kind reassured evangelicals that they could reclaim more and more of the "world" as their own by filling it with "consecrated" teens. But the line between public influence and public relations often blurred. Indeed, much like their Catholic counterparts, evangelicals were tempted to sell their good Christian teenagers to the public like some product that could prove the value of their religion.

Hamilton's vision for "branded" teenagers did not fare as well as he hoped not only because teenagers were more interested in having fun, but also because real persecution was in short supply in the high school world of the 1950s. Principals often visited Bible clubs. In Detroit, one principal spoke at the Bible club's welcome party for freshmen, urging the new students to join the club. Other principals allowed Youth for Christ leaders to plan school assemblies or to show Christian films to the student body. One principal even gave the "invitation" after a showing of the evangelistic film *Seventeen*, resulting in thirty-five conversions. In Savannah, another allowed the club to meet during a class period every other week. Not surprisingly, attendance went up. One principal expressed his enthusiasm for the clubs this way: "My problem is this. When God is put out of my high school, how can I keep anti-God from coming in?" Even less devout principals and teachers worried about discipline in the overcrowded schools of the 1950s. They also feared communist subversion and the menace of juvenile delinquency. When they saw the well-behaved students in YFC Bible clubs, school officials wanted to believe that such groups provided an answer.[21]

Even though YFC leaders and students liked to see themselves as "outsiders," school officials recognized them as allies in forming pious, law-abiding, patriotic Americans. The unofficial collaboration between some school officials and groups like Youth for Christ inspired evangelicals to hope for increasing influence in the public sphere. The result was anything but countercultural. Indeed, the Christian teens of the 1950s probably came to value authority and order even more than truth and justice. Such Christians also tended to assume, or at least hope, that simply being present in a worldly environment was enough to redeem it.

YFC leaders did worry at times about the new form of juvenilized Christianity they were creating. In 1956 Bob Cook warned a national conference of YFC directors that they must address "big issues" in their rallies, publications, and clubs, because "when you begin entertaining only . . . brother, you've had it!" Cook bemoaned rapid cultural change and the constant need to pronounce judgment on new artifacts of the youth culture. He claimed that young Christians cried out for direction in these matters, but worried that such struggles took energy away from the movement's evangelistic thrust and threatened to divide even its leaders. In 1957, Cook laughingly told fellow leaders that "I was probably the first man ever to have opened a drag race with prayer and a few appropriate remarks about the Lord." He was referring to a meeting of the "Boltin' Bishops" Christian hot rod club. Yet while he was not opposed to gimmicks, Cook warned YFC directors to guard against "evangelical gadgetry" by keeping their hearts "desperate for souls."[22]

By the early 1960s, leaders began to lay some of the blame for dulling YFC's evangelistic edge on Christian teenagers. President Ted Engstrom complained to leaders in 1962 that "far too much of our Youth for Christ ministry is geared to church kids." He urged leaders to create programs "more geared to the un-churched — lost, pagan kids, and not to pamper the spoiled church kids." He wondered, "are we going to evangelize our campuses by puncturing balloons, in slapstick and pie in the face?"

Engstrom insisted he was "not opposed to fun" but suggested — tellingly — that when it came to some of the YFC antics, "kids don't look for this today."[23] The evangelical youth culture had taken on a life of its own, and it needed to be fed with more up-to-date forms of entertainment and expression. But this form of Christianity might not necessarily end up looking much like what adults originally had in mind.

Popular Culture, Bodily Purity, and the Evangelical Virgin Testimony

Although some of their innovations may seem quaint today, the evangelical teenagers and youth leaders of the 1950s were engaged in a radical transformation of their religious tradition. During the 1940s and 1950s, Billy Graham and like-minded conservative Protestants were creating a new version of old time religion that they now formally called "evangelicalism" to distinguish it from the older, more negative label "fundamentalism." They wanted to keep a conservative view of Scripture and a strong commitment to saving souls, but at the same time to win public respect in society and collaborate with a broader spectrum of like-minded Christians. Some, like Carl Henry, wanted evangelicals to get involved in social and political issues as well. Their success in this project is best symbolized by Graham himself, who became the unofficial but highly visible chaplain to presidents. The National Association of Evangelicals became the official standard bearer of this movement. But organizations like Youth for Christ and Young Life became the places in which the new evangelicals worked out their relationship to popular culture and the preferences of younger generations. Staunch fundamentalists, meanwhile, refused to join the NAE and criticized YFC for being too "worldly."

Although the shift from fundamentalism to evangelicalism helped the new movement in many ways, it did accelerate the juvenilization of conservative Protestantism in America. By defining the Christian life as less countercultural and more fun and fulfilling, YFC leaders harnessed the appeal of youth culture to the cart of revivalism. But once harnessed, this horse began to dictate where the cart would go. When the appeal to teenagers became overwhelmingly important, the Christian standards so long taken for granted were not as self-evident as they had once seemed. How could Christians tell the difference between becoming worldly and beating the world at its own game?

In the end, YFC leaders turned to the purity of youthful bodies as the key distinguishing mark that separated cultural victory from worldly contamination. But this approach often led to poor choices. Some cultural elements were too easily accepted, while others were rejected on dubious grounds. Rather than developing sophisticated theological criteria for evaluating popular culture and entertainment, evangelicals relied on their shared instincts about what constituted bodily corruption. They also accepted anything that promised evangelistic success — or could at least draw a crowd of teenagers. They saw most pop culture forms as morally neutral and showed little awareness of the way that a change of medium can change the message it communicates.

The importance of bodily purity was continually reinforced in the activities of local Youth for Christ ministries. At a 1953 rally in Lansing, Michigan, the club time was interrupted by Bible club member Norm Hinton, who staggered down the aisle holding his stomach and feigning illness. Four young men planted in the audience jumped up to help. They carried Norm to a cot on the platform. Local YFC director Billy Walker immediately prescribed an operation. Lacking proper anesthetics, Walker removed one of Norm's shoes and placed it over the patient's nose and mouth. Using a knife and saw as make believe instruments, the "doctor" extracted dice, cards, cigarettes, tickets to the movies and a dance, comic books, and an empty bottle of whiskey. He replaced these with a picture of Jesus, a Bible, Christian tracts, a Christian novel, tickets to the Bible club and roller skating party, and a copy of *Youth for Christ Magazine*. After the successful operation, the patient got up "really alive, and gave a terrific testimony!" Such stunts made a big impact. One visitor who was not in on the stunt even jumped up to help the others carry Norm to the platform.[24] The skit illustrated in a humorous way one of the main messages of Youth for Christ: bodily purity was crucial to true Christianity.

YFC leaders had to figure out which forms of entertainment could support their evangelistic goals, and which could not. They condemned smoking, drinking, movies, dancing, card playing, "bebop" slang, petting, fan clubs, and rock 'n' roll. They even criticized jazzed-up gospel music. Yet they enthusiastically supported Christian movies and had little to criticize about mainstream television. They published reviews of Christian music and movies and contributed to a growing evangelical celebrity culture. They did not try to stamp out dating or the practice of going steady, but tried to control these activities. Although YFC leaders and their most devout followers tried to give the impression that "Christian standards" were clearly spelled out in the Bible and therefore non-negotiable, in fact they themselves changed some of those standards.[25] They justified a youth culture version of Christianity by claiming that nothing important had changed.

Even though evangelicals had long been suspicious of the film industry, Youth for Christ played a key role in the development of Christian films. Youth for Christ rallies and clubs became a key market that allowed fledgling organizations like Gospel Films to become financially viable. In the 1950s Youth for Christ collaborated with Gospel Films to produce a spate of films geared to teenagers. One of the most widely shown of these films, *Seventeen*, premiered at the 1956 YFC convention and dramatized the importance of YFC Bible clubs. In the film, a new student at "Broadview High" named Linda, "whose beautiful voice sings the Gospel unforgettably into the hearts of all those who hear her," talks her friend Jennifer into helping to start a Bible club in their school. Jennifer gets converted, but faces opposition from her football-star boyfriend and her "socially prominent parents." Meanwhile, Jennifer's father, as a member of the school board, must decide what to do about a motion to shut down the Bible club. He mistrusts the club, but cannot deny that his daughter has changed for the better. The film climaxes with the tragic death of a boy at school. Producers hoped to drive home the point that "every high school student in the world should have at least one chance to hear that Christ died for his sins." The teenage actors in the film, who were all YFC members, testified to the thrill they experienced from helping to save souls by starring in the movie. Later films like *Teenage Rock, Preacher's Kid, Silent Witness*, and *Going Steady* revisited this thematic combination of teen witnesses, conversion, romantic conflict, and juvenile delinquency.[26] As the extremes of juvenile delinquency and "socially prominent parents" indicate, evangelicals unconsciously fretted over their class position. They feared the spiritual dangers of both sinking too low and rising too high, and they often projected those fears onto their children. Such class anxiety contributed to the heated debates over changing cultural taboos.

In January 1954, *Youth for Christ Magazine* printed a debate about religious films between YFC regional director Evon Hedley and Rev. A. W. Tozer. Hedley praised Christian films for prompting many conversions and inspiring missionary vocations. He noted that the film *Mr. Texas*, sponsored by the Billy Graham Evangelistic Association and shown at many YFC high school clubs, had recently been credited with 135,000 "first time decisions" for Christ. He also insisted that Christians must press their advantage now that they had broken in on the "monopoly" of non-Christians in the entertainment world.[27] Hedley's defense of Christian films did not include a single scripture reference, and it proceeded from the assumption that film was a neutral cultural medium.

In contrast, evangelical elder statesman A. W. Tozer predicted that as a result of films, "the rising generation will come to look on religion as another, and inferior, form of amusement." Acting demanded insincerity, which would harm the souls of the actors: "To *pretend* to pray, to *simulate* Godly sorrow, to *play* at *worship* before the camera for effect — how utterly shocking to the reverent heart!" Tozer argued that "the movie is not the modernization or improvement of any scriptural method" since the Bible clearly endorsed only four methods for communicating the truth: prayer, song, preaching, and good works.[28] Although not all of his arguments have stood the test of time, Tozer rightly recognized the danger of turning the faith more and more into a "form of amusement."

In an evangelical subculture in which Christian films shown in Christian settings were still somewhat controversial, attending movies in the theater was out of the question. But in the 1950s, Hollywood began to cash in on popular religious sentiments with films like *The Ten Commandments, A Man Called Peter,* and *The Robe.* YFC president Bob Cook argued that such movies had "no place in the believer's heart and life" because they presented a "distorted, over-sexed, highly spiced view of life, coupled (where it is religious at all) with a watered-down version of the Gospel, carefully weakened until it is palatable to Jew and Gentile, Roman Catholic and Protestant, as well as to the thoughtful pagan." He believed that whether the believer saw them in the theater, a Christian meeting, or on television, such movies would "edge out of your heart the desire for God and the Bible, prayer and soul-winning." Cook noted that these films had already led some Christians to break their rule about going to the theater.[29] Indeed, what made Hollywood films sinful was not just their content, but the way that they could lure Christians into compromising their public witness by entering the worldly venue of the theater. But if Cook felt the need to condemn these films, clearly some Christian teenagers were watching them.

Television, on the other hand, while controversial at first, quickly won full acceptance from youth leaders and teenagers, in part because it did not compromise public witness by forcing a person to enter a "worldly" public space. Those who condemned television did so because it supposedly brought "temptation into the front parlor." Such critics insisted that the new medium would steal devotion, time, and money from the cause of Christ. Dr. David Otis Fuller even argued that "television is doubtless Satan's latest instrument" which he would use to prepare the way for "the entrance of Antichrist." But this apocalyptic view of television failed to capture the teenage imagination. Rev. Arvid Carlson warned YFC members that television had great potential for evil, but also insisted that "no greater medium has ever come to our hands by which we may invade the sanctuary of non-Christian homes." If a medium could be used to get the Christian message to more people, Youth for Christ leaders tended not to worry about how the medium might alter the message. In the case of television, it didn't even seem to matter that the medium was not in fact being used much for evangelistic purposes. At least YFC leaders could point to YFC musician Ralph Carmichael's Emmy-winning show *The Campus Christian Hour.*[30]

Although YFC teenagers called for more Christian programs and condemned advertisements for tobacco and alcohol, they fundamentally accepted television. As a member of a teen panel in *Youth for Christ Magazine,* Ray Marshall expressed a common view: "television is wonderful *IF* the Christian lets the Holy Spirit guide him in doing the Lord's will in determining which programs to watch." Although Ray hoped teenagers would rely on the guidance of the Holy Spirit, it is not likely that YFC members were getting much help in theologically evaluating the content of the television shows they watched. And teenagers who never darkened the door of a movie theater felt free to watch television in their homes because their public "witness" was not compromised. Like radio before it, television was quickly domesticated, and evangelical teenagers supported this process.[31] Since television did not compromise the public image of evangelicalism and the teenagers who were its walking advertisements, most white evangelicals eventually decided that all was well.

Popular music with religious themes became controversial among adults, but teenagers embraced it. During the 1950s popular musicians began releasing "juke box hymns" like "He," "I Believe," and "Church Twice on Sunday." YFC evangelist Carl Bihl insisted that *"the god of the juke box evidently is not the God of the Bible!"* He complained that this music communicated bad theology and omitted the name of Jesus. Obviously "the almighty dollar," not concern for souls, controlled this music. He argued that its "strong sensuous beat" led "the thoughts and emotions away from, rather than to, the things the Lord would have us love and cherish." Bihl thought these songs had their roots in the craft of the "voodoo artist." He was appalled that some "Gospel meetings" mistakenly used them. But in 1955 a panel of Christian teens seemed more favorable to such music. They were asked, "Do juke box hymns cheapen the Gospel?" Two of the panelists worried that these songs did not "glorify God" or lead to conversions; as one put it, "the unsaved teenager, while listening to music, pays little if any attention to the words." But another panelist, Theresa Overstreet, disagreed. She thought it depended "greatly on what the hymns say and who sings them." In her opinion, any "true Christian" would be able to recognize juke box hymns "sung for Jesus' glory and to win souls for Him."[32] Evidently some YFC members believed that the performer's godly intentions could shine through even "worldly" styles. Although they paid some attention to the words, evangelical teenagers relied just as heavily on their subjective perceptions of the artist's sincerity.

These juke box hymns proved to be an easy case compared to the "jazzy" gospel choruses and performance pieces in some YFC rallies. Nevertheless, three out of four teen panelists allowed some room for "jazzy" choruses so that "the unsaved person will realize that the Christian life is not dull." While all recognized that some songs went too far, they did not really know how to draw the line, except to say that "the Bible says that we should be different from the world." In practice, the fun side of evangelical youth spirituality trumped such vague scruples. Ruth Voskuyl worried that "jumpy, noisy, gay music" did not belong in worship, but insisted that on a hay ride the same music "expresses as no other music could, the happiness and thrill which one experiences in knowing the Lord Jesus Christ as Savior." The new evangelical youth culture taught teenagers to see emotional states like "happiness and thrill" as central to Christianity and to its appeal.

But Gunnar Urang, head of the music department at Trinity Seminary in Chicago, found little to commend in such music. He compared the musician who tried to appeal to unbelievers through "sensual harmonies and frenetic rhythms" to the unthinkable case of a "gospel preacher" who told a "smutty story" in the name of speaking "the language of the people." As a member of the older generation, Urang recognized the similarity between many gospel singers and the "torchy crooners" who sang suggestive love songs. He found it bitterly ironic that some of these very crooners knew better than to use such sensual styles when performing their occasional gospel numbers.[33] But voices like his fell on deaf ears. Evangelical teenagers demanded that Christian music reflect the emotionally intense, romantic spirituality they were creating in their youth groups. Teenagers didn't buy Urang's argument because they agreed with their youth leaders that most cultural forms were neutral vessels that could be filled with Christian content.

Music became a fearful frontier of cultural interchange because it stood at the intersection of evangelical spirituality and teenage bodily purity. Youth for Christ leaders taught teenagers to expect fun, fulfillment, and even pleasure from their relationship with God. But since youthful bodies were also expected to serve as visible "witnesses" for Christ, sensuality and a driving beat threatened to taint evangelicalism's public image and evangelistic success. Jerry Oas, a teenage member of Youth for Christ, warned that the religious songs topping the secular charts in the mid 1950s were spiritually dangerous because they might "draw Christians into a place where they would not go and to do things to ruin or cheapen their testimony."[34] Like virginity, a pure "testimony" could only be maintained by bodily control and avoiding sinful public spaces. Once lost, it could not easily be recovered, if at all.

Teenage sexuality, music, and public "witness" came together in the problem of dancing. In 1954, a hand-picked panel of YFC teenagers all agreed that it was wrong for Christians to attend the prom. The amusingly named Erwin Boring said, "I cannot, as a child of God, attend a worldly function which is geared primarily to the lust of the flesh." He especially feared publicly endorsing immorality by attending dances. Similarly, Joan Marshall noted that although some Christian young people claimed they "can be an effective witness on the dance floor," experience proved "it *can't* be done." To drive home her point, she told a story about a Christian teenager who attended a dance, only to be publicly rebuked by one of her non-Christian friends.[35] Evidently even "pagan" teenagers knew that Christians did not dance. Because the moral reasoning that condemned all dancing was weak, evangelicals often fell back on the importance of the pure bodily testimony.

Judging from how frequently they felt the need to condemn dancing, YFC leaders must have encountered resistance on this point from Christian teenagers. In 1957, Jim Smith, a YFC director in Charleston, West Virginia, noted that "again and again I am asked by kids and parents alike, 'What about dancing?'" He suspected that dancing was the "number one problem" Christian teens faced. He argued that by its very nature, dancing provoked sexual impurity. He claimed that psychologists and anthropologists had discovered the sexual roots of dancing. He also denounced dancing because of its association with drinking. Above all, he insisted that "I have never met a young person who danced who was a consistent soul-winner." To prove this point, he told the story of an evangelical "campus queen" who thought she could "witness on the dance floor." Her partner backed away and loudly confronted her with the words, "What in the world are you doing at a dance?"[36] These often repeated stories about non-Christian teenagers rebuking Christians for dancing look suspiciously like other apocryphal preachers' stories that get passed around the evangelical community. Like other such stories, this one may reveal more about the religious community that circulates it than about the real attitudes and behaviors of non-Christians. In this case, the main message was that a Christian teenager who dances ruins her chance to stand as a pure witness who wins friends to Christ.

YFC leaders reinforced this message by recounting stories of teenagers who made a spiritual impact on their friends by taking a public stand *against* dancing. One Saturday night in Missoula, Montana, the Youth for Christ rally and a dance met at the local high school on the same night. Bible club members arranged for their guest speakers, the singing team of Louis and Phil Palermo, to perform at the dance after the rally was over. Club members proudly reported that the "spirit of the dance was changed so much" that students only danced to one more song, and the dancing shut down completely after that.[37] When YFC club member Paddy Hanna got elected homecoming queen, she refused to dance. Although her crown hung in jeopardy for several days as friends prayed, in the end school officials respected her wishes and allowed a procession rather than a dance by the homecoming court to open the evening's activities. Paddy then left the dance and her parents drove her to a surprise party put on by her Christian friends.[38] Although Jack Hamilton presented these stories in *Youth for Christ Magazine* as spiritual victories, it is likely that other teenagers in these schools saw Paddy and other Christian teenagers as misguided people spoiling everyone's fun. And Paddy left the dance, retreating into her safe evangelical world.

Paddy's story illustrates how evangelical teens struggled to reconcile the competing claims of popularity and purity. Young women like Paddy faced such dilemmas precisely because they achieved the sort of popularity that Youth for Christ leaders had always promised. Not every YFC member faced such a difficult choice, but adults hoped that such stories would teach teens to view their bodily behavior as a way to make or break their "witness" for Christ. Evangelical scruples essentially made dancing into an act of foreplay which not only destroyed the individual's reputation but also disgraced Jesus. Perhaps more importantly, teenagers who refrained from dancing could be reassured by stories like Paddy's that their sacrifice would help the cause of Christ.

While it should come as no surprise that evangelicals condemned Elvis Presley and rock 'n' roll, the reasons they gave are revealing. Members of a YFC teen panel denounced Elvis in 1956. Larry Nelson thought teens thronged to Elvis because he seemed to fulfill their desires for "a thrill," "a buddy," and "security." Only Jesus could truly meet such needs, he argued. Marg Jones said, "watching gals 'moon' over a picture of his swinging body reminds me of their lost condition and my mind compares the picture with the heathen dances of darkest Africa." Elvis and other "teen idols" seemed threatening because they inspired aggressive, sensual bodily behaviors, especially in young women. But the desire to compete with the bodily "thrills" offered by such teen idols could push evangelical spirituality in dubious directions. One anonymous teenager wrote of her disillusionment with Elvis: "The fact of the matter is, I've found something else that has given me more of a thrill than a hundred Presley's ever could! It's a new friendship with the most wonderful Person I've ever met, a Man who has given me happiness and thrills and something worth living for."[39] Christian teenagers were coming to believe that the Christian life could best be described as falling in love with Jesus and experiencing the "thrills" and "happiness" of a romantic relationship with him. Perhaps because evangelicals believed so strongly in a "personal relationship" with Jesus as the center of Christianity, they didn't question what might be lost when that relationship was compared to an erotic, emotional attraction to a teen idol.

White evangelicals feared rock music because they associated it with sex, violence, and loss of bodily control. It also provoked visceral fears of corruption that were rooted in racism. Radio preacher William Ward Ayer argued in *Youth for Christ Magazine* that rock music contributed to juvenile crime and cited examples of stabbings at the new gatherings called "record hops." Ayer taught that rock music provoked "sex-crazed, irrational, irresponsible actions" because, like its voodoo precedents, it induced demon possession. Revealingly, he paraphrased the observations of anthropologists who had seen "savages" use the drum beat to help demons "mount" their victims. Ayer insisted that this music was "alien to our culture" and would destroy America. He bemoaned the fact that while communist radio stations played the classics, Radio Free Europe broadcast the music of "confusion, savagery and hopelessness." Ayer also denounced the commercial exploitation of young people by leaders of the music industry.

Acknowledging the competition between the sensual beat and the thrills of religious emotion, Ayer warned that rock music might "even provide a carnal substitute for the joys and exaltations of the Holy Spirit's indwelling presence."[40] While in hindsight most of these criticisms seem weak and perhaps even racist, Ayer's sense that rock music might transform religious emotions was prophetic.

YFC leaders insisted that cultural styles, practices, and tastes could be adapted only if they contributed to the salvation of souls. Television, movies, and some types of music seemed acceptable because they promised the ability to persuasively communicate a Christian message. With their location in homes, Bible clubs, churches, and youth rallies, these media did not compromise the evangelicals' commitment to bodily separation from worldly public spaces. Nor did they involve threatening uses of the body. In contrast, the frenzy, lawlessness, and sexuality associated with dancing and rock 'n' roll could not help but corrupt young Christians. Evangelicals did not compare popular music and dancing to "neutral media" like radio or television, but rather connected them with body-corrupting practices like drinking, smoking, and sexual immorality. Jazzy gospel songs proved the most troublesome precisely because they straddled the supposedly unbridgeable chasm between evangelism and sensuality. Adults wanted to grant teenagers limited freedom to have fun. But teenagers always pressed for more, and grew up not knowing any world but one in which Christianity was fun and a relationship with Jesus provided better "thrills" than Elvis Presley. This juvenilized version of Christianity proved highly popular, but was ill suited to address some of the pressing challenges of the day.

When a "Good Witness" Goes Bad:
Bodily Purity, Anti-Communism, Juvenile Delinquency, and Racism

YFC leaders thought they were bringing Christianity back into American public life and saving the world from communism by forging a band of consecrated teenage witnesses. But to gather that group of pure teenagers, they created a new juvenilized version of evangelicalism. And in order to create a Christian youth culture without compromising their sense of separation from the world, they adopted teenage bodily purity as a key marker of evangelical identity. Meanwhile, a desire to share the message of salvation with all types of teenagers prompted YFC leaders to establish ministries to juvenile delinquents and African Americans in an era when most conservative white Protestants ignored them. But even though they did some good in reaching out to African Americans and juvenile offenders, the members of YFC found it hard to escape the instinctive feeling that these groups might be sources of corruption for good white Christian teens.

In 1952, Bob Cook issued a resounding challenge to be "willing to die" for the sake of spreading the gospel. Drawing on a recent *Reader's Digest* article "Conquest by Terror," he exposed how communists "with devilish ingenuity" played upon youthful idealism and patriotism. By giving young people responsibility and meaningful activities, the communists turned them against their parents. Cook proposed that YFC counter this "devilish system" by sending born-again teenagers and adult leaders into every town and school in America. These messengers would spread the word that young people must choose whether America would be "free and godly" or turn into "a pig pen and a rat's nest and a place for subversivists and ter- mites and communists and atheists, a place of concentration camps and fearful horrors."[41] Cook was not alone in viewing communism as filthy and corrupting — the opposite of the teenage bodily purity taught by YFC.

Christian teenagers got the message. A panel of YFC teenagers declared the individual's "witness" or "testimony" as the antidote to communist sub- version. Harold Spencer said Christians should not "start swinging their fists and screaming against the Communists," but "we *do* have to outlive them in regard to our personal lives and our loyalty to Jesus Christ." Phil Spain agreed, and noted that Christianity and communism used parallel "methods and means of reaching men's souls." Only by exceeding the com- munists in devotion to their cause could Christians hope to triumph. In 1954 another YFC youth panel denied that congressional investigations of "un-American activities" had gone too far. Instead, these students suggested that such efforts to catch communists in America should be continued.[42]

The fear of communism was so great that almost any social evil or source of corruption came to be linked with it in the white evangelical mind. In 1954, a hand-picked panel of YFC teens agreed that "our school system has become anti-religious as opponents of the Gospel have used the separation of church and state principle to take God completely out of the classroom." Betsy Gray of Friendship, New York, noted the hypocrisy of educators who taught "dancing, but not the Bible, evolution but not the true story of Creation." She also noted with alarm that "Communism is finding its way into the vacuum."[43] Since it is hard to imagine communist doctrine being taught in any 1950s high school classroom, Betsy's comment revealed how communism could be tied to all that was evil and corrupting in the eyes of white evangelicals and other conservatives of the 1950s.

Juvenile delinquency proved to be a difficult issue precisely because evangelicals found themselves torn between wanting to evangelize this needy population and wanting to keep white middle-class teenagers away from corrupting influences. Like other social problems of the era, delinquency came to be associated with the communist threat. Gordon McLean, the first national director of YFC's Youth Guidance Department, paraphrased J. Edgar Hoover's statement that the juvenile delinquency problem was "as dangerous to America from within as Communism is from without!" Hoover's statements and articles appeared frequently in YFC publications. YFC leaders especially liked the fact that Hoover strongly endorsed religious efforts to help young people. "The churches are in the front trenches of America's crime prevention crusade!" he wrote in 1955.[44]

Some teenagers agreed that the problems of communism and juvenile delinquency were interconnected, and that YFC provided the answer to both. A 1951 editorial in the student newspaper at Kansas City's Manual High quoted J. Edgar Hoover: "The teenager today has drifted away from the old-time religion. If our nation is to survive, the high school students must get back on the thing that our nation was founded on, the Bible." The young writer then touted the YFC Bible club as an answer to this challenge, and concluded, "We count it a real privilege to have a meeting like this. We know that this is what our Nation was founded upon, what our boys in Korea are fighting for, and the thing that Communism is trying to stamp out around the world."[45]

YFC leaders specialized in tailoring their message to a specific audience, so they recognized immediately that youngsters in trouble with the law needed special programs. Beginning around 1950, several YFC leaders pioneered ministries to juvenile offenders. Roy McKeown pioneered Lifeline camps in Southern California, Morry Carlson founded Youth Haven Ranch in Western Michigan, and Gordon McLean started Youth Guidance in Washington. At Lifeline camps, counselors worked hard to befriend the boys, and avoided a preachy style. Only at the end of the week did they "draw in the net." These camps consistently reported high conversion rates (60 to 80 percent) and low rates of recidivism. Leaders worked to provide ongoing support and help to the boys throughout the year.[46] YFC established 18 such camps in the 1950s, and another 109 camps between 1960 and 1964. By 1965, YFC claimed to be contacting over 10,000 juvenile offenders yearly through camps and counseling.[47]

McLean's success brought him to the attention of YFC President Bob Cook, who appointed him "Youth Guidance National Representative" in 1952. McLean began conducting revival meetings in juvenile institutions across the country. These meetings often employed musicians and counselors drawn from the local YFC ranks. Montana Governor John Bonner appointed the eighteen-year-old McLean to the State Board of Terms and Paroles. McLean's growing status as an expert on juvenile delinquency made him a popular high school speaker. For example, in 1953, he spoke to 10,000 students in high school and junior high assemblies in Des Moines, Iowa. Meanwhile, some YFC leaders criticized McLean's efforts for detracting from the main mission of the organization. Others liked the program, but thought McLean was too young to direct it.[48] Eventually, such opposition drove McLean out of the national organization, but YFC's ministry to juvenile delinquents continued under leaders like Wendy Collins and Bruce Love. Perhaps one reason YFC did more for juvenile delinquents than they did for racial justice was that combating delinquency was particularly good for public relations during the 1950s and 1960s.

McLean and his successors in the Lifeline Department hoped that their converts would attend local YFC Bible clubs and rallies when they got out of training school or prison. Leaders made much of particular cases in which this worked well. A young gang leader who was converted at a Lifeline camp in Indiana went home and preached to his friends, resulting in many converts. In another case, YFC club members befriended a former gang member who had recently moved to their area. He was soon converted at the YFC rally and the next year became Bible club president. Yet well into the 1960s, Youth Guidance leaders complained that their ministry to juvenile delinquents was not well integrated into the total program of YFC.[49]

One barrier to integrating juvenile offenders into mainstream programs was the belief that every teenager was a potential delinquent. In the words of Bob Cook, "the seeds of delinquency are in every human heart." On the positive side, this theological observation tended to reduce the sense of distance between Christians and juvenile delinquents, and could lead to genuine sympathy and understanding. Gordon McLean described the typical delinquent as "a lot like your boy, or the kid next door."[50] Charles Holmes drew a parallel between his conversion at a YFC rally and the arrest of a young thief that same night. He realized that "that boy could have been me" because both of them were "looking for something exciting, something that would satisfy."[51]

On the other hand, adults were too quick to use the specter of delinquency to try to scare teenagers onto the straight and narrow. Articles in *Youth for Christ Magazine* with titles like "Are You Headed for Delinquency?" and "You Could Be a 'J. D.'" identified everything from a rebellious spirit to particular types of clothing as danger signs of delinquency. More commonly, YFC leaders condemned teenage amusements like dancing, rock 'n' roll, and comic books because they supposedly led to teenage crime. YFC leaders also reminded middle-class teens that delinquents presented sexual dangers. Following the advice of J. Edgar Hoover, they warned young women to avoid immodest clothing and "lovers' lanes" that made them vulnerable to "sex crimes."[52] Such uses of delinquency to discipline white, middle-class Christian teenagers made delinquency seem like a communicable disease. So it should have come as no surprise to white evangelicals that "too often Christian kids have a tendency to pull their self-righteous cloaks about them so they won't get contaminated by the fellow or girl with a special problem."[53] They were just doing what adults had told them to do.

Compared to their substantial efforts to reach juvenile offenders, YFC barely scratched the surface of ministry among African Americans during the 1950s. Some Bible clubs and rallies were racially integrated in northern, midwestern, and west coast states. But in the south, when blacks were involved at all, it was through segregated clubs and rallies. In 1954 Jimmy Stroud, director of YFC in Memphis, worked with black leaders to charter a "colored" rally, but this is the only such group mentioned in the YFC records.[54] For his part, Jack Hamilton presented positive images of young African Americans on the pages of *Youth for Christ Magazine*. In 1954, he printed a story on Rafer Johnson, a four-sport varsity athlete, student body president, and Bible club member from Kingsburg, California. In the same year, Ronie Haley of Peoria, Illinois, became one of the few African American students elected to the "court" of a local YFC group. In 1955, the magazine featured a new club at a black high school in Sweetwater, Tennessee, as well as profiles of African American club presidents from Dayton, Tennessee, and Peoria, Illinois.[55] But these news items did not distinguish between segregated and integrated high schools, or make any mention of race, for that matter. Instead, Hamilton presented these students as model Christians with no sense that their "witness" was any different from that of the white students who more often appeared in the magazine. These stories and photos may have challenged some white readers to rethink their racial stereotypes. Appearing as they did just after *Brown v. Board of Education*, the stories may have also been intended as evidence that YFC was not an all-white or racist organization.

Occasionally, YFC leaders took public stands against racism, particularly when Christian racists threatened to exclude blacks from revival meetings. Gordon McLean remembered a case from the early 1950s in which a prominent pastor in Tacoma, Washington, refused to participate in a citywide youth crusade if organizers invited the black churches. McLean and the other organizers invited them anyway.[56]

More commonly, YFC leaders tried to avoid talking about race because they knew it would alienate large segments of their white audience. In 1956, when Bob Cook called on YFC staff to address "big issues" in their rallies, he cautioned that he did not mean debating segregation in the South, because this might be "meddling" and would certainly be divisive. On the other hand, he recounted an incident in which he had spoken "feebly" on the topic of smoking at a rally in Memphis. Afterwards, he apologized to local director Jimmy Stroud for potentially alienating some of his financial contributors. Stroud told him not to worry: "They don't get mad at you. They just don't pay any attention to you." Just as sermons against smoking fell on deaf ears with some Southern evangelicals, Cook sensed that preaching against segregation would convince no one and could therefore only be a liability in winning converts.[57]

Cook could lump together smoking and segregation because both were issues of teenage purity. Although they seldom said anything about it directly, white evangelical youth leaders knew that sexual fears added a significant stigma to integration. One rare exception to this general silence came in 1963, when a group of YFC staff discussed the advisability of integrating Bible clubs. They agreed that in some areas integrated clubs worked well, but worried that if such clubs fostered "inter-racial dating" it could "hinder the Club ministry."[58] These YFC leaders realized that whatever teenagers might want, white parents deeply feared interracial romances.

Like many white evangelical adults, teenage members of Youth for Christ tended to favor integration in theory, but spoke only vaguely about action steps to promote it. In 1957, a youth panel discussed the question, "What should be the Christian attitude on the segregation-integration problem?" Orma Jones of Vancouver said, "I fail to see how it is fair to isolate some people from others, simply because of the color of their skin," but called on white Christians simply to pray and to model "the spirit of understanding, tolerance, and love." Wayne Augustine of Erie, Pennsylvania, thought that the Christian "answer" was clear from Jesus' command "love thy neighbor as thyself," yet he did not spell out how to put this into practice. Benny Curtis of Jackson, Mississippi, said, "I am in favor of the advancement of the colored people," but not by integration. He claimed that "because of cultural, moral, economic, and educational" differences, "all of the Negro people with whom I have talked do not want it." The best way to help "the colored people" was to "reach them with the gospel of Christ."[59] It is probably significant that in this controlled sample of teen opinions, the editor chose to include at least one person opposed to integration. Most likely such a choice reflected a desire not to offend segregationist constituents. Even the white Christian teenagers who supported integration suggested that individual moral behavior and evangelism, not changing the system, would be the answer.

As in the case of popular music, racial prejudice combined with fears about teenage bodily purity and Cold War politics to trigger a negative reaction to the civil rights movement among white evangelical adults. Once adults associated civil rights activism with lawlessness and communism, they could not possibly support it. Like other "gradualists," white evangelical youth leaders worried about social and political disruption more than they worried about racial injustice. In 1961, Harold Myra kept a close eye on the communist youth paper *New Horizons for Youth* and sent regular bulletins on communist activities to YFC directors. Myra viewed the freedom riders and other civil rights activists with suspicion in part because the communists praised them. He noted with dismay that the communists encouraged young people to "tear down beliefs in rightly constituted authority" by participating in protests against segregation. Nor did it help when *New Horizons for Youth* actually included Youth for Christ among its list of "extreme right wing youth groups." Myra noted parenthetically, "wouldn't it be nice if we had the support of the big financial interests as they say we have?" He seemed pleased that YFC was the only religious organization denounced by the communists, since it proved that "we must be accomplishing things!"[60] Myra and other white evangelicals reasoned that if the communists supported the civil rights movement and also attacked YFC, then the civil rights movement must be suspect.

Yet it would be wrong to characterize Harold Myra or any other YFC leader as a virulent racist. In fact, it was under Myra's leadership that *Youth for Christ Magazine* began to publish articles attacking racial prejudice and discussing other social issues in the mid 1960s. YFC leaders were quick to detect a change in racial attitudes among young evangelicals and tried to hurry that change along. Myra found that younger rally directors and their teenage followers liked these new articles, but some of the older financial supporters of the movement did not.[61] This quick about-face suggests that for white evangelicals, the turning point in perceptions of the civil rights movement may have come when segregationists were finally exposed as more lawless and violent than protesters. It also dramatizes the limitations of YFC's market-driven approach to youth ministry. If the number one priority is to gather as big a crowd as possible, then controversial issues are taboo. Yet YFC leaders didn't shy away from controversial condemnations of dancing, movies, and worldly music. The real problem with integration was not that it was controversial, but that white adults feared it would corrupt their children. The obsession with teenage bodily purity made effective action for racial justice nearly impossible for conservative white evangelicals of the 1950s.

Yet many white evangelicals recognized that racism and segregation were wrong. In 1964, Larry Fuhrer authored the first article in *Youth for Christ Magazine* to tackle teenage racism, entitled "Prejudice and the Christian Teenager." Fuhrer highlighted parallels between the black experience and the experience of white Bible club members. He hoped to appeal to his readers' experiences of rejection and persecution to build empathy with minority groups. Just as sinners attacked Christians out of a sense of guilt or persecuted them for abstaining from various worldly activities, so whites persecuted blacks for being different and reminding them of their failings. Fuhrer also noted that whites often projected their own shortcomings on minorities, "so they can consider themselves clean, industrious, intelligent, capable and energetic." He admitted that while a minority group might have some genuinely objectionable traits, these could come from "social, economic, or cultural disadvantages." He concluded that "prejudice is usually a person's unconscious attempt to create a world of security," but that "as Christians we can face our world realistically."[62]

For the first time, YFC constituents were encouraged to use their sense of minority status as a source of empathy with African Americans. Yet the impulse toward sympathy could not overcome the more powerful drive toward purity. Indeed, the youth spirituality fostered in YFC valued comfort, security, and moral purity in a way that roughly paralleled the traits that Fuhrer had identified as causes of racism. During the 1950s, evangelicals like those in Youth for Christ helped add a religious component to white middle-class fears about corruption. In this world view, rock 'n' roll threatened to corrupt young bodies because it subverted them with the sensual, demonic rhythms of Africa. Integration, especially of schools, tapped religiously enhanced fears of sexual impurity, juvenile delinquency, and communism. White evangelicals had identified these very evils as key competitors for the souls and bodies of youth — and therefore as key enemies that threatened to destroy America. Even when they saw racism and class prejudices as wrong, YFC members found themselves trapped in their own middle-class, white adolescent version of Christianity that prevented them from taking action.

Evangelicalism and Youth Culture on the Eve of the Sixties

Youth leaders and teenagers created a full-fledged juvenilized version of evangelical Christianity during the 1950s. This version of Christianity embraced fun and entertainment while maintaining strict rules about bodily purity. Although God demanded "consecration," he also offered "thrills" and a personalized faith that supposedly met all the needs of the typical high school student. Teenagers embraced this new version of Christian faith in part because it was much more appealing than the version they saw among their parents. For the most part, they went along with the required abstinence from sex, drinking, smoking, and dancing, though the thrills of these vices were clearly tempting to many. It helped that as they attended weekly Bible clubs and youth rallies, they could see other young people coming to faith. They could believe that by keeping pure and carrying their Bibles to school, they served as public, bodily "witnesses" and contributed to the salvation of souls. So teenagers could link the sacrifices of their daily lives to the most important mission in the world. On the other hand, with so much emphasis on bodily purity, evangelicals found themselves stuck when it came to truly embracing juvenile delinquents and African Americans. By catering to the tastes of white, middle-class teenagers, evangelicals became captive to the prejudices and besetting sins of that cultural group.

Yet at the same time, the juvenilized version of Christianity created in Youth for Christ and similar youth ministries in the 1950s prepared evangelicalism to weather the storms of the decade to come. In an era in which young people would become increasingly disillusioned with traditional churches, evangelicals had well-established ministries outside the church walls which were devoted to reaching the indifferent. The pioneers of the 1950s also convinced most evangelicals that adapting to youth culture should be a normal part of teen evangelism, and eventually of church life itself. Teenagers who grew up in Youth for Christ during the 1950s and early 1960s were primed to accept the Jesus People movement, Christian rock music, and small groups that would be needed to reach later generations. Evangelical youth leaders popularized the idea that most cultural forms were morally neutral, a principle that would eventually be applied even to forms of entertainment like Hollywood movies and rock music. Of course, in their race to appeal to teenagers, evangelical youth leaders did not establish theological and moral criteria that might help Christians make better decisions about pop culture in the future. Still, they did create an enduring and adaptive way to sustain a conservative Christian identity in American society. Some of the growth of conservative churches over the subsequent decades would come from this ability to foster and sustain religious commitment among the young.

CHAPTER 7

Youth, Christianity, and the 1960s Apocalypse

To those who lived through it, the decade of the 1960s seemed to bring apocalyptic changes in which young people played prominent and often disturbing roles. At the beginning of the decade, college students wore coats and ties while attending weekly dinners with their dorm housemothers. By the end of the decade, long-haired, pot smoking, cursing college students occupied administrative offices and forced universities to abolish student behavior codes. The decade began with well-mannered and well-dressed African American young people staging nonviolent protests. It ended with young people smashing windows, setting fires, throwing rocks at police, and looting businesses in cities across the country. Parents and school administrators fought losing battles with teenagers over clothing styles, hair length, music, dating, sex, drugs, and support for the war in Vietnam. Adults embraced the concept of "the generation gap" as an apt description of what seemed like a new and permanent antagonism between young and old.

For many conservative Christian adults, these trends seemed at best disorienting, and at worst disgusting. At the opposite extreme, politically progressive Christians saw the youthful alienation of the age as a justifiable response to a sick society. They hoped youthful political activism might create a new and better America. Whether they see the events of the decade as liberating or destructive, Americans still look back on the sixties as an "apocalypse," a time when violent events heralded the end of one world and the beginning of another.

Yet an even better way to understand the 1960s is to recognize how the decade matched the original meaning of the word "apocalypse," which comes from a Greek word meaning not dramatic destruction, but revelation. Thus the last book of the Bible is "The Revelation (Apocalypse) of Jesus Christ." Because that book describes cataclysmic events and the end of the world, the word "apocalypse" took on those meanings. In a similar way, the dramatic events of the 1960s have often distracted us from more important truths about Americans and their society that those events revealed. The cataclysms of the 1960s dramatically revealed changes that had been percolating at least since World War II, if not earlier. The peace movement, black power, women's liberation, and the hippie counterculture all had roots in an earlier era.

It's also important to remember that only a minority of young Americans plunged into the "sex, drugs, and rock 'n' roll" or the political protests of the era. These more extreme manifestations were like the foam at the crest of a wave that was indeed sweeping over all Americans and leaving a changed landscape in its wake. The ways that ordinary Americans responded to the dramatic events of the sixties would be at least as influential in the long run as those events themselves. Even those who hated the hippies eventually accepted some elements of the youth counterculture. Everything seemed to be changing suddenly in the 1960s, but in reality, the long-term trend toward the juvenilization of American society simply became more visible.

The sixties first revealed what would be the consequences of various Christian approaches to youth culture. Some ways of managing juvenilization were nimble enough to adapt to the seismic shifts of the sixties; others were overly dependent upon the old era that was rapidly disappearing. The times revealed who would be the winners and losers when it came to motivating teenage religious commitment in the decades to come. A look back at the sixties also reveals that Christian youth ministries pioneered many of the religious trends that have come to dominate American church life in subsequent decades. Most of all, the sixties revealed that juvenilization was here to stay, and that the dilemmas of juvenilization would continue to shape American churches for the foreseeable future.

Left Behind to Pick up the Pieces:
The Black Church and Youth in the 1960s

In 1960, African American Christians launched a youth-led movement of social protest. In its initial stages, this movement was deeply Christian, nonviolent, and produced activists who were mature, courageous, and confident. By the end of the decade, the student movement had become increasingly strident and even self-destructive. Young black people became increasingly critical of the church and considerable numbers even left it behind. What had gone wrong?

Young activists became increasingly impatient with what they believed were the overly cautious tactics of older leaders like Martin Luther King Jr. For example, during the Washington March for Jobs and Freedom in 1963, a major argument took place between younger and older leaders over the proposed content of John Lewis's speech. Lewis toned down his speech but still felt good that he was able to express "defiance" through it. He even compared the civil rights movement to General Sherman's march to the sea during the Civil War — hardly a nonviolent image. Still, other members of his Student Non-Violent Coordinating Committee thought he had sold out. In addition, when foundation funds became available to the movement, older clergymen snapped up much of the $800,000 for their organizations, leaving SNCC with a mere $15,000.[1] The student leaders came to believe that, as the ones on the front lines taking the risks, they were not receiving the respect and support they deserved. And since most of the older leaders were ministers, young people who became alienated from them also became increasingly disillusioned with the church and Christian nonviolence.

As they took the movement into the Deep South, young activists endured beatings, imprisonment, and even the murder of their friends. Many white Christians eagerly joined in, or at least tacitly supported this violent opposition to civil rights. Even a good many African American Christians were not particularly enthusiastic. The full-time work of political organizing under constant threat of death took an emotional toll. Anger and fear boiled over into resentment toward the church and even toward God. As one young leader put it,

> No prayer is necessary to open this meeting. We shall be concerned with social problems and it is too late for God or the Church to pretend to have any concern. We know better.

In today's terms, many of these young people were probably suffering from post-traumatic stress disorder. Full-time activists who traveled away from their home communities suffered the most and were most vulnerable to burnout and alienation from the church. In contrast, young people who participated in the movement for shorter periods and in their home communities drew more strength from their faith and the adults in their lives and so tended to be less alienated from the church.[2]

But it is not as if the older generation intentionally abandoned the student leaders. The younger generation wanted to be as independent as possible, and they got their wish. They accomplished amazing feats: they sparked voter registration drives and brought down the walls of segregation. But in their stress and isolation, they also developed an increasingly militant and anti-Christian youth culture. In 1966 Stokely Carmichael ousted the more religious John Lewis as chairman of SNCC, denouncing him as "a Christ-loving damn fool." Some members of SNCC started calling Martin Luther King Jr. "De Lawd" as they distanced themselves from the piety that had launched their movement. Others, like Cleveland Sellers, tried to promote black liberation as a replacement for what they considered to be the outmoded Christian spirituality of the black community. For their part, older leaders coined the phrase "freedom high" to describe the way some young activists recklessly put themselves in danger. Instead of helping people overcome anger and fear with Christian love, young leaders like Carmichael took to stirring up resentment. In 1967 his speaking tour of Nashville campuses sparked three days of riots. SNCC eventually collapsed because of heated ideological battles and internal power struggles. Its leaders not only kicked out white members, but also distanced themselves from the local black citizens they were supposedly representing.[3]

Meanwhile, some older leaders in the movement strained to put a positive spin on the increasingly militant movement youth culture. Kelly Miller Smith hoped that "the terms of the rebellion of today's youth are properly spiritual." He did admit that "there are justifiable reservations about some of the settled conclusions youthful, frustrated, inexperienced minds may reach." But he blamed adults: "their frustrations are, in large measure, due to the fact that we have failed them." He noted that "although many of today's youths will not admit it, the nonviolence discipline is closely akin to the words of One who said, 'but I say unto you, Love your enemies, bless them that curse you, do good to them that hate you, and pray for them which despitefully use you, and persecute you.'" He concluded, "The young people of our day are in quest of something. Their quest confronts us with a challenge."[4] Language of spiritual searching among young people was everywhere in the 1960s. But the leaders of SNCC were not searching for ways to forge a stronger relationship with the black church and its spirituality. Instead their political activism was spiraling out of control in anti-Christian and self-destructive ways. Because church leaders like Smith had idealized the youth movement at its beginnings, they could not bring themselves to criticize this emerging juvenilized form of civil rights politics.

Disenchantment with adults in the black church was not limited to radicals and revolutionaries. When Christian educator Benjamin Perkins interviewed young people in ten different schools across the country, he uncovered considerable criticisms of the church. Many young people complained that the church seemed adult-centered and unresponsive to their needs. One student observed, "the main reason most black ministers don't do more for black youth is that they are frightened . . . they're afraid of the older black adults' reactions." A sixteen-year-old complained, "Unlike music and fashion, the black Christian church has not kept up with the times. To reach us, religion should be geared to us." Most of all, these black teenagers wanted adults to listen to them and give them more personalized attention. One pastor's son said that ministers "should spend some time with us young black people, learn what we like and most of all, learn what we need . . . my own father doesn't know me, much less the other young people of his church."[5] Young African Americans wanted more personal attention and understanding from adults, but felt they were not getting it.

Even those who called on the black church to do more for its young people sometimes had little to offer in the way of innovative approaches. Perkins noted that "too many black leaders still operate on the assumption that the present problems of black youth's rejection of the Christian church can be solved by an expansion of presently existing church services." He called for better Christian education, noting that only 20 percent of the young people he surveyed could pass a simple Bible literacy test. But he did not describe in any detail his ideas for reforming Christian education. Similarly, Dr. Horace N. Mays told his fellow black Baptists in 1966 that "we are obligated to explore every available channel of usefulness in an effort to help solve the vexing problems that besiege our youth" but offered little specific advice for how to proceed with that task.[6]

Even during the height of the student civil rights movement, many young African Americans continued their lives much as they had before, focusing on getting an education and having fun. After his release from prison in Mississippi, John Lewis enrolled in Fisk University and wrote a scathing editorial in the student paper denouncing "black bourgeoisie groups." One day, while walking across the Fisk campus, he stumbled upon a fraternity hazing in progress, complete with pledges in dog collars "barking like hounds." He recalled, "It struck me as completely distasteful, very disappointing, very distressing, to see these young black men swept up in this trivial silliness at the very moment that people their own age, young men and women just like them, were risking their lives down in Mississippi." Cleveland Sellers remembers that his college roommate told him, "You and Martin Luther King can take care of the demonstrating and protesting. I have *no* use for them." All he wanted from life was "a degree, a good job, a good woman, and a good living."[7] African American leaders either neglected this group or found it hard to bridge the gap between the black church culture and their youth culture.

Not all African American young people got caught up in either trivial youth culture pursuits or the civil rights movement. Considerable numbers of the best and brightest left the church behind to pursue the new educational and career opportunities opening up before them. Like their counterparts in the civil rights movement, these young people were carrying out instructions they had learned at home and in church. Pam Shaw was typical of her generation in remembering her mother drumming into her the idea that "you could be whatever you wanted to be." Upon their arrival at state universities, especially in the later 1960s, these upwardly mobile young people encountered an exciting world in which black students were staging sit-ins of university administrative offices. Such protests swept the nation and led to the hiring of black faculty members and the establishment of black studies departments. The slogans "black power" and "black is beautiful" were in the air. How did the churches respond? Students like Beverly Hall Lawrence saw them as weak and stuck in old ways:

> My generation was one that fled churches filled with those who appeared to us to be helpless, sitting and waiting for (a white) God to intervene and solve problems for them. Many of my friends and I admit now that at times the idea of going to church was simply embarrassing, because it taught people to wait for change to come.

These young people could have just as easily celebrated the Christian elements in the movement for change. But they chose to criticize the church in part because of what they had heard from their young, militant black power heroes. Living through the pain caused by the assassinations of Martin Luther King and Malcolm X as well as the disillusionment caused by the failure to integrate schools and secure economic equality, some lost faith in God completely. Sheila Dixon remembered, "I looked around at all the ills in the world and began wondering, how could there be a God?" Lawrence's book documents a common experience of members of her generation: many upwardly mobile young blacks of the late sixties and early seventies left the church. Although some would return twenty years later, in the meantime the church lost many young, gifted leaders who could have helped the church weather turbulent times.[8]

Meanwhile, other institutions in the African American community that could have helped young people were not faring well either. As some of the barriers erected by segregation and discrimination came down, upwardly mobile African Americans moved out of the inner cities in unprecedented numbers. Black-owned businesses hit hard times as much of their customer base disappeared. Schools serving African American children faced increasing internal and external pressures. Funding dried up as more and more businesses and wealthier homeowners fled the inner cities. Many of those families that remained were the ones most trapped in poverty and the problems it brings. The behavior of children and teenagers in schools changed too. Virginia Bright, a Sunday school and high school teacher in the Nashville area, remembered a distinct change in the behavior of her students beginning around the mid-sixties. Young people went from being "very submissive" to displaying "a bit more freedom, a bit more speaking up." While this change had some positive elements, it also created more discipline problems in schools, distracting from educational efforts. And many young people became increasingly cynical about their ability to escape poverty through education.

Even the limited integration of schools that took place often did little to help African American students and teachers. Bright had to take matters into her own hands to deal with racial slurs from a white student; her white principal had told her to not do anything to discipline students who broke rules or insulted her. Bright also remembered being passed over as department head in favor of a much younger, less experienced white teacher. Even worse, in one integrated school in which she worked, none of the African American students could afford the fees required for membership in extracurricular activities.[9] In short, integration did little to overcome racism in those early days. During the 1960s, the African American community urgently needed its best leaders to be creatively addressing the problems of its young people, but many of those leaders were bogged down in protracted battles with whites who did their best to make sure that if institutions had to integrate, white people were still going to be very much in charge.

African American leaders found themselves in crisis mode by the late sixties and early seventies. With their communities in turmoil and their best young people leaving for what they hoped would be greener pastures, the church was left behind to pick up the pieces. The challenges to the African American community and its churches were unprecedented — and not of their own making. Some significant losses among young people were almost inevitable.

Yet to a surprising degree, the black churches seemed paralyzed and unable to respond creatively to these challenges. In sharp contrast to white leaders, African Americans did not invest heavily in retooling their youth work during the 1960s. The decade revealed that the African American church had become mesmerized by the student civil rights movement and unable to see beyond it to the needs of ordinary young people. Even when they devoted their best efforts to youth work, black church members were all too often abandoned by their children. Yet it was Christian adults who had taught their young people that "you can be anything you want to be" and that the passions of the young should set the agenda for the church.

Leaving the Church to Get in on the Revolution

The 1960s revealed that white Methodist youth leaders were not as good as they thought at interpreting the signs of the times. They thought that naturally idealistic young people would embrace the activism of the sixties. A few did, but for the most part, the sixties generation of white Methodists was not much more active than their predecessors of the "silent generation."

The ongoing struggle to mobilize young people for social action revealed that liberal Methodists believed in their ideal of social justice more than they believed in the church itself. They ever more stridently denounced the church as an obstacle to true Christianity. At gatherings like the 1961 North American Ecumenical Youth Assembly, young Methodists heard strong statements denouncing denominations as a hindrance to Christian integrity and mission.[10]

By the end of the decade, Methodists and other mainline Protestant churches began to hemorrhage young people. The sixties revealed that neither social activists nor more ordinary young people found much to attract them to the Methodist church. At a deeper level, the successes and failures of liberal Protestant youth leaders during the 1960s exposed a lot about the limits of sixties-style political activism, especially as a tool for recruiting and retaining young people in the church.

Around 1960, national Methodist youth leaders entered a major phase of reevaluation of their work, provoked in large part by their limited success in mobilizing young people for social action during the previous decade. They formed an Interboard Staff on Youth Work to discuss ministry philosophy and coordinate their efforts. This group commissioned several position papers and launched a series of experimental projects called the "Youth Exploration." In the report that recommended the Youth Exploration, the committee condemned the typical youth program for contributing to a process of decay in which the church was "losing its soul" and becoming "synonymous with society." Yet they also complained that Christians had been too concerned with "preserving an institution" and needed to move out into the world.[11] This confusion about whether the church was to remain distinct from the world or be absorbed into it would prove crucial in the decade ahead.

Liberal Protestant youth professionals like those who ran the Methodist Youth Department actually became some of the earliest promoters of youth rebellion as a cure for society's ills. As we have seen, by the late 1950s, Methodist Youth Department staff members became convinced that the "organized society" was producing a generation of politically apathetic conformists. They prescribed a little healthy rebellion as the antidote not just for youthful apathy, but for the problems of society itself. By the early sixties, Christian education departments in colleges and seminaries as well as manuals for local youth leaders commonly drew on social critics like David Riesman, Margaret Mead, Edgar Friedenberg, Paul Goodman, and William Whyte.[12] Methodist youth leaders also turned to Erik Erikson's model of adolescent development that demanded a time of struggle towards adult identity.[13] Ross Snyder, a professor of religious education at Chicago Theological Seminary, recommended a new style of education he called the "Ministry of Meanings." When he turned this idea into a curriculum, the book cover showed Scrabble tiles arranged to spell interlocking words that included "Experiencings," "Identity," "Meaning," and "Risk."[14] As these buzzwords suggest, liberal religious educators combined psychology and existentialism in what they hoped would be a potent antidote to the deadening effects of modernity upon youth.[15] Experts in adolescent psychology and critics of the organized society all tended to glorify individual choice and autonomy and to portray institutions as obstacles to achieving healthy adult identity. As early as 1960, it became commonplace for national Methodist youth leaders to argue that teenagers needed to be "free to rebel." The institutional church and its youth programs could now be condemned for constraining this healthy process of self-definition through struggle and rebellion.[16] This view that set adolescent identity and institutions in opposition to one another took hold among liberal Methodist leaders well before the dramatic days of the late 1960s "youth rebellion."

The leaders of the Methodist Youth Department had always struggled with the problem of how to create a prophetic youth movement within denominational structures. In 1964 and 1965 Methodist youth leaders established several "intentional communities" as part of their Youth Exploration. The idea for this new kind of Christian community came from sources as diverse as the Methodist youth work camps of the 1940s and 1950s and the "secular theology" of Harvey Cox. Small groups of high school and college students lived together for ten weeks in the summer. Participants pooled their money and served the poor. They also shared a common life of prayer and study. They read and discussed books like Bonhoeffer's *Life Together* and Cox's *The Secular City*. These authors, in very different ways, called the church to abandon its separation from the world, by embracing "secularism" or "religionless Christianity." Young people in these "intentional communities" participated in new and exciting forms of socially engaged Christianity. But they also learned that "normal" church life and its structures were all but useless.[17]

Liberal Methodists not only embraced the civil rights movement, they interpreted it as a further indictment of the institutional church and its youth. Socially concerned young Methodists especially worried that the civil rights revolution would leave them behind if they stuck with a church that still could not agree to end segregation within its own structure. In 1963, the National Conference of Methodist Youth appointed John Newman as "Youth Associate for Race Relations." His job was simply to act as a participant observer in the civil rights movement and report back to the Conference on how young Methodists could contribute. Newman's assessment was pessimistic. He doubted that the Methodist Youth Fellowship could work with civil rights organizations or "any other social or political action group" because the average Methodist teenager only knew "his own middle-class white 'churchy' world." Even worse, Newman believed that the average white teenager could not endure any encounter with difference, because such an experience would be too threatening to his identity.[18] Newman was right about one thing: there was plenty of racism in the church. But he and his fellow progressives seemed blind to their own prejudice against "normal" church life and the people who lived it. Despite at least four decades of effort on the part of liberal Methodists, the "middle-class white 'churchy' world" of mainstream Methodism remained intact. Perhaps it endured because it performed some important and even healthy religious functions for adults and young people. But such a possibility was not one progressive Methodists bothered to consider.

Young Methodist liberals correctly judged that much of their predecessors' efforts had gone into preserving an institution. But by mid-decade some of them took the further step of claiming that the key to spiritual vitality and social effectiveness was to abandon that institution. Linda Hutchinson, Judy Lewis, and Tom Welch spent the summer of 1966 traveling the country as representatives of the National Conference of Methodist Youth. They too were disappointed at the "apathy" and racism they saw among young Methodists, which led to "youth groups that went nowhere and accomplished nothing." These activists found teenage apathy especially tragic because they thought that "social revolution is a given in our world." Progressive politics and "revolution" were everything to young Christians like these. The church meant little to them by comparison. They concluded that young Methodists should stop serving the "institutional church" and start working in secular social service organizations. Instead of building up the church, they wanted to "lose our identity and become reconciled with the people of the world." They questioned the assumption that youth "can or even want to become full members of the laity." While these ideas could become a valuable resource for renewal and reform in the church, their impact would be dissipated if young people like these simply gave up on the church. Even worse, the idea that great things can be accomplished without institutions was a naïve and adolescent way to view the nature of human society and change. Yet by the mid 1960s, the young Methodists most on board with the progressive Christian social agenda spoke as if they were ready to abandon the church. Of course, such rhetoric was just the latest in a long string of attempts to shake up their white, middle-class constituents. Not all liberal young people actually abandoned the church. But by the late sixties, even those who stayed became increasingly antagonistic, staging protests at Methodist conferences.[19]

Other young Methodists found the anti-institutional trend bewildering. In August 1967, 125 elected representatives attended the National Conference of the Methodist Youth Fellowship held in San Francisco. They visited the Methodist Glide Urban Center, where they participated in jazz worship services that attracted people described by one young participant as "homosexuals, hippies, drug addicts, drunks, Negroes from the slums, and prostitutes." Arthur Foster, a theologian, and Don Garrity, a sociologist, both assured the young people that the church needed to discard much of its traditional structure in order to serve the city. The teenagers worked at a soup kitchen and went on a guided tour of the Haight-Ashbury district. They brought soap bubbles, balloons, and banners as their contribution to the hippie scene. The encounter provoked cultural vertigo for some, especially when they visited the Psychedelic Shop's meditation room. Seventeen-year-old Johnny Cook of Kingston, Tennessee, said, "It was scary, particularly since you don't know what they were doing." Still, at the conclusion of the tour, their anarchist "Digger" guide, Don Cochran, said,

> I'm surprised. I really am. Who would have thought they'd go in the meditation room. That really blew my mind. It shows, I guess, that I'm thinking in stereotypes too.[20]

Later, Johnny Cook wrote a report on his experiences at the conference in which he expressed appreciation for being immersed in the city, but judged that "instead of Glide Methodist converting people to the way of the church . . . the people were converting Glide Methodist." Here was a young Methodist who supported his church's social concern; he got the message of the conference that "the institutional world of the church and the secular world of man should be united," but he was not sure he agreed.[21]

The contrast between Johnny Cook and civil rights activists like John Newman suggests the range of options created by Methodist youth programs in the postwar era. A Methodist teenager of the early 1960s who faithfully internalized the message of national leaders would most likely see herself at the center of a dramatic contest for the future of the world, which depended heavily on her existential choice and commitment. She would be eager to work for social justice outside church structures, and would have only a vague understanding of traditional doctrines about Jesus, sin, and salvation. She would view America as a land of injustice and militarism, and might wonder if Russia had something to teach the United States. She would value organizations that operated "democratically" and would be familiar with communal living. She would have spent long hours discussing racism and segregation and may have even participated in in-

terracial activities. She would be familiar with the concepts of "nonviolence" and "direct action." She might well labor under the fear that her
church was impotent in an age of revolution. She would likely see institutions as obstacles to positive social change and personal development.

In other words, such a young Methodist would be sympathetic to
many of the aspirations of the New Left on America's campuses. Not surprisingly, one study uncovered connections between Christian existentialism, the social gospel movement, and the New Left at the University of
Texas. Methodists figured prominently in this tale. At national conferences
and through campus ministry centers across the country, Methodist and
other liberal Protestant youth leaders helped create the college political activism of the sixties.[22] Ideas that seemed radical at the time, such as racial
integration or equal rights for women, have now been embraced in the
wider culture. In that sense, mainline Protestant youth leaders of the sixties could be said to have succeeded in their project of liberalizing church
and society by influencing young people. Of course, a good number of
these same young people became increasingly disillusioned with the
church itself. Others just left the church behind, since it no longer provided them something unavailable in the secular world. And after all, even
the youth leaders who represented the church in their eyes were telling
them to leave the church and get in on the revolution.

Meanwhile, most Methodist young people were not radicals; they were
more likely to be spiritually adrift. One study of a heavily Methodist community in New Jersey demonstrates that many in the high school class of
1966 wore their Methodism lightly. They tended to participate freely in the
high school culture of dancing and drinking. They showed little political
awareness, and certainly did not get the messages sent by the liberal Youth
Department. While at college, mostly at non-elite institutions, they were
relatively untouched by student radicalism and the counterculture. They
did not oppose the Vietnam War on principle; rather, they tried to find
safe ways to serve by enlisting in the National Guard or the Coast Guard.
They often felt stifled by their high school environment, and consistently
reported that teachers and guidance counselors showed little personal interest in their talents and future prospects.[23]

By banking on the supposedly innate idealism and political activism
of youth, national Methodist youth leaders and their counterparts in other
denominations contributed to the decline of the mainline that would become apparent in the 1970s. Much of the growth of the mainline denominations during the 1950s came through the addition of young families ea-

ger to find a spiritual home that was not too demanding. Even in the 1960s, these churches continued to receive members fleeing more stifling religious traditions. But the children in these families found few reasons for loyalty to an institution that made no strong lifestyle demands and officially questioned its own reason for existence. The average local MYF program sustained youthful loyalty in a supportive environment, but once society abandoned the expectation that "good people" went to church, its charms could fade. Such expectations did decline during the 1960s — a transition no doubt eased by the qualms of the church's own leaders about the institutional church.

Viewed in the longer sweep of history, postwar mainline Protestant youth groups emerged as a halfway house between the old-time religion and the more recent trend toward being spiritual without being tied to any institution. While they searched for the magic key that would unlock the supposedly inexhaustible social idealism of youth, mainline leaders neglected the more basic question of why young people should stay in their churches in the meantime. In the absence of clearly articulated core beliefs sustained by a vibrant adolescent spirituality, other options seemed too appealing to young people. Liberal Methodist leaders faced a difficult choice: they could build loyalty to an institution that seemed content with racism and other injustices, or they could build alternative communities of social action. In effect they chose neither, preferring to denounce the institutional church while only dabbling in other forms of religious community. Mainline Protestant youth leaders made significant contributions to the progressive legacy of the sixties by adapting the faith to the student radicals of the decade. But in the process they left the majority of young Methodists without a vibrant form of the faith that fit the realities of their lives.

Too Little Too Late:
Catholic Youth Work and the Collapse of the Catholic Ghetto

The decade of the 1960s was especially turbulent for American Catholics. Not only did they have to endure the political protests, assassinations, urban riots, sexual revolution, and other dramatic events that shook all Americans, they also lived through the aftermath of the Second Vatican Council. Mass was suddenly in English, eating meat on Fridays was no longer a sin, and reformers of all stripes felt empowered to push their agendas.

Although it launched many positive reforms, the council also provoked a crisis of authority in the minds of many Catholics. How could eating meat on Fridays be a serious sin one day, and not a sin the next? If religious leaders like priests and nuns were questioning the church and abandoning their vows, what were lay people supposed to think about the church's authority? Even for those who longed for simpler times, unquestioning obedience was no longer an option, since church leaders could not even agree on what the new rules required. It was especially disorienting to see the church in turmoil at the very time when everything else in society also seemed to be shaking. Catholic identity, which had seemed so stable, was in flux.

Besieged on every side, Catholic youth leaders needed all their creativity and courage to adapt the faith to the changing needs of young people. Some pioneered new forms of youth ministry that juvenilized the faith in ways that held promise for the future. But because adults were so divided, these efforts never won the wide support they would have needed to succeed. Meanwhile, to make matters worse, other Catholic young people and adults seemed eager to tear down the spiritually formative institutions of the Catholic ghetto without much thought for what would replace them.

Despite the dominance of all-American Catholicism and the defensiveness of the Catholic ghetto during the 1950s, a significant minority of young Catholics had grown up with a desire for a new kind of Catholic faith that was fully engaged with the world. Some of those young people became influential youth leaders in the 1960s. For example, Monsignor Frederick J. Stevenson, the new director of the NCWC Youth Department, initiated a movement to reform Catholic youth work in the early 1960s, and he was not alone. Articles in the Catholic press denouncing ineffective CYO programs proliferated.[24] Like their Methodist counterparts, these Catholic reformers bemoaned teenage apathy and tried to encourage teenagers to rebel against the deadening structures of "mass society." Catholic sociologist Fr. Andrew Greeley spoke at numerous youth events in the early sixties promoting the message of his 1961 book, *Strangers in the House*. Greeley insisted that only an apostolic program like the Young Christian Students could overcome the materialism and conformity of the young "organization man" Catholic. Youth panels at the 1961 CYO convention discussed topics like "Conformity vs. Individuality — Do Catholic Teenagers Dare 'To Be Different'?" and "How Catholic are Catholics? Does the Catholic Youth Keep His Identity in Our Society?"[25] Youth work reformers wanted to push teenagers to forge a new sort of Catholic identity characterized by social service, not by withdrawal into the Catholic ghetto.

Some young Catholics shared their elders' obsession with apathy and took on a sense of their own importance for the future of the church and the nation. At the 1963 national CYO convention, Francis Darigan identified "Materialism, Communism, and I Don't Care-ism" as the three great enemies precipitating the "moral degradation and indolence" of American society. Catholic teenagers felt the pressure adults were placing on them to save the world. As one 1964 high school graduate put it:

> In High School we were told over and over that we were the hope of the future; the triumph of America in its technological and ideological war with Communism was entirely in our hands. I began to feel that I was the most important commodity of the gross national product.[26]

Youth work reformers took heart from stirrings of social concern among the young. Leadership training programs designed to produce socially concerned young Catholics proliferated. In Minneapolis, Fr. Joseph Baglio created the Contact Leaders' Corps, which brought together outstanding young Catholics for a three-day seminar intended to deepen their personal faith and make them into community service leaders. During the seminar, the participants lived as a "family" at the Youth Center and participated in a communal life of worship and service. This experience of communal living paralleled Protestant "intentional communities" of the era. After the seminar, a team of six full-time lay workers continued to meet in small groups with the teenage participants. Members of the Contact Leaders' Corps in turn led their own cells for young apostles in their schools. These young people collected food for the needy, served as Big Brothers, and taught catechism classes. In the summers, the Contact Leaders' Corps mobilized students for the "Peace Corps, Junior Grade" and sent them out to work in Grail centers, Native American missions, the Chicago Friendship House, and the Minneapolis House of Charity for transient men. Contact members also participated in interracial and interfaith projects several years before the Vatican Council endorsed such activities.[27]

Some Catholic teenagers also seemed to be embracing the civil rights movement. The 1961 CYO convention featured a teen panel on the topic "Racial Relations and Teen Attitudes." The National CYO Board, made up of teenage and young adult officers, passed a resolution endorsing the Student Non-Violent Coordinating Committee in 1962. In Washington, D.C., Rev. Geno C. Baroni led a parish Catholic Action group that mobilized young adults to help organize the March for Jobs and Freedom in 1963.

Other young Catholics participated in a "Behold Your Brother" march in Kansas City in which an interracial, interfaith group of 400 young people descended on City Hall singing "C'mon people and smile on your brother/ Let's see you get together and love one another — Right Now!"[28] The "silent generation" seemed to have passed the baton to a more activist one.

Yet there were signs that most Catholic teenagers did not fit the stereotype of socially concerned sixties youth. In an article describing his successes in mobilizing young Catholics for civil rights, Fr. Baroni asked, "are we to continue to foster in our 'social-life'-oriented youth activity the development of middle-class, status-conscious young Catholics?"[29] Comparing his adolescence in the 1930s to that of the teenagers of 1964, Andrew Greeley wrote, "in my day, teenagers weren't generally so apathetic, but none of us were so dedicated as these few, either." He argued that a feeling of impotence combined with affluence to rob most teenagers of their "moral outrage." In other words, he assumed that "moral outrage" was normal for adolescents, while apathy was an anomaly to be explained. Like other youth work reformers of the era, he blamed parents:

> They want to go into lay mission work, or teach catechism in a Negro parish, and their parents are horrified. The most tragic thing I've seen in dealing with young people is seeing their ideals crushed by adults who force their children into the same ruts that they themselves are in.[30]

Many parents probably were suspicious of the new push toward socially concerned Catholicism. But teenagers resisted it as well. It was teenage interest that kept panels on communism and going steady on the agenda of CYO conferences and did not allow social justice concerns to dominate.[31] Merton Strommen's study of Lutheran youth must have troubled youth leaders when it appeared in the Catholic press in 1964. Strommen found that teenagers' top concerns clustered into several categories: "family, opposite sex, personal faith, self acceptance, acceptance by others, conflict of standards and morality." Strommen admitted that these concerns "define a pretty small world" and suggested that "the church must be in the business of creating problems" as well as solving them, since teenagers did not naturally concern themselves with social issues.[32] Yet like their liberal Protestant counterparts, progressive Catholics ignored such evidence and clung to the mistaken belief that most young people were eager to embrace a life of sacrificial social service.

But in fact, the reform agenda made little headway in the average parish. Throughout the 1960s, the majority of local CYO clubs operated on the old model that stressed keeping teenagers Catholic by keeping them busy. Peter Kesling of Seattle won the Catholic Youth of the Year Award in 1963 for his role in leading just such a local CYO branch. Catholic youth in Seattle sponsored a full round of dances, banquets, athletics, contests, and panel discussions. These Catholic teenagers served their parish community by "baby-sitting at Masses, mowing the church lawn when the custodian gets sick, helping a family move furniture, building a stage, running miles of errands." Similarly, a 1964 profile of the CYO at St. John the Baptist Parish in Kenmore, New York, noted that it operated "better than many a big business." This CYO club recruited from a pool of 800 young people and raised $12,000 each year. Dances, plays, communion breakfasts, Catholic Youth week celebrations, and Sports Night banquets drew crowds of one hundred or more. Neither of these exemplary groups paid much attention to social concern, although they did sponsor a few charitable projects. Even a reformer like Youth Department director Msgr. Frederick Stevenson felt obliged to praise such traditional groups, which obviously appealed to a significant segment of young Catholics.[33]

As late as 1969, National CYO President Mike McGown complained that most local groups were still "dance-of-the-month clubs," and that his fellow national CYO officers were tired of convention panels on "how to have a better CYO." Instead, they wanted to push racial integration and service to the poor, and to inspire young Catholics to get out and make a difference in their communities.[34] Despite nine years of advocacy during a time when youthful activism seemed to be on the rise everywhere in American society, Catholic reformers had failed to convince most teenagers to get on board.

At the same time, the traditional CYO model was not exactly thriving. Numerous influences inside and outside the church were undermining it. First, young Catholics seemed increasingly unwilling to abide by the church's teachings on sex. In 1961 the Legion of Decency conducted a nationwide survey of 6,000 Catholic teenagers' views on entertainment. Only 37 percent of Catholic teens consulted the Legion of Decency ratings before going to the movies, and as many as 39 percent read "immoral" books or magazines at least once a month. Even worse, many Catholic teens frequented drive-in theaters, even though they admitted that they knew church teaching warned them away from such "near occasions of sin." By 1968, a survey of CYO members in Brooklyn found that 62 percent of the boys and 28 percent of the girls thought it was fine for boys to have premarital sex, while 46 percent of the boys and 13 percent of the girls thought it was acceptable for girls. Only girls still seemed to be accepting church teaching. Although it was difficult to get reliable information about how many Catholic teenagers were engaging in premarital sex, many youth leaders assumed that it was a growing problem. A few called for drastic measures to teach sexual purity in more positive ways, but such proposals never gained much traction until after the sexual revolution had already done its work.[35]

Second, teenagers increasingly found traditional Catholic devotions uninspiring — and some youth work reformers urged this trend along. At the 1963 CYO convention, President Francis Darigan felt the need to defend traditional devotions to his fellow youth delegates, insisting that the CYO had no place for anyone who "thinks it is foolish or childish to carry a rosary, to make a visit to the blessed sacrament, or thinks it is nonsense to receive the Sacraments or make a novena." But youth work reformer Albert Nimeth insisted that teenagers found devotions "stuffy." He advocated teaching them that "the spiritual life does not consist in a multitude of devotional practices" and that it should be characterized by "virility," not sentimentality. Reformers associated traditional prayer practices with a feminine, weak spirituality ill-suited to engage the modern world, and assumed that traditional devotions appealed to girls more than boys. Innovative youth leaders tried to replace traditional devotions with youth masses, but like attempts to reform sexual teaching, these experiments often faced local resistance from parents and priests.[36]

Third, Catholic youth leaders overreacted to the anti-institutional and anti-authoritarian trends among 1960s young adults and scrapped anything that smacked of indoctrination, even for younger teenagers. Catholic youth leaders noticed that young people seemed less willing to listen to adults than ever before. For example, a 1966 survey of boys in a Jesuit high school revealed that one-fourth of the graduating class no longer considered themselves Catholics, while twice that number said they did not believe in "organized churches." Four-fifths of the boys disagreed with the church's teaching on birth control. Yet these trends were not simply the result of external pressures. As early as 1961, Catholic youth experts had warned adults not to try to impose their will on teenagers because "few groups of adolescents will choose to remain under adult domination."[37] Perhaps because of their own frustrations with the conservatism of the Catholic ghetto, youth work reformers were not just responding to a rebellious trend among teenagers — they were urging it along.

In their rush to be relevant and to escape the perils of indoctrination, Catholic educators sometimes went too far. In 1967, Catholic youth expert Fr. Joseph McGloin, S. J., observed, "I have encountered religion classes which consisted only of discussion where the teacher said nothing, corrected nothing and taught nothing." By the late sixties and early seventies, discussions of films portraying social problems like racism and poverty became popular. Even when teenagers found these sessions engaging, they seldom learned much distinctively Catholic theology. Experiments with ecumenical youth activities in the late sixties also led to the production of generic Christian education materials with little distinctively Catholic content.[38] And worst of all, American Catholics no longer came close to agreeing on what their faith was, so they were hardly prepared to pass it on to the next generation in a coherent fashion.

Meanwhile, youth work pioneers created new programs that promised to juvenilize the faith in creative ways. One such pioneer was Fr. Peter Armstrong of San Francisco, who wanted to make his youth retreats more effective. While discussing retreat problems with CYO members, Armstrong casually threw out the comment, "it's too bad you kids can't give the retreats." The idea sparked interest in his team of young leaders, and with the help of some insights from the Cursillo movement, the "Search for Christian Maturity" was born in March 1963.[39] Like the Cursillo, the Search weekend aimed to revitalize the faith of nominal Catholics through an intensive experience of Christian community living. The key innovation was to have young adults give the talks and lead the retreat. Armstrong and his team carefully controlled the environment. They segregated the Search weekends by sex, and made sure that no more than four participants came from the same high school. Once at the camp, they split up friends in the room and discussion-group assignments. Young people led the discussion sessions that followed each talk, and the adults could not even sit in on these groups.[40]

The Search weekend often revitalized teenage loyalty to the church. One of the earliest searchers said, "the influence, manliness, and maturity of the young adults, who are so close to us in age, showed me that I have a place and responsibility just as they in the Apostolate of Christ." During the day on Saturday, each discussion group made a visit to the chapel and their young adult leader showed them how to pray spontaneous prayers. Students learned that they should be active participants in the Mass, a theme that anticipated the main thrust of post-Vatican II liturgical spirituality. Search weekends took advantage of the permissive atmosphere of the times and incorporated into the Mass pop music like "Kum Bah Yah" and a Christianized version of "Blowin' in the Wind" with a chorus that went, "The answer, my friend, is living in all men/The answer is living in all men." All the innovations seemed justified when on the last day of the retreat the group readily absorbed a two-hour talk on the sacraments. Once they got home, some participants attended classes to learn how to lead a Search weekend, others taught catechism classes, and still others participated in periodic follow-up meetings.[41] The Search weekend was such a success that the NCWC Youth Department promoted it in its publications and conferences. Similar intensive leadership development programs emerged in other places.[42]

The Search weekend and its imitators succeeded through aggressive juvenilization of Catholic piety and social concern. The retreat capitalized on the growing desire for community, autonomy, and emotional intimacy among American teenagers. It also played into an emerging teen spirituality that preferred "searching" over indoctrination. And it perpetuated the myth that young people needed to do everything themselves and would not listen to adult leaders. The whole package was a sixties-style "happening" complete with emotionally intense experiences, popular music, and film. Indeed, activities like the Search weekend helped create these religious tastes among the sixties generation.

Despite their limitations, intensive youth formation programs like the Search weekend were the best thing going in Catholic youth work during the 1960s. An all-out effort to help every Catholic teenager experience this kind of revitalized faith and sustain it through follow-up programs would have been the best hope for weathering the storms of the late sixties. But Search weekends and similar programs worked best when numbers were small, usually no more than fifty people at a time. Even the most active dioceses only sponsored ten to twenty Searches per year. So the vast majority of Catholic teenagers never benefited from the Search experience. Also, leaders of the Search movement admitted that such retreats would only be effective if adults and teenagers invested their time in providing follow-up activities that could make the gains permanent. Yet effective follow-up programs were rare, and attracted even fewer teenagers than the retreats themselves.[43]

The very existence of the Search program as a separate retreat experience demonstrated that normal parish life was inhospitable to its ideals and methods. Indeed, a good many Catholic parents of the late 1960s angrily fought against anything that seemed to be connected to the new youth counterculture. Mary Reed Newland, a Catholic religious education expert, received hate mail in the late sixties for allowing her sons to wear their hair long. Catholic parents who bitterly condemned young people for wearing long hair were not likely to embrace radical new ways to do youth ministry.[44]

But the real reason that programs like the Search weekend did not succeed as well as they might have was that by the late sixties, Catholic adults were actually investing less of their time and money in young people than they had in the previous two decades. In the early 1970s, Catholic youth leader Rev. William McNulty noted that many of the priests and religious sisters who had recently renounced their vows had been involved in youth work and teaching. The spectacle of their teachers and youth leaders renouncing their vows probably had a devastating effect on many young people. It certainly marked the end of an era. McNulty concluded, "the days of a parish being organized around the school, the Holy Name Society, the Altar & Rosary Society and the Youth Club with the youngest associate [pastor] being in charge of youth activities are history."[45] The upheavals of the sixties traumatized not just priests and sisters, but also rank-and-file Catholic adults. With so many adults questioning their own faith and relationship to the institutional church, there was a sudden collapse of adult investment in youth work. Clear answers to young people's questions about the faith and what it meant to be Catholic were in especially short supply.

A 1973 report on the "Status of the Youth Apostolate" in the Archdiocese of Chicago summarized the results of ten years of tumult: "Frankly, the picture is not an encouraging one." Catholic school enrollments had declined despite an increase in the teenage population. Young Catholics weren't learning about their faith in extracurricular catechism classes either, since "CCD programs on the high school level have almost ceased to exist." Young people no longer went to confession. Many had stopped attending mass, and those who did attend found plenty to criticize. Meanwhile, YCS, YCW, CISCA, and Marian sodalities had "disappeared" as well. Some teenagers seemed willing to participate in Catholic youth groups when they were available, but few adult sponsors could be found to lead them. Scouting and athletics seemed to be surviving the best, but these activities provided little spiritual content or doctrinal instruction.[46] The institutions of the Catholic ghetto were collapsing due to lack of interest on the part of both teenagers and adults.

In the end, few youth leaders mourned the passing of the Catholic ghetto, even though it left devastation in its wake. Writing to his fellow youth leaders in 1971, Rev. P. David Finks could assume agreement when he looked back with amazement on the late-fifties world of "Mary-like Fashions." "For all the tumult of today, thank God, we have moved away from the 'never-never land' of the antiseptic Catholic ghetto," he wrote.[47] Yet whether they eagerly escaped the ghetto or suffered through its dramatic collapse, most young Catholics of the late 1960s did not receive a coherent spiritual formation powerful enough to produce enduring commitment to their church. Research on the Vatican II generation indicates that members of that generation conceived of their religious identity in less institutional terms than did the previous generation. They also showed slightly *less* social concern as adults than either the prior or subsequent Catholic birth cohorts. The same study found that the most effective Catholic religious training over the past forty years had focused on promoting strong childhood religiosity and traditional beliefs. Efforts to promote Catholic social teaching among young people had proven less effective.[48]

The sixties revealed that Catholics no longer knew what their faith was about or how to teach it to the young. They were hopelessly divided between those who wanted to foster a socially engaged youth movement, those who wanted to create a sixties-style juvenilized Catholicism, and those who wanted to cling to the older and increasingly unworkable CYO model. None of these options appealed to the majority of young Catholics. The Catholic ghetto had produced dramatic results with only a superficial juvenilization that had not conceded much to the deeper trends in youth culture. As a result, Catholic youth leaders had little practice in creatively appealing to young people who were no longer forced to attend their programs and who were less and less likely to believe something just because a religious authority figure said it. The effective juvenilization they did accomplish, in programs like the Search weekend, was too little, too late.

The Price of Success:
Evangelicalism and the Future of Christian Youth Work

If political activism was really the most powerful force shaping young people during the 1960s, then politically progressive youth leaders should have attracted throngs of young people and conservative Protestants should have fared the worst. Yet the opposite happened. How could this be?

The sixties revealed that white evangelicals were more united than other Christian youth leaders regarding their goals for young people and their strategies for reaching those goals. Evangelicals successfully attracted and retained young people because they aggressively marketed their version of Christian faith using the styles of the sixties youth counterculture. The sixties revealed that the evangelical model of youth work was extremely adaptive to changes in youth culture. As a result, it would become the dominant model across the spectrum of American churches in the decades to come. But the price was indeed high at times, as evangelical youth environments increasingly glorified entertainment and self-fulfillment and downplayed calls to spiritual maturity.

While other youth leaders struggled to capitalize on the rise in youthful political activism, the leaders of YFC cashed in on a trend that would prove more enduring. During the 1960s, a few far-sighted advertising companies began to market products to adults by packaging them in the images and styles of youth culture. This new "hip consumerism" did not really promote the "sex, drugs and rock 'n' roll" of the sixties youth culture. Rather it offered adults the feeling of being young and free by consuming products. In a similar way, Youth for Christ leaders developed a hip Christian youth culture that continues even now to win customers. As early as 1961, YFC leaders conducted seminars that trained thousands of church youth workers, and even drew a few Catholic nuns.[49] And since adults were coming to value youthfulness more and more, this attention to adolescent styles would eventually pay off in winning the loyalty of adults as well.

Although they were not generally motivated by the same social concerns, the leaders of Youth for Christ joined other youth workers in conducting a serious reevaluation of their programs around 1960. President Ted Engstrom called for "new rally centers — we have fewer every year!" Bible clubs came under close scrutiny as well. Jack Hamilton feared that "our YFC kids are substituting know-how for the power of God" and so "duplicating *our* mistakes." After spending 200 days on the road in 1960, the new National Club Director Bill Eakin told the national staff, "There are a lot of sick clubs." Eakin especially worried about the declining "quality and caliber" of the young men in the Bible clubs.[50] The leaders of Youth for Christ sensed that large youth rallies no longer appealed to teenagers, and that their approach to youth work had become more about technique than about the power of God.

YFC leaders adopted a two-pronged approach to these perceived challenges. First, they tried to revitalize rallies by more aggressively catering to teenage tastes. In 1961 Tedd Bryson addressed a national gathering of adult leaders on the topic "The Teen Emphasis in the Rally." He told rally directors, "don't be afraid to 'entertain' and give teens what they want." He advised them to avoid Christian jargon and eliminate "church furniture" like a pulpit and rows of chairs on stage. Such an unabashed endorsement of entertainment was new for Youth for Christ, even though they had been in the entertainment business from the beginning. At the same conference in 1961, Al Kuhnle taught on "How to Be in the 'Teen Know.'" He told leaders to "learn to live where they do — lose yourself in their world." He advised them to attend school functions and visit youth hangouts. Most of all, he encouraged fellow staff members to show a genuine personal interest in teenagers and listen to their problems. Much like employees of advertising agencies who were starting to dress and act more "young," the leaders of YFC learned to immerse themselves in the youth culture.[51] Rather than assuming they knew what youth "really" wanted, the leaders of Youth for Christ set out to do some market research.

The most innovative rally directors and musicians, often based on the West Coast, began to experiment with folk and folk-rock styles. In Fresno, California, YFC director Larry Ballenger made some drastic changes around 1963. He sought out musical performers who could approximate the sound of groups like The Association or Simon and Garfunkel. He realized that the "warm-up music" used at the beginning of his rallies was for entertainment and audience participation, not for spiritual impact. "Let 'em sing 'Georgy Girl,'" he suggested. He warned that if adults became too attached to a particular musical style, it would "slow us up in the communication of the message." For innovators like Ballenger, musical style and the message it could communicate were almost completely separable.[52] The most innovative musical groups of the 1960s even performed non-Christian "problem" songs like the theme song from the film *The Valley of the Dolls* or "Who Will Answer" by Ed Ames. Ray Nickel and his folk group The New Creation performed the latter song and followed it with their own original song "God Will Answer." YFC musician Ralph Carmichael used a rock beat in the score he wrote for the 1965 Billy Graham Evangelistic Association film *The Restless Ones*. Carmichael was among a group of musicians who pioneered the use of folk-rock styles and wrote musicals that introduced these styles in churches. YFC musicians like Carmichael were also key players in the emergence of the Christian recording industry.[53] The leaders of YFC were way ahead of other evangelical adults of the day, who typically didn't allow drums or guitars in church and insisted that rock music was of the devil.

When Youth for Christ leaders discussed the merits of aggressive use of adolescent musical styles, they recognized that they were potentially changing how people experienced the faith. But in the end, they decided the powerful appeal to youth justified the potential costs. In 1967, Ralph Carmichael addressed a national meeting of YFC leaders, warning them that "yesterday's progressive is usually the greatest deterrent to today's progress." He called on youth leaders to do some "market research" and insisted that any musical style could be adopted if it communicated the message clearly and was performed sincerely. Like some other musicians of his generation, he claimed to dislike folk and rock music. But he noted that "even the adult taste in music has become top-40 oriented." He admitted that "the music that was used at the time of a person's conversion is ordinarily the music that he'll want to stay with and worship with unless there are some drastic changes." Thus he predicted that teenagers evangelized with the new folk-rock sound would eventually "want to worship to" that sound. This way of talking about worship was parallel to the way contemporary teenage stars of American Bandstand talked about dance music: "nice beat, easy to dance to." More importantly, Carmichael was right when he predicted that the teenagers of the sixties would bring their Christian rock music with them into the "adult" worship services of the future.

Just as rock music was increasingly becoming the soundtrack of adolescent love, contemporary worship music was becoming the new soundtrack for falling in love with Jesus. As distressing as some might find that prospect, Carmichael took it philosophically: "It would shock the britches off the good saints of two or three hundred years ago if they got into one of our YFC meetings and heard us ripping through a couple of fast choruses of 'Do Lord,' 'Safe am I' [and] 'Happy Now.'"[54] In other words, YFC leaders had been using controversial music for a long time, so they had no business stopping now. The juvenilization that had taken place in the youth groups of the 1950s helped prepare the evangelical movement to accept the "Jesus People" and "Jesus Rock" of the 1960s and early 1970s.[55] If it attracted teenagers to Christian events and provided an appealing soundtrack for worship and conversion experiences, youth leaders thought that new styles of music and other cultural adaptations were perfectly acceptable. They gave little thought to ways that worship might become more and more like a dance or a rock concert.

The second major change in the Youth for Christ strategy was to retool their youth environments to be more informal, intimate, and personalized. One reason that YFC rallies may have faltered during the sixties was that the sheer size of the baby boom cohort had made its members hungry for small, informal groupings that fostered personal attention. In part because of the need for crowd control, the high schools of the 1950s and early 1960s could be institutions that specialized in petty tyrannies. In 1964, young men got sent home from school for wearing boots that resembled those worn by the Beatles.[56] Immersion in such environments contributed to the teenage hunger for less restrictive social settings.

YFC leaders trying to follow up on teen conversions at rallies also ran up against this trend. In the 1950s, follow-up consisted of a conversation with a counselor at the end of the rally, a one-time visit at a later date, and a correspondence course. This system worked well throughout the 1950s, a decade that Jim Wright, head of the follow-up department, called "the heyday of correspondence follow up." Wright's successor Ray Curry found around 1960 that few converts successfully completed the correspondence course.[57] A group of leaders discussing follow-up at a 1963 convention stressed that "we can only help those we know, hence the need for many individuals who can take personal interest in a convert."[58] Although a relatively impersonal system of follow-up had worked fine in the fifties, YFC leaders realized that if they wanted to see young converts sustain spiritual growth in the sixties, they would have to develop a more personal touch.

Meanwhile, ongoing discussions among Bible club directors pointed in a similar direction. Beginning at a directors' conference in 1962, Bill Eakin began to emphasize "Training Teen Leaders." Participants in these discussions stressed that YFC staff could only train teen leaders by spending time with them and demonstrating "a personal CONCERN for every aspect of the kid's life." They also agreed that *"spirituality is not necessarily leadership."* A teen leader must be an "attention getter" or "extrovert" that "constantly has other kids following him." The participants in this discussion claimed that they did not need "the football hero type of teen," but one "whose life is well-balanced in the fields of the mental, physical and social."[59]

Eakin and other Bible club innovators drew on business advice literature for some of these principles of leadership. He strongly recommended *The Technique of Getting Things Done* by Donald Laird and *Think and Grow Rich* by Napoleon Hill. Eakin especially liked Hill's questions for evaluating leadership effectiveness. These questions highlighted the importance of setting goals and improving working relationships. Eakin also offered advice on "How to Manage People" that honed in on the need for YFC staff to learn how to motivate teen leaders by learning to "treat them as human beings." Students would respond better if the club director tried to "make them feel important" and made the effort to "get to know the individual." Eakin observed that psychological testing had invalidated the old management model that sought to motivate employees through "compulsion." Instead, management experts now confirmed that "you must arouse a desire in them to do their work well."[60] While Christian liberals tried to catch the wave of anti-institutional student activism, YFC leaders adapted the new theories of business management to create more relationally warm institutions. They also subtly redefined spiritual leadership by making it look a lot more like business leadership.

Over the next few years Eakin and other YFC leaders built these insights into a new club format they eventually called Campus Life. This model closely paralleled the approach that Young Life had been taking for the past twenty years. The pattern called for alternating "Impact" and "Insight" club meetings. The Impact meetings were fun evangelistic club meetings; the Insight meetings were for training teenage Christians to be evangelists. Ken Overstreet in San Diego led the way in developing the evangelistic "Impact" meetings. Adult leaders carefully planned and led these meetings, which often met in homes rather than at school. The goal of each meeting was to provide a fun, informal environment that appealed to non-Christian teenagers and offered them a small dose of Christian teaching. Pioneers like Overstreet honed these one-hour sessions into step-by-step plans, and Bill Eakin distributed them nationally. The session on "Is There a God?" led off with the "Campus Life Clap" in which the leader moved his arms up and down, scissors-like, in front of his body, while the crowd tried to clap whenever his hands passed each other. Then the leader pulled two guys from the crowd and had them take off their shoes. He blindfolded them and put gloves on their hands. The boys raced to put on a pair of nylons up to their knees, while the crowd roared with laughter. The loser's penalty was a trip to the "electric chair," which had been specially wired to deliver a mild shock. This was followed by "egg roulette" in which five guys broke open eggs over each other's heads. One of the eggs was raw, the others hard boiled. At this point, the leader started a discussion on the topic "Is there a God?" He asked questions like "Do you believe in God? Why or why not?" "What is your concept of God?" and "What difference does it make to you if you believe in a God?" The leader did not answer any of the questions, and had privately instructed the Christian club members to hold back on answering until their non-Christian friends spoke up. Finally, the leader gave his personal testimony of meeting God, being sure to avoid religious jargon. Although the leader would usually say a few words in the "wrap-up," student participation through discussion and games dominated these meetings.[61]

Unlike the old clubs and rallies, leaders did not usually call on teens to get converted at these meetings. Instead, they urged them to simply come back next time, or to come to the next Campus Life social event. They also tried to arrange individual meetings with students who looked interested. This format required more staff both to put on the meetings and to meet with students individually. As a byproduct of this change, for the first time significant numbers of young women began to join the YFC staff in the late 1960s. According to their manual, the role of these "girl staff" members was to support the male leader by helping to organize the meetings and by meeting individually with the girls who attended the clubs.[62]

Such environments taught young people that Christianity was centered on them, and that their opinions mattered. The point of Christianity was not to get indoctrinated in a complicated set of theological beliefs, but to engage in open-ended discussions with peers that culminated in a simple gospel message. Teenagers at these meetings also learned that Christianity could be fun and that religious meetings need not be boring, but could be a good place to feel at home with friends. These religious values would shape the future of evangelical churches and of American Christianity more broadly.

Leaders hoped the bi-weekly "Insight" meetings would train Christian teenagers in the "balanced life" that would make them better evangelists. The focus of these sessions was clearly teenagers and their problems. One such session called "What's Buggin' You?" invited students to talk about the frustrations they encountered as they tried to live as Christians. Later sessions taught principles of spiritual growth and gave tips for how to have a daily "quiet time" of prayer and Bible reading. Students also learned how to share the gospel with friends.[63] Although the aim of the Impact meetings was to train evangelists, even here youth leaders sensed that personal attention and help with internal struggles was key to effective ministry among youth.

In the hands of Youth for Christ leaders, this same informality made it even into the sacred precincts of Scripture. Beginning in 1966, YFC developed "teenage editions" of the Bible, using the new "Living Letters" paraphrase. Interspersed with the biblical text were photos of teenagers and captions related to the passages at hand. Some of these images depicted problems like war, juvenile delinquency, suicide, consumerism, and racism in order to draw out the contemporary relevance of the biblical text. Indeed, the back cover of one such Scripture edition featured counterculture-style lettering with the promise that

> *a new kind of experience awaits you*. . . . In this life one's nationality or race or education or social position is unimportant. Such things mean nothing; whether a person has Christ is what matters, and He is equally available to all. *Colossians 3:11 (Living Letters)*

The accompanying photograph showed a racially mixed group of young people. But the majority of the images and captions in these Scripture editions evoked the humor, play, and dating relationships that dominated both YFC clubs and white, middle-class teenage life.[64]

In short, YFC leaders laid the foundation for a new evangelical spirituality that seemed to embrace the intimacy, the authenticity, and even the "revolution" of the counterculture. Much like the advertising that employed the images and metaphors of youth rebellion in order to sell products, the evangelicals of the late 1960s and early 1970s would use rebellion to sell Christianity to youth. The titles of three books published in 1969 that each went through multiple printings illustrate this trend: *Revolution Now!*, *Will the Real Phony Please Stand Up?* and *Love Is Now*.[65] Judging by the brisk sales of these books, the evangelical version of the counterculture found a receptive market. Youth leaders had succeeded in creating a juvenilized version of Christianity that marketed the old-time religion in the trappings of the youth counterculture. And in subsequent decades, seeker-service pioneers like Bill Hybels and Rick Warren would use the same techniques to attract Baby Boomer adults to church.

Juvenilization Revealed

Some young Christians who lived through the 1960s learned to value the political dimensions of their faith more than members of previous generations. But even more of them began to see the institutional church as an impediment to personal fulfillment. They wanted a Christian faith that was emotionally engaging, informal, and intimate. They demanded personal attention and expected to be able to discuss their personal opinions, rather than just being told what to believe. They created adolescent versions of the faith seasoned with pop culture and individualized spiritual searching. The sixties revealed that only those churches that creatively adapted the faith to the tastes and needs of large numbers of young people would continue to thrive. The religious styles that began as techniques for appealing to young people would eventually become the preferred ways to reach adults as well.

Those who saw youthful political activism as the wave of the future tended to assume that most young people were already politically progressive and only needed to be mobilized. They also believed that the best politics was youth-led political protest. Yet many young people were uninterested in the political revolutions of their times. And the increasing violence and decreasing political impact of protests in the late 1960s shouted that all was not well in the newly juvenilized political movements. Politically progressive youth leaders from the African American, mainline Protestant, and Roman Catholic churches ignored this evidence. Their strategy for saving America might have worked if they had put all their efforts into forming young social activists and supporting them with a compelling social justice spirituality. Instead, they wrongly assumed that both loyalty to the church and zeal for political activism would take care of themselves, so that all they had to do was encourage young people to leave the church behind and get in on the revolution. Liberals firmly entrenched in institutions that stood to lose a great deal from the anti-institutional ethos of the times nevertheless felt the inspiring thrill of identification with countercultural student activists. White mainline Protestant leaders were especially short-sighted in the way they attacked their own church and taught young people to do the same.

African Americans and Roman Catholics also suffered significant setbacks as their networks of supportive institutions began to unravel in the sixties. It's hard to see a way that these institutions could have survived, and in many cases they were badly in need of reform. But leaders in both groups made matters worse by underestimating what it would take to continue to provide adequate spiritual formation for their young people. The sixties revealed that neither mainline Protestants nor African Americans nor Roman Catholics were ready to creatively and effectively adapt to youth culture on anything like the scale that would be necessary in the future. Some of them had juvenilized Christian politics; others had created various "hip" versions of Christianity; but few in these groups found ways to powerfully connect with the majority of their young people. Their efforts left most alienated or bored.

In the long run, the rebellious *styles* of sixties youth proved more popular among the middle class than the substance of their social vision. Youth for Christ leaders sensed this trend and quickly capitalized on it. Although adults in their own constituency worried about the "devil's music" and the anarchy of the youth culture, the most innovative leaders in YFC believed that it was easy enough to separate youth culture styles from their ideological content. Meanwhile, the leaders of YFC shared with all other Christian youth leaders of the sixties a tendency to create informal environments designed to give teenagers a sense of personal attention. In so doing, evangelicals led the way in developing a version of adolescent Christianity that would come to dominate both youth ministries and the churches in the decades ahead. Unfortunately, their success came at some cost. By assuming that teen tastes in music and spirituality were essentially neutral, they allowed youth culture the power to reshape Christian faith. While some of these changes were beneficial, others would create a chronic immaturity among American Christians. The sixties revealed once and for all that adolescent Christianity would shape the future of the churches one way or the other. It could not be ignored.

CHAPTER 8

The Triumph and Taming of Juvenilization

Juvenilization has kept American Christianity vibrant. Visit any suburban community in America and you will find a rapidly growing white
evangelical church that uses the "seeker-friendly" approach pioneered by
Bill Hybels and Willow Creek Community Church or the "purpose-
driven" model pioneered by Rick Warren and Saddleback Church. These
churches reach thousands of "unchurched" Americans by providing an informal, entertaining, fast-paced worship experience set to upbeat contemporary music.

The musical styles and multimedia sophistication may be new, but the
ministry philosophy is the same one that created the Youth for Christ rallies of the 1950s. Not surprisingly, Bill Hybels first experimented with the
seeker-friendly model and church market research while serving as a youth
pastor in the 1970s. The white evangelical churches that are growing the
fastest in America are the ones that look the most like the successful youth
ministries of the 1950s and 1960s.[1]

Although white evangelicals have been the most aggressive juve-
nilizers, other branches of American Christianity are not far behind.
Some of the most fervent young Catholics are combining traditionalist
faith and youth culture styles. One observer described "the new faithful"
this way:

> They sing evangelical songs. They tell their conversion stories and facili-
> tate the conversion of others. They stress the importance of a "personal
> relationship with Christ." They wear T-shirts with messages like
> "Eucharistic Adoration: Do It 24/7" and "Top 10 Reasons to Be Catholic."

In groups like Life Teen and other Catholic youth ministries, rock bands and youth-friendly eucharistic liturgies are successfully attracting teenagers. When asked why they attend these youth liturgies, teenagers report that they like the "intense experience" that serves as a "stress reliever" and they "love the music." In a similar move, some African American church leaders are experimenting with hip-hop worship in order to reach young people who are alienated from traditional black churches.[2] Over time, we can expect that these innovations will filter into adult church life. And even if adults are not yet singing the latest youth-friendly music in church, they have already been affected by juvenilization in other ways. What have been the major effects of juvenilization on American Christianity? What can be done to minimize the negative ones?

Youth Ministry Revitalizes the Churches

Youth ministries and juvenilization have encouraged generations of Americans to keep coming to church and to take their faith seriously. The United States continues to enjoy unusually high levels of religious commitment compared to similar industrialized nations. Church attendance hit an all-time high during the 1950s; as we have seen, there was an explosion of new youth ministries during this period. Although the leaders of these ministries did not always understand the changes affecting young people, they did sense something important was happening. They all proclaimed that young people held the key to the "crisis of civilization." American adults responded by investing heavily in youth programs. Their investment bore long-term fruit by forming generations of young people who were committed to their faith. Studies confirm that thriving congregations consistently provide strong programs for children and teenagers.[3]

This enduring religious vitality in America is all the more remarkable because no one saw it coming. Even during the 1950s many experts were predicting that the "religious revival" would not last. And then the cultural storms of the sixties seemed to confirm that America was becoming more secular. The late sixties and early seventies were a bad time for church attendance, but a dramatic downward trend did not appear. On any given Sunday, about 40 percent of Americans still attend church, and that number has held steady since 1970. A full 90 percent of Americans consistently report belief in God. The percentage of Americans who agreed with the statement "religion can help with today's problems" remained high from the 1970s through the 1990s.[4] Not everyone who answers opinion polls with favorable answers to such questions is really a devoted follower of Jesus, but many are. Millions of Christians devote themselves to evangelism, political activism, service to the poor, education, the arts, and myriad other socially and spiritually beneficial activities. For all its flaws, Christianity in America is remarkably resilient, with a proven ability to overcome significant challenges. The persistent prophecies of doom for the church in America should be laid to rest once and for all.

Youth ministries and the process of juvenilization they fostered contributed to this religious vitality by helping the churches adapt to cultural changes. Whether it was civil rights protests or Jesus Rock, youth-friendly activities in the church helped win the loyalty of young people. In 1924, a major sociological study of Muncie, Indiana, called *Middletown* found many signs that Christianity was in decline. A key indicator was that young people seemed less religious than their parents. In 1978, the Middletown surveys were repeated; this time they revealed that the predicted decline in religion never materialized. Both youth and adults had more positive views of the church and Christianity in 1978 than their predecessors did in 1924. The percentage of people who attended church regularly actually increased dramatically, and attendance by high school students remained strong. The top reason people gave for going to church had changed from "habit" to "enjoyment."[5] Youth ministries helped make the Christian life more emotionally satisfying. Passion was in, duty was out. But this kind of individualized, emotional connection to God played a crucial role in a changing society in which custom, tradition, and social pressure would no longer motivate people to care about faith or attend church.

As we have seen, some of the religious interest that was fostered in youth groups could be superficial and did not necessarily lead to a mature adult commitment to the church. But even many of those who gave up going to church in their young adult years retained the positive views of God and religion they learned in church youth groups. If their faith was a bit immature, that should not be surprising, since structured input into their spiritual lives stopped in adolescence for some, and for others continued in adolescent mode well into their adult years. It is in youth groups that teenagers and adults negotiate ways to make Christianity more appealing to more people by making it more Americanized and adolescent. But it is also in youth ministries that American Christianity has become more emotionally vibrant and socially relevant. Youth ministries will continue to serve as crucial laboratories of religious innovation. And like other institutions, churches need creative thinking and adaptive change if they are to survive and fulfill their missions.

Church Growth and Decline among White Protestants

Churches have not benefited equally from the power of youth ministries and juvenilization to sustain religious vitality. Mainline Protestant denominations such as the Methodists, Presbyterians, Episcopalians, and the United Church of Christ have declined in membership. Meanwhile, conservative Protestant churches such as Southern Baptists, the Assemblies of God, and non-denominational churches have grown.[6]

Church attendance numbers are by no means the only measure of spiritual vitality. Big churches are not inherently better than small churches. A faithful remnant can serve a prophetic role by proclaiming an important message or pursuing a unique mission that is not popular. Such faithfulness to the call of God is to be celebrated. The desire to gather a crowd can easily push leaders to compromise the message of the gospel and downplay spiritual maturity. Yet while attendance figures cannot guarantee that Christians are fulfilling Jesus' command to "go and make disciples of all nations" (Matt. 28:19), declining numbers are a bad sign. Leaders of churches that cannot sustain membership over time should take a hard look at how well they are fostering lifelong faith in the lives of their children. A church cannot fulfill the mission God has given it if it has no members.

Several theories have been advanced to explain why evangelical churches have fared better than mainline churches in motivating religious commitment. Some say that conservative churches attract more members because their strongly held, clearly articulated beliefs and strict lifestyle demands help people achieve a more stable, satisfying religious identity. Others claim that conservative Christianity offers people greater rewards both in this life and the next. Another theory is that the conservative Protestant churches that are growing are actually the ones that have made the most adaptations to modern American culture, suggesting that they succeed not so much because they make strict demands, but because they market a version of Christianity that helps people retain a religiously invigorating sense of tension with the surrounding culture even as they mostly fit into it.[7]

The history of evangelical youth ministries suggests that it is a combination of strictness and creative adaptation to culture that has sustained the appeal of conservative Protestantism. A key strength of organizations like Youth for Christ and Young Life was the way they wove together powerful conversion experiences, strict moral purity, and fun with a sense of participation in a world-changing mission. Teenagers could believe that by conversion, consecration, and abstaining from drinking, dancing, and sex they were witnessing to their friends and fighting communism. They could even come to see the celebrities, Christian pop music, stunts, skits, and games of their youth groups as powerful religious tools for evangelizing the world. Although youth ministries pioneered this approach, growing conservative churches have perfected it in the past thirty years.

In an ironic twist, some argue that it was the very cultural and political successes of liberal Protestants that caused their denominations to decline numerically. Liberal Protestants promoted values like individualism, freedom, pluralism, tolerance, democracy, and intellectual inquiry. They worked to convince church members that these values were not only the best elements of the Christian faith, but the most useful tools for reforming society. But as these values became more and more embraced in American society as a whole, liberal Protestant churches lost some of their appeal.

This cultural success led to numerical decline for at least two reasons. First, liberal values tended to undermine the sort of loyalty and commitment that institutions like churches need to remain vital. People who learn to question authority and value their individual freedom tend to have looser attachments to institutions, or push for weaker institutions that make fewer demands. Second, as their values and political goals became more widely approved in society, liberal church leaders found themselves without a distinctive niche in the religious marketplace. In the 1950s, it was difficult to be a political liberal without getting labeled a communist, but being a *Christian* liberal helped. In subsequent decades, many liberal causes could be just as easily pursued through secular institutions. In addition, since the 1960s religion has become tainted in the eyes of many political liberals because so many Christians have opposed progressive political causes and embraced conservative ones. As a result, many of the people otherwise most likely to join liberal churches have become increasingly wary of religion.[8]

The history of the Methodist Youth Department suggests that this story of numerical decline through cultural success is incomplete. It ignores the hidden cost of the failed campaign to liberalize several generations of reluctant young people. Liberal Methodist youth leaders succeeded in convincing a vocal minority of young people to embrace the liberal political agenda even if they had to leave the church behind to do so. These same leaders then squandered the rest of their limited resources in an unsuccessful bid to create a mass movement of Christian social progressives. Their efforts alienated most young Methodists and their parents. Few resources went into fostering a Christian spirituality that could appeal to the masses. As a result, thousands of young people found little to capture their imaginations or sustain their spiritual health in the Methodist Youth Fellowship. Over time, these factors contributed to numerical decline in the United Methodist Church.

And this mainline decline began not in the sixties, but already in the 1950s. In the early 1950s, Methodist Youth Department officials estimated that in order to keep its 14 percent share of American Protestant youth, the Methodist Youth Fellowship would need to expand its membership from 1.125 million to 4.6 million by 1960. But in 1964, the Methodist church claimed only 1,388,378 students aged twelve to twenty-one in its Sunday school system. Even if the Methodist Youth Fellowship meetings reached an additional 1 million — which was unlikely — Methodists had still failed to keep up with the Baby Boom.[9] The decline in membership that became more visible in the 1960s and 1970s resulted in part from a failure to win and keep the loyalty of the young.

Others deny that the church beliefs and practices have had much to do with growth and decline. Recently, an important study of fertility rates found that as much as 76 percent of the change in church membership in recent decades could be explained by the simple fact that over the past forty years, conservative Protestants have had more children than liberal ones. The effects of church switching, apostasy, and recruitment of the non-religious all seem to be small compared to the effect of birth rates.[10] But high birth rates only produce church growth if many of those children keep going to church. Liberal Protestants did worse at retaining young people because they were not as good as conservative Protestants at turning juvenilization to their advantage. Liberal Protestants chose to ignore the fun, entertainment, and emotional comfort that increasing numbers of American teenagers *and* adults wanted from their faith. Some Methodist attempts to tap into youth culture were awkward, such as the "rhythmic games" they tried to substitute for dancing. Others were highbrow and offensive to many in the laity, like jazz dancers or dramas ridiculing patriotism. In the end, Methodist youth leaders mistakenly believed that a "natural" youthful idealism would do their work for them, so they could ignore trends in youth culture that made sacrificial service for unpopular causes increasingly unappealing. Their error was not in believing that Christian young people should work for racial justice; rather, it was underestimating what it would take to form large numbers of countercultural young people. Even worse, decades of stumbling attempts to deploy youth culture did not prepare mainline church leaders to adapt to the increasingly adolescent religious preferences of adults.

Mainline Protestants have also invested less in youth ministry over the past thirty years than their conservative Protestant counterparts. The protracted struggle over how best to shape Methodist young people probably contributed to the decision to restructure the denomination's youth-serving agencies in the late sixties and early seventies. Like many other mainline Protestant denominations, the Methodists dismantled much of their national youth ministry structure at that time. Leaders justified these changes by claiming that young people needed to be fully integrated into the church and become full members of the laity.[11] But the net effect was less institutional investment in young people and therefore less retention of young people in the churches.

In contrast, evangelical Protestants aggressively adapted their practices to teenage tastes. In the early seventies they even repackaged the long hair, rock music, and rebellion of the youth counterculture as a new conservative Protestant way to follow Jesus. Unlike mainline Protestants, who were in the unenviable position of trying to create a countercultural political movement from within a denominational bureaucracy, the leaders of independent organizations like Youth for Christ and Young Life were free to innovate. Of course this flexibility came at some cost. In the name of evangelizing teenagers, the leaders of parachurch youth ministries experimented freely with ways of being Christian that would create an ever more immature evangelical church. As time went on, more and more white evangelicals of all ages began to demand this new combination of old-time religion and adolescent spirituality.

Beginning in the 1970s, white conservative Protestants far outpaced all other American Christians in their institutional investments in youth ministry. They eagerly united around the techniques pioneered in Youth for Christ and Young Life. Leaders who had grown up in these youth groups or in church youth groups modeled on them founded organizations like Youth Specialties and Group Publishing to promote this approach. Conferences and publications designed to train and support youth ministers proliferated. Christian pop music went from being a small-time operation with performances at Youth for Christ rallies to a multimillion-dollar industry. This contemporary Christian music industry both fostered and benefited from the boom in conservative Protestant youth ministry. Conservative churches also hired youth pastors in unprecedented numbers; by the 1990s, the demand for youth pastors was strong enough to sustain dozens of youth ministry degree programs at evangelical colleges and seminaries across the nation. Predictably, these investments in youth ministry have led to greater retention of young people in evangelical churches. Continuing these investments will be more important than ever, because now conservative Protestant birth rates are declining as well.[12]

Growth and Decline in Roman Catholic and African American Churches

In the 1950s and early 1960s both African American and Roman Catholic churches in the United States depended upon a strong network of mutually supportive institutions to form young people in the faith. In both cases, that network collapsed or was severely weakened in the late sixties and early seventies. Both faith traditions have yet to provide an equally effective replacement for their pre-1970 youth-forming institutions. Yet African American church attendance has remained strong, while Roman Catholic attendance has declined. In the National Study of Youth and Religion, black Protestant teenagers fared better on many measures of religious vitality than young Roman Catholics.[13] Yet neither faith tradition has juvenilized as aggressively as white conservative Protestants. What factors account for these different outcomes?

Church attendance by Roman Catholics has declined dramatically in recent decades, even though the percentage of Americans who identify themselves as Roman Catholics has held steady or increased slightly. During the 1950s about 75 percent of American Catholics attended mass weekly. That percentage decreased steadily during the 1960s, until in 1969 only 63 percent attended weekly. In the 1970s, the percentage hovered between 51 and 55 percent. The downward trend has continued in recent decades, with only 44 percent attending mass weekly in 1987 and 37 percent doing so in 1999. On the other hand, 84 percent of those who attended mass weekly in 1995 received communion, compared with only 57 percent of those who attended weekly in the 1950s.[14]

This decline in church attendance usually gets blamed on some combination of the social upheavals of the sixties, the theological and liturgical confusion that followed the Second Vatican Council, and the fallout from the 1968 papal encyclical *Humanae Vitae*, which renewed the church's ban on birth control. But the confusion, conflict, and collapse in Catholic youth ministries during the 1960s and 1970s also contributed. The decline in mass attendance started among younger Catholics. Between 1957 and 1974, weekly attendance at Mass by 18-to-29-year-olds went from being a nearly universal practice to one observed by 53 percent of college graduates and 36 percent of high school graduates.[15]

Why did young people stop going to church? One factor could be the rise of youth counterculture. Catholic young people who participated in political protests and elements of the hippie lifestyle faced hostility from adults. The Catholic youth ministries of the 1950s were also partly to blame for this generation gap, because they had adapted all too well to the clean-cut, white middle-class youth culture of the 1950s and early 1960s. Indeed, for many older Catholics, this "all-American Catholicism" had become central to their conception of the faith. As a result, young Catholics inspired by the youth counterculture were especially primed to see their church as part of the evil "establishment." Other teenagers who just wanted to wear long hair were often treated like criminals by adults in their parishes. Still, most young Catholics did not participate in the sexual immorality, drugs, and left-wing political activism of the era. In fact, the FBI and CIA especially targeted places like the University of Notre Dame to recruit agents during the sixties because they could count on finding more staunchly anti-communist young men there than at many state universities. So the exodus of young people from the Catholic church in the late sixties can't simply be blamed on the youth counterculture.[16]

There were huge external challenges to Catholic faith in the sixties, but internal confusion in youth work and catechesis made matters worse. Those who experimented with promising innovations in youth ministry faced considerable opposition from other adults. Other catechists overreacted to the "spirit of the sixties" and scrapped anything that smacked of indoctrination. As a result, young people often had only vague notions of the content of the faith and little emotional commitment to it. This situation has not improved much in more recent decades. One study of the religious attitudes of young adult Catholics conducted in the late 1990s found that they had overwhelmingly negative memories of their religious education. They remembered fun, but little substance. Leaders drilled into them the importance of social concern, but did little to explicitly connect that concern to the Catholic faith.

In the late sixties, institutional investment in young people slumped in the Catholic world, and has not yet fully recovered. The number of Catholic schools has declined steadily. Catholics were among the last American Christians to hire youth ministers. Catholic youth ministers enjoy lower job satisfaction and support from their fellow Catholics than other full-time workers in the Catholic church.[17] Catholics adapted quite well to the relatively conservative youth culture of the 1950s, but have not learned how to adapt on a large scale to the newer, more voluntary religious climate.

Despite facing some of the same challenges as the Roman Catholic Church, African American Protestant churches have done better at retaining loyalty over time. One study found that only conservative white Protestants ranked higher than black Protestants in their average level of church commitment. Black church membership seems to have held steady after a brief downturn in the early 1960s.[18]

Why have African American churches continued to motivate a high level of religious commitment compared to their Roman Catholic counterparts? For one thing, black churches serve as guardians and promoters of African American identity, culture, and political action. A good number of upwardly mobile members of the Black Power generation who left the church in the late sixties and early seventies returned in middle age. They did so in part because even their successes in the "white" world revealed both the enduring power of racism and their need for nurture and support of their African American identity. As Beverly Hall Lawrence put it, "our rejoining the church" was "an overt political statement . . . a suggestion that we were part of a new generation of 'believers' seeking to revive the church as an instrument of change." The black church also serves as a haven and a source of emotional consolation; as Lawrence notes, "I no longer *choose* to go, but often *need* to go; it is a place to which I am drawn. Church is the temple of the familiar — my filling station, where I revive my spirits." For successful professionals like Lawrence, church becomes one of the few places to connect with what she calls "real black people" and their culture.[19]

Second, African American churches have been more successful than their Roman Catholic counterparts in connecting with adolescents. Roman Catholics sometimes struggle to get adolescents and their parents to view confirmation as something other than a rite of passage out of active church participation. Although both faith traditions practice intergenerational worship, African American churches do better at helping young people connect emotionally with that worship. Youth choirs are often cited as one of the most effective youth programs in black churches. Despite grumbling by old timers, black churches have adapted to changing musical tastes and provided the sort of upbeat, emotionally expressive music that connects with younger worshippers. This juvenilization of black church music has helped the black church retain an emotional link to each subsequent generation. The new hip-hop worship is just the latest example of this musical innovation. Meanwhile, American Catholics are still singing the folk songs of the seventies in their masses.[20]

Black churches have also adapted to the beliefs of younger generations by embracing the cause of black consciousness. Not all black church leaders were comfortable with the slogan "black power" and other elements of the black consciousness movement that began among young people in the 1960s and early 1970s. But by the 1980s, a full 64 percent of African American pastors said their sermons reflected themes of "black pride, black is beautiful, black power, etc." Similarly, 71 percent of black pastors claim that the children in their church are taught about their black heritage. As one pastor put it, "The church has an obligation to teach about the contributions of our race. If we don't do this, where are our kids gonna get it?"[21] The black church has succeeded in convincing each generation of African Americans that it is a crucial spiritual repository of racial pride, identity, and empowerment. In contrast, white Roman Catholics may see their Catholic identity as personally important, but are less likely to see the church as one of the primary institutions representing their interests.

However, the news is not all good for African American churches. There has been a rise in the percentage of African Americans who declare no religious affiliation, and that increase has been greater than among white Christians. Post–civil rights generations seem to be leaving the church in greater numbers than those of earlier generations. And the church has done especially poorly at attracting young, urban males living outside the South. Compared to their white evangelical and mainline counterparts, black Protestant teenagers are more likely to hold religious beliefs that are different from those of their parents. Many church leaders are deeply concerned that they have not done as much as they should to address the problems in urban communities caused by poverty and racism. Churches are working hard to overcome the gap between "church people" and the urban poor, but the existence of that gap is a bad sign for the future of Christianity among poor young black men.[22] The religious innovators who are trying to create a Christianized version of hip-hop culture may well reverse these negative trends. But they will need to be careful to avoid the pitfalls of juvenilization that have plagued white churches.

Feeling Good about God

During the 1950s, observers of the "religious revival" bemoaned the fact that not many Christian believers seemed to know much about their faith. An often-cited example was a poll that revealed that a majority could not name even one of the four Gospels. The problem of high religious interest combined with low religious literacy may well have worsened in recent decades. In their landmark National Study of Youth and Religion, Christian Smith and his team of researchers found that the majority of American teenagers are not alienated from religion or the church; on the contrary, even teenagers not personally involved in religious activities think that religion is basically a good thing. Many of them have learned this favorable view of religion through contact with church youth groups. An astonishing 69 percent of all teenagers in America have attended a religious youth group at one time or another.[23]

But Smith's research team also found that American teenagers are surprisingly inarticulate about their faith. When asked what they believed, even some young people who attend church and youth group regularly said things like "Um, Jesus and God and all them guys." The researchers found that the biblical language of faith is a foreign language to American teenagers. Teenage Christians seldom used words like "faith," "salvation," "sin," or even "Jesus" to describe their beliefs. Instead, they returned again and again to the language of personal fulfillment and happiness to describe why God and Christianity were important to them. The phrase "feel happy" appeared over 2,000 times in their 267 interviews.[24]

Smith and his research team came up with the label "Moralistic, Therapeutic Deism" to describe the religious beliefs that emerged in their in-depth interviews with teenagers. Teenagers learn these beliefs from the adults in their lives. It is the American culture religion. Teenagers are "moralistic" in that they believe that God wants us to be good, and that the main purpose of religion is to help people be good. But many think that it is possible to be good without being religious, so religion is an optional tool for being good that can be chosen by those who find it helpful. Further, they believe most people are good and will go to heaven. American Christianity is "therapeutic" in that, like the teenagers in the study, we believe that God and religion are valuable because they help us feel better about our problems. Finally, American teenagers show their "deism" in that they believe in a God who remains in the background of their lives — always watching over them, ready to help them with their problems, but not at the center of their lives.[25]

Given the history of youth ministry and juvenilization, it should not be surprising to find that many Americans have an inarticulate faith characterized by moralistic, therapeutic deism. As early as the 1950s, youth ministry was low on content and high on emotional fulfillment. Religious illiteracy may not have begun in youth ministry, but most youth ministries did little to reverse the trend. Most youth ministries since the 1960s have followed the club model pioneered in Young Life and later adopted by Youth for Christ in its Campus Life program. Songs, games, skits, and other youth culture entertainments are followed by talks or discussions that feature simple truths packaged with humor, stories, and personal testimonies. This pattern works because it appeals to teenage desires for fun and belonging. It casts a wide net — by dumbing down Christianity to the lowest common denominator of adolescent cognitive development and religious motivation.

The pressure exerted by youth culture makes some such accommodations necessary. It is difficult to attract young people to a voluntary youth group by making it look more like school. Yet it should come as no surprise that the Mormons did the best on many measures of religious literacy in the National Study of Youth and Religion. Young Mormons participate in some of the most rigorous religious education classes being offered to teenagers in America today.[26]

At their best, youth ministries attract and at least temporarily retain teenagers who might otherwise leave the church. But the relentless attention to teenage tastes ends up communicating that God exists to make us feel good. Christianity operates as a lifestyle enhancement like the movies, music, dances, amusement parks, sports teams, and clubs that dominate teenage life. If you're getting something out of it, by all means, go. If not, find what makes you happy and get involved in that.

As they listen to years of simplified messages that emphasize an emotional relationship with Jesus over intellectual content, teenagers learn that a well-articulated belief system is unimportant and might even become an obstacle to authentic faith. Fortunately there are exceptions to this pattern. Smith's research team did find the occasional teenager who could articulate a meaningful set of Christian beliefs. But in far too many youth groups, teenagers learn to feel good about God without learning much about God. And increasingly, Americans of all generations take it for granted that emotional fulfillment is one of the main purposes of religious faith. Youth groups and the juvenilization they fostered helped create this insatiable appetite for a feel-good faith. According to the Bible and Christian tradition, God does help people with their problems, including their emotional problems. But reducing the faith to this function neglects other important elements of the faith, such as submitting to Christ as Lord and enduring suffering for the sake of the Kingdom of God.

Another way that juvenilization has affected religious beliefs is by training people to pick and choose what to believe and to be suspicious of religious orthodoxies and authorities. This change is especially striking in the case of Roman Catholics, who were more likely than other believers to accept official church teaching before the sixties. Between 1961 and 1971, the number of Catholic students at Marquette University who approved of "heavy necking with a steady date" rose from 6 percent to 75 percent. The number condoning serious dating relationships with non-Catholics rose from 17 percent to 92 percent. In 1961 only 1 percent of Catholic students thought it acceptable to miss a major part of the Mass by arriving late, but 55 percent condoned this infraction in 1971. The number who thought it acceptable to consistently neglect evening prayers rose from 17 percent to 70 percent. The number willing to accept serious religious doubts as a normal part of life rose from 48 percent to 82 percent in the same period.[27]

This trend that began among young people in the sixties has continued among adults of all generations. For example, the percentage of Catholics who said that a person could be a good Catholic without obeying the church's teaching regarding abortion rose from 39 percent in 1987 to 53 percent in 1999. The percentage who believed that someone could be a good Catholic without donating time or money to the poor rose from 44 percent in 1987 to 56 percent in 1999. The number who thought you could be a good Catholic without going to church every Sunday (despite the fact that every Catholic knows the rule about this) rose from 70 percent in 1987 to 76 percent in 1999. On the other hand, in 1999 only 23 percent agreed that a person could be a good Catholic without believing that Jesus physically rose from the dead and only 38 percent believed someone could be a good Catholic without believing that during mass the bread and wine become Jesus' body and blood.[28] It seems that most Catholics still believe some important church teachings, but they consider themselves empowered to determine which teachings are central and which can be ignored.

Juvenilized Catholics seem especially likely to ignore church teachings that impose behavior restrictions. This freedom of choice might be a sign of adult autonomy, but it may well be the legacy of teenage rebelliousness. Indeed, it looks suspiciously like an adult version of the typical adolescent distaste for institutions and their rules.

Teenagers from all religious traditions tend to practice a pluralistic tolerance and to believe that all people have to decide for themselves what to believe when it comes to religion. As one teenager put it, "each person decides for himself," or as another said, "if it works for them, fine." The Middletown studies confirm that religious tolerance and distaste for imposing one's beliefs on others have increased over time. In 1924, 94 percent of high school students in Muncie agreed with the statement "Christianity is the one true religion and all peoples should be converted to it," but only 40 percent agreed in 1977. Adults show the same discomfort with the idea of exclusive religious beliefs. Gallup polls taken in the mid 1980s found that 62 percent of Americans agreed that "God reveals himself through a variety of religious beliefs and traditions" and a majority also agreed that "people should just believe in God and not argue about religion."[29] On the positive side, younger generations of Americans are much less likely than their parents or grandparents to reject their fellow Christians just because they belong to a different church or have different theological beliefs. On the other hand, the new tolerance reinforces the idea that the theological content of one's faith is unimportant.

It should come as no surprise that Americans create individualized faiths and are reluctant to discuss ways that some religious beliefs may be better than others. They have been learning to approach religious beliefs this way for decades in their youth groups. Think, for example, of Methodist youth leaders in the 1950s and 1960s who exhorted young people to "live the questions," or Roman Catholics of the 1960s and 70s who glorified religious searching. Not surprisingly, more members of those churches doubt the existence of absolute truth than do members of evangelical churches.[30] For many youth leaders and religious educators in America, "indoctrination" is still a bad word. The most important thing, they say, is for each individual to decide for himself or herself what to believe and to embrace the fact that one's beliefs will be always changing.

Making space for religious questioning and searching fits very well with the developmental needs of older adolescents. Older teenagers and emerging adults are in the process of figuring out their beliefs and commitments, and some enter a "moratorium" in which they seriously question what they have been taught. Often this process results in an adult acceptance of childhood beliefs, although in a modified form. What is new in the last forty years is that some adults working with young people have come to celebrate such searching and to speak in ways that imply that always searching and never finding might be a sign of authentic spirituality. And more and more adults are embracing a lifelong religious identity search. But open-ended religious searching may not in fact be well suited to younger adolescents. The National Study of Youth and Religion found that only 2 percent of teenagers are "religious seekers" who are interested in questioning theological beliefs and experimenting with other religions.[31] The proponents of religious seeking may be imposing a young-adult mode of religious exploration upon younger adolescents and older adults. Confusion about developmental differences between older and younger adolescents has often led to the juvenilization of the adult church without much perceptible benefit to teenagers.

Even in youth groups in which the leader is trying to communicate some clear beliefs that he or she hopes young people will come to accept, the teaching methods used often reinforce the cultural imperative toward individualized belief systems. Youth ministries pioneered group discussions and simplified, entertaining teaching styles. Many leaders idealized young people and hoped to remake the church in the image of youth. Some youth leaders actively criticized the adult church and taught young people to feel religiously superior to adults. In short, youth ministry activities communicated to young people that they and their opinions were all-important.

It is a good thing for young people and adults to forge supportive relationships that help them apply their faith to the challenges of daily life. Such groups can help people make a personal commitment to the teachings of the faith. The old systems of indoctrination certainly had their flaws; as we have seen, many in the pre–Vatican II generation of Catholics rebelled against the rigid dogmatism and refusal to entertain questions that they encountered in Catholic schools. But at least the young people of that generation knew the content of the Baltimore Catechism. The problem is that by glorifying the process of individual choice and by constantly trying to please young people and attract them to religious faith, youth ministries have formed generations of Americans who believe it is their privilege to pick and choose what to believe. Even worse, perhaps, is the widespread assumption that it doesn't really matter what you believe, so long as you believe it "sincerely."

The Christian small groups that began in youth ministries and that have become pervasive among adults reveal the same patterns. Participation in these groups helps people strengthen their religious feelings. In one survey, the top five perceived benefits of group participation were "support each other emotionally" (92 percent), "feel better about yourself" (84 percent), "feel like you are not alone" (82 percent), "give encouragement when you are feeling down" (72 percent), and "feel closer to God" (66 percent). Although many groups report praying together and discussing the Bible, the only item on the list of perceived benefits that related to development of religious beliefs was "improve understanding of those with different religious perspectives" (55 percent). Other studies support the idea that membership in a church-based small group often encourages people to value relational intimacy and practical application of their faith more than formal theology or denominational loyalty. Small groups do help people learn about their faith. But sometimes this way of learning encourages people to think that their opinions are every bit as important as what the Bible or the church teaches. The discussion format may sometimes reinforce the idea that all theological beliefs are a matter of personal preference.[32]

So juvenilization has made the process of finding, maintaining, and submitting to religious truth more problematic. And the faith that Americans choose is increasingly the faith of "moralistic, therapeutic deism." To put it simply, they continue to believe what they learned in adolescence. And more and more often, they hear the same messages as adults. God, faith, and the church all exist to help me with my problems. Religious institutions are bad; only my "personal relationship with Jesus" matters. In other words, large numbers of Americans of all ages not only accept a Christianized version of adolescent narcissism, they often celebrate it as authentic spirituality.

The Costs and Benefits of Feel-Good Faith

Many larger American churches have remained vibrant by adapting to the preferences of younger generations. Many of those adaptations have enriched the church. In 1950, many people who went to church did so out of a sense of social obligation. While at church, they didn't expect either to have fun or to be challenged to work for social justice. Just as many people go to church today, but now, by and large, they want to be there because their faith is providing them with strong feelings of connection to God, to others, and to a spiritual mission. As a result of juvenilization, they are more likely to have intense experiences of God, participate in a service or mission trip, and engage in Christian political activism. Evangelical youth ministries made religious conservatives less dour and legalistic. Progressive Protestant, Catholic, and African American youth leaders eventually won the battle to get Christians to see social and political concerns as legitimate elements of their faith.

Of course these changes came at some cost. White evangelicals invested heavily in young people and aggressively adapted to their preferences for an informal, entertaining, feel-good faith. They ended up with churches full of Christians who think that the purpose of God and the Christian faith is to help them feel better. Liberal Protestant youth leaders seriously misjudged the cultural tastes of young people and underestimated how much effort it would take to form countercultural social activists. They ended up with aging congregations and declining numbers. Roman Catholics were slow to juvenilize their churches and invested less in the spiritual formation of youth than they had before the crises of the sixties. They ended up with thousands of nominal Catholic adherents with relatively low levels of religious knowledge and commitment. African American churches managed to retain a high level of religious loyalty without much juvenilization, thanks to the close identification between racial and religious identities among African Americans. But there are signs that younger generations of African Americans may now be less automatically connecting with the church, particularly in urban areas outside the South.

Although juvenilization has renewed American Christianity, it has also undermined Christian maturity. First, the faith has become overly identified with emotional comfort. And it is only a short step from a personalized, emotionally comforting faith to a self-centered one. Second, far too many Christians are inarticulate, indifferent, or confused about their theological beliefs. They view theology as an optional extra to faith, and assume that religious beliefs are a matter of personal preference. Many would be uncomfortable with the idea of believing something just because the Bible, the church, or some other religious authority teaches it. And they are particularly resistant to church teachings that impose behavioral restrictions. If we believe that a mature faith involves more than good feelings, vague beliefs, and living however we want, we must conclude that juvenilization has revitalized American Christianity at the cost of leaving many individuals mired in spiritual immaturity.

Taming Juvenilization

Youth ministries and the juvenilization they bring are crucial to the ongoing vitality of American churches. And as the line between adolescence and adulthood continues to blur, eliminating youth ministries would only hurt long-term church attendance without doing much to counter the trend toward spiritual immaturity. Without major changes in American society, juvenilization cannot be eliminated. But it can be tamed in local congregations that build an intergenerational way of life that fosters spiritual maturity. Pastors, youth leaders, church members of all ages, and youth ministry educators all have a role to play.

Pastors and youth leaders need to teach what the Bible says about spiritual maturity, with a special emphasis on those elements that are neglected by juvenilized Christians. Both teenagers and adults need to hear what Jesus and the apostles taught: that every Christian should reach spiritual maturity after a reasonable period of growth. Those who do not mature are abnormal, like babies who never progress from drinking milk to eating solid food. They are in spiritual danger, just as a tree that produces no fruit might be cut down (Heb. 5:11–6:2, Matt. 7:15-20, Matt. 12:33-37, Luke 13:6-9). Those who are mature know the basic content of the faith (Heb. 5:12-14, 6:1-2) and live a godly way of life that is "worthy" of the salvation they have received (Eph. 4:1–5:2, Col. 3:1–4:1). Like Jesus, they lay down their lives in sacrificial service for others in the body of Christ (Mark 10:41-45, John 13:1-17, 2 Cor. 4:7-12, Eph. 5:1-2, Phil. 2:1-11). They do not view the Christian life as a solitary endeavor, but are deeply committed to their spiritual family, the church (1 Cor. 12:12-26, Eph. 4:1-16). They recognize that the call to follow Jesus includes not only an easy yoke and a light burden, but also taking up their cross daily (Matt. 11:28-30, Luke 9:23). They expect both emotional comfort and suffering as normal parts of the Christian life and embrace both as ways to union with Christ (James 1:4, 1 Pet. 1:6-8, Rom. 5:3-5, 2 Cor. 1:3-11, 4:7-15). Mature disciples of Jesus center their lives on following Christ and partnering with him in his kingdom mission (Phil. 1:21, Matt. 6:33, Matt. 28:16-20, John 20:21). Teachers need to present spiritual maturity as it really is: a beautiful life of love shared with others. Jesus died and rose again to purify a people of his own (Titus 2:11-14) full of "love, joy, peace, patience, kindness, generosity, faithfulness, gentleness, and self control" (Gal. 5:22-23) who "shine like stars" in a dark world (Phil. 2:15).

It is not enough for juvenilized Americans to hear that spiritual maturity is possible and desirable. It is not even enough for them to be able to explain what a spiritually mature believer should look like. They need practices and environments that will help them grow into spiritual maturity. After all, it is easier to say "it's not all about me" than it is to really think, feel, and act that way. It is here that church leaders need cultural discernment. They need to ask hard questions about the music they sing, the curriculum materials they use, and the ways they structure the activities of the church. Is what we are doing together reinforcing mature or immature versions of the faith? In our attempts to "reach" people in our community, are we conceding too much to the characteristic weaknesses and besetting sins of our culture? We will always have to build cultural bridges to people outside the church (Acts 17:16-34, 1 Cor. 9:19-27). But which direction is the traffic flowing on those bridges? Are unbelievers crossing the bridge to reach a countercultural, spiritually mature way of life, or are believers crossing back into the spiritually immature ways of the world?

For example, is the music we sing in church fostering a self-centered, romantic spirituality in which following Jesus is compared to "falling in love"? If so, we should not be surprised if some people have a relationship with Jesus that has all the maturity and staying power of an adolescent infatuation. Do we ask every church member to master a shared body of basic truths, or is all of our Christian education on an "a la carte" basis? If the latter, then we should not be surprised if people pick and choose which parts of Christian truth to believe and live. Are we training leaders to disciple others through one-on-one and small-group relationships? If not, we should not complain when people remain stuck in immature ways of believing and behaving. Do we model service, teach about it, and provide opportunities for every believer to serve others? If not, we should not be surprised if people continue to think the faith is "all about me."

Youth ministry educators need to teach future youth ministers about juvenilization and equip them to serve as responsible cultural gatekeepers in the church. Youth pastors need to be taught to ask themselves, "In what ways would the rest of the church be improved and in what ways would it be impoverished if it looked exactly like my youth ministry?" They need to learn that cultural forms are not neutral. Every enculturation of Christianity highlights some elements of the faith and obscures others. Youth ministry leaders need to ask, "If we adapt to the needs or preferences of young people in this particular way, what are we going to do to help them transcend the limitations of youth culture and strive toward biblical spiritual maturity?"

Youth ministry educators also need to challenge youth ministers to love *both* young people *and* the church. Especially since many new youth ministers are emerging adults who may be struggling with a lingering adolescent aversion to "organized religion," they need older adults to help them love the church and value its heritage. Youth leaders who only tolerate the church will not tame juvenilization, because they will not care what happens to the church in the future. And the young people they influence will be more likely leave the church behind, or at least spend their lives stuck in a self-centered, "me and Jesus" faith.

Our vision for Christian maturity should neither stigmatize adolescents nor let adults off the hook. Although the Bible uses the metaphor of growing from infancy to adulthood to describe the process of spiritual maturation, there is nothing in the nature of the biblical traits of maturity that restricts them to people of a certain age. Adolescents can behave in spiritually mature ways, and many adults are still in spiritual diapers. All life stages have characteristic strengths and weaknesses when it comes to living the Christian gospel. For example, in the "worship wars" that have raged in some churches in recent years, both adults and young people have displayed the worst traits of their respective life stages. Adults have rigidly clung to the worship practices of the past and accused young people of corrupting the faith. They have used their power to block changes without listening to young people. They have often complained about the tastes of young people but have not recognized their own subjective preferences. They have not provided convincing theological reasons for their resistance to change. For their part, young people have grown frustrated with the slow pace of change. They have shown little respect for the traditions of the past or of the "old people" who love those ways. Both groups have seen each other as enemies and have not tried very hard to understand each other's perspectives. They have allowed the cultural gap between generations to trump their unity in Christ. Instead of being enriched by one another and learning from one another, we are in danger of *both* losing the treasures of the past *and* missing out on the best of the new.

Theological and cultural disagreements like these would look very different among Christians who shared a vision for spiritual maturity and understood the positive contributions that people in all life stages can make toward that goal. Adults need children and adolescents to draw out their committed love and provide concrete opportunities to care for others. Adolescents can help adults reconnect with the passion of a life devoted to Christ, what he called the "first love" of the Christians at Ephesus

(Rev. 2:4).[33] Young people need adults in their lives who are teaching and modeling an attractive spiritual maturity. The church is an intergenerational family in which each person has a unique role in helping the others toward their shared goal of maturity in Christ (Titus 2:1-15, Eph. 5:21–6:4, Col. 3:18–4:1, 1 John 2:12-14).

Adults should not try to be teenagers, but instead need to set adult examples. Teenagers can legitimately follow Christ in adolescent ways, but they need to grow up spiritually as well as physically. All of us, whether teenagers or adults, should be devoting ourselves to helping one another grow toward spiritual maturity. After all, churches full of people who are committed to helping each other toward spiritual maturity are not only the best antidote to juvenilization in the church, but also a powerful countercultural witness in a juvenilized world.

Notes

Notes to the Introduction

1. James Cote, *Arrested Adulthood: The Changing Nature of Maturity and Identity* (New York: New York University Press, 2000), 206-7; Gary Cross, *Men to Boys: The Making of Modern Immaturity* (New York: Columbia University Press, 2008).

2. See "Frontline: The Merchants of Cool," directed by Barack Goodman (PBS Home Video, 2005), and "Frontline: The Persuaders," directed by Goodman and Rachel Dretzin (PBS Home Video, 2005); Jennings Bryant and Susan Thompson, *Fundamentals of Media Effects* (Boston: McGraw-Hill, 2002). Extensive literatures exist that explore both the effects of consumerism and the dynamics of the American religious marketplace. For the most part, the literature on the religious marketplace has said little about the way that markets foster immaturity.

3. The developmental characteristics described here can be found in any standard textbook on adolescent psychology. See, for example, Jeffrey Arnett, *Adolescence and Emerging Adulthood: A Cultural Approach* (Upper Saddle River, N.J.: Prentice Hall, 2001) and John Santrock, *Adolescence*, 11th edition (New York: McGraw-Hill, 2005).

4. Thomas Hine, *The Rise and Fall of the American Teenager* (New York: Harper, 2000).

5. See "Frontline: The Merchants of Cool."

6. Barbara Ehrenreich, *Fear of Falling: The Inner Life of the Middle Class* (New York: Pantheon, 1989).

7. Dick Hebdige, *Subculture: The Meaning of Style* (New York: Routledge, 1988, originally published 1979); Mike Brake, *The Sociology of Youth Culture and Youth Subcultures* (London: Routledge & Kegan Paul, 1980).

8. Jeffrey Jensen Arnett, *Emerging Adulthood: The Winding Road from the Late Teens through the Twenties* (Oxford: Oxford University Press, 2004). The Society for the Study of Emerging Adulthood was established in 2003; see www.ssea.org.

Notes to Pages 20-23

Notes to Chapter 1

1. For unemployment statistics, see Maxwell S. Stewart, *Youth in the World of Today* (New York: American Council on Education, Public Affairs Committee, 1938), 3. For the anecdote about young transients, see Kingsley Davis, *Youth in the Depression* (Chicago: University of Chicago Press, 1935), 1-4. For descriptions of the Scottsboro case, see James Goodman, *Stories of Scottsboro* (New York: Pantheon, 1994), and Clarence Norris and Sybil D. Washington, *The Last of the Scottsboro Boys* (New York: G. P. Putnam's Sons, 1979).

2. Katherine Glover, *Youth . . . Leisure for Living* (Washington, D.C.: Committee on Youth Problems, Office of Education, U.S. Department of the Interior, 1936), 1-2. For the struggle between young people and adults over use of leisure time, see Suzanne Wasserman, "Cafes, Clubs, Corners, and Candy Stores: Youth Leisure Culture in New York City's Lower East Side during the 1930s," *Journal of American Culture* 14 (Winter 1991): 43-48. For the role of new educational expectations in exacerbating the sense of crisis, see Stephen Lassonde, "The Real, Real Youth Problem," *Reviews in American History* 22 (1994): 149-55.

3. M. M. Chambers, *Looking Ahead with Youth* (Washington, D.C.: American Council on Education, 1942), 30. See also *Teen Trouble: What Recreation Can Do About It* (New York: National Recreation Association, 1943), University of Notre Dame Archives, Edward V. Cardinal Papers CCRD 12-4.

4. For examples of adult fears about youthful political radicalism, see Homer P. Rainey, *How Fare American Youth?* (New York: D. Appleton-Century Company, 1938), W. Thatcher Winslow, *Youth a World Problem* (Washington, D.C.: National Youth Administration, 1937), Murray Plavner, *Here Are the Facts: Is the American Youth Congress a Communist Front?* (New York: Murray Plavner, 1939), and Maxine Davis, *The Lost Generation: A Portrait of American Youth Today* (New York: Macmillan, 1936). For information on the student movement and youth march on Washington, see Ralph S. Brax, *The First Student Movement: Student Activism in the United States During the 1930s* (Port Washington, N.Y.: National University Publications, 1981), and Louis de Rochemont, Exec. Producer, "1940: America's Youth" in *The March of Time: America's Youth 1940-1950* (New Line Home Video, 1995).

5. See titles already cited by Rainey, Winslow, Davis, and Kingsley as well as *Christian Youth and the Economic Problem* (Chicago: United Christian Youth Movement, 1944), Wyndham Lewis, *Doom of Youth* (London: Chatto & Windus, 1932). See also Chambers, *Looking Ahead with Youth*.

6. *Facing Life with Jesus Christ: Record of the Proceedings of the Methodist Young People's Conference Held in the Municipal Auditorium, Memphis, Tennessee, December 27-31, 1935* (Nashville: General Board of Christian Education, Methodist Episcopal Church, South, 1936), 15-17, 82-89, 125-33, 169-77.

7. Torrey Johnson, "Accepting the Challenge!" in *Minutes of the First Annual Convention* (July 23-29, 1945), 17-19, Billy Graham Center Archives (hereafter BGCA), collection 48, box 13, folder 36.

8. George E. Haynes, "The Crisis Confronting the American Negro and the Negro Churches," *National Baptist Voice* (Oct. 20, 1934): 1, 6-8. *Proceedings of the 1945 Session of the National Sunday School and Baptist Training Union Congress Held in St. Louis, MO, June 18-24* (Nashville: Sunday School Publishing Board, 1945), 14-18.

9. *The Call to Youth* (Washington, D.C.: National Council of Catholic Women, 1937), 16-21.

231

10. *A Program of Action for American Youth* (Washington, D.C.: American Youth Commission of the American Council on Education, 1939), 3-5.

11. *A Program of Action,* 3, 19. Other American Youth Commission publications praised the efforts of religious organizations, although the authors sometimes worried that such groups might be losing their effectiveness. See Stewart, *Youth in the World of Today,* 28-29, 34-35.

12. Richard A. Reiman, *The New Deal and American Youth: Ideas and Ideals in a Depression Decade* (Athens: University of Georgia Press, 1992), 1-10.

13. "Msgr. George Johnson Dies While Delivering Address at Commencement Exercises," 6/5/44, Archives of the Catholic University of America, National Catholic Welfare Conference (hereafter ACUA, NCWC), Press Department, 10-51.

14. Reiman, *The New Deal and American Youth,* 39-44.

15. For the story of Wyrtzen's military influence, see Forrest Forbes, *God Hath Chosen: The Story of Jack Wyrtzen and the Word of Life Hour* (Grand Rapids: Zondervan, 1948), 63. For the public reception of Youth for Christ, see Joel Carpenter, *Revive Us Again: The Reawakening of American Fundamentalism* (New York: Oxford University Press, 1997), 161-76; Clarence Woodbury, "Bobby Soxers Sing Hallelujah," *American Magazine* 141 (March 1946): 26-27; "Youth for Christ," *Time,* Feb. 4, 1946, 46-47; "Wanted: A Miracle of Good Weather, and the 'Youth for Christ' Rally Got It," *Newsweek,* June 11, 1945, 84; and William F. McDermott, "Bobby Soxers Find the Sawdust Trail," *Colliers,* March 26, 1945, 22.

16. Blaine E. Kirkpatrick, *Adventures in Christian Leadership: A Guide to Young People's Work in Church Schools and the Epworth League* (Chicago: Board of Education, Methodist Episcopal Church, n.d.), 3-5, 33-34. See also the other titles in the series: Roy E. Burt, *Adventures in Building a Better World* (Chicago: Board of Education, Methodist Episcopal Church, 1933); Owen M. Geer, *Adventures in the Devotional Life* (Chicago: Board of Education, Methodist Episcopal Church, 1936); Owen M. Geer, *Adventures in Recreation* (Chicago: Board of Education, Methodist Episcopal Church, 1934).

17. T. Otto Nall, ed., *Christian Fellowship in a World of Conflict: Report of the National Conference of Methodist Youth in Biennial Session at the University of Colorado, Boulder, Colorado, August 30-September 4, 1938* (Chicago: National Council of Methodist Youth, 1938), 82, 108-10. "The Story of a Movement," *Newsletter of the National Conference of Methodist Youth* (July, August 1941): 12, Methodist Center for Archives and History, General Board of Discipleship Records 1124-4-2:41.

18. *Being Christian in Times Like These: A Report of the Second National Conference of Methodist Youth Held at Berea College, Berea, Kentucky September 2 to 6, 1936* (Chicago: National Council of Methodist Youth, 1936), 12-18, 83-84, 102, MCAH, GBD 1124-4-1:15. "The Story of a Movement," 4, 12. For other examples of generational conflict, see "Youth Serves in New Ways" *Newsletter* (March 1942): 1, MCAH, GBD 1124-5-2:08; *Third Annual Report of the National Conference of the Methodist Youth Fellowship August 29-September 4, 1943,* 13-15, MCAH, GBD 1124-5-2:13; *Our World for Christ: Report of the Second National Convocation of the Methodist Youth Fellowship Held at College Campus, Lake Geneva, WI, August 25-30, 1944* (Nashville: National Conference of the Methodist Youth Fellowship, 1945), 59, MCAH, GBD 1124-4-3:03; and *The Fifth Annual Meeting of the National Conference of the Methodist Youth Fellowship, Adrian College, Adrian, Michigan, August 24-30, 1945,* 51-54, MCAH, GBD 1124-5-2:13.

19. Harvey Seifert, ed., *Methodist Youth United: The Report of the First National Confer-*

ence of the Methodist Youth Fellowship, Baker University, Baldwin, Kansas, August 29-September 2, 1941 (Nashville: National Conference of the Methodist Youth Fellowship, 1941), 21-24, MCAH, GBD 1124-4-2:39. Alfred E. Moore, ed., *For the Living of These Days: Report of the First National Convocation of the Methodist Youth Fellowship Held at Oxford, Ohio, September 1-5, 1942* (Nashville: National Convocation of the Methodist Youth Fellowship, 1942), 24-25, 30-31, 32-33, 38-39.

20. Moore, *For the Living of These Days*, 44-47, 51. For more on service to Japanese Americans, see *Third Annual Report*, 24, "Send *Power* to Japanese," *The Planner* (Apr., May, June 1943): 2, MCAH, GBD 1184-3-1:22; "Best Attempted," *The Planner* (Oct., Nov., Dec. 1943): 3, MCAH, GBD 1184-3-1:22; *The Fifth Annual Meeting of the National Conference of the Methodist Youth Fellowship*, 14-20, 42; and "Three Hostels to Assist in Relocation," *Newsletter* (Apr. 1945): 1, MCAH, GBD 1124-5-2:08. For integration of Methodist youth gatherings, see "Reports of Interracial Camps," *Brotherhood Builder* (Nov. 1945): 1, MCAH, GBD 1126-6-3:14; photographs on front and back covers and inside front page of *Our World for Christ: Report of the Second National Convocation of the Methodist Youth Fellowship* (Nashville: National Conference of the Methodist Youth Fellowship, 1945). For youth protests leading to camp integration, see "A Statement from the Mount Sequoyah Board of Trustees to the 1940 Young People's Leadership Conference," August 1, 1940, MCAH, GBD 1126-6-2:41; and J. Q. Schisler to Bishop Paul E. Martin, November 28, 1945, MCAH, GBD 1126-6-2:41.

21. Seifert, *Methodist Youth United*, 8-11. "The Aims, Purposes, and Philosophy of Catholic Youth Work: Proceedings of the Buzz Sessions of the Seventh National Conference on Catholic Youth Work, Nov 17-20, 1958," 8-10, ACUA, NCWC, Education Department Papers, 10-84.

22. "History of the 1946 Conference, Mt. Sequoyah, Fayetteville, Arkansas, August 5-15, 1946," MCAH, GBD 1126-6-2:33. For similar optimism regarding Methodist political influence, see "Program Suggestions for Meetings," *The Planner* (Oct., Nov., Dec. 1943): 1-3, MCAH, GBD 1184-3-1:22; and "The Crusade for a New World Order," *The Planner* (July, Aug., Sept. 1943): 1-4, MCAH, GBD 1184-3-1:22. For youth protests of segregation at the Mt. Sequoyah campground, see "Prepare the Way: Report of the 1939 Young People's Leadership Conference," 22-24, 28-29, MCAH, GBD 1126-6-2:35; J. Fisher Simpson, "A Statement from one Member of the Board of Trustees with Reference to the Entertainment of Negro Speakers at Mount Sequoyah," Aug. 24, 1939, MCAH, GBD 1126-6-2:41. In 1946, after about ten years of complaints from campers, the camp directors relented and allowed a black speaker to be housed on the grounds. Joseph Bell to Mrs. Retha L. Sadler August 20, 1965, MCAH, GBD 1126-6-2:41.

23. Torrey Johnson and Robert Cook, *Reaching Youth for Christ* (Chicago: Moody Press, 1944), 44-62.

24. For a description of the typical Youth for Christ rally and directions on how to duplicate it in your own city, see Torrey Johnson and Robert Cook, *Reaching Youth for Christ* (Chicago: Moody Press, 1944). For a description of an early rally by an outside observer, see McDermott, "Bobby-Soxers." For reprints of several early descriptions of the movement written by insiders, see Joel Carpenter, ed., *The Youth for Christ Movement and Its Pioneers* (New York: Garland, 1988).

25. McDermott, "Bobby-Soxers Find the Sawdust Trail," 23.

26. "Victory Youth Rally, Chicago Stadium, Saturday, Oct. 21, 1944," 5, Billy Graham Center Archives 48-14-32. Interview with Torrey Johnson, tape 3, side 2, tape 6, side 1, BGCA,

collection 48. Johnson remembered that more War Bonds were sold at the Soldier Field rally than at any other single gathering during the war because "we wanted to prove that Evangelical Christians were loyal, patriotic Americans."

27. Johnson and Cook, *Reaching Youth for Christ*, 20. "Minutes of the Second Annual Convention, Youth for Christ International, July 22-29, 1946," 6-7, 37, 44-45, BGCA 48-9-4. See also BGCA 17-18.

28. Carpenter, *Revive Us Again*, 161-76. See also Joel Carpenter, ed., *The Youth for Christ Movement and Its Pioneers* (New York: Garland, 1988), and James C. Hefley, *God Goes to High School* (Waco, Tex.: Word Books, 1970). For claims that YFC rallies prevented juvenile delinquency, see Johnson and Cook, *Reaching Youth for Christ*, 20.

29. Torrey Johnson, "Accepting the Challenge!" in *Minutes of the First Annual Convention* (July 23-29, 1945), 17-19, BGCA 48-13-36.

30. Torrey Johnson, "God Is in It!" in *Minutes of the First Annual Convention*, 26-32.

31. Harold E. Fey, "What About Youth for Christ?" *Christian Century* (June 20, 1945): 729-31, and "Has Youth for Christ Gone Fascist?" *Christian Century* (Nov. 14, 1945): 1243-44.

32. "Youth for Christ," *Time*, Feb. 4, 1946, 46-47. *What Is Youth for Christ International?* (Chicago: Youth for Christ International, 1946), BGCA 48-17-9. "Brief Facts about Youth for Christ International" (Chicago: Youth for Christ International, 1946), BGCA 48-17-9. Rev. G. Richard Kuch, "Youth for Christ a Challenge to Liberal Youth," *American Unitarian Youth and Universalist Youth Fellowship*, Dec. 1945, 8, 9, 11, MCAH, GBD 1184-3-2:02. See also "Why We Are Opposed to Youth for Christ," *Youth for Action*, n.d., MCAH, GBD 1184-3-2:02.

33. For a good summary of *The Christian Education of Youth*, see Harold A. Buetow, *Of Singular Benefit: The Story of Catholic Education in the United States* (New York: Macmillan, 1970), 229-30.

34. *Summary of Catholic Education, 1944-45* (Washington D.C.: Department of Education, National Catholic Welfare Conference, 1946), 22. "Religion and the High School Student," *Catholic Action* 35 (Sept. 1953): 12. For the dangers of non-Catholic education as a justification for new youth programs, see "Secularization of Education Today's Greatest Danger to Youth, Says Archbishop McNicholas," *Catholic Action* 19 (Sept. 1937): 6, and "February Study Topic — 'The Catholic Family and the Youth Movement,'" *Catholic Action* 17 (Feb. 1935): 19-20. For calls from educators to supplement school activities, see Aloysius Croft, "The Catholic Youth Movement and the Parish School," *Catholic School Journal* 37 (Feb. 1937): 48-49, and Leon A. McNeill, "What Shall We Do for Our Boys and Girls in Public High Schools?" *The Catholic Educational Review* 32 (Jan. 1934): 37-42.

35. "Growing Interest in Meeting Problems of Catholic Youth," "N.C.C.W. Plans for Girls' Welfare," "Youth Leaders Confer with N.C.C.M.," *Catholic Action* 16 (March 1934): 4-5, 14. "Need of a Catholic Program for Youth," *Catholic Action* 16 (Oct. 1934): 14, 18.

36. *Youth Today and Tomorrow* (Washington D.C.: National Council of Catholic Women, 1935). *The Call to Youth* (Washington D.C.: National Council of Catholic Women, 1938), 10-12. For more on the four-fold program, see *Youth Leaders' Handbook* (Washington D.C.: National Council of Catholic Women, 1939), 6-9, 14-18, 25-27, 31-32, 34, 39-41.

37. "A World to Reconstruct," *Diocesan Directors Bulletin* 5:2 (Sept. 1944): 5, ACUA NCWC Youth Department 10-54. For similar views, see "Victory in War and in Peace," *Diocesan Directors Bulletin* 3:3 (Nov. 1942): 3-19, ACUA, NCWC, YD 10-54; "Trial By Fire," *Diocesan Directors Bulletin* 3:1 (Sept. 1942): 3-4, ACUA, NCWC, YD 10-54; "A Parable from Mars," *Diocesan Directors Bulletin* 1:5 (May 15, 1941): 8, ACUA, NCWC, YD 10-54; and Rev.

V. Brennan, S.M., "The Parish Youth Council," *Diocesan Directors Bulletin* 2:2 (Oct. 1941): 13-19, ACUA, NCWC, YD 10-54.

38. For background on the Catholic Action movement, see Philip Gleason, *Contending with Modernity: Catholic Higher Education in the Twentieth Century* (New York: Oxford University Press, 1995), 152-54. For the easy coexistence of Catholic and American values in some minds, see David J. O'Brien, "Catholicism and Americanism," in Edward R. Kantowicz, ed., *Modern American Catholicism, 1900-1965: Selected Historical Essays* (New York: Garland, 1988), 98-115.

39. Bernard J. Sheil, "Social Readjustment — A Problem of Youth," *American Catholic Sociological Review* 1 (March 1940): 10-12. Sheil claimed to be replacing worldly ideals with Catholic ones in "The Catholic Youth Organization," University of Notre Dame Archives, Edward V. Cardinal Papers CCRD, box 12, folder 5. For his claim to be restoring young lapsed Catholics through boxing, see "The Records Speak," UNDA, CCRD 12-5. For the "youth is not a problem" quote, see "The Problem of Youth," UNDA, CCRD 12-5. For summaries of Sheil's work with the CYO, see Roger L. Treat, *Bishop Sheil and the CYO* (New York: Julian Messner, 1951); Edward R. Kantowicz, *Corporation Sole: Cardinal Mundelein and Chicago Catholicism* (Notre Dame: University of Notre Dame Press, 1983), 173-202; Steven M. Avella, "The Rise and Fall of Bernard Sheil," in Ellen Skerrett, Edward R. Kantowicz, and Steven M. Avella, *Catholicism, Chicago Style* (Chicago: Loyola University Press, 1993), 95-108, and Steven M. Avella, *This Confident Church: Catholic Leadership and Life in Chicago, 1940-1965* (Notre Dame: University of Notre Dame Press, 1992), 109-49. Early reports and pamphlets published by the CYO presented the organization as a benefit to the church, to the general population of Chicago, and to the nation. See "Facts on the Catholic Youth Organization of the Archdiocese of Chicago," UNDA, CCRD 11-8; "Facts on the CYO," UNDA, CCRD 11-8; "Historical Survey of the Catholic Youth Organization," UNDA, CCRD 11-8; "Catholic Youth Organization Nov. 1949," UNDA, CCRD 11-1; and "CYO Vacation Schools: Manual for Leaders," 10-11, UNDA, CCRD 11-09.

40. Gleason, *Contending with Modernity*, 152-54; Mary Irene Zotti, *A Time of Awakening: The Young Christian Worker Story in the United States, 1938 to 1970* (Chicago: Loyola University Press, 1991), 11-12, 37-39, 96.

41. "The World Outlook for Young Baptists," *National Baptist Voice* (hereafter *NBV*) (Mar. 2, 1935): 3, 7-8.

42. Lethia Craig, "Junior Missionaries," *Star of Hope* 1:4 (Jan. 1938): 21.

43. First Baptist Church of Nashville kept young people and adults together for worship and for many other activities. Ben Harris, interview by author, 27 October 1999, Nashville, tape recording, author's personal collection. Evelyn Gaines and Mary Wickware, interview by author, 20 October 1999, Nashville, Tennessee, tape recording, author's personal collection. For the youth activities of the Women's Auxiliary Convention, see *Proceedings of the 61st Annual Session of the National Baptist Convention, USA, Inc.* (Nashville: Sunday School Publishing Board, 1941), 256-63; *Proceedings of the 62nd Annual Session of the National Baptist Convention, USA, Inc.* (Nashville: Sunday School Publishing Board, 1942), 232-83; *Proceedings of the 63rd Annual Session of the National Baptist Convention, USA, Inc.* (Nashville: Sunday School Publishing Board, 1943), 304-55.

44. "First Baptist through the Years: A Twin Anniversary Celebration," March 12, 13, 14, 16, 1952, Vanderbilt University Archives, Kelly Miller Smith Papers, Box 37, Folder 7. For Youth Sunday sermons, see Rev. M. D. Dickson, Peoria, Ill., "Youth's Seat Reserved at the Ta-

ble," *NBV* (Jan. 19, 1935): 5; Wade Hampton McKinney, "Windows of Experience," Sept. 1, 1935, Western Reserve Historical Society, Wade Hampton McKinney Papers, Box 4, Folder 3, and Wade Hampton McKinney, "Still with Thee," May 4, 1937, WRHS, WHM 4-4. For postwar examples, see Kelly Miller Smith, "God in the Morning," 1951, VUA, KMS 23-5; and Kelly Miller Smith, "Toward a More Consecrated Youth," VUA, KMS, 27-13.

45. For close ties between black churches and schools in Nashville during the 1940s and 1950s, see Gaines and Wickware, interview by author, and Zelma Ewing, interview by author, 23 October 1999, Nashville, Tennessee, tape recording, author's personal collection.

46. Kelly Miller Smith, "Accent on Youth," VUA, KMS 112-7.

47. W. H. Jernagin, "The Most Important People in the World Challenge the Home, the Church and the State." *NBV* (Apr. 6, 1935): 3, 8. W. H. Jernagin, "The Responsibility of the Present Day Church," *NBV* (June 29, 1935): 1, 7-8.

48. "My Spiritual Pilgrimage," Jan. 12, 1947, WRHS, WHM 5-4. For McKinney's message of personal conversion, see "The New Birth," Fourth Anniversary of the Junior Church, March 10, 1940, WRHS, WHM 6-1. For denunciations of injustice, see "While Cleveland Sleeps!" WRHS, WHM 4-2; "Why This Concentration of Crime in the Negro District?" Aug. 23, 1942, WRHS, WHM 5-1; and "The Central Area," address to the City Club, Feb. 3, 1945, WRHS, WHM 5-2. "The Reign of Sin," 4-12-42, WRHS, WHM 5-1. "The Church on the New Frontier," Pittsburgh, Oct. 22, 1945, WRHS, WHM 5-2. For the young church member's praise of McKinney, see "Dr. McKinney as an Example and Leader of Youth," delivered by Samuel B. Dickerson, Twentieth Anniversary Program of Dr. W. H. McKinney, Pastor, Antioch Baptist Church, Friday, July 23, 1948, 8:30 p.m., WRHS, WHM 1-1. For a summary of McKinney's youth programs, see "The McKinney Era," n.d., WRHS, WHM 1-1.

Notes to Chapter 2

1. Louis de Rochemont, "Youth in Crisis," *The March of Time* 10:3 (New York: Time, Inc., 1943), re-released in *The March of Time: American Lifestyles — American Youth* (New Line Home Video, 1987). For similar concerns about youth and suggestions of "teen canteens" as the answer, see *Teen Trouble: What Recreation Can Do About It* (New York: National Recreation Association, 1943). Although some social scientists tried to temper wartime exaggerations of the "youth problem," their findings did not often make it into the press. See Ray H. Abrams, ed., *The American Family in World War II* (Philadelphia: American Academy of Political and Social Science, 1943), 69-78, 157-63, and Wayne W. Soper, *A Study of Youth in Wartime* (Albany: The University of the State of New York, 1943).

2. *Young Life*, March 1944, 3. For a similar use of contrasting photographs in a Methodist publication, see John E. Marvin, *Crusade for Christ Manual for Pastors and Church Leaders* (Chicago: Crusade for Christ, n.d.).

3. Louis de Rochement, "Teen Age Girls," *The March of Time* 11:11 (New York: Time, Inc., 1945), re-released in *The March of Time: American Lifestyles — American Youth* (New Line Home Video, 1987).

4. James Gilbert, *A Cycle of Outrage: America's Reaction to the Juvenile Delinquent in the 1950s* (New York: Oxford University Press, 1988).

5. Thomas Hine, *The Rise and Fall of the American Teenager* (New York: Harper Collins,

1999), 234-43. Grace Palladino, *Teenagers: An American History* (New York: Basic Books, 1996), 50-55, 74-91, 109-10.

6. "Youth Meeting Saturday, May 23, 1942," MCAH, GBD 1184-3-1:09. For similar discussions, see "Minutes, Youth Worker's Commission, Methodist Conference on Christian Education, November 29-December 3, 1943," MCAH, GBD 1122-5-3:13, and "Minutes of the Youth Department Staff Retreat October 14-17, 1946," MCAH, GBD 1124-2-3:07. For evidence of low participation in work camps, see *Fifth Annual Meeting of the National Conference*, 14-20, 42.

7. Isaac Kelley Beckes, *Young Leaders in Action* (Nashville: Abingdon-Cokesbury Press, 1941), 6-7, 16-25.

8. For declining numbers at Sunday School and MYF meetings see "Compel Them to Come In," *The Planner* (July, Aug., Sept. 1944), 1, MCAH, GBD 1184-3-1:22, and "Meeting of Jurisdictional Youth Leaders, February 19, 1943," 7, MCAH, GBD 1184-2-2:04. High school enrollments dropped 17 percent between 1940 and 1944 according to Palladino, *Teenagers*, 66.

9. "Youth Meeting," 5, 8. "Meeting of Jurisdictional Youth Leaders," 19-25.

10. "Meeting of Jurisdictional Youth Leaders," 20. For examples of weak conference resolutions on "commercialized recreation," see Seifert, 25-26, and Moore, 38-40. For criticisms of teen centers, see "Youth Centers," *The Planner* (Oct., Nov., Dec. 1944): 2. For Methodist alternatives, see "Fun Fair Flashes," *The Planner* (Oct., Nov., Dec. 1944): 2. For exhortations to keep pure for the sake of the war and returning soldiers, see "When Johnny Comes Marching Home," *The Planner* (Oct., Nov., Dec. 1944): 1. See also "Temperance and Leisure Time," *Newsletter of the NCMYF*, Sept. 1941, MCAH, GBD 1124-5-2:08.

11. *Our World for Christ*, 13-14. *The Fifth Annual Meeting*, 20.

12. Mel Larson, *Youth for Christ: Twentieth Century Wonder* (Grand Rapids, MI: Zondervan, 1947). William F. McDermott, "Bobby Soxers Find the Sawdust Trail," *Colliers*, Mar. 26, 1945, 22-23. "Wanted: A Miracle of Good Weather and the 'Youth for Christ' Rally Got It," *Newsweek*, June 11, 1945, 84.

13. Rupert, "Field Report: Youth for Christ Rally," 1.

14. "Minutes of the Second Annual Convention," 38-39. For the forties as an age of anxiety, see William Graebner, *The Age of Doubt: American Thought and Culture in the 1940s* (Boston: Twayne, 1991). For the cultural role of delinquency in postwar America, see Gilbert, *A Cycle of Outrage*.

15. Joel Carpenter, ed., *The Early Billy Graham: Sermon and Revival Accounts* (New York: Garland, 1988), 49-50, 63-76, 89-96. "Young Life: A Special Anniversary Booklet Commemorating the First Twenty-Five Years Service of Young Life," BGCA 20-69-1. See also Char Meredith, *It's a Sin to Bore a Kid: The Story of Young Life* (Waco, Tex.: Word, 1978).

16. Johnson and Cook, *Reaching Youth for Christ*, 35-36. "But Brother, It Did Happen in Grand Rapids, Mich.!" YFC brochure, BGCA 48-14-14.

17. Hoover Rupert, "Report on Youth for Christ Rally, Nashville, Tennessee, December 8, 1945," MCAH 1184-3-2:02. For an overview of reactions to YFC, including the "gospel horse," see Carpenter, *Revive Us Again*, 161-76.

18. Hoover Rupert, "Field Report: Youth for Christ Rally, Kansas City, Missouri, January 11, 1947," MCAH 1184-3-2:02.

19. Staff of the Youth Department of the International Council of Religious Education, "Youth for Christ and Other Non-Denominational Youth Movements," Dec. 1945, MCAH

1184-3-2:02. Rev. G. Richard Kuch, "Youth For Christ: A Challenge to Liberal Youth," *American Unitarian Youth Universalist Youth Fellowship*, Dec. 1945, 8-9, 11, MCAH 1184-3-2:02.

20. "Minutes of the Second Annual Convention," 3, 8-9.

21. "Wanted: A Miracle of Good Weather," 84.

22. Bob Cook, "What Happens Next?" *Youth for Christ Magazine* (hereafter YFCM), July 1949, 4-8. "What's Cookin? A monthly chat with Bob Cook," *YFCM*, Apr. 1949, 25, 75.

23. Joseph E. Schieder, "You and Your Parish — The Strength of the Church," *Catholic Action* 33 (Mar. 1951): 6-8.

24. Joseph E. Schieder, "Youth and the Community," *Catholic Action* 34 (Mar. 1952): 10-12.

25. *Youth United for a Better Home Town* (Youth Division, National Social Welfare Assembly), UNDA, CCRD, 12-4. "Youth and the Community — a Prophecy," *Newsnotes* 1:4 (Apr. 1948): 15, ACUA, NCWC, Youth Department, 10:52.

26. "Northeastern Area Directors Meet at Washington," *Newsnotes* 1:6 (June 1948): 1-3, ACUA, NCWC, YD, 10:52.

27. For ongoing struggles to make the youth council plan a reality, see "Objective Number Two," *Diocesan Directors Bulletin* 6:2 (Nov. 1, 1945): 3, ACUA, NCWC, YD 10-55. See also *National Federation of Catholic College Students: Handbook for Student Leaders* (Washington, D.C.: Youth Department, NCWC, 1941). Joseph E. Schieder, "The Value of a Diocesan Youth Council and the Value and Power of a National Youth Council," in *Second Annual Conference Youth Department National Catholic Welfare Conference* (Washington, D.C.: National Catholic Welfare Conference, 1949), 33-35.

28. For concerns about national YCS efforts, see Patricia Groom, "Student Leaders and Two-Legged Answers," *Today*, May 1950, 5, UNDA, John Cogley Papers (CCOG) 6. For complaints about high school YCS elitism see "Catholic Action is Different," *Today*, Mar. 15, 1948, 19, UNDA, CCOG 6.

29. Mary Irene Zotti, *A Time of Awakening: The Young Christian Worker Story in the United States, 1938 to 1970* (Chicago: Loyola University Press, 1991), 46-47, 64-66. Dennis Michael Robb, "Specialized Catholic Action in the United States, 1936-1949: Ideology, Leadership and Organization" (Ph.D. dissertation, University of Minnesota, 1972), 172, 182.

30. "CISCA — The Story of an Idea," *Today*, Apr. 1946, 16, UNDA, CCOG 6. "Today Toasts: Rev. Martin Carrabine, S. J.," *Today*, Apr. 1950, 23, UNDA, CCOG 6.

31. "God or Mammon: Sanctity in This Highly Mechanized World," *Today*, Dec. 1947, 19, UNDA, John Cogley Papers, CCOG 6.

32. "The Movies: Here's Where We Came In," *Today*, May 1946, 16, UNDA, CCOG 6. "The Reader's Digest," *Today*, Sept. 1946, 16, UNDA, CCOG 6. "Perfume Patter," *Today*, Oct. 1946, 16, UNDA, CCOG 6. "The Comics," *Today*, Nov. 1946, 16, UNDA, CCOG 6. "Star System: In Hollywood, the Name's the Thing," *Today*, Nov. 1946, 16, UNDA, CCOG 6. "The Bells: A Minority Report," *Today*, Apr. 1946, 10, UNDA, CCOG 6. Marguerite McDonough, "Brideshead Revisited: The Critics and Evelyn Waugh," *Today*, Apr. 1946, 10-11, UNDA, CCOG 6. For negative reader reactions to these articles on popular culture see "Our Critical Readers: 'The Bells of St. Mary's,'" *Today*, May 1946, 15, UNDA, CCOG 6, and "Our Letter-Writing Readers," *Today*, Nov. 1946, 13, UNDA, CCOG 6.

33. "The Back Pages: A Further Explanation of Why Certain Pieces Have Appeared Here," *Today*, May 1947, 16, UNDA, CCOG 6. "The Need for Criticism: The Source of Popu-

lar Neo-Paganism is Found in Innocuous-Seeming Streams," *Today*, Jan. 1947, 2, UNDA, CCOG 6.

34. Marguerite Ratty, "Open Letter to Frank Sinatra," *Today*, Jan. 1947, 3, UNDA, CCOG 6. Charles C. Smith, "One Man's Answer to the Charges Made against Frank Sinatra," *Today*, Jan. 1947, 3, UNDA, CCOG 6. "Frank Sinatra," *Today*, Feb. 1947, 11, UNDA, CCOG 6. "The Greatest Fan of Them All — How it Started and What Came of It," *Today*, Apr. 1947, 3, UNDA, CCOG 6.

35. J. Pius Barbour, "The Decline of the B.Y.P.U.," *NBV*, Mar. 1, 1945, 4. "The Terrell Plan to Hold the Baptist Youth," *NBV*, Dec. 1, 1945, 2.

36. R. C. Barbour, "The Fire Still Burns," *NBV*, June 15, 1940, 4.

37. R. C. Barbour, "A Religion for Youth," *NBV*, June 30, 1934, 2.

38. Rev. M. D. Dickson, "Youth's Seat Reserved at the Table," *NBV*, Jan. 19, 1935, 5.

39. W. H. Jernagin, "The Most Important People in the World Challenge the Home, the Church and the State," *NBV*, Apr. 6, 1935, 3, 8. W. H. Jernagin, "The Responsibility of the Present Day Church," *NBV*, June 29, 1935, 1, 7-8.

40. "President W. H. Jernagin Delivers Key-Note Address to S.S. & B.T.U. Congress at Houston, June 17-22," *NBV*, July 1, 1941, 1. "President Jernagin Delivers Key-Note Message to Congress Delegates at Atlanta," *NBV*, July 15, 1942, 2, 13. See also "Pres. Jernagin Outlines Future of Religious Education in Annual Message to Baptist Youth at Cincinnati," *NBV*, July 15, 1943, 1, 10, 12, 15.

41. R. C. Barbour, "Two Brilliant Negro Sociologists Submit Facts and Comments on the Negro Church and Youth," *NBV*, Mar. 15, 1941, 10. See also Pauline Slade, "California Youth Pay Tribute to Rev. and Mrs. A. Wendell Ross of Los Angeles," *NBV*, Aug. 1, 1943, 2. Wade Hampton McKinney, "The Central Area" Address to the City Club, Feb. 3, 1945, WRHS, WHM 5-2. "Why This Concentration of Crime in the Negro District?" Aug. 23, 1942, WRHS, WHM 5-1. See also "While Cleveland Sleeps!" 1931, WRHS, WHM 4-2. McKinney delivered the latter talk in numerous settings over the next ten years. He blamed city officials, not black residents in the Central District, for the high crime rates there.

42. Jesse Jai McNeil, "Jehovah Versus Jazz," *NBV*, May 1, 1941, 14. See also Henry T. McCrary, "Jazz Band Evangelism," *NBV*, May 19, 1934, 6.

43. McCrary, "Jazz Band Evangelism," 6.

44. Barbour, "A Religion for Youth," 2. Rev. D. V. Jemison, "Baleful Influence of Church Members Indulging in Social Dancing," *NBV*, Aug. 4, 1934, 6.

45. Luvenia A. George, "Lucie E. Campbell: Her Nurturing and Expansion of Gospel Music in the National Baptist Convention, U.S.A., Inc.," in Bernice Johnson Reagon, ed., *We'll Understand It Better By and By* (Washington, D.C.: Smithsonian Institution Press, 1992), 109-19. For Dorsey's complaints about some gospel music, see Thomas A. Dorsey, "Who Took Worship out of Gospel Singing?" *NBV*, Mar. 15, 1951, 2.

46. E. Franklin Frazier, *Negro Youth at the Crossways: Their Personality Development in the Middle States* (New York: Schocken Books, 1967), 112-33. This is a reprint of the 1940 study published by the American Youth Commission of the American Council on Education.

Notes to Chapter 3

1. George Harper, "Statement from the Administrative Secretary," in "Twelfth Annual Meeting, National Conference of Methodist Youth, Lafayette, Indiana, August 21-24, 1952," MCAH, GBD, 1124-4-1:08. Such uses of crisis and comparison to communists as goads to liberal social activism were not unusual in the 1950s. G. Baez-Camargo, "The Christian World Pattern of Brotherhood," in Hoover Rupert, ed., *Christ Above All: The Message of Cleveland* (New York: Abingdon-Cokesbury, 1948), 29-72. "Youth Night, General Conference, San Francisco, California, April 25, 1952: Youth and the Church," MCAH, GBD, 1120-4-3:20. Miss Rowena Ferguson, "Youth in the Church," addresses delivered at the National Methodist Youth Fellowship Commission, Purdue University, West Lafayette, Indiana, August 16-23, 1959, MCAH, GBD, 1124-4-2:05.

2. Rev. Harold W. Ewing, "Thy Will Be Done," September 6, 1953, 2, 4, MCAH, GBD, 1184-3-1:28.

3. "Statistical Report of the Youth Division in Methodist Church Schools 1943-1953," MCAH, GBD, 1124-4-1:19. *Turning the Tide*, July 1954, 1, MCAH, GBD, 1124-4-1:19. "An Open Letter to Methodist Pastors from C. Glenn Mingledorff," June 1955, MCAH, GBD, 1124-4-1:19. *Turning the Tide*, November 1955, 4, MCAH, GBD, 1124-5-1:19.

4. "Draft, Minutes of Unofficial Meeting of National Conference of Methodist Youth, Shubert Room, Pantlind Hotel, September 3, 1948," MCAH, GBD, 1124-4-1:12; "Report of the Annual Meeting, National Conference of Methodist Youth, Denver, Colorado, 1950," MCAH, GBD, 1124-4-1:10. Nona M. Brierley, News Release on National Conference of Methodist Youth Annual Meeting, August 1954, MCAH, GBD, 1124-4-1:06.

5. For mention of congressional testimony, see "Twelfth Annual Meeting, National Conference of Methodist Youth," 4. "Report on the Case of James M. Lawson and the Appeal Made in His Behalf," February 8, 1952, MCAH, GBD, 1124-4-1:08.

6. Charles B. Copher to Dean Seymour, August 23, 1949, MCAH, GBD, 1126-6-2:41. Virginia Henry to Executive Secretaries and Conference Directors of Youth Work, May 18, 1949, MCAH, GBD, 1126-6-2:41; Wallace Chappell to Rev. Leland Moore, August 21, 1956, MCAH, GBD, 1126-6-2:41; Wallace Chappell to Rev. Leland Moore, September 13, 1956, MCAH, GBD, 1126-6-2:41. Dr. A. Y. Brown to Harold W. Ewing, August 30, 1957, MCAH, GBD, 1126-6-2:41. At least one church boycotted Lake Junaluska and sent a resolution against integration to the Youth Department office. N. C. Oakes, Chairman, Special Committee, Official Board of First Methodist Church, Starkville, Mississippi, to Harold W. Ewing, August 15, 1957, MCAH, GBD, 1126-6-2:41. For Rebecca Owen's story of participating in a boycott at Lake Junaluska, see Sara M. Evans, ed., *Journeys that Opened up the World: Women, Student Christian Movements, and Social Justice, 1955-1975* (New Brunswick, N.J.: Rutgers University Press, 2003), 66-69.

7. News Release, Camden, South Carolina, July 11, 1956, MCAH, GBD, 1184-3-1:52. Untitled transcript of meeting between work camp members and Camden city council, MCAH, GBD, 1184-3-1:52. Methodist opposition to integration was not uncommon in the 1950s. Methodists were prominent in some White Citizens Councils. Donald E. Collins, *When the Church Bell Rang Racist: The Methodist Church and the Civil Rights Movement in Alabama* (Macon: Mercer University Press, 1998), 18-20.

8. Stanley High, "Methodism's Pink Fringe," *Reader's Digest*, February 1950, 134-38.

9. For a description of the Houston watchdog groups, see Martin Marty, *Modern Amer-*

ican Religion, vol. 3: Under God, Indivisible, 1941-1960 (Chicago: University of Chicago Press, 1996), 362-66. For Oxnam and HUAC, see Robert Moats Miller, *Bishop G. Bromley Oxnam: Paladin of Liberal Protestantism* (Nashville: Abingdon, 1990), 567-98. "Ask Yourself!" newsletter of Houston chapter of Circuit Riders, Inc. 1:4 (July-August 1955), MCAH, GBD, 1124-4-2:06. Rev. J. Claude Evans lost his job as associate pastor of a Methodist church in Columbia, South Carolina, after preaching a sermon against segregation in 1942. See Evans, *Journeys That Opened Up the World,* 11-12. See also Collins, *When the Church Bell Rang Racist,* and Timothy B. Tyson, *Blood Done Sign My Name* (New York: Three Rivers Press, 2004). Birmingham, Alabama, had a large population of white Methodists, some of whom formed the Methodist Layman's Union in the 1950s to fight integration. One of the main functions of this group was to harass fellow Methodists who favored racial integration. See Diane McWhorter, *Carry Me Home* (New York: Simon & Schuster, 2001), 140-42, 169-73.

10. "Right down the Line," *The High Point Enterprise,* October 4, 1951, MCAH, GBD, 1124-4-1:22. George Harper to Robert L. Thompson, November 1, 1951, MCAH, GBD, 1124-4-1:22.

11. News release, "National Conference of Methodist Youth Council Meets in Kansas City, Kansas," December 31-January 3, 1948-1949, MCAH, GBD, 1124-4-1:11. See also George Harper, "Statement from the Administrative Secretary." For evidence of debate within the Conference and weakening of its resolutions, see "Draft, Minutes of Unofficial Meeting of National Conference of Methodist Youth, Shubert Room, Pantlind Hotel, September 3, 1948," MCAH, GBD, 1124-4-1:12; "Committee on the Domestic Situation," in "NCMY Annual Meeting, Denver, 1950," MCAH, GBD, 1124-4-1:10; and "Annual Meeting, Purdue, 1955," NCMY," MCAH, GBD, 1124-4-1:05.

12. *Here's How to Win Youth for Christ, to Build Your MYF Membership* (Nashville: Board of Education of the Methodist Church, 1949).

13. Joseph W. Bell, "Field Report: Western Regional Christian Witness Mission and Workshop, Denver, Colorado, February 17-21, 1956," MCAH, GBD, 1126-6-3:56.

14. Luke G. Beauchamp, *Evangelism in the Church School* (Nashville: General Board of Education of the Methodist Church, 1957), 4, MCAH, GBD, 2577-5-3:14. See also *Evangelistic Teaching for Leaders of Youth,* March 1960, MCAH, GBHE, 2577-5-3:14; Ted McEachern, "Areas of Concern for a National Consultation on Youth Evangelism," September 14, 1960, MCAH, GBD, 1122-6-2:17; and "I Am a Teen-Ager," n.d., MCAH, GBD, 1120-2-3:37. For an example of the debates about how to elicit "commitment" to social activism, see "Minutes, Joint Committee on Youth Evangelism May 11, 1956," MCAH, GBD, 1124-3-1:03. For attempts to introduce confirmation programs, see James E. Kirby, Russell E. Richey, and Kenneth E. Rowe, *The Methodists* (Westport, Conn.: Greenwood Press, 1996), 231-54.

15. Wallace Chappell, "Report on the Study of the Young Life Campaign," presented to the Joint Staff on Youth and Student Work, December 4, 1953, MCAH, GBD, 1124-2-3:06. Hoover Rupert, "Field Report: Youth for Christ Rally, Grand Avenue Methodist Temple, Kansas City, Missouri, January 11, 1947," MCAH, GBD, 1184-3-2:02. Hoover Rupert, "Report on Youth for Christ Rally, Dixie Tabernacle, Nashville, Tennessee, December 8, 1945," MCAH, GBD, 1184-3-2:02. Methodist concern about these groups was typical of mainline Protestant youth leaders. See Flavius Leslie Conrad Jr., "A Study of Four Non-Denominational Youth Movements" (M.A. thesis, Temple University, 1955), MCAH, GBD, 1184-3-2:02. A modified version of this thesis became the official report of the National Council of Churches on these groups. See Wallace Chappell to Mrs. DeFresne, n.d., MCAH,

Notes to Pages 75-77

GBD, 1184-3-2:03. For correspondence showing the appeal of evangelical groups to Methodists, see Joseph W. Bell to Rev. Reynold B. Connett, October 23, 1963, MCAH, GBD, 1184-3-2:02. This file is full of such correspondence. "Young Life in Competition With the Church," *Classmate*, Aug. 1964, 20-22, MCAH, GBD, 1184-3-2:02. See also Ruth Emory, "Nondenominational Youth Groups," *Workers With Youth*, Sept. 1960, 14-15, MCAH, GBD, 1184-3-2:02; Lorenz Boyd, "Straight Talk on 'Youth for Christ,'" *Classmate*, Oct. 1960, 22-23, 28, MCAH, GBD, 1184-3-2:02.

16. The National Conference of Methodist Youth denounced the use of alcohol during the 1950s. "Annual Meeting Purdue, 1955, NCMY," MCAH, GBD, 1124-4-1:05. Alcohol also made it onto the agenda of the Quadrennial Emphasis on Youth. *What's Yours? Your answer to — Your action on — The Alcohol Problem*, MCAH, GBD, 1184-3-1:24. Aubrey B. Speer, *Helping Youth Meet the Alcohol Problem* (Nashville: Service Department, General Board of Discipleship, The Methodist Church, 1954), MCAH, GBD, 1184-3-1:24. And, of course, Sunday school and MYF curriculum materials condemned it. See "Home Should Never Be Like This," *Studies in Christian Living*, Summer 1955, 52-56. On caravans, see *Methodist Youth Caravans: A Project for Methodist Youth* (Nashville: Methodist Youth Caravans, 1958), MCAH, GBD, 1126-6-3:19. "Methodist Youth Caravan Statistics," MCAH, GBD, 1126-3-3:19. For alternatives to dancing, see "Methodists Substitute 'Play-Party Games' for Dancing," *Life*, Aug. 19, 1946, 12-14. For the survey of Methodist youth attitudes, see Murray H. Leiffer, "Methodists Don't Do That . . . or Do They?" *Christian Advocate*, Jan. 5, 1956, 10-11.

17. For advice regarding petting, reckless driving, and popularity, see "Respect for Personal Relations," *Studies in Christian Living* 2:3 (Summer 1954): 41-43. For one of the few mentions of popular music in Methodist materials, see "Radio Station Hits Off-Color Pop Songs," *Concern*, May 13, 1955, 7. This youth magazine devoted to social concerns virtually ignored such music; this article reports on one radio station in Durham, North Carolina, that pledged to ban songs with suggestive lyrics — hardly a long-term solution to the problem. For calls to "sublimate" desires, see "Nobody Finds It Easy," *Studies in Christian Living*, Fall 1953, 12; "To See God Clearly," *Studies in Christian Living*, Summer 1954, 20-21. The latter article, which treated the commandment against idolatry, identified cars and popularity as tempting idols for boys and girls respectively. See also Robert R. Powell, "Growing Up in the World Today," *Studies in Christian Living*, Fall 1953, 3-13; and R. P. Marshall, "Old Wisdom for New Times," *Studies in Christian Living*, Summer 1954, 20-21, 41-43.

18. *Studies for Youth* (Jan., Feb., Mar. 1944). *Studies for Youth* (Apr., May, June 1944). *Studies for Youth* (Oct., Nov., Dec. 1944). These themes and their urgency were prominent in this Sunday school quarterly for senior high students between 1941 and 1945.

19. See the four-week series "Making Our Community More Christian," in *Studies in Christian Living*, Summer 1953. See also the four-week series "The Christian in His Community," *Studies in Christian Living*, Summer 1955, 41-57. It may not be an accident that these lessons appeared in the summer quarter, a time when Sunday school attendance was typically down. The 1950s curriculum also switched to a cycle of lessons that included New and Old Testament surveys, a series on church history, a series on the Ten Commandments, and a series on church mission work in different regions of the world. Even though some of these lessons touched on the agenda of the old "social gospel," less space was devoted exclusively to investigations of political and social issues. Instead of focusing in on race, the postwar curriculum buried it in a larger series called "Across Border Lines," *Studies in Christian*

Living, Spring 1954. Here again, supposedly sound principles of Christian education actually blunted the force of the message.

20. Douglas E. Wingeier, "The Treatment of Negro-White Relations in the Curriculum Materials of the Methodist Church for Intermediate Youth 1941-1960" (Ph.D. dissertation, Boston University, 1962).

21. For example, Fred Cloud, "Christian Citizenship" and "Good Will Versus Prejudice," *Roundtable*, July 1953, 2-17. See subsequent issues of *Roundtable* for similar program suggestions.

22. "Report of Editorial Division to the Board of Education of the Methodist Church," Annual Meeting, April 20-24, 1954, 1-5, MCAH, General Board of Higher Education Records, 2577-5-3:12.

23. "The Significance of Methodist Summer Agencies: Conference on Youth Summer Agencies Atlanta, Georgia, January 24-27, 1956," MCAH, GBD, 1184-3-1:42. Methodist youth leaders seemed to be continually rediscovering this democratic principle. See for example the papers from a 1955 consultation on philosophy of youth work: Lucile Desjardins, "How Youth Learn," January 24, 1955, MCAH, GBD, 1184-3-1:21; and L. E. D., "The Adult Worker with Youth and the Methodist Youth Fellowship," January 24, 1955, MCAH, GBD, 1184-3-1:21. Staff member Rene Pino even advised "democratic" procedure when choosing activities for junior high groups: Rene F. Pino, "Principles of Intermediate Work," March 1957, MCAH, GBD, 1126-6-3:20. See also the MYF manuals *Guidebook for Workers with Youth* (Nashville: Methodist Publishing House, 1953) and *Handbook of the Methodist Youth Fellowship* (Nashville: Methodist Publishing House, 1955).

24. "Seminar on Training Adult Workers with Youth," Nashville, Tennessee, January 6-13, 1949, MCAH, GBD, 1124-2-3:06. Harold W. Ewing, "A Philosophy of Youth Work," address delivered to the Youth Commission, the Methodist Conference on Christian Education, Grand Rapids, Michigan, November 7, 1951, MCAH, GBD, 1184-3-1:21. Ewing admitted that adult guidance was more crucial than they had once thought, but still held out for young people taking a prominent role in the learning process. "Youth Department Staff, October 11, 1955," MCAH, GBD, 1124-2-3:06. "Report of the General Advisory Committee on the Youth Emphasis," Chicago, Illinois, March 11-12, 1953, 29, MCAH, GBD, 1124-4-1:19. For a published anthology of suggestions for overcoming "insipid" programs, see Nathaniel F. Forsyth, ed., *Your Church Can Win and Hold Young People* (Nashville: Division of the Local Church, General Board of Education of the Methodist Church, 1953).

25. *The Tell-Tale Arm*, MCAH, Audio-Visual Collection. MYF manuals of the 1950s presented the same club pattern, although their program suggestions included education on social issues; see Hoover Rupert, *Handbook of the Methodist Youth Fellowship* (Nashville: Methodist Publishing House, 1949); Miller C. Lovett, *The Methodist Youth Fellowship Local Church Program Planning Manual* (Nashville: Methodist Youth Department, 1950); *Handbook of the Methodist Youth Fellowship*; and *Guidebook for Workers with Youth*.

26. David Riesman, *The Lonely Crowd: A Study of the Changing American Character* (New Haven: Yale University Press, 1950), v-vi, 5, 24, 40, 273-74, 281. Paul Goodman, *Growing Up Absurd: Problems of Youth in the Organized System* (New York: Random House, 1956), x, 13-14, 17-19, 35, 70, 87, 135, 138-43, 169, 192-94. William H. Whyte Jr., *The Organization Man* (New York: Simon and Schuster, 1956), 5-6, 10, 14.

27. "Statement by Ehrensperger," Supplement, Minutes on Worship Committee Convocation Methodist Youth, MCAH, GBD, 1124-4-2:27.

28. "To Be a Pilgrim," MCAH, GBD, 1124-4-2:24.

29. "Statement by Ehrensperger." For evidence of the ongoing appeal of existentialism in Methodist youth circles see Richard H. Rice, "Nature of the Christian Faith," Jan. 25, 1955, MCAH, GBD, 1184-3-1:21; and "Working Documents for the 1964 National Convocation of Methodist Youth," especially Ross Snyder, "An Existential Mode of Christianity," MCAH, GBD, 1124-4-3:34. By 1961, the pervasiveness of existentialism in liberal Protestant circles could be assumed, as seen at the North American Ecumenical Youth Assembly; see *Assembly Bulletin* 1:5 (Tuesday, August 22, 1961), MCAH, GBD, 1124-4-3:15. Existentialism especially appealed to the most socially active, like those involved in the "Intentional Communities" projects of the 1960s. See "Evaluation of Atlanta Intentional Community (First Three Weeks)," 1965, MCAH, GBD, 1124-5-2:05; and Sue Ellen Gray, "Report on the Intentional Community Project," August 20, 1965, MCAH, GBD, 1124-4-3:11.

30. Rowena Ferguson, ed., *Our Christian Witness in the World of Struggle: A Summary and Interpretation of the National Convocation of Methodist Youth Purdue University, West Lafayette, Ind., August 22-26, 1955* (Nashville: Methodist Youth Department, 1955), 6-8, 20-23, MCAH, GBD, 1124-4-2:25.

31. Ferguson, *Our Christian Witness,* 12-17, 30-40.

32. Evans, *Journeys That Opened Up the World,* 68.

33. "Minutes of the Planning Committee for the 1959 Convocation," MCAH, GBD, 1124-4-2:07.

34. They should have read the Sunday school lesson on the commandment "Thou shalt not commit adultery," which noted the need to "sublimate" sexual desires into work for "worth-while causes." "Respect for Personal Relations," *Studies in Christian Living* 2:2 (Spring 1954): 41-43.

35. "National Convocation of Methodist Youth, Minutes of the Directing Committee, November 24, 1958," 2-3, MCAH, GBD, 1124-4-2:07.

36. "National Convocation of Methodist Youth, Minutes of the Directing Committee, November 24, 1958," MCAH, GBD, 1124-4-2:07. Charles H. Boyles to Directing Committee, August 5, 1959, MCAH, GBD, 1124-4-2:07. *The Program* (National Convocation of Methodist Youth, 1959), MCAH, GBD, 1124-4-2:05. *Concern: Seventh National Convocation of Methodist Youth,* Friday, August 28, 1959, MCAH, GBD, 1124-4-2:12.

37. "Report, National Convocation of Methodist Youth 1959."

38. "Report, National Convocation of Methodist Youth 1959." Eugene Laubach to Charles Boyles, September 25, 1959, MCAH, GBD, 1124-4-2:06. Judy Carr, "Convocation 1959," MCAH, GBD, 1124-4-2:06. Chester A. Pennington to Charles Boyles, September 15, 1959, MCAH, GBD, 1124-4-2:06.

39. Roy Grant to Charles Boyles, September 25, 1959, MCAH, GBD, 1124-4-2:06. Grant mentions an unfavorable editorial in the North Carolina Conference *Christian Advocate.* For mention of Boyles's resignation, see Neil Winslow to Charles Boyles, September 23, 1959, MCAH, GBD, 1124-4-2:06.

40. Eugene Laubach to Charles Boyles, September 25, 1959; Neil Winslow to Charles Boyles, September 23, 1959; Rev. Ray Poindexter to Mr. Moore, September 18, 1959; Forrest L. White to Charles Boyles, September 1, 1959; Joseph W. Bell, "Field Report: Quadrennial National Convocation of Methodist Youth," Sept. 1, 1959; Don Barnes to Charles Boyles, September 1, 1959, MCAH, GBD, 1124-4-2:06.

41. "The Convocation: 'From Jazz to Communion,'" *Information Bulletin* 16 (Jan. 1960):

1-3, MCAH, GBD, 1124-4-2:06. This article, prepared by members of the Louisiana Association of Methodist Laymen, drew its title and quoted extensively from a news release on the convocation by William M. Hearn.

42. Mrs. Bernard Miller to Youth Department, August 31, 1959; John N. Grenfell to Edgar A. Gossard, September 27, 1959; and Mrs. Edwin Close to Youth Department Staff, September 8, 1959, MCAH, GBD, 1124-4-2:06.

43. Judy Carr, "Convocation 1959," MCAH, GBD, 1124-4-2:06.

44. See David J. Garrow, *Bearing the Cross: Martin Luther King, Jr., and the Southern Christian Leadership Conference* (New York: Random House, 1986), 132-33. For a more extended treatment of Lawson's activities, see David Halberstam, *The Children* (New York: Random House, 1998).

45. Alice G. Knotts, *Fellowship of Love: Methodist Women Changing American Racial Attitudes, 1920-1968* (Nashville: Abingdon, 1996), 110-14. For similar stories, including the story of Rebecca Owen, see Evans, *Journeys That Opened Up the World.*

46. Murray H. Leiffer, "Segregation in Churches," *Christian Advocate,* March 15, 1956, 10-12, 29-30.

Notes to Chapter 4

1. Henry Louis Gates, *Colored People* (New York: Vintage Books, 1994), xi. Gates reports that his children had a hard time believing his childhood stories about segregation and other forms of racial injustice. And it must be noted that this is true even of Gates, who has been criticized for painting too rosy a picture of the Jim Crow era in his memoir. See Jennifer Jensen Wallach, *Closer to the Truth than Any Fact: Memoir, Memory and Jim Crow* (Athens: University of Georgia Press, 2008), 88-98.

2. Ellen Levine, *Freedom's Children: Young Civil Rights Activists Tell Their Own Stories* (New York: Puffin Books, 1993), 3-16.

3. Melba Patillo Beals, *Warriors Don't Cry: A Searing Memoir of the Battle to Integrate Little Rock's Central High* (New York: Washington Square Books, 1994), 22-28.

4. Sellers is quoted in Tom Brokaw, *Boom! Voices of the Sixties* (New York: Random House, 2007), 329-30. Levine, *Freedom's Children,* 10, 22.

5. Victoria W. Wolcott, "Recreation and Race in the Postwar City: Buffalo's 1956 Crystal Beach Riot," *The Journal of American History* 93:1 (June 2006): 63-90.

6. For racialized views of teen sexuality and pregnancy see Rickie Solinger, *Wake Up Little Susie: Single Pregnancy and Race Before Roe v. Wade* (Routledge, 2000).

7. For information on Christian racism and resistance to integration see Donald E. Collins, *When the Church Bell Rang Racist: The Methodist Church and the Civil Rights Movement in Alabama* (Macon, Ga.: Mercer University Press, 1998); Evans, *Journeys That Opened Up the World;* Andrew M. Manis, *Southern Civil Religions in Conflict: Black and White Baptists and Civil Rights 1947-1957* (University of Georgia Press, 1987); Charles Marsh, *God's Long Summer: Stories of Faith and Civil Rights* (Princeton, N.J.: Princeton University Press, 2008); Charles Marsh, *The Last Days: A Son's Story of Sin and Segregation at the Dawn of a New South* (New York: Basic Books, 2001); John McGreevy, *Parish Boundaries: The Catholic Encounter with Race in the Twentieth-Century Urban North* (Chicago: University of Chicago Press, 1998). For documentation of the close working relationship between the Klan and

civic authorities in Birmingham, Alabama, see Diane McWhorter, *Carry Me Home* (New York: Simon and Schuster, 2001). Jane Dailey, "Sex, Segregation, and the Sacred after Brown," *The Journal of American History* 91:1 (June 2004): 119-44.

8. Murray H. Leiffer, "Segregation in Churches," *Christian Advocate*, March 15, 1956, 10-12, 29-30.

9. "Jernagin's Youngsters Take Over Brooklyn," *NBV*, July 1953, 1, 14.

10. "Jernagin's Youngsters," 1, 14.

11. "Jernagin, 84, Smashes Jim-Crow in Capital," *NBV*, Nov. 1953, 12.

12. *Proceedings of the 70th Annual Session of the National Baptist Convention USA, Inc.,* 1950 (Nashville: Sunday School Publications Board, 1950), 382, 418. For an example of the use of "Are Ye Able?" and "Lift Him Up" see *Proceedings of the 72nd Annual Session of the National Baptist Convention USA, Inc., Chicago, Illinois, 1952* (Nashville: Sunday School Publishing Board, 1952), 481-83.

13. *Proceedings of the 70th Annual Session*, 382, 419, 423.

14. *Proceedings of the 73rd Annual Session of the National Baptist Convention USA, Inc., Miami Florida, Sept 9-13, 1953* (Nashville: Sunday School Publishing Board, 1953), 336-52.

15. *Proceedings of the 75th Annual Session of the National Baptist Convention, USA, Inc., Memphis, Tennessee, Sept 2-11, 1955* (Nashville: Sunday School Publishing Board, 1955), 380-83.

16. *Proceedings of the 75th Annual Session*, 380-83.

17. *Proceedings of the 75th Annual Session*, 382-83. *Proceedings of the 73rd Annual Session*, 342-56.

18. Opal V. Easter, *Nannie Helen Burroughs* (New York: Garland Publishing, 1995), 66-67. For references to the Women's Auxiliary Queen competition for young women, see "Young People's Department Holds 26th Annual Session," *NBV*, Feb. 1952, 10, 14; *Proceedings of the 75th Annual Session*, 447.

19. *Proceedings of the 77th Annual Session of the National Baptist Convention USA, Inc.* (Nashville: Sunday School Publications Board, 1957), 313. For the importance of music in attracting and keeping young people in the black church, see C. Eric Lincoln and Lawrence H. Mamiya, *The Black Church in the African American Experience* (Durham: Duke University Press, 1990), 330.

20. Horace Clarence Boyer, "Lucie E. Campbell: Composer for the National Baptist Convention," in Bernice Johnson Reagon, ed., *We'll Understand It Better By and By* (Washington, DC: Smithsonian Institution Press, 1992), 81-108. For the story about James Bevel, see David Halberstam, *The Children* (New York: Random House, 1998), 342.

21. Interview with Mary Wickware and Evelyn Gaines, Oct. 20, 1999; Interview with Virginia Bright, Oct. 27, 1999; Interview with Zelma Ewing, Oct. 23, 1999; and Interview with Sherman and Dorothy Webster, Oct. 21, 1999, tape recordings, author's personal collection.

22. Interview with Zelma Ewing, Oct. 23, 1999. Interview with Dorothy Fort, October 21, 1999.

23. "First Baptist Youth Minister Called to Mt. Nebo," *The Messenger* 1:1 (Nov. 1954): 1, VUA, KMS, 43-12. "Reverend Nichols Acting Youth Minister," *The Messenger* 1:1 (Nov. 1954): 1, VUA, KMS, 43-12. For other programs mentioned here, see "First Baptist through the Years," A Twin Anniversary Celebration, March 12, 13, 14, 16, 1952, VUA, KMS 37-7, and "Ninety-fourth Anniversary Celebration: First Baptist Church — Forward with Faith," April 1959, VUA, KMS, 37-9. For Smith's influence in reducing the number of teenagers skipping

the adult worship service, see Interview with Mary Wickware and Evelyn Gaines, and Interview with Zelma Ewing.

24. For the Youth Committee, see Interview with Ben Harris. For youth serving on other committees, see Interview with Mary Wickware and Evelyn Gaines. "Youth Day," Feb. 1, 1959, Archives of First Baptist Church, Nashville. "Youth Day," March 8, 1959, Archives of First Baptist Church, Nashville.

25. "Youth Week" 1954, VUA, KMS, 31-12.

26. Kelly Miller Smith, "God in the Morning" 1951, 1-3, VUA, KMS, 23-5.

27. Kelly Miller Smith, "Consecrated Through Faith," 1-3, VUA, KMS, 27-1.

28. Smith, "Consecrated Through Faith," 1-3.

29. Smith, "The General Situation," 3-9, VUA, KMS, 112-7.

30. For: Dr. W. L. Crump, From: Mrs. Carrie R. Hull, Social Action Committee, February 15, 1958, VUA, KMS, 47-16. "First Baptist Church Presents its Ninth Annual Spring Lecture Series March 7-11, 1960, 7:30 p.m.," VUA, KMS, 31-15.

31. Halberstam, *The Children*, 52-56. Kelly Miller Smith, "Where We Are in Human Relations and Where are We Going," NAACP Freedom Mass Meeting, April 9, 1963, VUA, KMS, 23-6. For the Youth March, see "Nashville Christian Leadership Council Minutes, April 4, 1959," VUA, KMS, 75-22. "Certificate of Appreciation," Pearl High School, 1981, VUA, KMS. For another example of the powerful impression made by ministers who insisted on nonviolence during the 1950s, see James Roberson's memories of Rev. Fred Shuttlesworth's reaction to the bombing of his home in Levine, *Freedom's Children*, 7-8.

32. Kelly Miller Smith, "Chapter 6: Day of Crisis," 7-8, in "The Pursuit of a Dream," VUA, KMS, 28-8.

33. Halberstam, *The Children*. Aldon D. Morris, *The Origins of the Civil Rights Movement: Black Communities Organizing for Change* (New York: The Free Press, 1984), 205-15.

34. Kelly Miller Smith, "Chapter 2: Inspired Amateurs," in "The Pursuit of a Dream," VUA, KMS, 28-7.

35. Smith, "Inspired Amateurs."

36. Kelly Miller Smith, "Chapter 1: Shame and Glory," 18, in "The Pursuit of a Dream," VUA, KMS, 28-7. See also, Kelly Miller Smith, "The Movement in Nashville, Tennessee commonly called the Student Sit-in Movement . . . ," VUA, KMS, 76-6.

37. "Report on the Case of James M. Lawson and the Appeal Made in His Behalf," February 8, 1952, MCAH, GBD, 1124-4-1:08. See also Halberstam, *The Children*, 30-42.

38. Halberstam, *The Children*, 67-68, 95, 238-46, 412-15.

39. Halberstam, *The Children*, 347-86.

40. Guy and Candie Carawan, eds., *Sing for Freedom: The Story of the Civil Rights Movement Through Its Songs* (Bethlehem, Penn.: Sing Out Publication, 1990), 16.

41. Halberstam, *The Children*, 63, 66, 69, 73-74, 151.

42. Lewis, *Walking with the Wind*, 84-88, 93. See also Halberstam, *The Children*, 59-64, 73-81.

43. Lewis, *Walking with the Wind*, 84.

44. Smith, "Day of Crisis," 1-8.

45. Smith remembered it was James Bevel who prophesied that the protest would draw out support from the black community. Smith, "Day of Crisis," 8-11. But John Lewis claimed that Bevel was still hesitating about becoming a protester and only showed up late that day after hearing his friends had been jailed. Lewis also places the primary debate between

adults and students at a meeting the week before the protest. Lewis, *Walking with the Wind*, 100, 109-10. The name of the principal student speaker and the timing of the meeting are not as important as the fact that Smith saw such interactions between adults and students as typical and memorable.

46. Smith, "Day of Crisis," 1, 12-22. For the use of "Everybody Sing Freedom" adapted from "Amen," see Carawan, *Sing for Freedom*, 24.

47. Interview with Ben Harris. Interview with Sherman and Dorothy Webster. For other evidence of adult support, see Wallace Westfeldt, "A Report On Nashville," Nashville Community Relations Conference, VUA, KMS, 76-6, and Wallace Westfeldt, "Settling a Sit-In," Nashville Community Relations Conference, VUA, KMS, 76-6. See also Halberstam, *The Children*, 177-79, and Morris, *Origins*, 205-13.

48. Lewis, *Walking with the Wind*, 108.

49. Student Central Committee of the Nashville "Non-Violent" Movement, "Why We Must Fight Segregation," October 1960, VUA, KMS, 89-15. Student Non-Violent Movement Central Committee, "Dear Freedom Fighter," January 1961, VUA, KMS, 89-15. The Nashville Non-Violent Movement, "To All the Citizens of Nashville," VUA, KMS, 75-13.

50. Carawan, *Sing for Freedom*, 15, 17, 18, 25, 37.

51. Carawan, *Sing for Freedom*, 5, 30-36. Lewis, *Walking with the Wind*, 70. *Sit-In* (New York: Folkways Records, FH 5590, 1960).

52. Morris, *Origins*, 208.

53. Smith, "Where We Are in Human Relations," 3. For the power of youth and children to provoke adult tears, see Jack Katz, *How Emotions Work* (Chicago: University of Chicago Press, 1999), 199-202.

54. Kelly Miller Smith, "The Misfits," VUA, KMS, 27-6.

55. Kelly Miller Smith, "Creative Disruption," VUA, KMS, 27-2.

56. Clayborne Carson, *In Struggle: SNCC and the Black Awakening of the 1960s* (Cambridge, Mass.: Harvard University Press, 1981), 23.

57. Carson, *In Struggle*, 23.

58. See Emily Stoper, *The Student Nonviolent Coordinating Committee* (Brooklyn: Carlson Pub., 1989), 105-33. Although Stoper used the terms "moralist" and later "redemptive" to describe the organizational style of SNCC, she largely ignored religious factors as possible source of this ethos.

Notes to Chapter 5

1. Donald F. Crosby, S.J., *God, Church, and Flag: Senator Joseph R. McCarthy and the Catholic Church, 1950-1957* (Chapel Hill: University of North Carolina Press, 1978).

2. Mary Irene Zotti, *A Time of Awakening: The Young Christian Worker Story in the United States, 1938 to 1970* (Chicago: Loyola University Press, 1991), 129, 131, 137, 139, 177-78, 191-192, 208, 225-46. See also Steven M. Avella, *This Confident Church: Catholic Leadership and Life in Chicago, 1940-1965* (Notre Dame: University of Notre Dame Press, 1992), 151-86.

3. James O. Supple, "Putting God in a Pigeonhole," *Today*, Jan. 10, 1948, 10-11, UNDA, CCOG 6.

4. "Going Too Far," *Today*, Apr. 30, 1947, 10, UNDA, CCOG 6.

5. Lucile Hasley, "To Catholic Youth — With Love from Catholic Middle Age," *Today*,

Oct. 1, 1947, 17, UNDA, CCOG 6. "Catholicism and Compromise," *Today,* Oct. 1, 1947, 2, UNDA, CCOG 6.

6. For the early development of Hillenbrand's movements, see Edward R. Kantowicz, *Corporation Sole: Cardinal Mundelein and Chicago Catholicism* (Notre Dame: University of Notre Dame Press, 1983), 197-202, and Dennis Michael Robb, "Specialized Catholic Action in the United States, 1936-1949" (Ph.D. dissertation, University of Minnesota, 1972). For an assessment of these movements in the 1950s, see Zotti, *A Time of Awakening,* 129, 131, 137, 139, 177-78, 191-92, 208, 225-46, and Avella, *This Confident Church,* 151-86. Bob W. to Msgr. Hillenbrand, 1954, UNDA, Reynold Hillenbrand Papers, CMRH 8-8. For episcopal support for CYO and opposition to YCW, see Zotti, *A Time of Awakening,* 105, 110-11, 192-93.

7. For examples of the key role Schieder and the Youth Department played in establishing and supporting diocesan youth programs, see "Spotlight on Little Rock," *Vision* 1:2 (Mar. 1952): 12-13, ACUA, NCWC, YD 10-55. "Let's Look at Hartford," *Vision* 1:5 (June 1952): 12-13, ACUA, NCWC, YD 10-55; Joseph R. Thomas, "Let's Look at Newark," *Vision* 2:1 (Sept. 1952): 15, ACUA, NCWC, YD 10-55; Patricia Mills and Geraldine Richards, "Spotlight on Crookston," *Vision* 2:3 (Nov. 1952): 14-15, ACUA, NCWC, YD 10-55; "The Story of Richmond and How it Grew," *Youth* 5:3 (Mar. 1958): 6, ACUA, NCWC, YD 10-55.

8. "165 Youngsters Display Plenty of Ability in Perfecting the New National Council of Catholic Youth," *Youth Newsnotes* 4:9 (Nov. 1951): 3-4, ACUA, NCWC, YD 10-52. William J. Kernan Jr., "The National Convention," *Youth Newsnotes* 4:10 (Dec. 1951): 11, ACUA, NCWC, YD 10-52. "William Stuart, Navy Veteran, Chosen President of National Federation of Diocesan Catholic Youth Councils," *Youth Newsnotes* 4:9 (Nov. 1951): 1-2, ACUA, NCWC, YD 10-52.

9. "St. Louis Meetings Finest in History," *Youth* 3:1 (Jan. 1956): 11-14, ACUA, NCWC, YD 10-53.

10. "Here's What the Stars Have to Say about National CYO Week, October 21-28, 1951," *Youth Newsnotes* 4:8 (Oct. 1951): 13, ACUA, NCWC, YD 10-52. "National CYO Week Proclaimed in New York as 5,000 Attend Mammoth City Hall Ceremony," *Youth Newsnotes* 4:9 (Nov. 1951): 16, ACUA, NCWC, YD 10-52. For other celebrity endorsements of Youth Week 1960, see "Youth Week Messages," ACUA, NCWC, YD 10:51.

11. "Catholic Youth Week Round-Up," *Youth Newsnotes* 5:9 (Nov. 1953): 9-10, ACUA, NCWC, YD 10-52. "Trust in Youth Pays," *Youth* 3:8 (Oct. 1956): 1, ACUA, NCWC, YD 10-53. "1956 Youth Week Challenges Youth and Adults," *Youth* 3:8 (Oct. 1956): 3-4, ACUA, NCWC, YD 10-53. "May 25, 1958." "National Catholic Youth Week 1959," *Youth* (Oct. 1959): 2, ACUA, NCWC, YD 10-53.

12. "Youth — Our Hope," Poster for 1955 National Catholic Youth Week, ACUA, NCWC, YD 10-52. "Spiritualize Youth — Vitalize Nations," Poster, Youth Week, 1959, ACUA, NCWC, YD 10-50.

13. "Visiting with Catholic Youth," *Youth* 1:9 (Dec. 1954): 7, ACUA, NCWC, YD 10-53. For posters and promotional materials used in Youth Week, see ACUA, NCWC, YD 10-52.

14. Garry Wills, *Bare Ruined Choirs: Doubt, Prophecy, and Radical Religion* (New York: Doubleday, 1972), 32-37.

15. Wills, *Bare Ruined Choirs,* 24, 65, 69, 71.

16. For a description of a typical diocesan youth rally, see "More than 900 Young People Attend Diocesan Youth Rally and Holy Hour in Springfield," *Youth Newsnotes* 4:10 (Dec. 1951): 10, ACUA, NCWC, YD 10-52. The pages of *Newsnotes, Youth Newsnotes,* and *Youth* be-

tween 1948 and 1959 are full of reports of communion crusades, communion breakfasts, holy hours, benedictions, and youth rallies taking place all over the country. Msgr. Joseph E. Schieder, *Spiritual Lifts for Youth* (Washington, D.C.: NCWC, 1956), 22.

17. Peter Occhiogrosso, *Once a Catholic: Prominent Catholics and Ex-Catholics Reveal the Influence of the Church on Their Lives and Work* (Boston: Houghton Mifflin, 1987), 72-73. Wills, *Bare Ruined Choirs*, 36.

18. Edward Stirender, *Still Catholic After All These Fears* (Little Rock, AK: August House Publishes, 1995), 184-93. Richard B. Schwartz, *The Biggest City in America: A Fifties Boyhood in Ohio* (Akron, OH: University of Akron Press, 1999). Louis Morrow, *My Catholic Faith* (Kenosha: My Mission House, 1959), 86, 230-33.

19. "Diocesan Data," *Youth Newsnotes* 4:1 (Jan. 1951): 30-31, ACUA, NCWC, YD 10-52. "Korea for Christ," *Youth Newsnotes* 3:8 (Nov. 1950): 15, ACUA, NCWC, YD 10-52. Wills, *Bare Ruined Choirs*, 36.

20. "O Beautiful Mother," *Youth Newsnotes* 4:6 (June 1, 1951): 16, ACUA, NCWC, YD 10-52. "Councils of Men, Women, and Youth Sponsor *Mary's Greatest Day* in the Detroit Archdiocese," *Youth* 1:5 (June 1954): 6, ACUA, NCWC, YD 10-53. For similar Marian Year observances, see "Turn to Mary," *Youth Newsnotes* 5:9 (Nov. 1953): 5, ACUA 10-52; "Archdiocesan CYC Announces Special Marian Year Program," *Youth* 1:1 (Jan. 1954): 8, ACUA, NCWC, YD 10-53; "For Our Lady," *Youth* 1:4 (May 1954): 10, ACUA, NCWC, YD 10-53; "Observer . . . Team! Over 25,000 Honor Our Lady in Eight CYO Marian Rallies," *Youth* 1:5 (June 1954): 7, ACUA, NCWC, YD 10-53; "Salute to Youth," *Youth* 1:6 (Sept. 1954): 8, ACUA, NCWC, YD 10-53; "Brooklyn CYO Holds Youth Day," *Youth Newsnotes* 3:8 (Nov. 1950): 1-2, ACUA, NCWC, YD 10-52.

21. "1956 Youth Week Challenges Youth and Adults," *Youth* 3:8 (Oct. 1956): 3-4, ACUA, NCWC, YD 10-53. "May 25, 1958 — Second National Youth Adoration Day," *Youth* 5:5 (May 1958): 2-3, ACUA, NCWC, YD 10-53.

22. For the bus charter, see "Diocesan Data," *Youth Newsnotes* 5:9 (Nov. 1953): 23, ACUA, NCWC, YD 10-52. "Spiritual Committee Adopts Advertising Technique," *Youth* 3:4 (Apr. 1956): 18, ACUA, NCWC, YD 10-53.

23. In 1958, 74 percent of American Catholics reported weekly church attendance. "Religion in America, 50 Years: 1935-1985," *The Gallup Report* 236 (May 1985): 42.

24. Edward Stivender, *Raised Catholic (Can You Tell?)* (Little Rock: August House Publishers, 1992), 13-51. Stivender, *Still Catholic After All These Fears*, 13-37.

25. Occhiogrosso, *Once a Catholic*, 2, 74-75.

26. Wills, *Bare Ruined Choirs*, 16-17. See also Occhiogrosso, *Once a Catholic*, xiii.

27. Occhiogrosso, *Once a Catholic*, 70-71.

28. Stivender, *Raised Catholic*, 186-87.

29. Occhiogrosso, *Once a Catholic*, 116.

30. The experience of questioning church teaching and not receiving satisfactory answers appears in most of the stories in Occhiogrosso's book. See also Wills, *Bare Ruined Choirs*, 19-30. Here Wills gives his extended explanation of why pre-Vatican II Catholicism was intellectually weak at the local parish and school level.

31. "Sports Can Develop Christian Virtues," *Youth* (Dec. 1959): 5, ACUA NCWC, YD 10-53. For pregame prayers, see "Indianapolis CYO Successfully Mixes Sports and Prayer," *Youth Newsnotes* 4:1 (Jan. 1951): 10, ACUA, NCWC, YD 10-52; and "Prayer — An Unfair Disadvantage?" *Youth Newsnotes* 5:2 (Feb. 1953): 15, ACUA, NCWC, YD 10-52. For an example of a

Holy Hour for athletes, see "Salute to Youth," *Youth* 3:2 (Feb. 1956): 12-13, ACUA, NCWC, YD 10-53. For CYO sports leagues, see the monthly column "Diocesan Data" in *Youth Newsnotes*. For the Chicago inter-league games, see Sister Mary Innocenta Montay, *The History of Catholic Secondary Education in the Archdiocese of Chicago* (Washington, D.C.: Catholic University of America Press, 1953), 342. For the importance of sports to adolescent identity and status in the fifties, see James S. Coleman, *The Adolescent Society* (New York: the Free Press, 1961). For a non-Catholic teenager's perspective on this point, albeit from a slightly later period, see Bob Greene, *Be True to Your School: A Diary of 1964* (New York: Atheneum, 1987), 44, 95. For the cultural function of Notre Dame football, see Mark Massa, *Catholics and American Culture* (New York: Crossroad, 1999), 195-213.

32. "Russell Aldrich Wins Hartford CYO Oratory Contest," *Youth Newsnotes* 4:4 (Apr. 1951): 26, ACUA, NCWC, YD 10-52. "Diocesan Data," *Youth Newsnotes* 4:8 (Oct. 1951): 30-31, ACUA, NCWC, YD 10-52. For religious quizzes, see "Diocesan Data," *Youth Newsnotes* 5:7 (Sept. 1953): 19-21, ACUA, NCWC, YD 10-52; and "Diocesan Data," *Youth Newsnotes* 5:8 (Oct. 1953): 19-24, ACUA, NCWC, YD 10-52. For other contests see "Diocesan Data," *Youth Newsnotes* 3:9 (Dec. 1950): 30-31, ACUA, NCWC, YD 10-52; and the monthly "Diocesan Data" column throughout the 1950s.

33. For a typical dance queen contest, see "A CYO Snow Queen," *Youth Newsnotes* 4:3 (Mar. 1951): 18, ACUA, NCWC, YD 10-52. For "Mr. and Miss CYO" see "Visiting With Catholic Youth," *Youth* 1:6 (Sept. 1954): 7, ACUA, NCWC, YD 10-53. For the Los Angeles "Girl of the Year Award," see "Diocesan Data," *Youth Newsnotes* 3:9 (Dec. 1950): 30-31, ACUA, NCWC, YD 10-52. "Springfield, IL CYO Holds 12th Annual May Day Celebration," *Youth Newsnotes* 5:6 (June 1953): 13, ACUA, NCWC, YD 10-52. Rev. Louis F. Meyer, "St. Louis Crowns a Queen," *Youth* 4:3 (Mar. 1957): 19-20, ACUA, NCWC, YD 10-53. For evidence that CYO queens still won by virtue of their fundraising abilities, see "Salute to Youth," *Youth* 4:8 (Oct. 1957): 12-13, ACUA, NCWC, YD 10-53; and "Spotlight on Youth," *Youth* (Dec. 1959): 8-9, ACUA, NCWC, YD 10-53.

34. "Highest Catholic Youth Award Presented in Albany," *Youth* 3:4 (Apr. 1956): 3, ACUA, NCWC, YD 10-53. "T'was a Most Unusual Day," *Youth* 5:4 (Apr. 1958): 2-3, ACUA, NCWC, YD 10-53. B. J. Plunkett, "Personality of the Month: Outstanding in 1958!" *Youth* (Jan. 1959): 5, ACUA, NCWC, YD 10-53.

35. See editorials in *Youth* for Jan., Feb., May, Sept., 1958, ACUA, NCWC, YD 10-53.

36. "Salute to Youth," *Youth* 5:5 (May 1958): 12-13, ACUA, NCWC, YD 10-53. "Salute to Youth," *Youth* 5:3 (Mar. 1958): 12-13, ACUA, NCWC, YD 10-53.

37. "Catholic Youth May Be Fed Up on Spoon Feeding," *Youth Newsnotes* 5:2 (Feb. 1953): 3, ACUA, NCWC, YD 10-52.

38. "5,000 Boys Counseled on Proper Living at Mass Honoring 15-Year-Old Blessed Dominic Savio," *Youth Newsnotes* 3:9 (Dec. 1950): 4, ACUA, NCWC, YD 10-52. "Delegates to Lincoln CYO Rally Told That Teen-Agers' System of Dating Is Sometimes an Occasion of Sin," *Youth Newsnotes* 4:9 (Nov. 1, 1951): 28, ACUA, NCWC, YD 10-52.

39. Occhiogrosso, *Once a Catholic*, 68-69.

40. "The Magic Whispers . . . Explanation of the Mass Plays Important Part in Catholic Youth Day Rally," *Youth* 1:3 (Apr. 1954): 17, ACUA, NCWC, YD 10-53. "Hartford CYO Survey Reveals that High School Students are Eager to Solve Their Problems," *Youth Newsnotes* 4:8 (Oct. 1951): 25, ACUA, NCWC, YD 10-52. A survey at a youth conference in Minnesota turned up dating, juvenile delinquency, drinking, drugs, choice of vocation, and recreation

as the topics of most interest to young Catholics. Patricia Mills and Geraldine Richards, "Spotlight on Crookston," *Vision* 2:3 (Nov. 1952): 14-15, ACUA, NCWC, YD 10-55. For examples of programs on dating, see "Diocesan Data," *Youth* 4:5 (May 1957): 12-13, ACUA, NCWC, YD 10-53.

41. For teenage behavior codes, see "All Teenagers of Berea, OH Follow Code of Behavior," *Youth Newsnotes* 5:2 (Feb. 1953): 4, ACUA, NCWC, YD 10-52; "Salute to Youth," *Youth* 3:2 (Feb. 1956): 12-13, ACUA, NCWC, YD 10-53; "A Teen-Age Code," *Youth* 4:6 (June 1957): 20, ACUA, NCWC, YD 10-53; "Spotlight on Youth," *Youth* (Oct. 1959): 8-9, ACUA, NCWC, YD 10-53; "Spotlight on Youth," *Youth* (Feb. 1962): 8-9, ACUA, NCWC, YD 10-53; "Spotlight on Youth," *Youth* (Mar. 1962): 8-9, ACUA, NCWC, YD 10-53; "Code for Youth," *Youth Program Service* 1:1 (Sept./Oct. 1962): 12, ACUA, NCWC, YD 10-53; and Clare F. Adams, "Spirituality in 3-D," *Youth Program Service* 1:2 (Nov./Dec. 1962): 11, ACUA, NCWC, YD 10-53.

42. "Marriage Forums Attract Large Number of Young People: Now in Third Year," *Youth Newsnotes* 4:5 (May 1951): 29, ACUA, NCWC, YD 10-52. See also "Fourth Annual Marriage Forum of Essex County CYO Opened Feb 27," *Youth Newsnotes* 4:3 (Mar. 1951): 19, ACUA, NCWC, YD 10-52; and "San Antonio Round-Up," *Youth Newsnotes* 4:1 (Jan. 1951): 8, ACUA, NCWC, YD 10-52. "The Spiritual Program," *Youth* 1:7 (Oct. 1954): 3, ACUA, NCWC, YD 10-53. For examples of the sort of advice given at these events, see George A. Kelly, *The Catholic Youth's Guide to Life and Love* (New York: Random House, 1960), and John J. Kane, *Together in Marriage* (Chicago: Fides Publishers, 1957).

43. "Rural Catholic Youth Take a Bow . . . ," *Youth Newsnotes* 5:8 (Oct. 1953): 19, ACUA, NCWC, YD 10-52.

44. Mary Jo Wahle, "Ro Could Be You without CYO," *Vision* 2:3 (Nov. 1952): 20, ACUA, NCWC, YD 10:55. For a similar sentiment among Catholic young people see "Article in May *Youth Newsnotes* Provokes Query by Parish Priest," *Youth Newsnotes* 5:6 (June 1953): 9, ACUA, NCWC, YD 10-52. For the Marquette survey, see Raymond H. Potvin, Dean R. Hoge, and Hart M. Nelson, *Religion and American Youth* (Washington, D.C.: United States Catholic Conference, 1976), 34.

45. "All Aboard," *Youth* 1:4 (May 1954): 20, ACUA, NCWC, YD 10-53. "Salute to Youth," *Youth* 4:5 (May 1957): 12-13, ACUA, NCWC, YD 10-53.

46. "Salute to Youth," *Youth* 1:6 (Sept. 1954): 8, ACUA, NCWC, YD 10-53. "Salute to Youth," *Youth* 4:5 (May 1957): 12-13, ACUA, NCWC, YD 10-53. "Salute to Youth," *Youth* 4:7 (Sept. 1957): 12, ACUA, NCWC, YD 10-53.

47. "Report of CISCA: Thursday, May 19, 1960," UNDA, CMRH, 8-8. For examples of modest dress crusades and coverage of Supply the Demand for the Supply, see "Diocesan Data," *Youth Newsnotes* 3:8 (Nov. 1950): 30-31, ACUA, NCWC, YD 10-52; "Diocesan Data," *Youth Newsnotes* 5:9 (Nov. 1953): 19-24, ACUA, NCWC, YD 10-52; and "Modest Dress Campaign Sweeps Nation as More Girls Demand 'Marylike' Dresses," *Youth* 1:1 (Jan. 1954): 13, ACUA, NCWC, YD 10-53. "Salute to Youth," *Youth* 1:6 (Sept. 1954): 8, ACUA, NCWC, YD 10-53 records one of many "Create Your Own" formal dress competitions. For drawings of Marian dresses, see Morrow, *My Catholic Faith*, 386.

48. "The Question of Decency: Our Big Problem is Not Solved by Picket-Lines and Protests," *Today* 2:11 (March 18, 1947): 2, UNDA, CCOG 6.

49. "Diocesan Data," *Youth Newsnotes* 3:2 (Feb. 1950): 30, ACUA, NCWC, YD 10-52. "165 Youngsters Display Plenty of Ability in Perfecting the New National Council of Catholic Youth," *Youth Newsnotes* 4:9 (Nov. 1951): 3-4, ACUA, NCWC, YD 10-52.

50. Stivender, *Still Catholic,* 183-85.

51. As of 1959, slightly more than half of all Catholic high schools were co-ed. Of single-sex schools, those for girls outnumbered those for boys two to one. Neil G. McCluskey, S.J., *Catholic Viewpoint on Education* (Garden City, NY: Hanover House, 1959), 111-13.

52. Stivender, *Raised Catholic,* 179-83. Schwartz, *The Biggest City in America,* 20.

53. Stivender, *Raised Catholic,* 181-86. For similar if less strict dating etiquette persisting in 1964 among non-religious public high school students, see Greene, *Be True to Your School.*

54. Schwartz, *The Biggest City in America,* 156.

55. Stivender, *Raised Catholic,* 186-88. See also Morrow, *My Catholic Faith,* 86, 230-33. This illustrated catechism showed a drawing of a man held at gunpoint to illustrate the condition of a person who had forfeited the "state of grace" by a mortal sin.

56. Beth Bailey, *From Front Porch to Back Seat: Courtship in Twentieth-Century America* (Baltimore: Johns Hopkins University Press, 1988).

57. For a historical investigation of ways that sexual "freedom" has had negative consequences for many young women, see Joan Jacobs Brumberg, *The Body Project: An Intimate History of American Girls* (New York: Random House, 1997).

58. Occhiogrosso, *Once a Catholic,* 72.

59. The crucial role of sexual issues in problematizing Catholic identity emerges as a recurring theme in interviews with well-educated, successful Catholics and former-Catholics in Occhiogrosso, *Once a Catholic.* Potvin, *Religion and American Youth,* 34.

60. Schwartz, *The Biggest City in America,* 152-53.

61. Occhiogrosso, *Once a Catholic,* 79. Joseph M. White, *Worthy of the Gospel of Christ: A History of the Catholic Diocese of Fort Wayne-South Bend* (Fort Wayne: Diocese of Fort Wayne-South Bend, 2007), 386.

62. "The Aims, Purposes, and Philosophy of Catholic Youth Work: Proceedings of the Buzz Sessions of the Seventh National Conference on Catholic Youth Work, November 17-20, 1958," 3-10, ACUA, NCWC, Education Department, 10-84, file: "National Conference on Catholic Youth Work Nov 17-20, 1958."

63. "Proceedings, Fifth National Convention, National Council of Catholic Youth, Diocesan Section," Kansas City, Mo., Nov. 11-15, 1959, 65-68, ACUA, NCWC, YD 10-44.

64. Potvin, *Religion and American Youth,* 34, 44-45.

Notes to Chapter 6

1. "YFC Launches 'Counter Attack,' New Documentary Film," *YFCM,* Dec. 1951, 40-42.

2. Frank C. Phillips, Robert A. Cook, and Cliff Barrows, eds., *Singing Youth for Christ* (Chicago: Youth for Christ International, 1948), 61. The first stanza of this song is quoted at the beginning of the chapter.

3. Lewis Sperry Chafer, *He That Is Spiritual* (Philadelphia: Sunday School Times, 1924), 68-69. Char Meredith, *It's a Sin to Bore a Kid* (Waco, TX: Word Books, 1978), 15-16. Emile Cailliet, *Young Life* (New York: Harper & Row, 1963), 8-10. For a similar sentiment in one of Billy Graham's youth sermons, see Joel A. Carpenter, ed., *The Early Billy Graham: Sermon and Revival Accounts* (New York: Garland, 1988), 69-72.

4. Joel A. Carpenter, ed., *Sacrificial Lives: Young Martyrs and Fundamentalist Idealism*

(New York: Garland, 1988). "Minutes of the Third Annual Convention, Youth for Christ International, July 1947," 47, BGCA 48-13-38.

5. Norman E. King, "Time is Now Fleeting," *YFCM*, Aug. 1949, 6-8.

6. For a similar argument about the appeal of Graham's calls for conversion, see Mark Silk, *Spiritual Politics: Religion and America Since World War II* (New York: Simon & Schuster, 1988), 64-68. Dr. Bob Cook, "President's Report," in "Minutes, YFCI Mid-Winter Hotel Convention, North Park Hotel, Chicago, January 4-6, 1956," 18-28, BGCA 48-13-3.

7. "Youth Poll," *YFCM*, Jan. 1953, 35.

8. "200 at Detroit Funspiration with 20 Decisions," and "200 at Selma, Calif. Hayride with 18 Decisions," *YFCM*, Dec. 1951, 57-59. See also "YFC Clubs," *YFCM*, Sept. 1951, 37.

9. "Teen-Agers Answer Teen Age Problems," *YFCM* (Sept. 1951), 10-12.

10. James Hefley, *God Goes to High School* (Waco: Word Books, 1970), 47-49. See also "Teen-Agers Answer Teen Age Problems," 11.

11. "Bible Club Know How," BGCA 48-18-14. Gene French, *Here's How: YFC Club Student Manual* (Wheaton, Ill.: Youth for Christ International, 1954), 17-24. For an example of sending visiting rally talent to all the local clubs, see Frank C. Phillips, "How I Organized My Area," in "Minutes, 3rd Annual Convention YFCI, Winona Lake, IN, July 1947," 11-13, BGCA 48-13-38.

12. Kansas City YFC, *Beam* (1948-1957), BGCA 48-12. For many examples of YFC banquets and their "courts," see the regular column "YFC Hi-School Clubs," *YFCM*, 1950-60. The 1959 Kansas City yearbook, renamed *Conqueror,* reported a film lending library boasting over sixty films and serving an eight-state region. These yearbooks, and similar ones for Portland, Grand Rapids, Modesto, Gary, and several other cities, are in BGCA 48-12. "Scrapbook on YFC Activities" [c. 1957], BGCA 48-20-2. "YFCI Information Book," 1957, BGCA 48-18-2. "Information: Screen Tests, Gospel Films, Inc.," BGCA 48-1-41.

13. Mark Senter, "The Youth for Christ Movement as an Educational Agency and Its Impact Upon Protestant Churches 1931-1979" (Ph.D. dissertation, Loyola University of Chicago, 1989), 241-44. "High School Bible Quiz Team Finals, Winona Lake, July 12, 1958," BGCA 48-T19. See also "Quizzing Can Change Your Life," *YFCM*, July 1963, 8-11.

14. David Halberstam, *The Fifties* (New York: Villard Books, 1993) 646-47. Interestingly, the YFC Bible Quiz began before the huge success of *The $64,000 Question.* Rather than being simply imitative, perhaps the YFC Bible Quiz contributed to a broader cultural trend of which the TV quiz shows were another manifestation.

15. "Dull Time Oh No! This Gridder Finds," and "She Sparks Her Club's 'One a Week' Goal," *YFCM*, Jan. 1953, 39.

16. Jim Smith, "From 3 to 147 in 5 Months!" *YFCM*, Apr. 1957, 24-25. For similar examples of dramatic growth see "St. Albans, West Va., Club Influences Life of Entire School," *YFCM*, Feb. 1958, 30-31; Paul Nix, "Club of the Month: Forest Hill, Jackson, Mississippi," *YFCM*, May 1958, 8; "Club of the Month, Falls Church, Virginia," *YFCM*, June 1958, 35; and "Three New Ones, Growing Pains at Grand Rapids, Michigan," *YFCM*, Jan. 1953, 37. For club statistics, see Jack Hamilton, "YFCI Club Department Report," in "YFCI Mid-Winter Hotel Convention, North Park Hotel, Chicago, Jan 4-6, 1956," 8, BGCA 48-13-3. Of 300 chartered rallies surveyed, only 59 reports came in. Those 461 clubs averaged 25.3 per week. For Hamilton's gloss on club growth, see "Shooting Underway on YFC Club Film," *YFCM*, Sept. 1951, 13.

17. For typical club columns featuring athletes, student body presidents, and other high

school stars, see Jack Hamilton, "YFC Hi-School Clubs," *YFCM*, Jan. 1954, 45-46; Hamilton, "YFC Hi-School Clubs," *YFCM*, Mar. 1954, 57-65. Molly Eichert, "God Helped Me Be a Cheerleader," *YFCM*, Feb. 1954, 50. See also Robert A. Cook, "Can a Christian Kid Be Popular?" *YFCM*, Feb. 1954, 18-24. "Newburg, OR, 'Counter Attack' Assembly Has Impact on Entire School," *YFCM*, June 1952, 40.

18. Jack Hamilton, "Are High Schools Pagan?" *YFCM*, Feb. 1950, 9-10, 74. Hamilton, "Missionaries are Made in High School," *YFCM*, Mar. 1950, 17-18, 45, 96. Hamilton, "A Bible Club in Your High School," *YFCM*, Apr. 1950, 19-20, 76, 84.

19. Jack Hamilton, "Branded," *YFCM*, May 1953, 38-39.

20. For several examples of using teen bodies as club billboards, see "Bible Club Leaders Meet: Notes and Ideas," n.d., BGCA, 181-1-79. For the impromptu service in a train station, see "500 at Pacific NW Club Convention at Vancouver," *YFCM*, Mar. 1954, 59. For numerous mentions of floats and hayrides, see the regular column, "YFC Hi-School Clubs," *YFCM*, 1951-56.

21. For the story of the Detroit principal, see "Bible Club Leaders Meet: Notes and Ideas," BGCA, 181-7-79. For the Savannah story, see "Newscast Material — Club Reporter," BGCA, 181-1-80. For school assemblies, see "YFC Clubs," *YFCM*, Sept. 1951, 37. For the principal's concern about "anti-god" see "Teen-Agers Answer Teen Age Problems," 12. For the discipline concerns in postwar schools, see Robert L. Hampel, *The Last Little Citadel: American High Schools Since 1940* (Boston: Houghton Mifflin, 1986), 1-16. When asked to speak to a civic club on "outstanding teen-age activity" in his school, one principal brought several members of the YFC Club with him. See "Campus Chatter," *YFCM*, Dec. 1950, 51.

22. Dr. Bob Cook, "President's Report," in "Minutes, YFCI Mid-Winter Hotel Convention, North Park Hotel, Chicago, January 4-6, 1956," 18-28, BGCA 48-13-3. Cook, "Presidential Message," in "Minutes, YFCI Mid-Winter Hotel Convention, Midland Hotel, Chicago, January 2-4, 1957," 7-8, BGCA 48-13-4.

23. Ted W. Engstrom, "Presidential Message," in "Youth for Christ International 7th Annual Mid-Winter Convention Minneapolis, Minnesota, January 2-5, 1962," 10-11, 15, BGCA 48-13-12. For similar concerns, see also "YFC Club Committee Minutes," Mid-Winter Convention, Leamington Hotel, Minneapolis, Minnesota, Tuesday, January 2, 1962," 1, BGCA 181-1-81; and "YFCI 8th Mid-Winter Convention, March 1963, Denver, Colorado," 25, BGCA 48-13-14.

24. "Operation Salvation!" *YFCM*, July 1953, 37-38.

25. "Should Christian Kids Use the Bebop Talk?" in "Youth Speaks Up!" *YFCM*, July 1954, 17-18. Warren Wiersbe, "Well, What About Playing Cards?" *YFCM*, Dec. 1957, 22-23. Ken Anderson, "Film Reviews," *YFCM*, Dec. 1954, 30. Carl Bihl, "Record Reviews," *YFCM*, Dec. 1954, 32. "Do You Know These Christian Recording Artists?" *YFCM*, Mar. 1963, 17. Ben Weiss, "Christian Standards: 20 Questions, 20 Answers," *YFCM*, Apr. 1954, 19-23.

26. Ken Anderson, "Through the Studio with 'Seventeen,'" *YFCM*, Aug. 1956, 10-11. "What It Meant to Be in 'Seventeen,'" *YFCM*, Apr. 1957, 20-21. "Going Steady," *YFCM*, Oct. 1958, 32. "Preacher's Kid" and "Silent Witness," *YFCM*, Dec. 1957, inside back cover advertisement.

27. Evon Hedley, "Christian Movies? Yes," *YFCM*, Jan. 1954, 26, 28.

28. A. W. Tozer, "Christian Movies? No," *YFCM*, Jan. 1954, 27-30.

29. Robert A. Cook, "What About Hollywood Movies?" *YFCM*, Apr. 1957, 15-16. See also Mel Larson, "Hollywood Heartwash," *YFCM*, Sept. 1960, 32-33.

30. "Teen Agers & Television: A Symposium," *YFCM*, Aug. 1952, 39-43. "Television —
Does It Sabotage the Church?" *YFCM*, Aug. 1952, 32-38. Interview with Ralph Carmichael,
Aug. 8, 1969, in R. Bruce Horner, "The Function of Music in the Youth for Christ Program"
(MME thesis, Indiana University, 1970), 146-55, 219.

31. "Youth Speaks Up!" *YFCM*, Aug. 1954, 6-7. Lynn Spigel, *Make Room for TV: Television and the Family Ideal in Postwar America* (Chicago: University of Chicago Press, 1992).

32. "Youth Speaks Up!" *YFCM*, Nov. 1955, 22. Carl J. Bihl, "Blessing? or Blasphemy?"
YFCM, July 1957, 11.

33. "Youth Speaks Up!" *YFCM*, Aug. 1956, 12. Gunnar Urang, "Singing in the Holy
Spirit," *YFCM*, Apr. 1957, 26-27.

34. "Youth Speaks Up!" *YCFM*, Nov. 1955, 22.

35. "Youth Speaks Up!" *YFCM*, May 1954, 17-18.

36. Jim Smith, "Well, What About Dancing?" *YFCM*, Sept. 1957, 11, 33. This article reappeared in *YFCM*, Aug. 1960, 10-11.

37. "30 Towns in Montana Open to YFC Clubs," *YFCM*, Jan. 1952, 64.

38. Paddy Hanna, "My Lesson on Matthew 6:33," *YFCM*, July 1958, 16. For a parallel incident involving Joanne Jorgensen of Milwaukee, Wisconsin, see "Nice Goin' Joanne,"
YFCM, Jan. 1954, 45.

39. "Special Panel: What About Elvis Presley?" *YFCM*, Nov. 1956, 18-19. "The Last Time
I Saw Elvis," *YFCM*, Mar. 1960, 4.

40. For the cultural significance of rock 'n' roll and its critics, see George Lipsitz, "Land
of a Thousand Dances: Youth, Minorities, and the Rise of Rock and Roll," in Lary May, ed.,
Recasting America: Culture and Politics in the Age of Cold War (Chicago: University of Chicago Press, 1989), 267-84. For Youth for Christ opinions on the subject, see William Ward
Ayer, "Jungle Madness in American Music," *YFCM*, Nov. 1956, 19-21; Marlin "Butch"
Hardman, "Rock 'n' Roll: Music or Madness?" *YFCM*, Oct. 1958, 10-12; Hardman, "The Real
Scoop on Rock 'n' Roll," *YFCM*, Oct. 1959, 10-12; Ron Wilson, "Who Did Invent the Twist?"
YFCM, July 1962, 7-8. For music celebrities as idols, see Thurlow Spurr, "How to Build an
Idol," *YFCM*, Sept. 1960, 14-15; "Should Christians Be Fan Clubbers?" *YFCM*, June 1959, 18-
19; and Norman King, "Teen-Age Idol Worship," *YFCM*, Mar. 1959, 6-7.

41. Billy Graham, "Report of the Vice President at Large," in "Minutes of the 2nd Annual Convention," 40. Bob Cook, "President's Report," in "Minutes, 8th Annual Convention,
YFCI, Winona Lake, IN, July 7-12, 1952," 16. Reprinted as Dr. Robert A. Cook, "Willing . . . to
Die?" *YFCM*, Sept. 1952, 12-22.

42. "Youth Speaks Up!" *YFCM*, Oct. 1954, 18. "Youth Speaks Up!" *YFCM*, Apr. 1954, 41-
42.

43. "Youth Speaks Up!" *YFCM*, Apr. 1954, 42-43.

44. Roy McKeown, "Youth for Christ's Role in Delinquent Evangelism," *YFCM*, Feb.
1951, 6-8. J. Edgar Hoover, "Crime Challenges the Churches," April 26, 1955, BGCA 181-4-60.
J. Edgar Hoover, "The Key to Life is God," *YFCM*, Feb. 1951, 9. J. Edgar Hoover, "Trade Softness for Firmness," *YFCM*, Aug. 1957, 12.

45. "Youth Meets the Challenge," editorial reprinted from *The Manual Craftsman*,
Manual High and Vocational School, Kansas City, Mo., in *YFCM*, Jan. 1952, 63.

46. Roy McKeown, "Lifeline," *YFCM*, Apr. 1953, 21-22.

47. "A Statistical Report of YFCI," in "Minutes, YFCI 9th Annual Mid-Winter Convention, January 7-10, 1964, Miami, Florida," BGCA 48-13-17; "The Other Side of America,"

YFCM, Apr. 1965, 11-12; and Bruce Love, "Lifeline," in "Minutes, YFCI Board Meeting, October 12-13, 1966," BGCA 48-9-9.

48. For a description of youth rallies held in prisons and for McLean's appointment to the state board, see "Youth Guidance News," *YFCM*, Aug. 1952, 65-66; and "Youth Guidance News," *YFCM*, Nov. 1952, 48. For McLean's school assemblies, see "Youth Guidance News," *YFCM*, Dec. 1953, 55. For the circumstances surrounding his departure from YFC, see Gordon McLean, *Cities of Lonesome Fear: God Among the Gangs* (Chicago: Moody Press, 1991), 36.

49. Gordon McLean, "America's New Frontier — Youth Guidance," *YFCM*, Apr. 1953, 13-17. "God Worked in This Young Fellow's Life," *YFCM*, Feb. 1957, 37. "No Room at Camp — 300 Applications Turned Down," in "Reports from Divisions of YFCI as Presented at Board of Trustees Meeting, Oct. 14-15, 1964," BGCA 48-9-9. Bruce Love, "Juvenile Delinquency," *YFCM*, May 1963, 26. For concerns about integrating former delinquents into the movement, see "Proposed Plans for Youth Guidance," in "Minutes, YFCI Board of Directors Meeting, San Francisco, May 6-7, 1958." This goal seemed just as remote nearly ten years later; see Bruce Love, "Lifeline Division," in "Reports and Agenda, YFCI Board Meeting, Oct. 11-12, 1967."

50. Robert Cook, "Are You Headed for Delinquency?" *YFCM*, Aug. 1957, 10-11. Gordon McLean, *Coming in on the Beam: A Look at America's Teenager* (Grand Rapids: Zondervan, 1956), 5-6.

51. For examples of YFC evangelism as delinquency prevention, see Caroline Lomier, "Problems Solved Feb. 23," *YFCM*, Oct. 1952, 36; "800 Kids, 15 Decisions at Post-Game Party at Fresno, Calif.," *YFCM*, Dec. 1952, 44; and McKeown, "Youth for Christ's Role in Delinquent Evangelism," 6-7. Charles A. Holmes Jr., "What Youth for Christ Has Meant to Me," *YFCM*, Oct. 1951, 18-19.

52. Cook, "Are You Headed for Delinquency?" 10-11. Billy Zeoli, "You Could Be a 'J. D.,'" *YFCM*, Aug. 1958, 4-5. "Youth Speaks Up!" *YFCM*, July 1954, 17-18. Warren Wiersbe, "I'm Fed Up With Smutty Literature," *YFCM*, Nov. 1957, 8-9. Ted Engstrom, "We Can Stop This Smut," *YFCM*, Nov. 1957, 10-11. "The Case for Modesty," *YFCM*, July 1958, 14-15. J. Edgar Hoover, "Warning to U.S. Teen-Agers," *YFCM*, Aug. 1958, 7.

53. Bruce Love, "The Truth About Juvenile Delinquents," *YFCM*, May 1961, 4-5. "The Other Side of America," 11-12.

54. In addition to the YFC club yearbooks cited above, see "Smiles, Classes are Over," *YFCM*, Feb. 1955, 30, which includes a photo of an integrated club meeting in Fremont High School in Los Angeles. For the "colored rally," see "Charter Time in Memphis," *YFCM*, Oct. 1954, 33.

55. "California Clubber Decathlon Champ," *YFCM*, Jan. 1954, 45-46. When Johnson later went on to collegiate sports fame, a longer interview appeared in *YFCM*, Nov. 1956. For Ronie Haley's election to the YFC court, see "YFC Hi-School Clubs," *YFCM*, Aug. 1954, 20. For black clubs and officers, see "New Club Going at Sweetwater, Tenn.," *YFCM*, Feb. 1955, 28; "All-Around Student Heads Dayton, Tenn., Club," *YFCM*, Feb. 1955, 28; and "Peoria President," *YFCM*, Feb. 1955, 31.

56. For the story of integration in Graham's rallies, see William Martin, *A Prophet with Honor: The Billy Graham Story* (New York: William Morrow, 1991), 168-72. McLean, *Cities*, 38.

57. Cook, "President's Report," Midwinter Convention 1956, 20.

58. "Research Session Notes, YFCI Mid-Winter Convention, Denver, Colorado, March 1963," 2, BGCA 48-13-14.
59. "Youth Speaks Up!" *YFCM*, Dec. 1957, 26.
60. Harold Myra, "What Are the Communists Saying?" *Monday Memo*, Oct. 23, 1961, 3, BGCA 48-15-39. "Synopsis of New Horizons for Youth (October)," *Monday Memo*, Nov 13, 1961, 6, BGCA 48-15-39. "New Horizons for Youth Synopsis," *Monday Memo*, Dec. 18, 1961, 3, BGCA 48-15-39.
61. Hefley, *God Goes to High School*, 90, 185.
62. Larry Fuhrer, "Prejudice and the Christian Teenager," *YFCM*, Sept. 1964, 18-20, 29.

Notes to Chapter 7

1. Lewis, *Walking with the Wind: A Memoir of the Movement* (San Diego, CA: Harvest Books, 1998), 218-31, 236.
2. For the quote from the young leader who said God and the church don't care, see Kelly Miller Smith, "Today's Youth in the Quest of Spiritual Values," n.d., KMS 27-13. Dr. Alvin Poussaint participated in the movement and remembers the severe emotional traumas and limited resources for recovery that young activists endured. He describes an occasion in which Stokely Carmichael "just totally lost it" due to anger and stress. See Juan Williams, *My Soul Looks Back in Wonder: Voices of the Civil Rights Movement* (New York: Sterling, 2004), 116, 129-33. For the positive relationship between local young people and their churches see Ellen Levine, *Freedom's Children: Young Civil Rights Activists Tell Their Own Stories* (New York: Puffin Books, 1993), 48, 63, 66, 69, 85, 87, 88, 109, 111, 117, 127, 133, 134. For the trend toward anti-Christian sentiments among full-time SNCC activists see Lewis, *Walking with the Wind*, 361-392 and Marsh, *God's Long Summer*, 166-91.
3. Marsh, *God's Long Summer: Stories of Faith and Civil Rights* (Princeton, NJ: Princeton University Press, 2008), 179-84. For a description of the "freedom high" phenomenon, see Tom Brokaw, *Boom! Voices of the Sixties* (New York: Random House, 2007), 58. For the riots in Nashville after Carmichael's visit see Jim Newton, "Carmichael, Race Oppression Blamed for Nashville Rioting," *National Baptist Voice*, June 1967, 2; and Dr. George Benson, "'Planned' Agitation: The Radicals and Riots," *National Baptist Voice*, Dec. 1967, 4. For the collapse of SNCC see Williams, *My Soul Looks Back in Wonder*, 138-39, and Carson, *In Struggle: SNCC and the Black Awakening of the 1960s* (Cambridge, MA: Harvard University Press, 1981), 287-303.
4. Smith, "Today's Youth in the Quest of Spiritual Values."
5. Benjamin Paul Perkins, *Black Christians' Tragedies: An Analysis of Black Youth and Their Church* (New York: Exposition Press, 1972), 10, 37-43.
6. Perkins, *Black Christians' Tragedies*, 27-28, 43, 46, 54. Dr. Horace N. Mays, "Unfinished Business as it Relates to New Areas of Concern," *National Baptist Voice*, Apr. 1966, 15-16.
7. Lewis, *Walking with the Wind*, 184. Marsh, *God's Long Summer*, 158.
8. Beverly Hall Lawrence, *Reviving the Spirit: A Generation of African Americans Goes Home to Church* (New York: Grove Press, 1996), 15-16, 32, 40.
9. Interview with Virginia Bright, Oct. 27, 1999, in author's personal collection.
10. "North American Youth Assembly, Ann Arbor, 1961," MCAH, GBD 1124-4-3:17.

11. See, for example, "Planning Committee for the Exploration." For other signs of intense reevaluation around 1960, see "1965 Division of the Local Church Annual Report," 73-74, MCAH, GBHE 2577-5-3:18. "Co-operative Curriculum Project," *DLC Reports* (Apr. 1961), MCAH, GBHE 2592-4-1:26. "Plans for a New Youth Curriculum," *DLC Reports* (Spring 1966), MCAH, GBHE 2592-4-1:26.

12. Friedenberg even lectured to Methodist youth workers in 1962. "Descriptions of Meetings of Conference Directors of Youth Work 1958-1962," MCAH, GBD 1124-2-3:02. "Report on the Graduate Seminar on Youth Work, Scarritt College, January 1961," MCAH, GBD 1184-2-1:26. For an example of a Methodist youth manual that drew explicitly on the critics of "organized society" see *Guidebook for Youth Work in the Church* (Nashville: Board of Education of the Methodist Church, 1961). David Riesman *The Lonely Crowd: A Study of the Changing American Character* (New Haven: Yale University Press, 1950), v-vi, 5, 24, 40. William H. Whyte Jr., *The Organization Man* (New York: Simon and Schuster, 1956), 23, 28-30, 44-45, 395-96, 398.

13. *Insights About a Youth Ministry: Papers from a Consultation On Ministry to Youth held at Chicago Theological Seminary* (Nashville: General Board of Education of the Methodist Church, 1962), MCAH, GBHE 2577-5-3:24.

14. Ross Snyder, *A Ministry of Meanings* (Nashville: General Board of Education of the Methodist Church, 1963), MCAH, GBD 1184-3-1:46. Ross Snyder, *The Ministry of Meaning* (Geneva: Youth Department of the World Council of Churches, 1965).

15. Psychology and existentialism were both heavily represented on the book table at the 1964 youth convocation; see "Books Suggested for Display and Use Eighth National Convocation of Methodist Youth, Purdue University — W. Lafayette, Indiana, July 27-31, 1964," MCAH, GBD 1124-5-1:03.

16. "Report of Consultation on Work Camps for Senior High Green Lake, Wisconsin October 7-9, 1960," MCAH, GBD 1184-3-1:50. "Planning Committee for the Exploration."

17. "An Invitation to be the Church in the World Summer 1964: 10 weeks in an Intentional Community," MCAH, GBD 1124-5-2:05. "Albuquerque Methodist Youth Intentional Community Log June 22 through August 21st, 1964," MCAH, GBD 1124-5-2:05. "Intentional communities Summer 1965," MCAH, GBD 1124-2-3:02. Sue Ellen Gray, "Report on the Intentional Community Project," Aug. 20, 1965, MCAH, GBD 1124-4-3:11. Ted McEachern, "The Kind of Christian Education This Day Calls For: The Significance of Dietrich Bonhoeffer's Theology for Christian Education," October 28, 1964, MCAH, GBHE 2592-4-1:24. The concept of faithfulness through abandoning the institutional needs of the church was later codified in "Some Directions in Youth Ministry 1966-1967," MCAH, GBD 1120-2:1:59.

18. John Newman, "Report: Youth Associate in Race Relations," 1-4, MCAH, GBD 1124-5-2:9.

19. Linda Hutchinson, Judy Lewis, and Tom Welch, "The Role of the Rebel: Report after Summer Spent in Travel as Representatives of NCMYF," Summer 1966, MCAH, GBD 1118-5-2:36. "Youth/Student Response to the Urban Crisis," Jan. 3, 1969, MCAH, GBD 1118-5-2:35. "To Participants of the Bishops-Youth Consultation from Millsaps Dye," December 30, 1969, MCAH, GBD 1118-5-2:30. "Statement of Concern from Convo Youth Caucus," Friday, March 7, 1969, MCAH, GBD 1118-5-2:30.

20. News Release, Berkeley, California, MCAH, GBD 1118-5-2:28. "Through Hippieland With Guide and God," *San Francisco Chronicle,* Aug. 23, 1967, 2, MCAH, GBD 1124-4-3:07.

21. Johnny Cook, "Report on National Conference of the Methodist Youth Fellowship, August 20-26, 1967," MCAH, GBD 1124-4-3:07.

22. Doug Rossinow, *The Politics of Authenticity: Liberalism, Christianity, and the New Left in America* (New York: Columbia University Press, 1998). For numerous examples of women whose mainline Protestant faith contributed to their campus political activism during the sixties, see Sara M. Evans, ed., *Journeys That Opened Up the World: Women, Student Christian Movements and Social Justice, 1955-1975* (New Brunswick, NJ: Rutgers University Press, 2003).

23. Paul Lyons, *Class of 1966: Living in Suburban Middle America* (Philadelphia: Temple University Press, 1994).

24. John J. Simons, "The Necessity for an Apostolic Approach to Catholic Youth Work," *American Journal of Catholic Youth Work* 2:2 (Spring 1961): 22-27, ACUA, NCWC, YD 10-55. Richard Stause, "Christianity and the Organized Approach — An Interview of Richard J. McCaffery," *AJCYW* 3:3 (Fall 1962): 19-23, ACUA, NCWC, YD 10-55. For examples outside the Youth Department publications, see Sheila McKeone, "The Catholic Youth Club," *Clergy Review* 48 (June 1963): 369-74; Rev. J. F. Sedlak, "Are We Really Helping Our Youth?" *Family Digest* 19 (Feb. 1964): 55-58.

25. "Spotlight on Youth," *Youth*, Nov. 1961, 9, ACUA, NCWC, YD 10-53. Andrew Greeley, *Strangers in the House: Catholic Youth in America* (New York: Sheed and Ward, 1961). See also Andrew Greeley, "A Spirituality for Young Americans," *AJCYW* 3:3 (Fall 1962): 3-9, ACUA, NCWC, YD 10-55. For teenage panel titles at the 1961 convention, see "Youth Wearing the Armor of Courage: 6th National Convention, National Council of Catholic Youth, Teenage and Young Adult Sections," 21-30, ACUA, NCWC, Education Department 10-82. For the late-sixties crisis of Catholic identity, see Philip Gleason, "Catholicism and Cultural Change in the 1960s," in *Keeping the Faith: American Catholicism Past and Present* (Notre Dame: University of Notre Dame Press, 1987), 82-96.

26. Douglas A. Fox, "The Alien Generation," *Spiritual Life* 12 (Spring 1966): 43-50.

27. Eleanor McGowan, "Contact Leaders' Corps," *AJCYW* 5 (Winter 1964): 43-47, ACUA, NCWC, YD 10-55. Rev. Joseph L. Baglio, "An Experiment in Forming the Christian," *AJCYW* 7:2 (Summer 1966): 27-32, ACUA, NCWC, YD 10-55.

28. "Whither the New Breed?" *AJCYW* 6:1 (Spring 1965): 35-39, ACUA, NCWC, YD 10-55. "Youth Wearing the Armor of Courage," 25. "National CYO Board Meets," *YPS* 1:1 (Sept./Oct. 1962): 2, ACUA, NCWC, YD 10-53.

29. Rev. Geno C. Baroni, "Youth Leadership in the Social Order," *AJCYW* 4:3 (Fall 1963): 29-35, ACUA, NCWC, YD 10-55. Rev. Leonard F. X. Mayhew, "Role of CYO Youth in Social Action," *AJCYW* 2:2 (Spring 1961): 28-33, ACUA, NCWC, YD 10-55.

30. James P. Gannon, "Teenagers: An Interview with Father Andrew Greeley," *AJCYW* 5:2 (Spring 1964): 30-34, ACUA, NCWC, YD 10-55. For youthful acceptance of social teaching, see "Proceedings, Tenth National Conference on Catholic Youth Work," New Orleans, Nov. 15-18, 1964, 7, ACUA, NCWC, ED 10-84.

31. "The Seventh National Convention, National Catholic Youth Organization Federation, Teenage and Young Adult Sections," New York, Nov. 14-17, 1963, 11-18, 59-66, ACUA, NCWC, YD 10-44. For conference sessions devoted to communism and going steady, see "Belleville Diocesan CYO Stages Annual Conference," *Youth*, Apr. 1962, 7, ACUA, NCWC, YD 10-53.

32. Merton P. Strommen, "Problems of Church Youth," *AJCYW* 5:2 (Spring 1964): 25-29, ACUA, NCWC, YD 10-55.

33. Elizabeth M. Gladych, "CYO: a Progress Report," *Catholic Digest* 27 (June 1963): 63-66. George Fischer, "Where CYO Really Works," *Catholic Digest* 28 (Jan. 1964): 14-17.

34. Marty Tharp, "CYO President Blasts 'Dance-of-the-Month,'" *Nebraska Register* 1969, ACUA, NCWC Education Department 10-83.

35. Rev. Paul J. Hayes, "Teenagers and Entertainment," *Catholic Review of Entertainment* 5 (Mar. 1961): 18-23. Rev. Paul J. Hayes, "Teens Talk About Entertainment," *Ave Maria* 93 (Mar. 25, 1961): 5-8. Carol F. Sinnott, M.S.W., "'Teens' — A Survey Summary," *AJCYW* 9:2 (Summer 1968): 17. For youth leader reactions to teen sexuality and calls for reform in how the church taught about sex, see "Youth's Influence in Modern Society," Symposium on Youth, Youth Department, United States Catholic Conference, March 6-7, 1967, ACUA NCWC Education Dept. 10-84.

36. Albert J. Nimeth, O.F.M., "Teen-ager's Spiritual Difficulties," *AJCYW* 9:3 (Fall 1962): 30-31. For evidence that adults assumed girls would still like traditional devotions, see Irene Shey, "Presenting the Ideal of Woman to the Adolescent Girl," *AJCYW* 2:3 (Fall 1962): 32-35. For examples of youth masses as national CYO conventions, see "1969 Convention Liturgy," ACUA, NCWC Ed. Dept. 10-83. Yet as late as 1973, priests in Chicago were calling for "more youth masses" because young people seemed alienated from regular masses. See "Report of the Presbyterial Senate Ad Hoc Commission on 'Youth,'" Presented to the Church Life Committee, Feb. 20, 1973, Association of Chicago Priests, CACP Box 4 File 33 University of Notre Dame Archives.

37. For the survey of Catholic high school boys, see "The Faith of the Young: An Emerging Problem," *America*, July 16, 1966, 54-55. For expert opinions that young people would no longer submit to adult leadership, see Dr. Jack Curtis with Barbara Moldraski, "Some Background Theory for Youth Workers," *AJCYW* 2:1 (Winter 1961): 9-11. See also Carroll F. Tageson, O.F.M., "Spiritual Direction of the Adolescent," *AJCYW* 3:2 (Fall 1962): 44-56, and Rev. James Finnegan, O.S.F.S., "A Salesian Approach to Youth," *AJCYW* 3:1 (Winter 1962): 14-18.

38. For McGloin's remarks, see the transcript of his talk in "Youth's Influence on Society." For examples of film discussions see Joan Benson, "Films: The Missing Media in Your Youth Program?" AJCYW 2:2 (Summer 1962), 90. Rev. Donald J. Bowen, "A Christian 'Live-In' Series," AJCYW 9:2 (Summer 1968): 4-7; and James Heft, S.M., and John Bakle, S.M., "NOW — A Retreat for Teenagers," AJCYW 9:2 (Summer 1968): 8-10. For the ecumenical youth curriculum and club manuals, see "Minutes of the 1969 Advisory Board Division of Youth Activities" and "Minutes of the 1970 Advisory Board Meeting Division of Youth Activities, USCC," ACUA NCWC Ed. Dept. 10-81.

39. Rev. Peter G. Armstrong, "Youth Mission Accomplished," *YPS*, May/June 1963, 6-7, ACUA, NCWC, YD 10-53. "Teenagers in Search," *YPS*, July/Aug. 1966, 3-5, ACUA, NCWC, YD 10-53.

40. Peter G. Armstrong, "The Search for Christian Maturity," in "Proceedings, the Eighth National Convention, National Catholic Youth Organization Federation," 151-60.

41. Rev. Peter G. Armstrong, Michael Nevin, Bob Perry, and Tim McSweeney, "A Search for Christian Maturity," *YPS*, July/Aug. 1963, 3, 19, ACUA, NCWC, YD 10-53. See also "Proceedings, the Eighth National Convention, National Catholic Youth Organization Federation," 151-60. For sample songs and liturgies, see *Search for Christian Maturity: Searcher's*

Manual (Washington, D.C.: National CYO Federation, 1966), 11-38, ACUA, NCWC, ED 10-84.

42. "Proceedings, the Eighth National Convention, National Catholic Youth Organization Federation," 151-60. For the ongoing use of the Search, see Rev. Paul Ouellette, O.M.I., "Search," *The Church World,* April 4, 1969, 5; Rick J. Quirk, "Search," *YPS* 8:1 (Jan./Feb. 1971): 20, ACUA, NCWC, YD 10-53; Rick Quirk, "Search," *YPS* 8:2 (Mar./Apr. 1971): 11, ACUA, NCWC, YD 10-53; "Program Features," *YPS* 8:3 (May/June 1971): 19, ACUA, NCWC, YD 10-53.

43. A national survey of Catholic youth leaders running Search programs in 1969 revealed that numbers were low and follow-up was not strong. "Replies to Questionnaire," *AJCYW* 10:3 (Fall/Winter 1969): 11, 20, 33-34.

44. Mary Reed Newland, *Youth: What Happened?* (Notre Dame: Ave Maria Press, 1970), 25-32.

45. Rev. William McNulty, "Youth and the Church," Catholic Action Federations, n.d., CACP Box 4 File 33, University of Notre Dame Archives.

46. "Report of the Presbyterial Senate Ad Hoc Commission on 'Youth.'"

47. Rev. P. David Finks, "To a New World," *YPS* 8:1 (Jan./Feb. 1971): 12, ACUA, NCWC, YD 10-53.

48. James D. Davidson et al., *The Search for Common Ground: What Unites and Divides Catholic Americans* (Huntington, Ind.: Our Sunday Visitor, 1997), 93-139.

49. Thomas Frank, *The Conquest of Cool: Business Culture, Counterculture and the Rise of Hip Consumerism* (Chicago: University of Chicago Press, 1997), 1-33, 53-73, 105-167. "Second Church Youth Director's Conference," July 1962, BGCA 48-19-26. "Adult Seminar on Teen Dynamics," 1968, BGCA 48-19-27. "New Dimensions in Teen Dynamics — A Service for Church Youth Workers Sponsored by YFCI," BGCA 48-19-28. James C. Hefley, *God Goes to High School* (Waco, TX: Word Books, 1970), 92. YFC reported 9,000 attending the Teen Dynamics seminars in 2 years.

50. "Minutes of YFCI Staff Retreat," May 5-6, 1959, 2-3, BGCA 48-19-13. For statistics on the number of YFC rallies, see Mark Senter, "The Youth for Christ Movement as an Educational Agency and Its Impact upon Protestant Churches 1931-1979" (Ph.D. dissertation, Loyola University of Chicago, 1989), 249, and "A Statistical Report of YFCI," in "Minutes, YFCI 9th Annual Mid-Winter Convention, January 7-10, 1964, Miami, Florida," BGCA 48-13-17. "YFCI Staff Retreat Minutes," May 10-11, 1960, 3, BGCA 48-19-14. For Eakin's travels, see "YFCI National Club Director" in "Memo to YFCI Board of Directors from Ted W. Engstrom, January 20, 1961," BGCA 48-9-8, and Bill Eakin, "YFCI Club Department" in "President's Report to the 17th Annual Convention of YFCI," July 2-16, 1961, BGCA 48-13-56.

51. "YFCI 6th Annual Mid-Winter Hotel Convention, Los Angeles, California, January 1961," 18-19, 22-23, BGCA 48-13-9. For the transformation of style among advertising employees see Frank, *The Conquest of Cool: Business Culture, Counterculture and the Rise of Hip Consumerism,* 112-14.

52. Interview with Larry Ballenger, July 9, 1969, in R. Bruce Horner, "The Function of Music in the Youth for Christ Program" (MME thesis, Indiana University, 1970), 136-41.

53. Horner, "The Function of Music," 77-109, 176, 210, 217, 220-21. For the success of folk musicals in the late 1960s and their role in opening the way for Jesus Rock, see Charlie Peacock, *At the Crossroads: An Insider's Look at the Past, Present, and Future of Contemporary Christian Music* (Nashville: Broadman Press, 1999), 60-64.

54. Horner, "The Function of Music," 222-26.

55. Larry Eskridge, "'One Way': Billy Graham, the Jesus Generation, and the Idea of an Evangelical Youth Culture," *Church History* 67:1 (March 1998): 83-106.

56. Hampel, *The Last Little Citadel*, 1-42. Greene, *Be True to Your School*, 308-9.

57. Interview with James Wright, Tape 2, Side 1, BGCA 326. "YFCI Department Goals," in "YFCI Staff Retreat Minutes, May 10-11, 1960, Lake Geneva, Wisconsin," BGCA 48-19-14. Ray Curry, "YFC Counseling and Follow Up," in "6th Annual YFCI Mid-Winter Convention," 40-47.

58. "YFCI 8th Mid-Winter Convention, March 1963, Research Session Notes," 28, BGCA 48-13-14.

59. "Research Session Notes," in "YFCI 7th Mid-Winter Convention, Minneapolis, January 1962," 8-10, BGCA 48-13-11.

60. For references to Hill and Laird see "Research Session Notes," 1962, 9-10, and *Dimension* 1:1 (Apr. 1962): 2, BGCA 48-15-40. "How to Manage People," *Dimension* 2:8 (Feb. 1964): 3-4, BGCA 48-15-42. "How to Manage People," *Dimension* 2:9 (Mar. 1964): 1-2, BGCA 48-15-42. The March 1964 issue also recommended the Nelson Doubleday "Personal Success Course" to improve YFC staff leadership skills.

61. *Campus Life Impact Manual* (Wheaton, Ill.: Youth for Christ International, 1968), 1-20, 34, BGCA 48-10-8.

62. Girl's Staff Manual, n.d., 17, 20-29, 44-51, BGCA 48-10-5.

63. *Campus Life Insight Manual* (Wheaton, Ill.: Youth for Christ International, 1968), BGCA 48-10-13.

64. Ken Taylor, Dean Merrill, Joan Nickerson, *Heads Up!* (Wheaton, Ill.: Tyndale House, 1968); see also Tom Schmerler, *Come Alive!* (Wheaton, Ill.: Tyndale House, 1966).

65. Bill Bright, *Revolution Now!* (San Bernardino, Calif.: Campus Crusade for Christ, 1969). Bright's book saw seven printings between 1969 and 1971. Ethel Barrett, *Will the Real Phony Please Stand Up?* (Glendale, Calif.: G/L Publications, 1969). This commentary on the Book of James sold 500,000 copies by 1974. Peter E. Gillquist, *Love Is Now* (Grand Rapids: Zondervan, 1970). Gillquist's book sold 35,000 copies and went through five printings by 1971.

Notes to Chapter 8

1. Mark H. Senter III, "The Groundwork for Willow Creek Community Church: An Interview with David Hulmbo," *Christian Education Journal* 5:1 (Spring 2001): 53-66. See also Kimon Howland Sargeant, *Seeker Churches: Promoting Traditional Religion in a Nontraditional Way* (New Brunswick, N.J.: Rutgers University Press, 2000), 190-201.

2. Colleen Carroll, *The New Faithful: Why Young Adults Are Embracing Christian Orthodoxy* (Chicago: Loyola Press, 2002), 42-44, 84-85, 97-98. The quotes about why teenagers attend youth liturgies are taken from William Dinges, "Comments on Colleen Carroll, *The New Faithful*," Cushwa Center for the Study of American Catholicism, University of Notre Dame, Seminar in American Religion, April 2003. Efrem Smith and Phil Jackson, *The Hip-Hop Church: Connecting with the Movement Shaping Our Culture* (Downers Grove, Ill.: InterVarsity Press, 2005).

3. "Children and Youth: High Priority Means High Performance," from "Ten Strengths

of US Congregations," report of the U.S. Congregational Life Survey, www.uscongregations
.org/10strengths-children.htm (retrieved July 21, 2008).

4. For a discussion of the superficiality of 1950s religious beliefs, see Mark Silk, *Spiritual Politics: Religion and America Since World War II* (New York: Simon and Schuster, 1988), 17-18. For the statistics on religious belief and church attendance as well as a persuasive argument that American Christianity is more vibrant than should be expected given the forces pushing in the other direction, see Robert Wuthnow, "A Puzzle: The Question of Religious Vitality," www.ucpress.edu/books/pages/9495 (accessed July 1, 2003).

5. Theodore Caplow, Howard M. Bahr, and Bruce A. Chadwick, *All Faithful People: Change and Continuity in Middletown's Religion* (Minneapolis: University of Minnesota Press, 1983), 39-42, 70, 73, 87-90, 100-102, 218-24, 230, 306, 308. For strong evidence that American teenagers continue to have positive views of the church and Christian faith, see Christian Smith and Melinda Lundquist Denton, *Soul Searching: The Religious and Spiritual Lives of American Teenagers* (New York: Oxford University Press, 2005), 39-42, 61-67, 124-27.

6. Wuthnow, "A Puzzle." James A. Mathisen, "Tell Me Again: Why Do Churches Grow?" *Books and Culture*, May/June 2004, 18-20, 41.

7. Mathisen, "Tell Me Again," 18-20, 41. Dean M. Kelley, *Why Conservative Churches are Growing* (New York: Harper & Row, 1972). Joseph B. Tamney, *The Resilience of Conservative Religion: The Case of Popular, Conservative Protestant Congregations* (Cambridge: Cambridge University Press, 2002). Christian Smith, *American Evangelicalism: Embattled and Thriving* (Chicago: University of Chicago Press, 1998).

8. N. J. Demerath III, "Cultural Victory and Organizational Defeat in the Paradoxical Decline of Liberal Protestantism," *Journal for the Scientific Study of Religion* 34:4 (1995): 458-69. For a similar argument, see Amanda Porterfield, *The Transformation of American Religion: The Story of a Late-Twentieth-Century Awakening* (New York: Oxford University Press, 2001), 1-12. A 1998 Gallup poll found that 55 percent of liberals, 47 percent of moderates, and only 35 percent of conservatives were unchurched. George Gallup Jr. and D. Michael Lindsay, *Surveying the Religious Landscape: Trends in U.S. Beliefs* (Harrisburg, Penn.: Morehouse Publishing, 1999), 96.

9. Memo to Youth Department Staff from Harold W. Ewing April 14, 1952, MCAH, GBD, 1184-3-1:26. "The Need for Emphasis on Youth in the Next Quadrennium 4-16-52," MCAH, GBD, 1184-3-1:26. *Methodist Fact Book* (Statistical Office, The Methodist Church, 1964), 170. For another example of concern over Methodists keeping their "market share" of American youth, see John Q. Schisler, "The Good Youth Leader," an address delivered before the General Youth Section of the National Conference of Methodist Youth at Purdue University, W. Lafayette, Indiana, Aug. 22, 1951, MCAH, GBD, 1124-4-2:30. Dean R. Hoge, Benton Johnson, and Donald A. Luidens, *Vanishing Boundaries: The Religion of Mainline Protestant Baby Boomers* (Louisville: Westminster, 1994), 1-6.

10. Michael A. Hout, Andrew Greeley, and Melissa J. Wilde, "The Demographic Imperative in Religious Change in the United States," *American Journal of Sociology* 107 (Sept. 2001): 468-500. Mathisen, "Tell Me Again," 20, 41.

11. Thomas E. Bergler, "The Place of History in Youth Ministry Education," *Journal of Youth Ministry* 1:1 (Fall 2002): 57-71.

12. Merton Strommen, "A Recent Invention: The Profession of Youth Ministry," in Merton Strommen, Karen E. Jones, and Dave Rahn, *Youth Ministry That Transforms* (Grand

Rapids: Zondervan, 2001), 30-33. For declining conservative Protestant birth rates, see Mathisen, "Tell Me Again," 42.

13. Smith and Denton, *Soul Searching,* 70.

14. William V. D'Antonio, James D. Davidson, Dean R. Hoge, and Katherine Meyer, *American Catholics: Gender, Generation, and Commitment* (New York: Rowman and Littlefield, 2001), 52-53.

15. Raymond H. Potvin, Dean R. Hoge, and Hart M. Nelson, *Religion and American Youth* (Washington, D.C.: United States Catholic Conference, 1976), 34, 44. The survey of Mass attendance cites 74 percent of high school graduates and 100 percent of college graduates attending weekly in 1957. Although the latter baseline figure is particularly suspect, a dramatic drop in attendance seems to have in fact occurred.

16. For Catholic adult opposition to long hair and the counterculture, see Newland, *Youth: What Happened?* For evidence that the FBI and CIA recruited heavily on Catholic campuses during the fifties and sixties, see James Carroll, *An American Requiem: God, My Father, and the War that Came Between Us* (Boston: Houghton Mifflin, 1996), and Mark Massa, *Catholics and American Culture* (Herder and Herder, 2001). A conversation with Stephen B. Clark, who attended the University of Notre Dame in the 1960s, confirmed that the FBI recruited heavily there.

17. Dinges, "Comments on Colleen Caroll." See also William Dinges et al., *Young Adult Catholics: Religion in the Culture of Choice* (Notre Dame: University of Notre Dame Press, 2001). Strommen et al., *Youth Ministry That Transforms,* 35.

18. For rankings of church commitment by religious family, see Wade Clark Roof and William McKinney, *American Mainline Religion: Its Changing Shape and Future* (New Brunswick, N.J.: Rutgers University Press, 1987), 100-102. For the decline in nonwhite church attendance from 1956 to 1966 see Norval D. Glenn and Erin Gotard, "The Religion of Blacks in the United States: Some Recent Trends and Current Characteristics," *American Journal of Sociology* 83:2 (Sept. 1977): 443-51. For regional differences in church attendance, see Hart M. Nelsen and Conrad L. Kanagy, "Churched and Unchurched Black Americans," in David A. Roozen and C. Kirk Hadaway, eds., *Church and Denominational Growth* (Nashville: Abingdon Press, 1993), 311-23.

19. For evidence of a return by some who left the church in the late sixties and early seventies, see Beverly Hall Lawrence, *Reviving the Spirit: A Generation of African Americans Goes Home to Church* (New York: Grove Press, 1996), 11, 13, 15, 17, 28, 38-39, 43, 49.

20. C. Eric Lincoln and Lawrence H. Mamiya, *The Black Church in the African-American Experience* (Durham: Duke University Press, 1990), 359-63, 377-81.

21. Lincoln and Mamiya, *The Black Church,* 164-76. See also Robert M. Franklin, *Another Day's Journey: Black Churches Confronting the American Crisis* (Minneapolis: Fortress Press, 1997), 59-62.

22. Christopher G. Ellison and Darren E. Sherkat, "Patterns of Religious Mobility among Black Americans," *The Sociological Quarterly* 31:4 (1990): 551-68. For regional differences see Nelson and Kanagy, "Churched and Unchurched," 311-23. For generational differences in apostasy among African Americans, see Darren E. Sherkat and Christopher G. Ellison, "The Politics of Black Religious Change: Disaffiliation from Black Mainline Denominations," *Social Forces* 70:2 (Dec. 1991): 431-54. For concerns about a growing gap between the black church and the urban poor, especially young males, see Andrew Billingsley, *Mighty Like a River: The Black Church and Social Reform* (New York: Oxford University

Press, 1999), xv, and Robert M. Franklin, *Crisis in the Village: Restoring Hope in African American Communities* (Minneapolis: Fortress Press, 2007). For conflict between urban black churches and their neighborhoods, often leading to heightened security at churches, see Franklin, *Another Day's Journey,* 58-59. For the gap between the religious beliefs of black teenagers and those of their parents, see Smith and Denton, *Soul Searching,* 35.

23. Smith and Denton, *Soul Searching,* 51, 61, 124-27.

24. Smith and Denton, *Soul Searching,* 118-71.

25. Smith and Denton, *Soul Searching,* 118-68.

26. For a glimpse of the Latter Day Saints seminary for teenagers, see Christian Smith, *Soul Searching,* directed by Michael Eaton and Timothy Eaton (79 min., Revelation Studios, 2007, DVD).

27. Potvin, *Religion and American Youth,* 34, 44.

28. D'Antonio et al., *American Catholics,* 43.

29. For studies of selective faith among younger generations, see Carol Lytch, *Choosing Church* (Louisville: Westminster John Knox, 2003), Robert Wuthnow, *After the Baby Boomers* (Princeton: Princeton University Press, 2007), Richard Cimino and Don Lattin, *Shopping for Faith* (San Francisco: Jossey-Bass, 1998). Smith and Denton, *Soul Searching,* 143-47. Caplow et al., *All Faithful People,* 218-21. George Gallup Jr. and Jim Castelli, *The People's Religion: American Faith in the 90s* (New York: Macmillan, 1989), 46. For similar results, see George Barna, *What Americans Believe* (Ventura, Calif.: Regal Books, 1991), 83-85.

30. Barna, *What Americans Believe,* 83-85.

31. Christian Smith, in "Consultation on the Christian Formation of Youth" (Lilly Endowment, Inc., Nov. 7-8, 2006), 83-84.

32. Gallup and Lindsay, *Surveying the Religious Landscape,* 91-92. Cimino and Lattin, *Shopping for Faith,* 80.

33. For a theological discussion of how adolescent developmental traits can benefit the church, see Kenda Creasy Dean, *Practicing Passion: Youth and the Quest for a Passionate Church* (Grand Rapids: Eerdmans, 2004).

Index

Index

Catholic "ghetto": Catholic schools as, 129-31; collapse of, 190, 197-98; defensive stance of, 145-46; discouraged, 56; formation of, 143-46; patriotism in, 135, 143, 144, 145, 216; role in juvenilization of faith, 119-20, 125-29; sexual purity emphasis, 135, 138
"Catholic guilt," 127
Catholicism, all-American: in Catholic "ghetto," 135, 143, 144, 145, 216; commodification of faith, 123, 128; NCWC programs, 121-25
Catholicism, integrated, 143-46
Catholic schools, 33, 129-31, 197
Catholic social teaching, 34-36
Catholic Youth Organization (CYO): apostolic mentality, 55-57, 65; civil rights support, 191-92; communist allegations, 35; competitions, 56, 131-35; creation of, 34-35; effectiveness questioned, 143-44, 190; factors undermining, 193-94; as juvenilized version of Catholicism, 121-22; public relations efforts, 123-24, 128-29, 132; sexual purity messages, 137, 138-39; sports events, 35, 132
Celebrities, Christian, 50, 54, 158
Celebrities, media, 60-61, 123
Chafer, Lewis Sperry, 148-49
Chappell, Wallace, 75
Chicago Inter-Student Catholic Action (CISCA), 58
Chicago Victory Rally, 28-29
Chittister, Sr. Joan, 130
Christian Century, 26, 31
The Christian Education of Youth (Pius XI), 32
Christians, adolescent: development of, 9-12; in social structures, 12-16
Christian social order, 26-28, 38
"Christian Witness Missions," 69-70
Church attendance: 1950s, 209, 224; African American, 215, 217-19; conservative Protestant, 214-15; effect of youth ministry on, 209-10; fertility rates and, 213, 215; mainline Protestant,

188-89, 211-14; Methodist, 183-89, 212-13, 225; Roman Catholic, 215-17
Churches, adolescent, 16
Cicognani, Amleto Giovanni, 33
Circuit Riders, 72
CISCA (Chicago Inter-Student Catholic Action), 58
Civilian Conservation Corps, 24
Civil rights movement. *See also* Nonviolence; Sit-ins: African American church support, 92, 97-100, 102-8, 112; Catholic youth support, 191-92; Christian opposition to, 72-73, 120, 172-73, 178; combativeness, 177-79; effect on interpretation of Christianity, 112-13, 118; and juvenilization of activism, 93; Methodist support, 68, 70-71, 185-86; as solution to crisis of civilization, 22-23
Class. *See* Middle class
Class anxiety, 14, 159
Close, Mrs. Edwin, 88
Cochran, Don, 187
Codes of conduct, teenage, 137
Cogley, John, 59-60
Cognitive development, adolescent, 10
Cold War: Catholic perspective on, 127, 134-36; rhetoric of, 67, 69, 134
Colliers, 49-50
Colvin, Claudette, 96
Commodification of faith: in Roman Catholic church, 123, 128, 129; by Youth for Christ, 53, 148, 154-55, 199
Commodification of youth, 191
Communion, 126
Communist Germany, 22, 98, 135, 167
Communist threat, perceived associations with: American Youth Congress, 21, 72; Catholic Action, 120; Catholic Youth Organization, 35; National Conference of Methodist Youth, 26, 67, 68, 72-73; as pressure on youth programs, 72; school systems, 167-68; social reformers, 73, 172; Youth for Christ, 31, 32
Communist threat, responses to: "Beat"

Index

Valentine, Helen, 45
Vatican II, 189-90, 198
"Victory girls," 42, 43
Voskuyl, Ruth, 162

Waggy, John, 85
Wahle, Mary Jo, 138
Walker, Billy, 158
War, rhetoric of, 136
Warren, Rick, 208
Washington March for Jobs and Freedom, 178
Watts, Corenne, 99
"We Are Soldiers," 114
Webster, Dorothy, 112
Weer, Betsy, 60
Wheeler, Sterling, 22
White Citizens Councils, 97
Whyte, William, 80
Will, Herman, 27
Williams, Sylvester, 39
Willock, Edward, 58-59
Willow Creek Community Church, 208
Wills, Garry, 125, 126, 130
Wilson, T. W., 50
Women in leadership, 89, 204
Women's Auxiliary of the National Baptist Convention, 37, 99, 100-101
World War II, 36. *See also* Crisis of civilization
Worship, 1-2, 201, 217-18
Wright, Jim, 202
Wyrtzen, Jack, 24-25, 29

YFC. *See* Youth for Christ
Young Christian Students, 57, 120-21
Young Christian Workers, 35-36, 57, 120-21
Young Leaders in Action (Beckes), 47
Young Life, 43, 75
Young Life magazine, 43
Youth, commodification of, 191
Youth, political power of: concern about, 21-22; overestimated, 42; public perception, 25, 31-32; in student protests, 107

Youth, viewed as more devoted than adults, 2, 10, 104-5, 117, 118
Youth, viewed as natural political progressives: in Catholic churches, 192; and declining youth involvement, 183, 188, 206; in Methodist churches, 27, 65, 78, 81, 90-91
Youth, viewed as solution to crisis of civilization: in African American churches, 23, 36-37; and declining youth involvement, 206; in evangelical Protestant churches, 22; and juvenilization of social activism, 39-40, 117, 118, 206; in mainline Protestant churches, 21-22; in Roman Catholic church, 23, 32-36, 124, 134, 191; by Youth for Christ, 30-31, 167
Youth, viewed as solution to racial problems, 23, 65, 111, 206
"Youth and World Trends" (Holt), 22
Youth Caravans, 75-76
Youth Committee, 103-4
Youth councils, CYO, 56-57
Youth culture (term), 44
Youth culture, Christian: Catholic youth programs, 55-58, 144; Youth for Christ, 148, 152-54, 157, 162, 199
Youth culture, secular, 41-67. *See also* Popular culture; in adolescent social structures, 12; adult perceptions of, 42-46; African American church responses to, 61-65, 93, 105; African American exclusion from, 64-65; Catholic critique of, 59-61; Catholic responses to, 55-61, 131-35, 196-97; competitions, 131; consumerism, 44-45; emergence of, 41-42; as factor in mainline Protestant declines, 68; influence on sit-in movement, 114-15; media forms viewed as neutral, 158, 162-63, 175, 227; Methodist responses to, 76, 91, 188; radical subcultures, 15-16; as rebellion against social constraints, 15; as result of age segregation, 12, 44; social concern diminished by, 46-49; Youth for Christ's